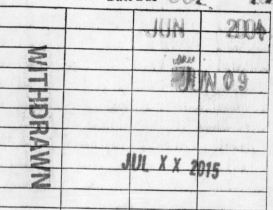

Fugue

HISTORY AND PRACTICE

IMOGENE HORSLEY

Fugue

HISTORY AND PRACTICE

The Free Press, *New York*
Collier-Macmillan Limited, *London*

Acknowledgments

My primary debt is to Darius Milhaud and Walter Piston under whom I studied fugue as a student. I should also like to thank Dr. Fred Blum of the Music Division of the Library of Congress, Professor Bathia Churgin of Vassar College, Professor Frederick Freedman of the University of California at Los Angeles, Professor Allen Forte of Yale University, and Professor Henry L. Woodward of Carleton College for their assistance and advice, and Mrs. Paul Stoughton for her patient help in preparing the manuscript.

I. H.

Contents

Fugue

HISTORY AND PRACTICE

Introduction

*I*n the nineteenth century, as fugue became less important in the field of composition, it was increasingly stressed as a necessary part of the musician's education. This was in part the result of academic conservatism but not wholly so. It was the function of fugue to act as a bridge between the student's exercises in harmony and counterpoint and the world of free composition. An artificial form, it combined the traditions of fugue with the rigors of scholastic contrapuntal devices and gave practice in such other procedures as the modulating sequence and pedal point. In addition, it was an exercise in form, in combining the various parts into a relatively fixed structure.

This academic fugue—or *fugue d'école* as it was named in France —was a fairly practical bridge between the schoolroom and the world of art, but it was no guide to the understanding of fugue. It was derived from the observation of extant fugue literature and in part from intensive theoretical speculation, and eventually it was the theory pedagogue who won out. The forms and procedures emphasized in academic tradition began to have the ring of true authority, and the fugues of Bach, Handel, Mozart, and Beethoven were forced by industrious analysis to fit into the scholastic forms or were criticized as wrong—all due to a misunderstanding of the original purpose of the academic fugue. A contrived model is a good teaching device, but it should never be mistaken for musical reality.

Modern fugue texts still rely on some such abstract model, and the artificiality of such a device is more obvious because the teaching of fugue today is even further removed from the realities of musical composition. Traditional fugue can no longer be called a bridge to free composition, since it is based on traditions that have been abandoned. It may help the would-be composer simply because it is an exercise in composition, and, while the skills learned in fugue do not transfer directly into the styles and structures used today, it does give practice in thinking polyphonically and in creating an extended form. But it is not a necessary part of a composer's training. Writing a sixteenth-century motet or a seventeenth-century ricercar would be as good an exercise and perhaps an even better one, since in writing these one faces the problem of building a long movement without the conventions of eighteenth- and nineteenth-century tonality.

On the other hand, the historical orientation of our musical culture means that the performer, conductor, theorist, musicologist, teacher—and the composer, too, if he must combine composing with one of these professions—needs a knowledge of fugue literature. For this reason, many contemporary courses in fugue stress fugue from the point of view of history and analysis, spending only so much time on writing as is needed to understand the basic elements of fugue. The historical study of fugue provides a broad background in literature from the late fifteenth through the nineteenth centuries, and fugue is unique in showing a close relationship between theory and practice in composition. It is unique also in that it involves the development of strict conventions and the constant adaptation of its conventions and procedures to different patterns of tonality, form, and aesthetic attitudes.

Although the need for learning to write a strict fugue has diminished for the composer, it has increased for those concentrating on other aspects of music, particularly theory and history. A musician worthy of the name should have experience in composition as well as in performance. Work in contemporary styles for the "non-composer" deepens his musical sensibilities and exercises his musical imagination, but he seldom gets to the point where he is so at home in a style that he can concern himself with the creation of larger forms. He rarely gets experience in composition in the sense of formal construction. Fugue is one of the best vehicles for learning how to put together a larger movement, since it includes sections of statement and transition and involves the development of a form based on tonality. At the same time, it gives experience in polyphony combined with harmony, in the conflict between the horizontal and the vertical components of music. It is also easy to work with because it uses a style that is familiar enough to the student for him to exercise musical judgment, and, for the musician who is self-critical and finds it hard to create themes that satisfy him, it is—in contrast to the song or the sonata—a form in which one can work successfully with a given theme.

This book attempts to provide the material for a course that combines the historical study of fugue with exercises in writing fugue, and, if this is an uneasy combination, it is because our musical culture today combines conflicting approaches to music. Because histories of fugue have been written from the point of view of the historian and musicologist, they do not provide enough historical material of a precise and detailed nature for the student of theory who wishes to analyze fugues of different eras in their proper historical context. The analysis has had to be made from the standpoint of nineteenth- and twentieth-century textbooks on fugue. This book is an attempt to remedy this situation. The history of the different elements of fugue—subject, answer, exposition, and so forth—has been given separately and from the point of view of musical structure and the theoretical rationalizations that contemporaries made about the details of that structure. Although the musicological approach has been observed insofar as reliance on and citing of primary historical sources is concerned, long lists of composers, works, and terms and their intricate relationship have been avoided so as to concentrate on the analysis of typical works. A listing of primary theoretical sources has also been provided in Appendix II, and current works on fugue history are listed in Appendix III.

The historical treatment of canon and fugue stresses their development from the beginning through the nineteenth century because during this time there is a continuous and unified growth in the traditions governing their construction. Projects in analysis are limited to this period so that the various facets of these traditions can be clearly observed. Twentieth-century usage has not yet arrived at the point where such conventions have become regularized, so that one is still free to contrive his own methods of composition and analysis. Those techniques found in twentieth-century canons and fugues that are echoes of the earlier tradition can be best understood by seeing them first in the musical milieu in which they originated.

The text is meant to be used flexibly, according to the purpose and extent of the course it serves. For each part of fugue, the historical background with suggested projects for analysis has been given first, followed by directions for and exercises in writing. The writing exercises are meant to be progressive. The fugue subjects and answers written in the first exercises in fugue are to be used later in the writing of expositions, and these expositions will eventually be made the basis of complete fugues.

Relatively fixed formal patterns have been given for the exercises in writing fugue forms, and, although these models do not have the complexity of the academic fugue or the *fugue d'école,* they are in that tradition and have been called "study fugues" to remind the student that they are artificial exercises designed to give practice in the problems of fugue writing and are not models by which to judge other fugues. The usages involved come from eighteenth- and nineteenth-century practice and theory.

It is intended that work in these study fugues should be preceded by at least the reading of the historical matter that introduces them, to make clear what the original practice was and to put the writing exercises into their proper perspective. Beyond this, the material is meant to be adapted to the needs of the course. If writing is to be stressed for the purpose of mastering the fugue of the eighteenth and nineteenth centuries, there is no need to spend much time on the material on sixteenth- and seventeenth-century fugue. If the emphasis is on analysis, writing may be kept to a minimum, but the writing of at least one fugue is necessary for an understanding of the technical difficulties involved in their composition. A number of suggested projects for analysis have been given, and they may be adjusted to the needs and materials at hand. Supplementary suggestions of materials for analysis are given in Appendix I.

A workbook correlated with this text includes exercises for mastering the difficulties of writing the different parts of the fugue. It has been taken for granted that, before using this text, the student has finished a course in music history as well as courses in harmony and tonal counterpoint. For those who have not had counterpoint recently, there is included in the workbook a short summary of the basic rules and exercises for review.

The text opens with a treatment of canon, since canon is the direct antecedent of fugue. A mastery of canon is not necessary for the understanding of fugue, but the writing of simple canon is important if the student plans to emphasize the writing of fugue, since the technique of canon is used to work out a stretto. The writing of a few canons will also make practical review exercise in tonal counterpoint, and exercises for the analysis, deciphering, and writing of canons are provided in the workbook. If the historical study of fugue is to be stressed, the chapter on the history of canon is the natural preparation for this study.

The compositions analyzed in the text have, wherever possible, been chosen from those historical collections of examples that are found in almost every music library, or from works available in inexpensive performing editions. Because so few average nineteenth-century piano fugues are in print today, two such fugues have been included in the workbook as additional material for analysis. The students should, as a matter of course, have available the *Well-Tempered Clavier* by Johann Sebastian Bach for reference.

For designating particular pitches the usual symbols are used: c' is middle "C"; c'', an octave above middle "C"; c, an octave below middle "C"; and C, two octaves below middle "C." Capitals in italics are also used when pitch is used in a general sense (*C,D,E* appearing in any octave).

For keys, if the letter is not modified by the terms major or minor (E major, E minor), lower case means minor (e stands for E minor; E, for E major).

For chords, upper case Roman numerals stand for major triads (I, III), and lower case for minor triads (i, iii). A superscript zero indicates a diminished triad (vii⁰, ii⁰).

Modal scales are identified by names (Dorian, Hypodorian) rather than by numbers (mode 1, mode 2).

Abbreviations

DDT *Denkmäler deutscher Tonkunst.* Leipzig, 1892–1931.

DTB *Denkmäler deutscher Tonkunst: Denkmäler der Tonkunst in Bayern.* Braunsscheig, 1900–1938.

DTÖ *Denkmäler der Tonkunst in Öesterreich.* Vienna, 1894–1956.

GMB Schering, Arnold (ed.). *Geschichte der Musik in Beispielen.* Leipzig: Breitkopf and Härtel, 1931. (New York: 1950.)

HAM Davison, Archibald T., and Apel, Willi (eds.). *Historical Anthology of Music.* 2 vols. Cambridge, Mass.: Harvard University Press, 1947, 1950.

HMS Abraham, Gerald (ed.). *The History of Music in Sound.* London: Oxford University Press, RCA Victor, 1953–.

MM Parrish, Carl, and Ohl, John F. (eds.). *Masterpieces of Music before 1750.* New York: Norton, Haydn Society, 1951.

MSO Starr, William J., and Devine, George F. (eds.). *Music Scores Omnibus.* Englewood Cliffs, N.J.: Prentice-Hall, 1964.

Chapter I

Canon in the Development

of Western Music

A historical study of fugue must start with
an investigation of canon, since canon preceded fugue as the major
imitative polyphonic device and thus provided fugue with some of its
main conventions. Even when fugue became a technique distinct
from canon, the two were usually linked pedagogically because of
their common use of strict imitation and their relation to contrapuntal skill.

In fact, the Latin word *fuga* (flight) that is the source of our
word "fugue," originally stood for what we call "canon." At that
time, the Latin *canon* (rule) meant a short motto or sentence that
indicated, in the manner of a riddle, the way in which a single part
was to be performed or another part derived from it—a well-known
example being the rondeau *Ma fin est mon commencement, et mon
commencement ma fin* by Guillaume de Machaut (*ca.* 1304–1377)
a three-voice work in which each part is sung as written and then, as
the "canon" implies, is sung backwards.[1] It was not until the eighteenth century that "canon" was used universally to mean what it
does today—the strict and continuous imitation of a leading part by
one or more following parts, usually at fixed intervals of time and
pitch. It is in this latter sense that the term will be used in this book.

[6]

Early Antecedents and Beginnings of Canon

Canon has been found in the music of certain primitive and exotic cultures,[2] but only in European music, where polyphony has been consciously cultivated, has it developed into complex and intricate forms. It has been an important technique in our music almost from the beginnings of polyphonic writing. Once the development of musical notation made possible the use of intricate polyphonic devices, hints of canonic imitation—the imitating of a complete phrase from one part in another part—began to appear.

Stimmtausch, the interchange of melodic segments between voices (see Ex. 1), is found in the music of the Parisian Notre Dame school at the close of the twelfth century and in motets of the thirteenth and fourteenth centuries. In some works, such as the motet *Alleluia psallat* (*HAM,* I, No. 57) when the two phrases interchanged (*a* and *b*) are of equal length, this is, in effect, invertible counterpoint. (See Chapter VIII.) In others, like *Alle psallite; Alleluia* (*HAM,* I, No. 33), where rests are used to make one fragment, *b,* shorter than the other, *a,* and *a* has a slight overlap with its second appearance, the imitation of the phrase *a* is more apparent. In neither case is the interchange obvious to the listener unless the parts are performed with contrasting timbres, since the exchange takes place at the unison resulting in the repetition of a single polyphonic unit, the combination of *a* and *b.*

The same is true of the fourteenth-century *rondellus* and *rota.* (See Ex. 1.) The *rondellus,* as described by the English theorist

EXAMPLE 1 (*a, b,* ETC., REPRESENT SHORT MELODIC PHRASES.)

MELODIC INTERCHANGE	RONDELLUS
a b	*a b c d e f*
b a	*b c a e f d*
c . . .	*c a b f d e*

ROTA OR ROUND

a b c a b c a b c, etc.
a b c a b c a b, etc.
a b c a b c a, etc.

Walter Odington, uses the principle of interchange to create a continuous form.[3] Although each part states a new melodic phrase at each repetition of a polyphonic unit, what the listener hears is simply the repetition of a series of polyphonic units. The *rota* likewise presents to the hearer the repetition of a polyphonic segment, but it is a single segment that is repeated, and the whole is produced by a different method of performance. (See Ex. 1.) The melodic fragments making up the vertical unit also must form a coherent melody (*a b c*), which each part sings as a whole. The voices enter one by one, and, once they are all singing, the polyphonic unit repeats continuously until the performers choose to stop.

The *rondellus* disappeared from the musical scene rather early. The *rota,* which is simply what we now call a "round," is a simple canon type found throughout our entire musical development. It is a form particularly attractive for amateur singing, and many rounds composed in the past, such as the ubiquitous *Three Blind Mice* (first published in a seventeenth-century collection of rounds for amateurs),[4] have become a part of popular lore. (See also Ex. 16.)

The fourteenth-century English *rota Sumer is icumen in* (*HAM,* I, No. 42), is the most famous *rota* of this early period, although it is perhaps most important because the four-part round is sung above a two-part *pes,* or ostinato, thus producing the earliest-known example of a six-voice texture. In the same century, a more sophisticated canon type appeared in the French *chace,* Italian *caccia,* or Spanish *caça*—settings of vernacular texts describing the hunt where the musical effect of one voice chasing after another in canon is a metaphorical expression of the text. Indeed, the terms *chace* and *caccia* are sometimes used to designate a canon even when the text is unrelated to the hunt;[5] the Latin *fuga,* which was first applied to this form by the fourteenth-century theorist Jacobus of Liège,[6] may have first been used as a Latin translation of the French term.

The *caccia* and *chace* provided the prototype for simple canons that have been composed ever since their time. Unlike the round, which is an "infinite canon" and continues until the performers decide to bring it to an end, the *caccia* ends the canon with a definite cadence. Also unlike the round, the leading part is a long melody without necessarily having any repetition, and the following part or parts may enter several measures later, so that the canon can be a long and complete composition. As a matter of fact, the *cacce* and related forms were made up of two separate canons, one after another, since the text was divided into two distinct parts. The first section of the text was set to one canon which came to a full stop with a complete cadence; then the second part of the text started up again with a second canon, the leading part starting alone with the following part entering after it, and this canon came also to a full stop with a complete cadence. The canons are, for the most part, at the unison and octave, although canons at other perfect intervals are found. The madrigal *De' dimmi tu* by Francesco Landini (1325–1397)[7] uses a canon at the fifth above in the first section and one at the fourth below in the *ritornello*. The canons are found in two or three contrapuntal parts and often in two parts with a third free instrumental part as accompaniment. Successive entrances are generally several measures apart, and the melodic lines are highly developed, especially in the *caccia* types where hocket and the imitation of the sounds of the hunt make for a highly complex and virtuoso vocal line. (Examples may be found in *HAM* I, No. 52; *HMS,* III, 13.)

The special relation that canon and canonic imitation had to the projection of the text in these early centuries should be pointed out, since in later periods composers tended to think of canon as an abstract musical construction. The projection is, of course, not directly emotional. At the simplest level, the use of the same text for each voice of a canon is significant for this early period when polytextual forms are so prominent in rhythmically differentiated polyphony. The symbolic use of canon to depict the hunt in the *cacce* has already been noted, but there are other equally interesting relationships between canon and text. A particularly interesting example of this is the thirteenth-century motet *En non Dieu; Quant voi la rose; Nobis.*[8] In general, the texture here is nonimitative, but the two vernacular texts have one line in common in each verse, and the music mirrors this textual construction by having the common line appear in canonic imitation at the unison. Another such example is Machaut's three-part ballade *Sans cuer; Amis, dolens; Dame, par vous.*[9] This is a three-part canon at the unison with the voice entries relatively close together. Each part has a different vernacular text, but the last line of each stanza is the same in all three texts, and the final syllables of corresponding lines in the three poems are alike. A canonic setting is ideal for pointing up these correspondences, and this work is an especially fine example of the interrelation of text and musical structure.

Fifteenth and Sixteenth Century: Creative Development

By the early fifteenth century, canonic procedure was used in sacred as well as secular music, and it became increasingly important in this new field. From the time of Guillaume Dufay (*ca.* 1400–1474) and his contemporaries, there was a steady growth in its use and in the invention of new canonic types. The Netherlanders took particular delight in creating works in this genre. Johannes Ockeghem (*ca.* 1430–1495), Josquin Des Près (*ca.* 1450–1521), and Pierre de la Rue (*d.* 1518), along with their contemporaries, wrote Masses in which each movement was a canon of some type (often, but not always, indicated by the title *Missa ad fugam*) as well as separate Mass movements and motets built on canon. Secular works, too, often had a canonic basis; in the French chanson particularly, a canon was frequently used as the structural skeleton.

With Josquin's generation, the use of canon reached its peak. From the time of Adrian Willaert (*ca.* 1490–1562) and Nicolaus Gombert (*ca.* 1490–1556), fugal writing took precedence over canon, but, throughout the century, composers of sacred works continued to write works in canon if for no other reason than to prove their skill. Giovanni Pierluigi da Palestrina (*ca.* 1524–1594) included five canonic Masses in his total output of 105. In the last half of the century, however, composers were skillfully re-using canonic techniques that were already well established; their use was a bow to tradition rather than the creation of new usage.

A detailed history of canon in this period has yet to be written.[10] Indeed, until all the music of the fifteenth and sixteenth centuries has been discovered and made available, it will be impossible to do so. But a study of the canonic works produced in this time is intriguing from the point of view of the theorist and composer as well as that of the historian, because it concerns musical structure. It must be pointed out that, in the fifteenth century, canon was still a new form that was alive with possibilities. It had been associated with projection of text and with the technique of formal construction—with practicality and not with pedantry. The exploration of possibilities in a new musical field must have been tremendously exciting, comparable perhaps to present-day experimentation with the possibilities inherent in musical organization by means of serial patterns in timbre. Then, as in many later periods, composers took pride in their technical skill and inventiveness, but that does not mean that they were not concerned with freedom and expressiveness. Ockeghem, who conceived that canonic masterpiece *Missa Prolationum,* also wrote the very free *Missa Mi-Mi;* Des Près, whose love of "ostentatious ingenuity"[11] was so evident in his Masses, was also celebrated for the dramatic and emotional power of his motets and chansons.

Parallel with the growth of canon went an increased use of short melodic motives in imitation as a means of organization. By the mid-sixteenth century, this had become so important that a more precise terminology was necessary for rational discussion, and this was supplied by a pupil of Willaert, the Venetian theorist and composer Gioseffo Zarlino, in his *Istitutione harmoniche*.[12] The terms *fuga, consequenza,* or *reditta* he applied to imitation at the perfect intervals —unison, fourth, fifth, octave, and their compounds—because it was at these intervals that exact intervallic imitation most easily takes place in our diatonic scales. For other intervals—second, third, sixth, seventh, and their compounds—he used *imitazione,* since here the imitation produces the generic intervals—second, third, and so forth—but a major second might be answered by a minor second, and so forth.

To these distinctions as to degree of intervallic exactness, he added two more. For imitation that lasted for a few notes after which the part moved on freely, he used the term *sciolta* (free)—thus, *fuga sciolta* and *imitazione sciolta.* For continuous imitation, he added the word *legata* (bound, strict) giving *fuga legata* and *imitazione legata.* The same categories were also applied to the types of imitation by inversion. Although Zarlino deplored the use of the term canon for the *fughe* or *imitazione legate,* it is this term that eventually triumphed, including within its category all types of continuous imitation. As for *fuga sciolta,* the *sciolta* was dropped in the seventeenth century, but *fuga* continued to mean short "points," or melodic fragments, in imitation at the prefect intervals. In some cases, "imitation" was used into the nineteenth century to mean imitation at intervals other than the perfect ones, but it also took on the generic meaning of imitation of all types.

Zarlino's categorization is significant because it indicates the need for more precise distinctions that was created by the many newly developed types, but it did not approach a listing of the canonic types then in use. Nor do the definitions seem clear when practically applied. Exact intervallic imitation, for example, does not necessarily take place at the fourth or fifth (above or below) without the addition of accidentals. In our Western diatonic system, the six notes *c, d, e, f, g,* and *a* and the six notes *g, a, b, c, d,* and *e* answer exactly to each other but cannot be extended in either direction and make exact imitation without chromatic alterations in one part so that most canons at the fifth and fourth require a different signature for the answering part or the addition of accidentals by the performer or editor.

After the early fifteenth century, composers rarely wrote out any but the leading part in a canon. Deciphering the canon was part of the game. The fact that another part or parts were to be derived from this part was sometimes indicated by a riddle "canon" but more often by more concrete directions such as *tenor faciens contratenorem* (the tenor makes the countertenor), *fuga in subdiatessaron* (canon a fourth below) or simply by two clefs. Often a sign (*signum congruentiae*)[13] is given to show points of entrance, but there are still cases where the editor must experiment to find the correct point at which the other parts enter.

Unless different signatures are indicated, the editor must decide whether or not different signatures or added accidentals should be used to make the answering part or parts precisely the same. If this is done, it means the answering parts will be in a transposed mode. Sometimes this works very well, but at other times the addition of accidentals to make exact imitation results in contrapuntal errors. The student should be aware of this problem when studying canonic works of this time, as it is one of the technical problems involved in both the writing and the transcription of canons at the fourth and fifth. In canons at intervals other than the perfect ones, this problem does not arise, since exact intervallic imitation is not prescribed for them.

The use of all diatonic intervals as proper intervals for canonic writing was one of the advances made in this period. Canons in which the answering part is an inversion of the leading part (mirror canon) or a retrograde of it (crab canon) do appear, but rarely outside of theory books. Also, composers began to experiment with the time element in canons. The entrances of the answering parts are found at very great and very small distances from the leading part. A special type is the canon *ad minimam,* usually in two parts only, where the second part follows the first a half-note behind, one part starting on the strong part of the beat and the other on the weak part.

A canon type peculiar to this period is the mensuration canon, which grew out of the rhythmic notation then in use wherein different mensuration signs applied to the same group of notes produced very different rhythms. Here, one line of music is given with two or three different mensuration signs (depending on the number of parts wanted) and, if the canon is not at the unison, there are different clefs to indicate the intervals of imitation. This is also one type of canon in which all the parts can begin together, since they move at different speeds and are soon separated. Canons by exact augmentation and diminution fit into this category but are less complex and do not directly depend on mensural notation; they thus survived beyond this period. Like the more complex mensuration canon, the parts can also start together, but it is not necessary that they do so.

To follow the technique of the mensuration canon in detail, one must understand the notation system in which they are written,[14] but the general idea can be made clear by looking at Example 2, the

EXAMPLE 2

BEGINNING OF KYRIE I FROM *Missa Prolationum*, JOHANNES OCKEGHEM.

beginning of the first Kyrie from Ockeghem's *Missa Prolationum.* This movement is a double canon, the two top voices coming from one part and the two lower from another. Since each of the canons is at the unison, each has only one clef. Each has, however, two mensuration signs so that each voice will move at a different speed. These four signs include the four "prolations" used in the notation of that time, and this is the source of the name of the Mass.

In the example given here the original note values are reduced so that the effect can be seen in our notation. In the canon presented in the top two voices the same melody moves in 2/4 and 3/4, and the voice moving in 2/4 moves faster than the other, getting farther and farther ahead as it moves on. In the canon sung by the two lower voices another melody moves in 9/8 against itself in a combination of 6/8 and 3/4, and here, too, the top melody moves ahead of the lower.

It can be clearly seen that this does not produce simple augmentation or diminution in which each note value is multiplied or divided by the same number, but produces a more complex system of relative movements. The first *e′* in the top canon, for example, is a quarter note in the soprano but a half in the alto. This is due to conventions within the mensural system that are absent from ours and that lend a particular subtlety to this type of canon. (Two complete mensural canons are given in *HAM,* I, No. 89—the Agnus Dei from Des Près, *Missa L'Homme armé,* including the original notation—and *HAM,* I, No. 92—the Kyrie I from the *Missa L'Homme armé* by Pierre de la Rue. The latter is accompanied by two free parts.)

In the late fifteenth and sixteenth centuries, there is also an increase in the number of parts that could appear in a canon. A single melody often generated canons of three, four, and more parts. Furthermore, combinations of single canons were used to create complex structures; two canons, each in two parts, were combined to make a double canon (as in the Ockeghem canon just mentioned), and this process was extended to produce combined canons of many parts. One of the most successful is the quadruple canon by Des Près in his setting of the psalm *Qui habitat in adjutorio.*[15] Here, the composer has created a quadruple canon, four canons each of six parts, combined to produce a twenty-four-part texture.

Another skillful use of multiple canon is found in Palestrina's *Missa ad fugam.*[16] The Kyrie, Gloria, and Credo are in four parts made up of two double canons. The interrelation of these canons is such that, by clever spacing of rests, arrangement of melodic motives and cadences, each movement sounds as if it were constructed of a series of points of imitation in the manner of most non-canonic works of the last half of the sixteenth century. The canonic structure is hidden from the listener.

All of these canon types are also found with free accompanying voices. One of the most interesting forms of this period is that in which a canon is used as the skeleton for polyphonic work. Here, it is generally used as was a cantus firmus, appearing often after the other free parts have entered. The relation of this skeletal canon to the rest of the parts varies widely with different composers and works, and a study of this form gives great insight into the contrapuntal and formal craftsmanship of the composers. A particularly complex relationship results when the canon takes part in the imitation of successive points as they appear. An excerpt from the chanson *Faulte d'argent* by Des Près (Ex. 3) shows how, by use of rests, the texture is kept clear and the canonic voices (marked by asterisks) are absorbed into the texture of the whole.

EXAMPLE 3

EXCERPT FROM *Faulte d'argent*, JOSQUIN DES PRÈS. (THE
TWO PARTS IN CANON ARE INDICATED BY ASTERISKS, THE
LEADING PART IN MEASURE 24 AND THE ANSWERING
PART IN MEASURE 27.)

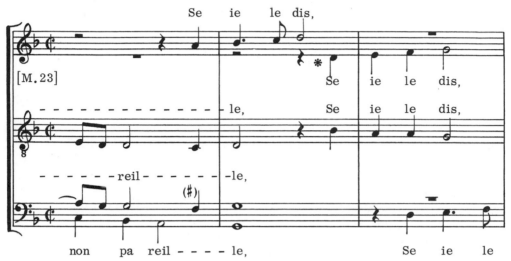

All the canons of the period were not strict. Variations were made
in the time interval by which the answering voices followed the
leading part. Jacob Obrecht (1453–1505) and Des Près were especially fond of this device.[17] In some canons, slight alterations might
be made in one part or another. The practice of improvising colora-
tura in performance was another way in which the fixed canon
structure must have been disguised from the listeners. Johannes

Buchner's *Fundamentbuch* for organ improvisation (*ca.* 1525)[18] includes a number of models for treatment of a chorale melody, one of which is to use it in canon with additional free parts imitating points from the canon. In these works, he often added short ornaments to all the lines, but, interestingly enough, the same motive was usually ornamented differently with each appearance, so that even the canon itself is not exact. Occasionally, he altered the time intervals separating the leading and answering parts as well.

A formal procedure directly related to canon was the use of a series of phrases in canonic imitation with short unrelated fragments interpolated here and there so that the time or pitch intervals of imitation could be smoothly changed—a movement, then, made up of a chain of canonic phrases with short fragments of transitional free material welding it together. Example 4 shows a short section of

EXAMPLE 4

FROM THE BENEDICTUS FROM *Missa Pange lingua,* JOSQUIN DES PRÈS (TEXT OMITTED).

the Benedictus from the *Missa Pange lingua* by Des Près. The material in parenthesis is free, not part of any canon. Numbers show the beginnings of new canonic phrases. Note that here the pitch interval of imitation, a fifth, remains the same, but the time interval gets closer until the third phrase and spaces out again for the fourth.

Clearly, these irregular and free uses of canon are not the result of ineptness on the part of the composers. Their skill at writing strict canons of all types is manifest. We must conclude, therefore, that these variants were consciously used for some particular aesthetic or structural effect. As the sixteenth century moved on, this type of freedom disappeared, and canons became more strict and rigid in their structure—a conscious show of skill rather than a means of construction. At the same time, canon ceased to be the dominant form in art music. But it still remained an important part of musical life. Skilled performers, singers and keyboard virtuosos, were expected to improvise canons above a cantus firmus at sight according to given rules.[19] And, in the many elementary texts written for the teaching of sight reading, rhythmic notation, solfege, and the modes, the musical exercises included for practice and examples were canons.

The Seventeenth and Early Eighteenth Centuries: Emphasis on Technique and Ingenuity

Among the many new styles and forms that grew up in the seventeenth century, canon still had a place. It was, however, no longer among the dominant forms of musical construction. It was found in all media, but the frequency of its use did not approach that of fugue, variation, ritornello, reprise, and similar forms. Its importance remained great mainly because of the prestige it still held as the final proof of a composer's contrapuntal skill; for, side by side with the new emphasis on dramatic and emotional expression, there remained a passion for craftsmanship and a respect for the labors involved in creating something within fixed limits.

In the early part of the century, there was a sudden resurgence in the production of canons originating primarily in Rome and associated not with the new style and radical composers, but with strict contrapuntal usage of the sixteenth century. Many of the composers involved were, in fact, followers of Palestrina or of Giovanni Maria Nanino (1545–1607) and his brother Giovanni Bernardino (1560–

1623) who, together with Palestrina, founded in Rome the first music school open to the public. From this school came the many Italian composers of Catholic church music of the century who clung to the old style, the *prima prattica,* of composition. Nearly all of them have long been forgotten, but, in their time, they achieved great eminence as skilled contrapuntists who wrote gigantic works for many voices; they were especially known for their skill in writing canons. One of their favorite exercises of musical and religious devotion was the writing of as many canons as possible on a single sacred cantus firmus. Giovanni Maria Nanino apparently started this trend by writing thirty different canon settings on a single cantus for his *Motecta,* published in 1586; his seventeenth-century followers outdid him in the numbers of canons they managed to create over a single cantus. Writing a canon on a given cantus firmus requires even more skill than writing a simple canon. In any canon the basic problem is to write a melody that will fit with itself at a fixed pitch and time interval, be interesting musically, and yet not depart from the harmonic and contrapuntal rules governing the music of the time. If the canon must also fit against a given cantus firmus—a melody in long notes—the difficulties are much greater.

A typical set is Francesco Soriano's *Canoni, et oblighi de cento, et dieci sorte sopra l'Ave Maris Stella,* published in Rome in 1610. The first group of two-part canons is ordered according to the interval at which the answering voice follows the leader (the canons are made upon the cantus firmus but do not imitate it), starting at the unison and going to the tenth. The time interval of imitation is fixed for these canons; except for the opening canon at the unison, where the second part enters after a half-note rest, the whole series of canons from the unison to the tenth are at the distance of a quarter rest. For each interval, Soriano makes a canon above and below the leading voice, omitting only the intervals of the second and seventh below and the ninth above and below, no doubt because these would not work at the fixed time interval. Then follows a second group of two-part canons moving through the intervals of unison to octave but with varying time intervals. These are followed by two "epilogues"—two canons at the interval of a whole-note rest in which the pitch intervals of imitation change within the canon. The first starts at the unison, and successive phrases imitate at the interval of a second, third, and so forth, up to the octave before coming to the end of the cantus; the second "epilogue" moves in a like manner from the octave down to the unison. Then comes a group of miscellaneous canons, including mirror canons and a few "enigmatic

canons." These latter are puzzle canons in which a short motto indicates how the canon is to be resolved. This is clearly a principle
derived from the "canon" of earlier periods, but, canon having pre-
empted the old term, the word "enigma" had to be added to give the
proper meaning. This section ends with some *oblighi,* and those that
follow, made up successively of works with three, four, and five parts
above the cantus firmus, include various canons and *oblighi.* The
whole collection ends with a canon in six parts above the cantus and
a work in eight parts divided into two choirs.

The concept of *obligo* was associated with canon, although all
oblighi were not canons. Like canon, *obligo* (bond or restriction),
intrigued the composer of this time because it provided him with
difficulties and restrictions that stimulated his imagination and tested
his skill. An *obligo,* an arbitrary restriction like the avoidance of
stepwise motion in the *Ricercar . . . obligo di non uscir di grado* of
Girolamo Frescobaldi (1583–1643),[20] was set up by the composer,
and he worked within this limitation. The invention of such *oblighi*
depended solely on the composer's imagination, and great pride was
taken in the number of new *oblighi* and canons that he could invent
and execute. If these were executed on a cantus firmus, the difficulty
and the pleasure of solving it was even greater. Soriano's *oblighi* in
the collection cited include No.74—where the tenor (the given
cantus) is in double whole notes, the alto in whole notes, the bass
in halves, and the soprano in quarters—and No. 77—where the
soprano continually repeats the melodic pattern la, sol, fa, re, mi.

One of Soriano's more ingenious combinations of *obligo* with
canon is No. 67, a three-voice work on the cantus firmus (Ex. 5). It
is a play on the lines and spaces of staff notation. The soprano, a free
part, is composed so that all the odd-numbered notes fall in the
spaces of the staff, and the even-numbered notes fall on the lines.
The alto and bass are in canon and are derived from a single part
that is a mixture of notes on lines and spaces. In the resolution,
thoughtfully included by Soriano, the alto takes out all the notes on
the lines, and the bass extracts those that fall on the spaces. These
make a strict canon in two parts.

Soriano's collection has been described in some detail not because
of its musical quality or its particular historical importance, but because it is typical of so many collections of its time and because it
illustrates so many of the trends in the use of canon from the late
sixteenth century through the time of Johann Sebastian Bach (1685–
1750). One of the most important is the tendency to make canon
stand out from the general musical scene. Although still used in all

EXAMPLE 5

CANON WITH *obligo*, FRANCESCO SORIANO.

(a) CANON: *In sub Dyapason. Altus lineas, bassus spatia percurrit; pausae a media linea sursum, spectant ad Altum; a media deorsum, ad Bassum.*

(b) RESOLUTION OF CANON, WITH FREE PART AND CANTUS FIRMUS

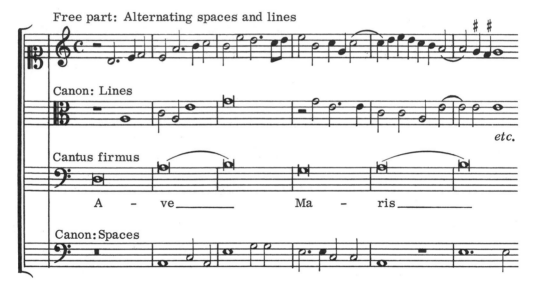

media and often as separate movements in larger works, canons began to appear more and more in separate collections or as a separate group in a miscellaneous collection of works. Sometimes, this was for a special occasion, like Bach's *Musical Offering* (1747), dedicated to Frederick the Great in memory of the composer's visit to the king's court. The collection is based on a theme of the king's that Bach improvised on in his presence and later used as the basis for a number of contrapuntal works including a series of canons using the theme as a cantus firmus and a second series using the theme itself in canon. Other collections were for pedagogical purposes, as examples for students, or for a frank exhibition of skill, like the collection of canons in Giovanni Battista Vitali's *Artificii musicali* published in Bologna in 1689.[21]

A correlative tendency was the habit of arranging these canons in some type of order. This was not new. Ockeghem's *Missa Prolationum*[22]—in which the canons proceed from the unison in the first Kyrie up by seconds, thirds, and so forth, to imitation at the octave in the final Agnus Dei—and Palestrina's *Missa Repleatur os meum*[23]—in which the canons start at the octave at the spacing of eight whole notes and move down in order to the first Agnus Dei, a canon at the unison at the distance of one whole note—are outstanding examples from the preceding period. But this ordering was not the general practice before the seventeenth and eighteenth centuries. Bach's *Goldberg Variations* (1742) are an outstanding example of eighteenth-century practice. Here is ordering on two different levels. First, the canons are grouped within the variations, every third variation being a canon. Then the canons themselves are ordered; starting at the unison, they progress in order up to the final canon at the ninth.

As has been mentioned, the writing of many canons on a sacred cantus firmus was, in part, an exercise of devotion—the labors involved being dedicated to the glory of God—and, as well, a display of contrapuntal skill. But it must also have been the fruit of a tradition of improvising canons on a cantus firmus that had its beginnings in the sixteenth century. Although sixteenth-century writers teaching counterpoint gave precise rules for the minutiae of counterpoint, cadences, and so forth, detailed rules for composing canons and like forms were not given. A few general directions and examples, with an admonition to look carefully at good compositions, were all that were included. This was, perhaps, a holdover from medieval custom wherein the secrets of every trade were jealously guarded. But, whatever the reason, it was in the teaching of improvised counterpoint (*contrapunto alla mente*) that systematic rules for making canons were first published.[24]

Zarlino was the first to make public precise rules for improvising two-part canons in free rhythmic style on a cantus firmus in long notes; in the 1573 edition of his *Istitutione harmoniche,* he added a long section giving clear and detailed directions.[25] Although he limited himself here to those at the unison, fifth, and octave, above and below the cantus firmus at the distance of a whole or half note between the leading and answering parts, his rules show how thoroughly the technique had been worked out. For each type of canon, the time interval by which one part follows the other and the melodic movement between the notes of the cantus are taken into consideration, and the available movements for the leading part of the canon on each possible melodic interval of a cantus firmus are explained.[26]

The seventeenth century saw a great increase of published texts on *alla mente* counterpoint. In regard to canon, Ludovico Zacconi's *Prattica di musica II,* which appeared in Venice in 1622, is perhaps the most interesting. He devoted the entire third part of this book to improvised counterpoint, giving examples of canons at all pitch intervals (and numerous time intervals) above a cantus. He further suggested the improvising of canons in two parts without any cantus, giving a few simple rules and many examples of canons at all intervals. The rules simply state that the counterpoint can move by successive thirds and that fifths, sixths, and octaves should come one after the other (that is, not two of a kind in succession) on the beats. This does not result in a very interesting canon, as can be seen in Example 6. But the rules for improvising canons, learned and practiced, gave the composer a sure foundation in this art, and most proponents of improvised counterpoint considered it a necessary foundation for the art of composing.

EXAMPLE 6

EXAMPLE OF IMPROVISED CANON AT THE FIFTH BELOW, AT THE INTERVAL OF A HALF REST, LUDOVICO ZACCONI.

Improvising canons on a cantus firmus was also practiced in Germany at this time, the only difference being that a chorale melody was used instead of a plainchant.[27] We are more familiar with the written counterpart of the German practice today, since it was used in organ chorale preludes that are still performed. The canons published by Samuel Scheidt (1587–1654) in his *Tabulatura nova*[28] are certainly a reflection of this practice, although only the first, fourth, eighth, and ninth canons show the common improvised form wherein the canon starts after or with the first note of the cantus firmus. Those canons that begin before the chorale tune, like the eleventh and twelfth, and like those found in Bach's monumental *Canonic Variations on Vom Himmel Hoch* (1747), are more in the tradition of composed cantus-firmus works, since in improvising singers would not anticipate the cantus on which they were building.

THE INVENTION OF NEW TYPES OF CANON

The seventeenth century also saw a resurgence of interest in the invention of new types of canons. These are often rather obscure and erudite, appearing mainly in theory books or in special collections of canons. Because of their obscurity and probably also because their difficulty precluded any musically effective realizations, most of these died out after a few examples were produced. However, some new types did survive along with older types that were used in the preceding century. There were also, for the first time, attempts to list and categorize these different types by theorists. Silverio Picerli, in his *Specchio di musica,*[29] divides them into three general classes: (1) those made on a cantus firmus that imitate it in canon; (2) those made on a cantus firmus or quasi cantus firmus (not all in long, even notes) in which the canon is thematically independent; and (3) those that are free of a cantus firmus and are limited only by the skill and invention of the composer.

Canons of the first type had been composed in earlier centuries but in a different context. Usually, they were found in works based on a cantus firmus in which the cantus was given a definite rhythmic pattern that was imitated in the other canonic parts, and this type of canon was normally combined with several free parts, used as a skeleton for a larger structure. Sixteenth-century examples of canons of this kind improvised on a cantus firmus in long, even notes show a very rudimentary type of organization (Ex. 7a), and most of those composed in later times show the effects of great effort and ingenuity. Since a plainchant melody in whole notes is unlikely to make a canon with itself in the usual way, this type of canon usually has an imitating part that is independent rhythmically; the imitation will be only exact in pitch. Even then, the composer often went to ridiculous lengths to accomplish this, starting the answering voice very late so that all of the cantus need not be imitated or using diminution so that the imitation is soon over and the added voice can move on freely. Elway Bevin, a theorist whose collection of canons in *A Brief and Short Instruction on the Art of Musicke* (London, 1631) includes some very ingenious types, solves it in one of his canons by combining diminution and inversion, so that the actual canonic imitation does not go on for very long. (See Ex. 7b.)

EXAMPLE 7

(a) IMPROVISED CANON ON A CANTUS FIRMUS AT THE FIFTH ABOVE, VINCENTIO LUSITANO (1553).

(b) CANON ON A CANTUS FIRMUS BY DIMINUTION AND INVERSION, ELWAY BEVIN (1631).

Strict canons of this type rarely appeared outside of theory books or special canon collections. When a two-part canon is attempted on a chorale tune, for example, the chorale is often imitated only in the beginning of the canon, and even there it is rhythmically varied, often with extra notes added. After the beginning the canon becomes independent of the chorale, since, in most cases, complete imitation of the chorale would be an impossibility. When, in his *Musical Offering,* Bach made canons of the theme given to him by the king, he had to transform it and extend it before it would make a canon with itself.

The second type, the canon made on a cantus firmus but thematically free of it, appeared in a variety of forms. It could be made at nearly all time and pitch intervals (depending, of course, on the shape of the cantus) and expanded to include a number of parts. The only problem was to get these canons to fit with the cantus firmus. A great many canons of this type were written, including some very ingenious ones, as shown in the Soriano collection. It also appears in art forms such as the chorale prelude and other church music and in secular forms, where the given "cantus firmus" is not necessarily taken from liturgical sources. Bach's *Musical Offering* also includes several canons of this type. (See Ex. 8.)

EXAMPLE 8

CANON AT THE OCTAVE ON THE KING'S THEME FROM THE *Musical Offering*, JOHANN SEBASTIAN BACH.

Most new types fit into Picerli's third category, the canon that is free of the cantus firmus, although almost all of them appear at times with a cantus firmus as well. As in the preceding century these are made in their simple form at all intervals of pitch and time and are likewise found combined to form double, triple, and quadruple canons, and so forth. Most theorists divide these simple canons into two classes: (1) finite, in which a definite cadence brings the canon to a close, and (2) infinite, in which the canon can go on, presumably, forever. The infinite canon is in this way similar to a round, but it differs from a round in that it is not made up of a series of strains of equal length that sound together with each new part entering as the preceding one finishes the first strain (see Ex. 16 in Chapter II), but can be made at any time interval. It does not seem to have been used much outside of theory books or special collections of canons, but evidently composers felt that they must show their skill in this form. Most collections of canons included at least one.

All the above canon types made much use of techniques first found in the fifteenth and sixteenth centuries. Canons by augmentation and diminution were common. Canons by inversion were likewise stressed, as well as combinations of inversion with augmentation and diminution. Crab canons, which appear only rarely in the sixteenth century, also came into prominence at this time. In contrast to other canons, the parts here usually start together and end together; many of them also were so composed that the total canon, once finished, could itself be played backward. (See Ex. 18 in Chapter II.) Retrograde movement was at times combined with inversion; in fact, all possible combinations of these particular devices were attempted at some time during this period with varying degrees of success.

The use of invertible counterpoint in canon, first described by Zarlino in 1573 along with his rules for improvising canons on a cantus firmus, became an important device in both improvised and composed canons. Zarlino's invertible canons were made without a cantus firmus, but, as this type of canon became more prevalent, it was used both with and without a given cantus. The technique of invertible counterpoint (which is explained more fully in Chapter VIII) is a way of creating a combination of melodies in which the relative positions of two or more melodies can be changed by transposing them by certain intervals to another pitch level. In a two-part texture, the top part would then become the bottom part, and the bottom would become the top. A three-part canon written in this way can appear in the following versions, reading from top to bottom: 1, 2, 3; 2, 3, 1; 3, 1, 2; 1, 3, 2; 2, 1, 3; 3, 2, 1. In certain types of invertible counterpoint, more than one transposition is possible for each part, so that even more versions are possible. A canon that has more than one possible solution was called a "polymorphous canon"; these canons were greatly in vogue during this period. The Roman Pier Francesco Valentini published in 1629 a canon *nel nodo Salomonis* that was capable of many solutions. New ones kept occurring to him, and the 1629 publication was followed by two others in 1631, *Canone nel nodo Salomonis à 96 voci con le sue resolutione* and *Resolutione seconda del canone nel nodo Salomonis à 512 voci in 128 chori.* The usual polymorphous canon, however, was capable of fewer solutions; in fact, two possible solutions were enough to merit the term "polymorphous." It should be pointed out, also, that, although invertible counterpoint is the simplest means of creating such a canon, all polymorphous canons are not necessarily in invertible counterpoint. By experimentation and by working with short, simple melodies, various canons with more than one solution can be devised.

Another new sort of canon that was subject to great development in the seventeenth and eighteenth centuries was the circular canon, a type of infinite canon in which the whole canon changes pitch at each repetition. At first this was done diatonically, each repetition rising a step (or falling a step) through the scale until it arrived at the octave of the pitch on which it started. By the eighteenth century, when the major–minor system—which included the possibility of using each scale in twelve different transpositions, or keys—was established, this type of canon could also move through a series of keys to fill out the octave or move through the whole circle of twelve keys. The techniques involved in doing this in the circle of keys depend to a great degree on the number of voices in the canon and the interval of imitation used. Bach's two-part modulating canon (*canon à 2 per tonos*) from the *Musical Offering* uses imitation at the fifth, so that each statement of the canon projects two keys, and the circle is completed after six statements. When more parts answering at the fifth are used, the movement through the twelve keys is more rapid, and the canon sometimes assumes another guise. This is true of the canon by Bach's pupil, Johann Philipp Kirnberger (1721–1783) shown in Example 9. Here, four parts are used in imitation at the fifth, and the circle of keys finishes after the third statement of the unit. Kirnberger managed to include all twelve keys within a single infinite canon; the repetition of a short canonic unit rising in pitch is included *within* the canon itself, so the repetition of the whole always starts on the same pitch. This example shows, too, how an infinite canon is managed in performance. The last three measures are the same as the first three measures except that all the voices take part and lead into measure four, which is indicated (by double-bar and repeat sign) as the point from which repetition should take place. This procedure is characteristic of all infinite canons, so that, once all parts have entered, the repetition may go on indefinitely without an awkward break in any of the parts.

There is one more type of canon that is relatively obscure but that merits attention because it is found as simple imitation in sonatas and other noncanonic works at this time and also because it is listed in several eighteenth-century theory books and thus perpetu-

EXAMPLE 9

CANON MODULATING THROUGH ALL TWELVE MAJOR
KEYS, JOHANN PHILIPP KIRNBERGER.

ated in nineteenth-century pedagogy. This is canon by interrupted imitation, spacing the answer by inserting rests in the melody of the leading part. In its earlier forms, like that from J. G. Walther's manuscript notes on composition[30] (*ca.* 1708), it seems to be a variant on the principle of augmentation, but examples like that taken from Friedrick Wilhelm Marpurg's *Abhandlung von der Fuge* (Berlin, 1753–1754) show a more sophisticated usage. (See Ex. 10.) It was often used in inversion as well as in regular imitation.

In addition to these main types of canon, composers and theorists took pride in inventing new kinds of canon that often appeared only

EXAMPLE 10

EXAMPLES OF CANON WITH INTERRUPTED IMITATION
FROM (a) J. G. WALTHER AND (b) W. F. MARPURG.

once or twice and never attained the status of a particular canon type.

A list of the canon types used in Bach's *Musical Offering* is interesting because of the kinship they show with the canonic traditions of the period. As noted earlier, some of these use Frederick the Great's theme as a cantus firmus, and others use variants of it as the thematic basis for canons. Except for the four-part canon, the canons are in two parts—some alone, some on the cantus firmus, and some with a free accompanying part. Although only two are called *canon perpetuus* (infinite canon), several others are written in this form. In addition to simple canons, there are canons using the main artifices of the time—retrograde, or crab, canon; canon by inversion and by inversion combined with augmentation; and the modulating canon discussed earlier. Some of these involve other familiar devices. The canon by inversion has a Latin motto, *Quaerendo invenietis* (seek and ye shall find), although the use of two clefs, one inverted, shows what is intended. Hans T. David[31] finds two solutions for this canon, which is written in invertible counterpoint, thus putting it in the polymorphous category. Finally, there is a special canon, particularly contrived by Bach; it is a *Fuga canonica,* where two canonic parts work out the form of an eighteenth-century fugue over a free accompanying bass line.

When, however, Bach used a canon as a self-sufficient work—such as a chorale prelude—or as a single movement in some larger form, it was not these learned canons that he wrote. Like other composers of his time, he was more likely to use a simple canon with one or more free accompanying parts, a type not specifically listed in theoretical treatises, although it had been in use since the fourteenth century. Like Des Près, who lived more than two centuries earlier, Bach also shows a strong feeling for canon in a structural sense, creating larger movements out of a series of short canons or fragments of canonic imitation. The final variation of the *Canonic Variations* is typical of his craftsmanship and ingenuity in building a larger form out of short canons. Here, each phrase of the chorale tune is treated in canon by inversion at different intervals, and these are used in continuous succession accompanied by one or two free parts. The whole movement ends with a stretto treatment of these four phrases and their inversions, some in diminution, building up a contrapuntal climax that is a fitting finish to the whole work.

A work that shows Bach's skill in putting together a larger form out of short phrases in canonic imitation is the duet *Et in unum Dominum* from his Mass in B Minor. Here, short phrases imitating one another canonically at changing time and pitch intervals are connected by fragments of free material in a way that is reminiscent of the structure of the duet in the Benedictus of the *Missa Pange lingua*. (See Ex. 4.) This and the canonic chorale preludes mentioned earlier show the strong continuity of tradition and technique that stretches from the fifteenth century through the time of Bach.

CANONS FOR AMATEUR PERFORMANCE

Probably the canons that were performed most often and with the greatest pleasure in this period were those written for amateur performance. Many of these were rounds, a type that is the easiest polyphonic form for amateur singers. In England particularly, this type of singing was a popular social diversion.[32] Many publications of "catches" (as this form was called in England) were brought forth again and again, and the singing of them was popular both in the taverns and in the many exclusive clubs formed for the express purpose of singing catches. In contrast to the seriousness that surrounds the learned canons of this time, these were contrived for the pleasure and amusement of those who performed them. In many, the musical form was combined with a clever play on words. A text that, sung as a single line, appeared to be innocent, could have an entirely different meaning when all the parts were combined. By using long rests in the beginning phrases, so that these gaps were filled in when combined with the final phrase, or by setting some words of the final phrases on a higher pitch than the beginning ones and thus bringing them to the fore, a new meaning was surprisingly revealed in performance.

By the early eighteenth century, the possibilities inherent in canon had been thoroughly explored. For theorists, this became a time of labeling and categorizing rather than inventing. In addition to the types already described, three other old forms were also listed: the canon in which the leader starts on the beat and the answer is on the up-beat (or vice versa); the canon of several voices in which each answer follows the leading voice at a different interval of pitch; and the enigmatic canon, which usually emphasized its erudite nature by keeping its motto in Latin.

Nor were there any secrets left about constructing canons. The technique of improvising canons according to certain fixed rules had long been common knowledge, and by the mid-eighteenth century the practice had almost died out. Since the early seventeenth century, theorists had revealed that, to write and invent a canon, one merely composed it in score, measure by measure, creating it in its fully realized form, and finally extracting the single line (or lines) that would be published and left for others to solve.

The Late Eighteenth and Nineteenth Centuries: Decline

The question of style has not been discussed so far because—except for the mensuration canon of the fifteenth and sixteenth centuries or the modulating canon of the eighteenth century—the canon forms were independent of style. New ones were invented and developed, but, even in the seventeenth century, many of these were written in the style of the sixteenth century with fixed rules for dissonance treatment. The problems of composing canon remained the same as long as the canons had to fit into some vertical control. When counterpoint became based on harmonic patterns and dissonances were simply notes not in the chord underpinning the texture at a certain point, dissonance treatment became less rigid, and the problems of writing canon eased somewhat, but it was still a difficult task. Canons now had to fit into a rational chord pattern.

Style became very important in the mid-eighteenth century because simple homophony became the preferred texture, and contrapuntal complexity and artifice fell into complete disrepute for the first time. The monodic reform of 1600 did not abolish the love of contrapuntal skill, but the new musical aesthetic that dominated the last half of the eighteenth century did. The emphasis on mood and on sudden and dramatic change of mood was in direct opposition to the genius of canon. The emphasis on melody and the objection to anything in the musical texture that detracted from the main melody also worked against contrapuntal forms. Perhaps most important of all was the growing feeling that music ought to be obvious and clear to the listener. Only the simplest of canons fulfilled this ideal.

Counterpoint and contrapuntal forms were still a part of the composer's training, and the learned style in contrast to the new free style was still a part of the composer's vocabulary, but it was no longer primary. Just as the new fugal forms pushed canon into the background in the seventeenth century, now the new homophonic forms pushed fugue into a subsidiary role and canon was removed even further from the center of musical life. The invention of new types virtually ceased, and complex canon forms are found only in pedagogical treatises. Marpurg's *Abhandlung von der Fuge* lists the main canon types found in the preceding period, and most contrapuntal texts of the nineteenth century repeat his listing. But these complex canons were considered to be dry exercises, impossible to make interesting in a musical sense, and calling forth a search to solve difficulties by "a cold and reasoned calculation" of interest only to the eye and not the ear.[33]

By the second half of the nineteenth century, most theorists considered even simple canons in more than two parts so very difficult that few composers had ever succeeded in making them attractive; they were thought to be "rather a musical artifice than a work of art," although a necessary discipline for students.[34] A two-part canon accompanied by one or more free parts was considered the only really attractive canon form.

The writing of canon was never completely abandoned during this period, but, after the deaths of Bach's sons and pupils, it steadily declined in importance. Canons for amateur singing were still popular. Franz Joseph Haydn (1732–1809), Wolfgang Amadeus Mozart (1756–1791), Ludwig van Beethoven (1770–1827), and Franz Peter Schubert (1797–1828) all wrote vocal canons of this type, many of them rounds.[35] Even Johannes Brahms (1833–1897) wrote thirteen rounds for women's voices, op. 113. Likewise, canons were written for special occasions—a memento of a visit or a birthday greeting—by composers of the late eighteenth and early nineteenth centuries. Haydn and Beethoven have left a number of these.

Canon was also used now and then in movements from larger forms. Canonic minuets for symphonies and sonatas were popular with the Classical composers and are found in certain minuets of Haydn (such as the minuets of his Symphonies No. 23, 44, and 47) and Mozart (for example, the minuet of his String Quintet in C Minor, K. 406). Even in the nineteenth century, this tradition suggests a connection between scherzo and canon. Among others, Beethoven's Sonata for Violin and Piano in C Minor, Op. 30, No. 2 and Brahms' Piano Quartet in A Major, Op. 26 have canonic trios to their scherzos. This does not mean that these pieces are complete canons, but merely that they use canon. The canon is used as the main period, returning after some free writing. That is, when the common $A :\|: BA' :\|$ form is used, as in the Mozart Quintet in C Minor or the Beethoven Violin and Piano Sonata in C Minor, the A is an accompanied canon, B is not a canon, and A' is then a variant of the first canon. This is decidedly different from Bach's use of the two-part form in the canons of the *Goldberg Variations,* where each section is a complete canon.

The adaptation of canon to a larger form, either by integration of a canon into a larger form or by shaping the canon itself into a particular form, may well be the contribution of this period to canonic usage. A well-known work that illustrates the former procedure is the finale of the Sonata for Violin and Piano in A Major by César Franck (1822–1890). Here, the main theme of the movement is a complete canon that recurs during the movement as a self-contained unit. The *Kanonisches Liedchen* by Robert Schumann (1810–1856) from his *Album for the Young* shows the use of canon to create a short $A :\|$ BA' form. The A sections are based on a canon in which the soprano part leads the tenor by one measure, and the B section is a canon in which the tenor leads the soprano by the same distance. Schumann managed the transition from one canon to the other very skillfully, without an awkward pause or break in the movement, but this apparent smoothness was not gained without a struggle.

Both of these works are based on simple two-voice canons at the octave with free accompanying parts that at times partake of thematic imitation. The interest is in the melodies and their spinning-out and the harmonic movement of the whole. Although the use of canon is the outgrowth of a tradition stressing technique, here it is not technique, but the musical effect that is the basis of the composer's effort. The composer's virtuosity during this time was just as important as in earlier periods, but it was melodic invention, thematic transformation, interesting harmonic progressions, and the like that showed his genius. The invention of a new type of canon was just not considered a creative accomplishment.

Whereas in the fifteenth, sixteenth, seventeenth, and, to a lesser degree, the eighteenth centuries, the composer who did not write some canon was an exception, in the nineteenth century, the opposite was true. The number of works for orchestra or chamber ensembles using canon can be listed on one page,[36] and the total for other media is likewise very small. The composers who wrote them were those who had a feeling of continuity with the past. As a form, it was associated with tradition and pedantry, not expression.

The Twentieth Century: A New Beginning

The change of style that took place in the first decades of the twentieth century brought about a resurgence in the use of canon but in a new context. During the past development of canon, the form had represented a strong tension between the horizontal and vertical elements in music. When the strict laws that had controlled the vertical aggregations of sound were abandoned, this tension was gone. Instead of being the most difficult form to compose, it became one of the easiest, subject only to the taste of the composer and to the aesthetic or musical criteria he established for its use. It was an organizing element, often the only strictly controlled element in a piece.

The strict canons of the past had represented a triumph of skill on the part of the composer. Now, in those styles not strictly organized in any aspect, there is no such prestige associated with exactness. A freer canonic structure with changes of pitch and time intervals of imitation and with interpolated free melodic segments—reminiscent of the technique used by Des Près (see Ex. 4) and used with such skill by Béla Bartòk (1881–1945)—is often preferred. The principle of augmentation and diminution is often applied to the melodic form of the answering part, augmenting or diminishing the intervals of the leading part by adding or subtracting a fixed interval (for example, a major second) or multiplying or dividing by some number (such as doubling or halving each interval).

Canon in the twelve-tone system, used so frequently by Arnold Schönberg (1874–1951) and Anton Webern (1883–1945) and their followers, shows a complete reversal of its role in past centuries. Here, the melodic organization is already strict, and exact pitch imitation at any interval in its original, inverted, retrograde, and inverted–retrograde forms is inherent in the style. What is often wanted is variation, which can be produced by having each part in the canon follow a flexible rhythmic pattern, so that the parts change function, one part and then the other taking the lead. Varying the octaves in which the different notes are sounded also gives variation in the shape and temporary direction of the lines. Changes in timbre or dynamics likewise give variety.

On the other hand, when these other elements—rhythm, timbre, dynamics—are often themselves organized serially and applied to different voices following one another closely, the basic principle of canon—exact imitation—is in force, and we have in effect canons of rhythm, dynamics, or timbre. Whether or not these coincide with one another—a combination of pitch and timbre or dynamic and rhythmic patterns, for example—the work is in fact organized by a number of canons.

Whatever the future holds for canon, there has been a distinct break in the tradition. Canon is no longer the supreme display of skill in which the composer struggles to create an attractive melody which will fit with itself in exact imitation and yet be so constructed that the parts combine vertically in such a way as to follow precise contrapuntal and harmonic rules. It is now an organizing element, giving a sense of unity and structure to a work, limited only by such constraints as the composer puts upon himself. There is no longer a universally accepted body of regulations within which he must work. Thus canon has lost its prestige as a high proof of the composer's skill and moved down to the level of a useful, but not inherently difficult, device.

Notes

1. Transcription (and recording) in *HMS,* III, 15–17; transcription in Gustave Reese, *Music in the Middle Ages* (New York: Norton, 1940), pp. 351–2.

2. See Bruno Nettl, *Music in Primitive Culture* (Cambridge, Mass.: Harvard University Press, 1956), pp. 85–8, Appendix, Ex. 45; see also Walter Blankenburg, "Kanon," *MGG,* VII, 515–8.

3. Walter Odington, "De speculatione musice," *Scriptorum de musica medii aevi nova series I,* ed. Edward de Coussemaker (Paris, 1864; facs. ed., Milan, 1931), p. 246*f.*; Odington's musical example in Percy C. Buck (ed.), *Oxford History of Music* (2nd ed.; London: Oxford University Press, 1929), I, 171–2.

4. First published in Thomas Ravenscroft (ed.), *Deuteromelia* (London: Thomas Ravenscroft, 1609).

5. Machaut applies this term to some of his polyphonic *lais* that are in three-voice canon. See Heinrich Besseler (ed.), *Guillaume de Machaut, Musikalische Werke* (Leipzig: Breitkopf & Härtel, 1943 and 1954), IV, 45*ff.*

6. [Jacobus of Liège], "Speculum musicae," Coussemaker, *op. cit.,* II, 395.

7. W. Thomas Marrocco, *Fourteenth-Century Italian Cacce* (Cambridge, Mass.: Medieval Academy of America, 1942), No. IX.

8. Pierre Aubrey (ed.), *Cent motets du XIIIᵉ siècle* (Paris: Lerolle & Cie, 1908), II, 180.

9. Friedrich Ludwig (ed.), *Guillaume de Machaut, Musikalische Werke* (Leipzig: Breitkopf & Härtel, 1926 and 1954), I, 16–17.

10. A concise history through Des Près's time is Laurence K. J. Feininger, *Die Frühgeschichte des Kanons bis Josquin des Prez* [*um 1500*] (Emsdetten: H. & J. Lechte, 1937).

11. Henry Glarean, *Dodekachordon* (Basel, 1547), p. 362.

12. Gioseffo Zarlino *Istitutione harmoniche* (Venice, 1558), pp. 212–20.

13. See Chapter II, Ex. 12; see also *Workbook,* section on canon, Problem 1.

14. Willi Apel, *The Notation of Polyphonic Music, 900–1600* (Cambridge, Mass.: Medieval Academy of America, 1942), chap. ii and pp. 179–88.

15. Found in J. N. Forkel, *Allgemeine Geschichte der Musik* (Leipzig, 1788–1804), II, 593–8.

16. Franz X. Haberl (ed.), *Pierluigi da Palestrina's Werke* (Leipzig: Breitkopf & Härtel, 1862–), XI, 57–70.

17. For example, Obrecht's *Cela sans plus* in Johannes Wolf (ed.),

Wereldlijke Werken (Amsterdam: Alsbach, n.d.), I, 12; and Des Près' *Plus nulz regrets* in A. Smijers (ed.), *Wereldlijke Werken* (Amsterdam: Alsbach, 1925), I, 74.

18. Johannes Buchner, *Fundamentbuch,* in *Vierteljahrsschrift für Musikwissenschaft,* ed. Carl Paesler (1889), V, 1–192.

19. Ernest T. Ferand, *Die Improvisation in der Musik* (Zurich: Rhein-Verlag, 1938), pp. 216*ff.*

20. Pierre Pidoux (ed.), *Girolamo Frescobaldi, Orgel und Klavier Werke,* Vol. I: *Il primo libro di capricci, canzone . . .* (Kassel: Bärenreiter, 1949), p. 76.

21. Giovanni Battista Vitali, *Artificii musicali* [1689], eds. Louise Rood and Gertrude P. Smith (Smith College Archives, Vol. XIV, Northampton, Mass., 1959).

22. Dragan Plamenac (ed.), *Johannes Ockeghem, Collected Works* (New York: Columbia University Press, 1947), II, 21–38.

23. Haberl, *op. cit.,* XII, 105–34.

24. Ernest T. Ferand, "Improvised Vocal Counterpoint in the Late Renaissance and Early Baroque," *Annales musicologiques* (Paris: Société de Musique d'Autrefois, 1956), IV, 129–74.

25. Zarlino, *op. cit.,* Part III, chap. lxiii.

26. Two of Zarlino's canons are reproduced in Ernest T. Ferand, *Improvisation in Nine Centuries of Western Music* (Cologne: Arno Volk, 1961), pp. 80, 81.

27. See examples in *ibid.,* p. 82.

28. Samuel Scheidt, *Tablatura nova,* in *DDT,* I, 78–83.

29. Silverio Picerli, *Specchio secondo di musica* (Naples, 1631), pp. 93*ff.*

30. Peter Benary (ed.), in the series *Jenaer Beiträge zur Musikforschung,* Vol. II (Leipzig: Breitkopf & Härtel, 1955). This technique is also described in the manuscript notes on composition compiled by Johann Adam Reincken (ca. 1670), in H. Gehrmann, ed., *Werken van Jan Pieterson* Sweelinck (Leipzig: Breitkopf & Härtel, 1901), Vol. X, pp. 90–1.

31. Hans T. David (ed.), *Musical Offering by Johann Sebastian Bach* (New York: G. Schirmer, 1944), pp. 63, 64.

32. John David Robinson, "The Vocal Canon of the Classical Era" (Ph.D. Dissertation, University of Indiana, 1959); examples of catches in *GMB,* No. 248.

33. Hippolyte Raymond Colet, *La panharmonie musicale* (3rd ed.; Paris, 1839), p. 216.

34. Solomon Jadassohn, *A Course of Instruction in Canon and Fugue* [1887], trans. Gustav Wolff (Leipzig, 1904), p. 51.

35. Listed in Robinson, *op. cit.,* pp. 27*ff.* Many of these are in Fritz Jöde (ed.), *Der Kanon: Ein Singbuch für Alle* (Berlin: Kallmeyer, 1932).

36. See list from P. Mies, reproduced in Blankenburg, *MGG,* VII, 541.

Chapter II

Analyzing and Writing

Canons

Since most canons were originally written in such a way that the performer had to decipher them, one should know something about the problems of deciphering before starting to analyze a canon. Usually, sufficient directions are given with the canons; if not, there is nothing to do but copy out the leading part (the part that is always given) and try to make it fit with itself at each pitch and time interval until a solution is found.

If the canon to be solved is an enigmatic canon, the meaning of the motto—which is nearly always in Latin—must be sought. In many cases, as in the direction *Contraria contrariis curantur* (opposites take care of opposites), the meaning is clear. This motto signifies a canon by inversion. However, in some cases, the meaning is obscure or may refer by pun to some musical term, as in *De minimis non curat Praetor* (the leader is not concerned with trivia). Here, *minimis* has reference to musical terminology, for *minima* means half note in Latin. The canon to which this is applied is written with a number of half notes inserted in the given line, and these must be removed before even the leading part can be written out correctly.

In most canons, however, the solution is clearly indicated. The interval of imitation is shown by different clefs given at the beginning or by very clearly written directions, such as "at the unison."

EXAMPLE 11

CLEFS FOR CANONS FROM THE *Musical Offering,* JOHANN
SEBASTIAN BACH: (a) FOUR-PART CANON; (b) TWO-PART
CANON BY INVERSION; (c) RETROGRADE CANON.

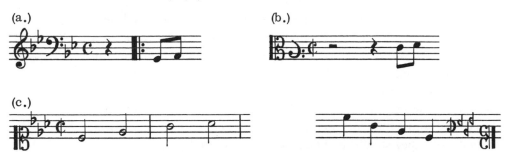

Example 11a shows a canon in which clefs give the clue. The first
clef (the old violin clef with the G-clef on the first line) indicates
that the top voice of the canon starts on *g'*; the second, the F-clef,
indicates that the other part starts on low G. Unfortunately, since
this is a four-part canon, it is up to the transcriber to decide which
octaves the other two parts will start in.

The inverted F-clef in Example 11b indicates that it is a canon
by inversion with the leading part starting on middle *c'* and the
second part on *d* below middle *c'*. A retrograde canon is indicated by
the combination in Example 11c, which shows the signs at the beginning and at the end of the canon as given by the composer. The
clef at the end must be looked at in a mirror to be seen as we are
used to seeing it, but it is clear that the leader is answered by a retrograde of itself, both starting on middle *c'*.

In these canons, none of the time intervals are indicated, and
they must be found out by experiment. (Bach has indicated this by
a motto affixed to the canon by inversion, *Quaerendo invenietis,*
seek and ye shall find.) A retrograde canon normally starts with the
answer directly above or below the leader, so the time interval
of this canon (*c*) is not in question. Usually, the spacing of entries is
clearly indicated in one of two ways—by describing it exactly in
words, for example, "at the third above after a quarter rest," or by
placing a sign at the note in the leading part where the answering
voice is to enter. In the case of a mensuration canon, or a canon in
augmentation or diminution when the parts begin together, a sign
may be used to indicate where the different parts end together. This
sign, called the *signum congruentiae,* appears in several different
forms, the most common of which are shown in Example 12.

[39]

EXAMPLE 12

COMMON FORMS OF THE *signum congruentiae.*

.?. ·$· ⚬$⚬ .|.

Canons by augmentation and diminution present no special problems not dealt with above; the student only needs to be accurate in
working them out. A few words of advice must be given about transcribing finite and infinite canons. (The types mentioned above fall
into these two categories.) The things to be watched in transcribing
each of the two types may seem obvious after they have been mentioned, but, until they are pointed out, the student is often unaware
of them, and they should be understood before analyzing canons.

The finite canon, with a cadence at the end, is always written so
that the leading part is never imitated in its entirety by the answering
parts, and all the parts must be written so that a final cadence is
made with the ending of the leader. (See Ex. 13.) On the other

EXAMPLE 13

(a) END OF CANON AS GIVEN IN A SINGLE LINE.

(b) END OF CANON IN REALIZED FORM.

hand, in an infinite canon, the leading part is always imitated in full
by the answering parts and there will, naturally, be no final cadence.
The canon "ends" when each part has stated the melody in full, and
a double bar with a repeat sign is placed at this point. By this time,
however, each part but that entering last has begun to repeat itself.
These entries will be the same as their beginning entries except that
all the parts will be sounding along with them. Thus, the end of the
canon leads naturally into the measure where the last part first entered. Going back to that bar, the transcriber will place another

double bar with repeat marks just before the entry of that last part. (See Ex. 9 in Chapter I.) The canon can then be sung or played *ad infinitum* between these two double bars. Often, there is a place within the canon where a cadence is indicated harmonically, and the editor may put a hold mark at that point for the salvation of the performers. If there is no such place, a cadence is sometimes added at the end, but if this is done it should be made note of by the transcriber. In most cases, an infinite canon is indicated by a repeat mark at the end of the single-line form given for solution. Sometimes, as well, the composer indicates the point where repetition commences by a double bar and repeat mark near the beginning as well. (See Ex. 11a.)

Aside from the above, the main problem that confronts one in the solution of canons not in direct motion at the unison or octave is the question of added accidentals. In music before the seventeenth century and in some seventeenth-century canons, this requires a knowledge of the workings of *musica ficta* as well as experience in the musical styles of these periods. In later periods, when harmonic procedures govern counterpoint, a knowledge of harmony is often the best guide. In both cases, it is experience with other music of the time that is the deciding factor as well, naturally, as experience in working with canon.

SUGGESTED PROBLEMS

Every music student should have at least minimum experience in solving canon. In the *Workbook* under "Canon," Problem 1, will be found two canons for solution. Other more difficult canons now available in their original unresolved forms in modern publications are those by Bach in the *Musical Offering.* These appear unresolved in Volume XXXV, Part II of the Bach *Gesellschaft* and editions derived from it. Their resolutions can be found in Hans T. David's edition.[1]

Analysis of Canons

In analyzing canons, one is generally working with the canon as it was resolved by some scholar, and this should be borne in mind in case of questions. But it must be remembered as well that a great deal of experience in historical scholarship is necessary before one can be sure of one's own solutions.

Because of the strictness of the canon form, there is not a great deal one can do with a canon from the point of view of its technique but admire it. The canon should, however, be checked for exactness and any variants noted. If the variant in question is the use of added or omitted accidentals, it may be illuminating to search for the musical reasons for these. Aside from this, the pitch and time intervals of the answering voices should be noted, as well as the manner in which they imitate the leading part—augmentation, diminution, retrograde, inversion, and so forth. In the case of inversion, note also whether the imitation is by exact or by generic intervals—that is, whether a major third or a minor sixth are answered by a major third and minor sixth or just by some kind of third or sixth. (It will be well, also, for the student to have some practice in finding the exact canon in an unusual situation. For practice in this, a canon by Elway Bevin is included in the *Workbook* in "Canon," Problem 1.)

The most interesting aspects of a canon are those not directly involved in the technique by which the canon was created. In general, one should observe the melodic and rhythmic movement of the parts and also of the whole, looking for climaxes or points of interest, the use of pauses, cadences and the like, and for harmonic variety and rate of harmonic change. All these, of course, should be related to the fact that the composer was working within a very restricted technique; their management by the composer within these restrictions is one way to judge his craftsmanship.

The canons that present the most interest to the analyst are those that were written not as a show of skill alone, but for performance and audience. These must, of necessity, have some musical appeal regardless of canonic technique. In many cases, this is brought about by elements found in music without canon, and their achievement within a canon is the result of great skill on the part of the composer. In many cases, too, the canon is used as a half-hidden basis for the work, and such free elements as interludes or accompanying parts tend to obscure the canon itself. In all, there are many relationships to be perceived and comprehended. The following problems point up some interesting interrelationships between canon and other compositional factors, although by no means all that exist. The examples chosen for analysis are those that are readily available in collections or in inexpensive editions in addition to the complete works of the composer. A list of some other works that can be used will be found in Appendix I. It is suggested that the student copy the work in question and make a graphic analysis, since in this way it is easier to see the relationship of the canon to the whole.

PROBLEMS WORKING WITH FORM WITHIN THE CANON

Des Près, *Royal Fanfare* (*GMB,* No. 62)
J. S. Bach, *Canon alla decima* from *The Art of Fugue*

In these, there is a repetition or recurrence of melodic motives throughout the canon, giving a sense of form. Pick out the repetitions, sequences, varied repetitions, and so forth, in the leading part; label them, and make note of those that occur close together and those that return after the introduction of other material. Note what effect the time and pitch intervals of imitation and the number of parts taking part have on the over-all sense of form and how the use of pauses and long notes help to make the different melodic ideas stand out.

PROBLEMS CONCERNED WITH THE AMALGAMATION OF CANON INTO LARGER FORMS

J. S. Bach, Two-Part Invention No. 2 in C Minor
Mozart, *Rex Tremendae* from the *Requiem*
Beethoven, Sonata for Violin and Piano in C Minor, Op. 30, No. 2: trio from the scherzo

In these, strict canons are used as thematic material, but none of the pieces is a canon throughout. First, identify and analyze the canons. Then, note how they are integrated into the whole form so that they seem to be a natural part of it. Take particular note of the nature of the noncanonic sections and the relation they have to the canons. Look for thematic relationships between the canons and these noncanonic sections.

PROBLEMS INVOLVING THE RELATION OF CANON TO FREE ACCOMPANYING PARTS

Palestrina, Sanctus from *Missa sine nomine à 5* (in *Workbook,* "Canon", Problem 2)
Des Près, *Faulte d'argent* (*HAM,* I, No. 91)

These both use canons as the skeletons of the works but, by imitation, parallel motion, and so forth, with the free parts, the canon is concealed from the listener. First, identify the canon and indicate it graphically by a line drawn over each part. Then, pick out the points of imitation in the free parts and the canon, labeling each different point, so that a graphic picture of the whole can be seen. Finally, note how the form of the whole has been made clear by the use of rests, cadences, and so forth, and also how the canon is made to fit into this design.

Mozart, String Quintet in C Minor, K. 406: minuetto

This involves a combination of techniques, the relation of canon to imitating free parts, and the integration of that canon into a form not wholly canonic.

Schumann, Étude IV (Variation III) from *Symphonic Études*

This represents a different sort of problem. Here, there are no accompanying melodies, but each voice of the canon is accompanied by a block chord. These chords are not always the same under identical notes in the canon. Notice where these harmonic changes occur, and look for reasons why they were made.

PROBLEMS IN FORMS BUILT FROM A CHAIN OF
SHORT CANONIC IMITATIONS

Des Près, *Pleni sunt cœli* from *Missa Pange lingua*[2]
Bach, *Et in unum Dominum* from Mass in B Minor (voice parts only)

This is a formal procedure that has been discussed in Chapter I. Use the same technique used in the analysis of Example 4 in that chapter. Identify the phrases used in strict canonic imitation, and indicate these by number, now noting also any changes in the time and pitch intervals of imitation. Put parentheses around all free material. When this is done, see how the free material is integrated into the whole, so that the change from one miniature canon to the next is not obvious to the hearer.

(In all the above projects, the individual works are suggested as independent units for analysis. A student with a strong background in music history could well devise studies in historical comparison, stressing, for example, the differences involved in using the same technique in widely separated periods. The list of other examples in Appendix I should be useful in selecting works for such a paper.)

The Writing of Canon

The actual process of writing a canon is not difficult in itself, no matter what type of canon is involved. Whether it is a canon at the octave at the distance of one measure, a canon by inversion at the ninth at three measures, or any other such canon, it is approached in the same way. The process is very simple. One writes the beginning of the leading part up to the point where the next part is to enter, and this is copied at the proper interval of imitation in the other part. The next section of the leading part is then composed to fit with this, and this new section is then copied into the other part. The canon must, however, be written so that it follows the rules of tonal counterpoint and this section must be checked and all mistakes corrected *in both the leading and following parts* before the composer can move on. He should be especially careful to see that, when a correction is made in one part, the exact melodic and rhythmic changes are made in the other part as well. Then he may compose the next fragment of the canon in the same way, and the procedure continues until the end where the parts must be adjusted so as to cadence in the key in which the canon is written.

Example 14 illustrates this process in a canon by augmentation

EXAMPLE 14

and inversion at the seventh below, entering one measure after the beginning of the leading part. The first measure of the leading part (*a*) is written, stopping at the end of the measure. This is then copied in the other part in inversion and augmentation starting at the seventh below (*a'*). Then the first part is continued to fit with the second (*b*), and this is copied into the other part in the proper form (*b'*). At this point in the second part, a good approach to a cadence in G major is possible, so the part can be brought to an end by coming up to *g* (*c*). This means, however, that the first beat of the fourth measure must be *a'*, and that can be arranged nicely by using it as an accented passing tone moving down to *g'* (*c'*). The imitation is now finished, and the top part may now move on freely to the end. Thus, a canon by augmentation and inversion, which sounds very complex, is shown to be quite simple to compose, and this is true of most canons.

In finite canons not using augmentation, the arrival of the cadence is solved in a slightly different way. Example 15a shows the

EXAMPLE 15

final measures of a canon at the ninth above, when it has arrived at the point where the composer wants to cadence. The process of adding to the canon measure by measure must be interrupted to accomplish this. To make a cadence in G major, the next measure in the bottom line must outline the dominant of G, so that the usual way of adding to the canon—which would require filling in the next measure in the upper (leading) part and copying it into the bottom (following) part—must be reversed. The composer must find something that implies the dominant in the fourth measure of the example and at the same time—transposed up a ninth—fits into the top part in the third measure. This is accomplished mainly by trial and error, but, once a satisfactory solution is discovered and copied in, the leading part can then be filled in with free material to the close.

(See Ex. 15b.) Here the a' in the top part in measure four is still in canon with the final g in the bottom part, but this may not work in every canon. Then the canon will have to be broken earlier.

While the *process* of composing a canon is simple, making a canon that is musically satisfying is not. Here, the conflict between the horizontal—the creation of a good melody—and the vertical—adjusting the melody to fit with itself according to strict contrapuntal rules—comes into play. In addition to a good melody, the canon should have contrapuntal variety—not too much unrelieved parallel motion—and good harmonic movement. It is when these three elements come into conflict that the composer's ingenuity is brought into play.

Each particular pitch and time interval has its special problems. A canon at the octave at the distance of one measure runs the danger of harmonic monotony. A canon at a close interval such as the unison or the second will necessitate much crossing of parts, and the canon will be difficult to hear. Canons at the second, third, sixth, or seventh will not be answered by exact intervallic imitation, but those at the fourth or fifth may well be so. This often means that the answering part will at times be in another key, dominant or subdominant, depending on the interval of imitation. Thus, in a canon in C major answered at the fifth above, the leading-tone, b, would be answered by an f'-sharp, moving this part into the key of G. In order to get the second part to return to C, the key of the canon, the leading part must introduce a b-flat in order to get an f'-natural in the answer and thus return to the original key. Exactness of imitation is not absolutely necessary in canon at the fourth and the fifth, but it is in the tradition of canon.

The difficulty of writing a good canon is increased when the number of parts is extended beyond two, and it is increased still more if the canon is being written on a given cantus firmus. On the other hand, a free accompanying part added to a canon can cover up many defects and is a great aid in making more logical or richer harmony. In any of these cases, however, the same process is used to create the canon; there are just more elements to be taken into consideration.

Writing an infinite canon is somewhat more difficult. It may be advisable to start by writing a round, which is an elementary form of the infinite canon. It differs mainly by the interval of time elapsing before the entries of the answering parts. A new voice always enters after the end of a phrase, or strain, so that, if there are three voices, the melody of the round will be composed in three equal strains—if four, in four equal strains. To make a good round, these strains must unite to make a logical and attractive melody. The round can be written completely in score, since that is the way it will sound once all the parts have entered. It must be planned so that it will end with a cadence, since, even though it may be repeated a number of times, it must still come to a stop eventually and sound finished. On the other hand, there must be some sort of melodic lead-in from the end of each phrase to the beginning of the next, to keep the melody moving. It is wise to make a harmonic plan in advance, even though it may be changed somewhat by the time the round is finished.

The structure can be grasped by looking at the simple round put in score form in Example 16. This is a round for three voices, the

EXAMPLE 16

ROUND, *Dreifach ist der Schritt der Zeit,* FRANZ SCHUBERT (TEXT OMITTED).

score showing how it will sound when all three parts have entered. The three lines sung successively give the round in its melodic form as it is sung by each voice. When the first part has reached the upbeat at the beginning of the second line, the second part enters, and so on. Once all the parts have entered, a repetition of the round as represented in the score is made until it is voluntarily brought to a close. The parts may be composed successively, line by line, or it may be worked out polyphonically, composing all three strains a measure at a time. The important thing is to see that the melody makes sense by itself, that it is kept moving to the end, and that each strain also gives the sense of being a unified phrase.

An infinite canon is a more sophisticated version of this. Like the round, it forms a polyphonic unit that can be repeated indefinitely, but the spacing of the entries is normally closer than in the round. Also, the entries may be planned at various pitch intervals, while the round is normally made so that the parts enter at the unison. The infinite canon may be composed like the finite canon until it approaches the point where the first part begins to repeat itself, for, at the entry of the last part, the infinite canon will begin to repeat the whole polyphonic unit in the manner of a round. The ending of each part must therefore be so formed that it leads naturally into its repetition. The best way to do this is to take the beginning of the canon through the first measure of the last entry and work back from there.

Example 17a shows the beginning of an infinite canon in three

EXAMPLE 17

parts entering at a one-measure interval. The double bar with the repeat marks after it is before the measure in which the last part enters, the measure in which the repetition of the whole canon will begin after each part has completed its first statement of the melody. Example 17b shows the next step to be taken in writing the canon. The composer starts with 17a and works backward, arranging it so that a melodic fragment (*a*) is contrived that will act as a lead into the beginning of the three entries. This fragment (*a*) is then copied

[49]

in the measure before the beginning of each part. A second fragment
(*b*) is then introduced that will lead into this and fit with the other
parts contrapuntally. These two melodies (*a* and *b*) will then act as
the end of the canon, and the composer must connect them smoothly
with the rest of the canon. The double bar with the repeat mark will
then be placed so that the end of the canon, in Example 17b, will
lead directly into the point for repetition marked by the double bar
in Example 17a.

A last canon type that requires a special mode of composition is
the crab, or retrograde, canon, where a part is so made that it will fit
with its retrograde form. The procedure for writing one of these is
very simple, although it is exceedingly difficult to make one of musical interest. Example 18 shows the beginning and end of such a

EXAMPLE 18

RETROGADE CANON.

(a) BEGINNING

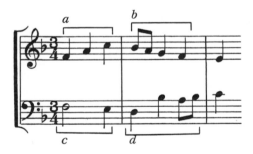

(b) ENDING

canon in the process of creation. Two melodies that fit together are
made in the first measure (*a* and *c*) and are copied in retrograde
form in the last measure, with their respective positions reversed, *a*
now on the bottom and *c* on top. This measure is important because
the first measure must be so formed that its retrograde will make a

satisfying cadence at the end. The process is then continued measure by measure.

It is evident that, at the point in the middle where the canon and its retrograde version meet, there will be a crossing over of parts, and this must be managed smoothly. Since they will not work in reverse, dissonant suspensions must be avoided, and rhythms that sound awkward in reverse must be guarded against. Treatment of dissonance must also be carefully watched. Once the canon is created, not only will the top part fit with its retrograde form, but also the whole canon may be repeated in retrograde order.

Problems in Writing Canon

The only direct application of canon in a fugue is in the stretto, but, in order to plan a stretto, the student should have some experience in writing a canon. Fortunately, in stretto the problems of cadencing and repetition are not involved. Nevertheless, to understand the process by which a canon is composed is an aid to understanding the canons that are part of our musical inheritance. For this reason, the student should write at least one infinite and one finite canon among those worked out under Problem 3 in the section on "Canon" in the *Workbook*.

For the student who needs review in the conventions of tonal counterpoint, which will be used in writing fugues, the writing of canons may well provide some practice. Any type of canon may be used. For one who has skill in working with words, the composing of a round can be very interesting. The round may be written in the manner of a catch, for example, where the text and music are so arranged that new meanings are brought to light when the round is sung as a polyphonic unit.

The writing of free parts to a canon may also give insight into the construction of works in this form that have been analyzed; in addition, it provides more practice in writing tonal counterpoint. Problem 4 in the section on canon in the *Workbook* provides a canon on which to do this. The student may also work with a canon of his own composition. Try writing a version with parts that are completely independent of the canon and also one where the added parts imitate short points found in the canon.

Notes

1. Hans T. David (ed.), *Musical Offering by Johann Sebastian Bach* (New York: G. Schirmer, 1944).

2. Found in Friedrich Blume (ed.), *Das Chorwerk,* Vol. I (Wolfenbüttel: Möseler, 1929 and 1938);

A. W. Ambrose, *Geschichte der Musik,* Vol. V, ed. Otto Kade (Breslau, 1882); and A. Smijers (ed.), *Werken van Josquin Des Prèz,* Vol. VIII (Amsterdam: Alsbach, 1952).

Chapter III

Fugue: Preliminaries

The Meaning of Fugue

*B*y 1558, when Zarlino first pointed out the difference between canon (*fuga legata*) and fugal imitation (*fuga sciolta*), the two had existed side by side for more than a century. Although there was a great difference in technique between canon or continuous imitation and the use of short points of imitation followed by free melodic continuation, these had both been known by the same term, *fuga*. The distinguishing feature of *fuga* was the interval of imitation used—the unison, fourth, fifth, or octave—because it was at these intervals that exact intervallic imitation took place.[1] Zarlino's definition of fugue followed this tradition and reasoning. His distinction between canon and fugal imitation was a reflection of the growing importance of the latter, which, by the second quarter of the sixteenth century, had become the dominant manner of composing. Although canon was still used, it moved into a subordinate position and, as we have seen, was often combined with free parts that used fugal imitation among themselves or even took motives used in the canon as material for fugal sections. Fugue in the sense of *fuga sciolta* became the primary form-building element in the second part of the century, and our failure to use the proper term has prevented full understanding of this music.

Despite Zarlino's precise differentiation between the *fuga legata* and *sciolta,* the unmodified term *fuga* was often used to designate either of these forms well into the seventeenth century. At the same time, its use became more and more associated with what Zarlino defined as *fuga sciolta.* In the late sixteenth and early seventeenth centuries, it is used to indicate a fugal section at the beginning or within a larger movement,[2] as a synonym for a work like the canzona,[3] which begins with fugal imitation, or the point or theme that is the subject for fugal imitation.[4] From early in the seventeenth century, it was also used as the name of a piece that starts with fugal entries in all parts and continues to use, in some form, the theme or themes on which the opening fugue is made.[5] It is in this latter sense that the word "fugue" was used in the eighteenth century and since, and it is in that sense that it is used today. This commonly accepted use of the term, as standing for a complete piece or movement and thus implying a form, prevents our applying the term to sixteenth- and early seventeenth-century music, as it was then used and as it should be used if we are to fully understand how this music is constructed.

The term "imitation" has become a free generic term for any statement of a theme in one part that is restated soon in one or more other parts. While this includes fugue and canon, it includes much more as well, and the use of "imitation" to describe a work based on fugal imitation—such as a Mass movement, a motet, madrigal, or ricercare—tends to obscure the real structure of the work so described. Even though Zarlino's use of the term—*imitatione legata* and *imitatione sciolta*—as representing, respectively, a canon and a short point imitated at the intervals of a second, third, sixth, or seventh (where exact intervallic imitation does not take place), did not remain long in effect, the musical difference between *fuga* and *imitatione* as he defined it is significant and particularly so in their *sciolta* forms.

As we have seen, the difference between *fuga* and *imitatione* in canon was not significant structurally, and all types of continuous imitation soon came to be called "canon." But the intervals of imitation used remained important in the *fuga sciolta.* Short points of imitation at the second, third, sixth, and seventh had been used since at least the late fourteenth century[6] but never as often as at the perfect intervals. By the time at which Zarlino was writing, a *fuga sciolta* was often used to start off a work or a section of a work, the theme being stated in each part as it entered at the interval of a unison, fourth, fifth, or octave. Only after it had been thus stated would it appear as *imitatione sciolta* at some other interval in relation to the opening part. Although the use of imitation at the perfect intervals was explained as preferable because it produced exact intervallic imitation, this was only part of the reason that it triumphed in the *fuga sciolta.* As a matter of fact, in some cases, this did not result in exact imitation, as we shall see. But, once the *fuga sciolta* became an important part in the building up of a form, it became intricately connected with the problem of tonality, and these intervals play an important role in defining the modes used in the sixteenth and seventeenth centuries and the keys used in the eighteenth and nineteenth centuries. Because of usage, it would be as confusing to call these early *fughe sciolte* "fugues" as it is misleading to call them "imitations," so they will be known in this text as "fugal imitations," to emphasize the part that fugue played in these works and to avoid the confusion of associating them with fugue as a self-contained form.

A great deal of effort has been expended in the attempt to define fugue exactly, but the fact remains that the meaning of fugue has changed a number of times so that it cannot be properly defined outside of the historical context. Because it is not a rigid form like canon, it has been particularly sensitive to the musical ideals, styles, and techniques of each period in which it has been used, adapting elements of the new to those that were traditional in its past. At the same time, certain of its aspects changed at one time and not at another, and elements strongly associated with it in one period do not appear in another.

The one thing that is characteristic of all fugues, including the *fuga sciolta,* is the beginning. The parts enter one at a time, the first to enter stating a short melodic subject and the others restating that subject on another pitch, rhythmically and melodically as exact as is possible. These later entries nearly always come at some perfect interval; they are found at other intervals but rarely, and these mainly in the nineteenth century and as a result of conscious experimentation. Variants of this opening pattern, such as the double fugue, are merely additions to not changes of the basic plan. Many fugues go on to include a number of other elements, but none of them can be claimed to be characteristic of all fugues.

This inherent flexibility of fugue makes it difficult to treat it as a fixed unit subject to historical fluctuations or to set up one particular type of fugue as an ideal form to be considered the goal of a process of musical evolution. In the historical treatment of fugue, then, the various elements to be found in fugues of different periods will be treated separately, along with exercises in analysis and composition, followed by a final summary of the place of fugue in the history of our music.

Tonality: The Modes

Before any serious study of fugue can be made, the elements of tonality as they apply to fugues must be clearly understood, because, from the sixteenth through the nineteenth century, fugue in all its aspects is bound up with the conventions of tonality. The understanding of the use and musical definition of the modes in the sixteenth century is especially important, because many conventions associated with later fugues had their beginnings in modal tradition. It is also a necessary background for the analysis of fugal imitation as a basic element in the building-up of longer forms, an important function of fugue in its early development.

Although the medieval modes were always important in the chants of the church, they were not strictly adhered to in early polyphonic music, and it is only with Ockeghem, Obrecht, and their followers that a concern with mode in relation to polyphonic music became evident. In the sixteenth century, theorists and composers continued to show interest in melodic structure, and an increased awareness and precision in analyzing and using the modes ran parallel to experiments in the chromatic and enharmonic genera. Throughout the whole period, a precise and detailed understanding of the modes was a basic part of all musical training,[7] and the different modes as well as the genera were consciously used for the expression of particular emotions.

The modes had their origin in monophonic music and thus are primarily melodic in their relation to musical organization. The placement of minor and major seconds is important in the pattern of each mode, but the half steps do not have the strongly felt need for melodic resolution that they have in the major–minor system, since they do not carry the harmonic implications associated with them in the major and minor scales. The melodic origin of the modes is also apparent in the fact that range was a factor in defining a mode —a factor that, in polyphonic music, could only be significant in the individual lines.

Each mode was defined by its octave range, the fifth and fourth into which the octave is divided, and its final and dominant notes. (See Ex. 19.) The authentic modes are the primary modes, the octave being divided into a fifth at the bottom and a fourth at the top with the final at the bottom of the fifth (in Dorian, *d–a–d′*).

EXAMPLE 19

THE MEDIEVAL MODES (FINALS INDICATED BY CAPITALS, DOMINANTS BY ITALICS).

Authentic Modes		*Plagal Modes*	
Dorian	D e f g *a* b c d	Hypodorian	a b c D e *f* g a
Phrygian	E f g a b *c* d e	Hypophrygian	b c d E f g *a* b
Lydian	F g a b *c* d e f	Hypolydian	c d e F g *a* b c
Mixolydian	G a b c *d* e f g	Hypomixolydian	d e f G a b *c* d

MODES ADDED IN THE SIXTEENTH CENTURY BY GLAREAN*

Aeolian	A b c d e f g a	Hypoaeolian	e f g A b c d e
Ionian	C d e f g a b c	Hypoionian	g a b C d e f g

* These appear so late in theory books that the old system of melodic dominants is never developed; they merge directly into major and minor.

The dominant in the authentic mode is the top note of the fifth, except in Phrygian where this falls on *b,* and *c′* is substituted for it as the dominant. The plagal modes are subordinate forms of the authentic modes; they are lower in range and share the characteristic fifth with the final at the bottom of it but differ in the octave that defines the range and in the location of the characteristic fourth below the fifth (in Hypodorian, *A–d–a*). The dominants of the plagal modes are a third below the dominants of their related authentic forms, except in Hypomixolydian where it falls on *b.* Here again, *c′* is substituted for the *b.*

To the four authentic modes (Dorian, Phrygian, Lydian, Mixolydian) and their correlative plagal forms (Hypodorian, Hypophrygian, Hypolydian, Hypomixolydian) that the theorists of preceding centuries had bequeathed him, the sixteenth-century theorist Henry Glarean added four more.[8] These had been in use for a long time—the Ionian and Hypoionian resulting from the use of *b*-flat in the Lydian pair and the Aeolian and Hypoaeolian from the use of *b*-flat in the Dorian pair. Glarean simply put these in the "natural" series, thus bringing the total to twelve modes. All of these were not, however, equally used; the Lydian pair was particularly rare. All of these modes could likewise be transposed, the transpositions by one flat (*b*-flat), one sharp (*f*-sharp), and two flats (*b*-flat and *e*-flat) being the most common, although the number of transpositions used increased as the use of more sharps and flats became common.

Strangely enough, the combination of a mode and its transposed form in a single melody or work—a concept basic to the major–minor system—was not considered regular in modal usage. Each of the modes created a particular melody type focused around the outer notes of its fifth, fourth, and octave. When the dominant was not the upper note of its fifth, as in the plagal modes or in Phrygian, it was an additional factor in the structure of the melody. The use of these tones as frequently recurring tones in the melody, as the outer limits for short melodic passages, or in skips, was considered more important than the last note of a melody in characterizing a mode.

Further, although a melody belonged as a whole to one particular mode, it could be mixed with other modes. If the melody included both the authentic and plagal forms of a mode, this was called a mixture of the two forms of the mode (in Latin, *mixtio*). If, however, the fifths of two different modes (such as *d–a* in Dorian and *e–b* in Phrygian) were used as skips or as prominent outer limits of melodic fragments in the same melody, this was a mixture of two different modes (in Latin, *commixtio*). (See Ex. 20.) These struc-

EXAMPLE 20

EXAMPLES OF *commixtio* FROM RENAISSANCE THEORISTS.
(a) *Commixtio* OF HYPODORIAN AND HYPOMIXOLYDIAN BY JOHANNES TINCTORIS (1476).

(b) *Commixtio* OF DORIAN AND PHRYGIAN BY ILLUMI- NATO AIJGUINO (1581).

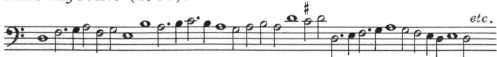

tural fifths, octaves, and fourths from the modes were thus associated with particular modes whenever they were used, and this must be borne in mind when working with sixteenth-century fugal works.

With a transposed mode, such as Dorian on *g* with a *b*-flat signature, the effect is that of the whole modal system transposed. The fifth *d–a* or the octave on *d* used in *g*-Dorian would therefore be considered a temporary insertion of *d*-Aeolian into *g*-Dorian and not a modulation to *d*-Dorian. The use of temporary accidentals (*musica ficta*) in a melodic line seems not to have been accorded structural significance unless an accidental was used so consistently as to affect the whole melody and thus define the mode of the whole. There are times when one is tempted to analyze a change of mode as transposition of the basic mode to another pitch, although clear examples are not readily found; but, if this is done, it must be done with the understanding that it is the application of a later concept to the music, perhaps a sign of the transition from modal tonality to the major–minor tonal system. As far as can be discovered, this was not consistent with modal theory. The modal system originated at a time when absolute, fixed pitches did not exist, and the modes were fixed only in relative relationships within the system. Transposition was primarily introduced to achieve a more convenient range and thus applied to a whole work. It did not fully achieve significance as a structural device within a piece until the advent of the major–minor system at the end of the seventeenth century.

Fortunately, a detailed analysis of the modal structure of a whole melody is not necessary to the understanding of fugal techniques.[9] The concept of *commixtio* is important here because it shows the close identification of the perfect intervals with specific modes. The tones bounding these intervals—Dorian, *d–a–d′;* Hypodorian, *A– d–a;* Phrygian, *e–b–e′,* and so forth—were known as the *corde del tuono,* the notes that define the mode. Their importance was rationalized mathematically by Glarean, thus adding theoretical backing to their musical prominence. Mathematically stated according to proportions, the authentic modes with the fifth at the bottom and the fourth at the top produce a harmonic division of the octave, 6 : 4 : 3, representing the ratio of the outer notes of the fifth (3 : 2 or 6 : 4) and of the outer notes of the fourth (4 : 3). The plagal modes, on the other hand, with the fourth at the bottom and the fifth at the top, produce an arithmetic division of the octave, 4 : 3 : 2.

These *corde del tuono* played an important part in the polyphonic elucidation of mode. In the early sixteenth century, when theorists began to interest themselves in the problem of mode in polyphonic music, they applied modal conventions found in the church chants to the analysis of contrapuntal works. Each melodic line was scrutinized according to patterns of melodic–modal construction and assigned to a particular mode. Since the tenor was almost universally accounted to be the most important part in a polyphonic work, the mode of the tenor part was the mode assigned to the whole work, although the other lines were often in other modes,[10] and the tenor itself might involve *commixtio*.

By mid-century, there was evident a narrowing-down of the possible choices allowed in composing in each mode, expressed most clearly in sacred music. Zarlino summed up these new restrictions in Part IV of his *Istitutione harmoniche,* where prescriptive rules are given for the polyphonic treatment of the modes. The tenor, which projected the mode of the whole, was to be written so that this mode was clearly projected. Unity of mode for all parts was preferred; the soprano (because of its similar range) should be in the same mode as the tenor, and the alto and bass should be in the correlative mode. Thus, if the tenor and soprano were in an authentic mode, the bass and alto would be in its plagal, and vice versa. This formation is typical of most sacred works in the last half of the century and of many other works as well, but it must be remembered that this refers to the over-all mode of a work. Any line could be in another mode temporarily, and often all parts at once would move for a time into a different mode. Two other elements were important in the polyphonic expression of mode—the pitches on which the entering parts began a work or a section of a work and the notes on which cadences could be made. Here, too, the wide choice allowed early in the century was narrowed down by mid-century. Depending on their analysis of chant melodies, many of which were irregular, early theorists listed as many as seven possible entry notes for certain modes. But they rarely agreed entirely among themselves as to what was correct for each mode. For example, Pietro Aaron in 1525,[11] Stephano Vanneo in 1533,[12] and Angelo da Picitono in 1547[13] all listed as initial notes for Dorian, *c, d, e, f, g, a, d':* but for Hypodorian Aaron gave *A, c, d, e, f;* Picitono and Vanneo, *A, c, d, e, f, g.* (These were given in the tenor range but naturally would be used in different octaves for the other parts.) Vanneo and Picitono, however, expressed a preference for the final and for the fifth and third above it for initial notes—in Dorian and Hypodorian, *d, f,* and *a.*

A like early freedom and later narrowing-down of allowable cadence notes is found in the theorists. It is interesting to note that, in the first part of the century, although a cadence on the final (*d* in Dorian and Hypodorian) was preferred, many others were allowed, and this must have been due in part to the fact that the works analyzed by these theorists had not always been written with a clear idea of mode in mind. It has become habitual to state that theorists lag behind practice, and this is true to a degree. But, in studying the development of musical techniques, one finds that certain theorists have had an influence on succeeding generations in perpetuating practices that they chose from compositions they studied and that they put forth as models to those who will be the composers of the future—an influence that tends to channel future development by emphasizing certain procedures they admired and considered to be "right."

Zarlino is one such theorist. It is he, again, who fixed and rationalized the polyphonic organization of modes in regard to the proper initial and cadence tones. Like Glarean, he found a mathematical rationale to reinforce his conclusions. He accepted Glarean's derivation of the modes by the harmonic and arithmetic divisions of the octave and carried this one step further, dividing the fifth harmonically to get the major triad and arithmetically to produce the minor triad. In each mode, then, the regular pitches for initial notes and for cadences became the notes of the triad built on the final of that mode—what later periods were to call the "tonic triad." Other initial or cadence notes were not forbidden, but were called "irregular," and, in succeeding generations, they were used only for special effects requiring a variant from the norm.

This stress on the tonic triad in determining and projecting mode had a strong influence on later fugal practice and on the future development of tonality. It meant, for one thing, that the difference between the authentic and plagal forms of the modes in polyphony was lessened. Since they shared the same initial and cadence notes, the main difference between the two forms remained a purely melodic one—the range—and, with the development of instrumental style, this ceased to be an important factor. It also tended to stress the fifth above the final at the expense of the old dominants of the plagal modes and of Phrygian—dominants that were purely melodic in origin and that a polyphonic and vertical orientation of mode tended to minimize.

The unity of mode was further emphasized by Zarlino in his emphasis on the tonic triad as the proper ending of a work, although he admitted that a work, and especially the first part of a work such as a madrigal with two self-contained parts, could end with a cadence on the fifth.

Zarlino had tremendous influence on the theorists who followed him, and his regulations regarding mode in polyphonic works were repeated with increasing refinement and dogmatism in the seventeenth century, until the major–minor system replaced the modes. Even though the first part of the seventeenth century saw the rise of new styles and musical ideals and was, tonally, a period of transition between modal and major–minor tonality, the conventions developed in the modes remained strong in polyphonic music, particularly in the realm of fugue.

Tonality: The Major–Minor System

The new order of tonal organization, based on the major and minor keys, was fully realized first in the music of Arcangelo Corelli (1653–1713) and, once established as the new order of things, was rationalized theoretically and codified into rules by Jean-Philippe Rameau in his *Traité de l'harmonie* published in Paris in 1722. Rameau's theories dominated the remainder of the eighteenth century and were further extended and developed in the nineteenth century until the music of Claude Debussy (1862–1918) forced a break with the principles on which they were based. It is still Rameau's theories—with additional accretions—that form the basis of harmony as it is taught to music students today.

Because the major and minor scales and the principles and procedures of harmonic progression are such a familiar part of music education, they need not be recapitulated here. But a summary of the elements of this system as they contrast with the modal procedures described above will be an aid to understanding the effects the shift to major–minor tonality had on fugue.

In contrast to modal tonality, this system uses only two main scales. But the loss in variety of melodic scales is balanced by the fact that each of these scales can appear in twelve different keys or transpositions. Moreover, the ordering of this system is not based on scales, but on the organization of chords in a relatively fixed order about the tonic triad. It might more accurately be termed "harmonic tonality" in contrast to the melodic tonality of the modes, since it defines tonality by the relatively rigid order in which the chords approach the tonic triad and in which the sense of gravitation toward the tonic increases in strength as this movement arrives at the dominant or dominant seventh chord that precedes the tonic. This gives to the music written in the harmonic system a strong feeling of forward movement that compensates for the diminished freedom of choice in chord movement.

As is so often true in the arts, these very restrictions carry with them possibilities for expansion in a new direction—in this case, toward the creation of long, unified forms. The fixed way in which a key is established makes possible an opposite effect—that of being in no key or, rather, of passing through a number of keys so rapidly that the listener feels unsettled. There is a possibility of moving from one key to another and of setting up a feeling of harmonic tension by exploiting the strong pull of the dominant or dominant seventh chord toward the tonic chord. In addition, there is a chance to combine unity with variety by repeating material in another key or by changing it from major to minor or from minor to major. And, above all, there is a potential for building up a large form by establishing a key, moving to other keys, and returning to the original key.

All of these procedures, separately or in combination, served to create the long forms developed in the eighteenth and nineteenth centuries. These procedures are first seen in Corelli's works, particularly in the fugal movements of his *Sonate a Violino Solo,* Op. 5, which he published in Rome in 1700. They are the same techniques that made possible the extension of fugue to form a unified piece of substantial length, the procedure that originated the eighteenth-century fugue form that reached its height in the fugues of J. S. Bach.

Notes

1. See Johannes Wolf (ed.), "Musica practica Bartolomei Rami da Pareia, 1482," *Publikationen der IMG, Beihaft II* (Leipzig, 1901), p. 68; see also Pietro Aaron, *Compendiolo di molti dubbi, segreti, et sentenze* (Milan, *ca.* 1550), Chap. LXX.

2. Hermann Finck, *Practica musica* (Wittenberg, 1556), f. Rii_v.

3. Bernhard Schmid, *Tabulatur-Buch* (Strassburg, 1607), index.

4. Claudio Sebastiani, *Bellum musicale* (Strassburg, 1563), ff. T₆, V, V₂; Scipione Cerreto, *Della prattica musica* (Naples, 1601), pp. 218f.; Giovanni Maria Trabaci, *Ricercate, canzone . . .* (Naples, 1603) and *Il secondo libro de ricercate* (Naples, 1615), in titles of works.

5. Adriano Banchieri, *L'organo suonarino* (Venice, 1605), in titles of works.

6. Johannes Ciconia (1340–ca. 1424) often used imitation at the second and third. See *DTÖ*, XXXI, 1–6.

7. Almost every theoretical treatise and teaching book published in the sixteenth century discusses the modes. A list of the most thorough ones is given in Appendix I under "Chapter III."

8. Glarean, *op. cit.*

9. Detailed analysis of particular works can be found in Bernhard Meier, "Bermerkungen zu Lechners 'Motectae Sacre' von 1575," *AfMW*, XIV (1957), 83–100; and "The Musica Reservata of Adrianus Petit Co-

clico and Its Relationship to Josquin," *MD,* X (1956), 67–105.

10. Glarean analyzes many works thus in Book III of his *Dodekachordon.* Translation and transcribed examples are in Clement Albion Miller, *The Dodekachordon of Heinrich Glarean* (Ph.D. Dissertation, University of Michigan, 1950).

11. Pietro Aaron, *Trattado della cognitione de tutti gli tuoni* (Venice, 1525), Chap. XXI.

12. Stephano Vanneo, *Recanetum de musica aurea* (Rome, 1533), Chap. XXXVIII.

13. Angelo da Picitono, *Fior Angelico di musica* (Venice, 1547), Chap. XL.

Chapter IV

The Subject and Answer

in Fugue: History

*T*he subject of a fugue—the melodic theme upon which it is based—and its answer—this same theme as it is stated at a different pitch—are so closely related that a technical discussion of one without the other is not feasible. Nor is it practical to write a subject to be used in composing a conventional fugue without thinking at the same time of the shape its answer must assume. The interrelationship of the two is such that the use of certain passages or particular combinations of notes in the subject may mean a distortion in its form as the answer, and beginning or ending with a "wrong" note may involve one in all sorts of difficulties in working out the rest of the fugue.

Early Concepts of the Subject–Answer Relationship

The history of the fugue subject and its relation to the answer provides an insight into the correlation between changing concepts of tonality, changing attitudes toward composition, and the theoretical and pedagogical codification of musical conventions. Around the turn of the sixteenth century, when fugal imitation was gaining importance as a structural device in choral music, there was as yet no theoretical division between fugal imitation and canon. The general rule that successive entries should be at the unison, fourth, fifth, or octave was evidently meant to apply to fugue in the sense of both canon and fugal imitation. In practice, it was applied more consistently to fugal sections than to canon, since canons at other intervals beside the perfect ones were accepted practice.

To consider fugal imitation at the interval of a fourth or fifth in the context of our experience with fugues of the eighteenth century and later is to misunderstand these early fugal works and their relation to the theory and conventions of their time. The fugal beginning of Obrecht's motet *Salve crux, arbor vitae* (see Ex. 21) illus-

EXAMPLE 21

BEGINNING OF THE MOTET *Salve crux, arbor vitae*, JACOB OBRECHT (TEXT OMITTED).

trates some of the differences between early and later usages in fugue. Here, the subject starting on *B*-flat is imitated properly at the fifth above starting on *f,* but the third entry comes in on *c',* a fifth above the second entry. (The fourth part to enter does not take part in the imitation, nor does the fifth part, which is the cantus firmus and enters much later in the piece.) Although they are foreign to our later concept of fugue, these entries agree perfectly with the traditions then associated with *fuga* as canon each following the other at the fifth and, perhaps, indicate that this newer technique was still associated with canon in the composer's mind.

Written before the polyphonic treatment of mode had been defined by composers or theorists, the pitches of these entries are not limited by strict modal requirements. The mode is Lydian with a *b*-flat; after Glarean's *Dodekachordon* (1547), this would more accurately be called "transposed Ionian on *f*," but at this time *b*-flat was commonly used in Lydian. It could not be called "transposed Lydian" because, in that case, the final of the mode would be *b*-flat, and here the tenor part—the part which indicates the mode—clearly defines Lydian as ending on *f*, and the final cadence is also on *f*. Before Zarlino, theorists listing proper initial notes for polyphonic works in Lydian all include *f*, *c'* and *g'* as correct Lydian, but *b*-flat, not even a legitimate note in the scale of the mode, certainly was not listed. It is rational musically but not controlled by strict modal limitations. Only as the composers and theorists begin to restrict the number of possible entering notes for a polyphonic composition did fugal imitations begin to approach what we have learned to accept as proper for fugue. The early history of the subject and answer is, in fact, the history of increasing limitations brought about by a growing sense of tonality.

Other fugal works by Obrecht, Des Près, and some of their contemporaries show answering imitation of the subject at similar combinations of fourths and fifths and with like freedom in the choice of initial notes. The great majority of the fugal works at this time limited their opening entries to statements of the subject at the unison or octave of the note on which it enters, and to an answer at either a fourth or fifth above or below the subject and repetitions of this answer at the unison or octave of the note on which it is first stated. This meant that the initial notes of the entering parts were limited to two different pitches which projected a certain perfect fifth or fourth. In some cases, in fact, only entries of the subject at the unison and octave were used, so that a single initial note was stressed.

Although these limitations produced expositions that are closer to the conventions of fugue as we know them, they still do not necessarily express clearly the mode in which the work was written. They are within the lists of legitimate initial notes listed by theorists (see Chapter III), but they do not clearly project a single mode. Statements of the subject and answer on *f* and *c'*, *a* and *e'*, or *d* and *g* would all be possible within the list of proper *initiae* for Dorian, but, if the *corde del tuono* (the notes that clearly define a mode) are considered, *f* and *c'* indicate Lydian, *a* and *e'* Aeolian, and *d* and *g* Mixolydian. Only *d* and *a* really project Dorian. In the case of the other entry pairs, it is only the melodic development of the parts and the cadences that fully reveals the mode as Dorian. The opening entries do not unequivocally define the mode.

In the second quarter of the century, there was a growing tendency to limit entries in fugal imitation to the exact fifth or fourth of a mode. This is apparent in the works of Gombert and of Willaert, who were the leaders of the generation in which fugal imitation became the preferred technique for writing choral movements. Other entry pairs are found but in lessening frequency in their works. As noted, it was Zarlino, Willaert's pupil, who, basing his conclusions on mathematical rationalization, prescribed the notes of the triad based on the final of the mode as the only regular initial notes for a mode. Zarlino himself did not discuss the relationship of these *initiae* to fugal imitation, but clearly the only imitative pair at the fourth or fifth included in this triad would be those entering on the final and the fifth above it (or the fourth below it)—in other words, the *corde del tuono*. The duets that he gives in the fourth book of his *Istitutione harmoniche* as illustrations of correct writing in the twelve modes bear this out. All but one of these duets begin with fugal imitation, and, except for two of these where the entries are at the octave, the initial notes outline the regular fifth or fourth of the mode.

With Zarlino, it should be pointed out, "irregular" did not necessarily mean "wrong." Some of the works that he cited as examples of correct polyphonic writing in the modes do have irregular beginnings. With Zarlino, it was still the form of the individual melodies, particularly that of the tenor, that really defined the mode, and he weighed these more than the entrance notes or the final cadence. But the composers of the last part of the century—perhaps influenced by Zarlino's prescriptive rules (which were repeated in more dogmatic form by theorists who followed him) and perhaps also because of a growing feeling for clarity of mode on the part of composers—tended to begin their opening sections on these notes that clearly define the mode. This is particularly true of sacred music. The modes were likewise used in secular music, and, when fugal imitation is found, the entrances normally define a mode. But it was also a time of experiment with chromaticism, and this usually meant working without the mode.

One of the irregular entry pairs that appeared fairly consistently even later in the century was a subject beginning on the final of the mode and an answer on the fourth degree above it—a "subdominant" answer, in eighteenth-century terminology. A look at the pat-

terns of major and minor seconds in the different modes will show
why this might occur. Example 22a shows the five authentic modes

EXAMPLE 22

(a) Scale patterns in the modes (minor seconds are indicated by ‿ ;
tetrachords of similar pattern are in brackets).

Dorian	d e‿f g	a b‿c d	Mixolydian	g a b‿c d e‿f g
Phrygian	e‿f g a	b‿c d e	Aeolian	a b‿c d e‿f g a
Ionian	c d e‿f	g a b‿c		

(b) Pairs of modes commonly combined (finals are in capitals; dominants are in italics).

Hypomixolydian	d e f G a b *c* d	Hypoaeolian	*e* f g A b c d e
Ionian	C d e f *g* a b c	Phrygian	E f g a b c d e

then in use. Lydian is omitted because it was used so rarely without
the flatted *b,* and with a *b*-flat it is simply transposed Ionian; and the
plagal forms of the modes are left out because their patterns follow
the patterns of the authentic modes.

The table shows that exact imitation at the fifth above the final
will take place naturally only in Dorian, Phrygian, and Ionian. In
Mixolydian and Aeolian, on the other hand, exact imitation will
occur only when the answer is made starting on the fourth degree.
However, a common use of the answer at the fourth is in the Phrygian
mode and, furthermore, imitation is found often at the fifth in
Mixolydian and Aeolian. Practice in this case is far removed from
what the theory of the time defined or what investigation of the
modal scales would imply.

The precise relation between fugal imitation and the pattern of
major and minor seconds found in each mode was not discussed by
theorists in the sixteenth century.[1] Two possible justifications for the
answers at the "subdominant" in the mode can be made according
to the modal theories of the time, and these give an interesting view
of the ambiguities involved in trying to apply a theory that is the outgrowth of a melodic sense of tonality to a polyphonic, or vertical,
expression of that tonality. These "subdominant" answers are in accord with two different explanations that Zarlino gave in discussing
works in which the mode is not immediately obvious.[2] One of these
explanations involves the mixture of two modes—the mixing together of an authentic mode with a plagal mode from a different
pair. He specifically mentioned the mixtures of Hypoaeolian with
Phrygian and Hypomixolydian with Ionian; these two combinations

can be seen side by side in Example 22b. As the juxtaposition of these shows, the two modes in each combination have a relationship that is, to us, an embryonic tonic–dominant relationship. A work ending in *G* but beginning with entries on *g* and *c′* could easily seem to be in Hypomixolydian mixed with Ionian, and one ending on E and beginning with entries on *e* and *a* could be seen as basically Phrygian but mixed with Hypoaeolian.

Zarlino's alternate explanation for modal ambiguity is more in line with eighteenth-century theories. This is the possibility of a composition being clearly in one mode but ending with a cadence on the fifth degree above the final. Here, entries on *g* and *c* in a work ending on *G* or entries on *e* and *a* in a work ending on *E* fit clearly into the pattern of future theories, as a work in *C* major and a work in *A* minor, each ending with a half cadence.

Either way, we are given an example of a theoretical rationalization of a musical practice that does not fit exactly into the theory current at the time. Looking back, from the point of view of the major–minor system, these conflicts between practice and theory are indicative of the amalgamation of the modes established by the conflict between horizontal and vertical expression of tonality, a conflict only to be finally settled with the advent of the major–minor system. This, however, was not the primary concern of the composer.

By manipulation of the material, composers managed to get the answers they wanted, using answers at the fifth as well as the fourth in these modes. By skillful omission of certain notes in the subject, an exact answer could still be obtained at the fifth; *g, a, c′* in Mixolydian, for example, could be answered exactly at the fifth by *d, e, g,* and similar techniques were used in Aeolian. As a matter of fact, musical practice was even freer at times. Zarlino and his followers defined fugue as exact intervallic imitation and chose the intervals of the unison, fourth, fifth, and octave because it was presumably at these intervals that exact intervallic imitation took place. But, as we have seen, exact imitation does not automatically take place at these intervals in every mode. A feeling for tonality expressed by the final and fifth of the mode was really the element that fixed the pitch of fugal entries. As a matter of fact, composers at times used answers that did not precisely follow all the intervals of the subject, a fact not alluded to by the major theorists.

The only description now known of these different types of answers is found in a work by Pietro Pontio, a theorist and composer and a pupil of the famous Cipriano de Rore (1516–1565). In a book published in Parma in 1595, the *Dialogo . . . ove si tratta della theorica, e prattica di musica,* he observed wisely that practice is more difficult and subtle than theory, and, in discussing the various ways of beginning a composition, he described the three general types of fugal answer then in use.[3] The first is the real answer (*reale*), in which both the rhythm and the precise intervals of the subject are kept. The other two are less exact and have no precise names. One keeps the exact intervals but not the exact rhythm; the other keeps the same rhythm and the generic but not exact intervals (it does not matter if a major third is answered by a minor third or a minor second by a major second). The real answer is a type of answer that has remained important throughout the history of fugue, whereas the other two types lost their significance as answers early in the seventeenth century, remaining only as variants of the subject to be used later in the body of a fugue. They were, however, frequently used in the sixteenth century, when fugal usage was still flexible. Example 23 shows the second type of answer. The third type is seen

EXAMPLE 23

BASS AND TENOR FROM MEASURES 89–91 OF *Miserere pie Jesu à 4,* NICOLAS GOMBERT (TEXT OMITTED).

in the Obrecht motet (Ex. 21) where the answer on *c′* would require a *b*-natural if exact intervallic imitation was desired.

Another type of answer that Pontio did not list with these others and that he discusses in a rather off-hand manner later in the book, is a type that was to become very significant in the seventeenth century and thereafter—the tonal answer. This form of answer, which was not intervallically exact but which conformed to the *corde del tuono,* is rarely found in the fifteenth century but appeared more and more frequently during the sixteenth century. Zarlino did not mention it in his section on fugue, but he used it in three of his duets illustrating the correct polyphonic treatment of the modes. Pontio, in discussing a four-voice fugal example where the subject *a, c′, d′, e′* is answered by *e, f, g, a,* points out that, although the two are not exact, each has the proper intervals of the mode (*del tuono*), one going by the fifth and the other by the fourth of the mode. The mode in this case is clearly Aeolian, defined by the fifth *a–e'* and the fourth *e–a*. He showed that the order of the two can be reversed—the form starting on *e* coming first and answered by the form starting on *a*—without destroying the sense of the mode, because the main notes of the mode are clearly outlined.

The tonal answer of this time was a melodic adjustment made in the answer so that both the subject and answer would fit within the main notes of the mode, the fifth and fourth into which the octave of the mode was divided. In the subject–answer pair given by Pontio, the subject *a, c', d', e'* fits within the Aeolian fifth, and its answer is so adjusted that, starting on the top note of the fifth, *e*, it fills in the Aeolian fourth, *e–a*, in the answer. If the subject had been *e, f, g, a*, then the answer would have gone through the opposite process, expanding to fill the fifth *a–e'*.

Other subject–answer relationships can be observed in the music of the time. If the subject skips a fifth, say the Dorian fifth *d–a*, the answer states the Dorian fourth *a–d'*; when the subject is *a–d'*, the answer is then *d–a*. When the tonic triad of a mode is the subject, for example *c, e, g* in Ionian, the adjustment of the answer to the fourth *g–c'* is often made in a way that is surprising to ears trained to listen to eighteenth-century fugues. The answer *g, a, c'* used in the sixteenth and early seventeenth centuries is a sharp reminder of the difference between the Ionian mode and C major with its strong harmonic implications. In an eighteenth-century fugue, the answer would always have been *g, b, c'*, because *b* is identified as the third of the dominant triad and is, therefore, the proper answer to *e*, the third of the tonic chord.[4]

As Pontio remarked in his discussion of the tonal answer, the subject and answer of this type can appear in any order since each of them defines the mode. Since the fact that this type of subject and answer clearly defines a mode melodically was well understood at the time, we can only conclude that the tonal answer was less used because fugal imitation had not yet lost its association with canon and that exact melodic imitation was therefore preferred. Both theory and practice at this time affirm that, if the initial notes of a fugal opening define the mode, this was considered enough. In Dorian, four entries on *d, a, d',* and *d'* would establish the mode beyond any doubt. If the subject started with *d–a* and the answer was a real answer, *a–e'*, the answer melodically asserted Aeolian. This apparently did not matter to the sixteenth-century musician, since a single line could at any time be temporarily in another mode, and the initial notes had already made clear what the mode of the piece was to be.

The increased use of the tonal answer in the late sixteenth century may well be indicative of a growing feeling for tonal unity, but the use of the tonal answer was even then not habitual. Not only would a composer use the same subject in one work with a tonal answer and in another work with a real answer, but also the two forms were often used in the same work or even in the same fugal section. In many cases, one feels that its use was a matter of convenience rather than conviction, a legitimate way to get more harmonic variety. An interesting combination of the two forms is found in one of the inner fugal sections of the motet by Orlando di Lasso (1532–1594) shown in Example 24. The work is in Hypomixo-

EXAMPLE 24

MEASURES 10–13 OF *Veni creator spiritus à 6,* ORLANDO DI LASSO (TEXT OMITTED).

lydian, and the initial entries of this fugal section, *G* and *D,* affirm this mode. The subject outlines the fifth of the mode, skipping a fifth down from *d″* to *g′* and back up. The second entry is a tonal answer outlining the fourth of the mode, *g′–d′,* and the third repeats the subject an octave lower. The next two entries, in the bass and baritone, are, however, real answers outlining the Ionian fifth, *g* to *c,* which is followed by the sixth entry, which is again a tonal answer, *g–d.* Subsequent statements of the theme are subjects and tonal answers affirming the mode.

We may speculate that the reason the tonal answer was not discussed in the directions for composing fugue at this time was that the answer did not exactly imitate the melodic outline of the subject; therefore, it was to be accounted imitation rather than true fugue, which was not yet fully divorced from canon in the theorists' minds. This view is supported by a comment made by the English theorist and composer Thomas Morley in *A Plaine and Easie Introduction to Practicall Musick,* which first appeared in London in 1597. In discussing an exercise in counterpoint where the beginning of a plainsong subject, *g–c',* is answered by *c–g,* he remarked of the answer, "Although it rise five notes yet it is the point, for if it were in Canon we might not rise one note higher, nor descend one note lower than the plainsong did, but in fugues we are not so straitly bound."[5]

Morley's observation gains weight by being an innocent observation of musical practice as he saw it rather than the result of theorizing; thus, he saw more clearly the practical separation between fugue and canon that was taking place. He seems not to have realized the tonal implications of this answer form. Although he was acquainted with the major Continental theorists, the relationship between the modes and composition is rarely touched on in his book. The relationship between mode and fugue is never discussed, and his ready acceptance of the tonal answer can only indicate its common use in the musical practice of his time.

One other form of fugal answer that developed in the sixteenth century is the answer by inversion. A type of imitation first developed in canon, it was used extensively in fugal imitation in the works of Willaert (Ex. 25) and frequently thereafter in fugal sections of secular madrigals and instrumental music as well as in sacred works. Its possibilities in canon and fugal imitations were mentioned, but not in detail, by Zarlino[6] and another of Willaert's pupils, Nicola

EXAMPLE 25

INVERTED ANSWER AT THE BEGINNING OF THE SECOND PART (*à 3*) OF *Confitebor tibi Domine à 4,* ADRIAN WILLAERT.

Vicentino. Both showed that it can be done by exact intervallic imitation and by freer imitation (where third is answered by third and second by second, but a major third may be answered by a minor third, and so forth), but neither gave precise rules as to how it can be accomplished. In the fugal imitation used in compositions of the period, it was generally the freer type that was used, since the intervals at which the answers enter are governed primarily by the initial notes allowed in the mode rather than by the intervals at which exact inverted imitation might take place. Vicentino showed this concern for mode in his description of this technique in his *L'antica musica ridotta alla moderna prattica,*[7] which was published in Rome three years before the appearance of Zarlino's *Istitutione harmoniche.* Here, he warned against making the subject leap a fifth upward when the answer imitates it at the interval of an octave, because the answer would have to skip down a fifth, and this would take it out of the mode. Only the answer of a fourth downward would be right for keeping the mode, and this is not correct imitation of the subject.

The Adoption of the Tonal Answer

The conviction that the entire subject and answer and not just their initial notes should establish the mode was articulated by Italian theorists in the early seventeenth century. Girolamo Diruta (1550–), organist, theorist, composer, and a pupil of Zarlino, insisted that the fifth and the fourth of the tone should be stated melodically at the beginning of a fugal composition; if one part stated the Dorian fifth *d–a,* the other must answer with its fourth, *a–d'* (or A–d). The reasons he gives were not new; to answer *d–a* by *a–e'* would mean going into the Aeolian mode, and to answer *a–d'* by *d–g'* would be using the Mixolydian fourth. What was new is the conviction that the subject and answer should present both the fourth and the fifth of the mode melodically as well as in their initial notes.[8]

Diruta also projected a theory that he claimed as his own—the idea that the subject in an authentic mode should ascend melodically, and the subject in a plagal mode should descend. This seems at first an unusual doctrine, but it does have some logic as its base. Theorists had always claimed that the plagal modes were opposite in nature to the authentic modes, and, when the power to induce a particular emotion was attributed to an authentic mode, a contrasting emotion was ascribed to its plagal.

At this time, too, the difference between the two forms of a mode had largely disappeared in polyphonic music. The only real difference was in melodic range, and even in choral music the ranges of the different parts were expanding, so that this was not always a clear criterion even for a single part. Also, the increase in the number of parts used in the new polychoral style tended to blur the differentiation in range between the authentic and plagal modes in the total polyphonic texture.[10] The modes were also losing their melodic purity as the result of the free use of chromaticism in polyphonic writing and the increasing use of the basso continuo, which forced the melodic parts to fit into a harmonic framework. Thus, it may have been that Diruta was searching for a way to musically identify these two forms of the mode. He clearly intended this to be a subject type that characterized the mode of the whole work, for he repeated the usual prescription that, when the tenor is in an authentic mode, the bass is to be in its plagal (and vice versa), but, when a "plagal subject" is used in a composition, the answer is also "plagal," the subject and answers in each part moving downward.

EXAMPLE 26

SUBJECT AND ANSWER PAIRS IN (a) DORIAN AND (b) HYPODORIAN FROM RICERCARS, LUZZASCO LUZZASCHI, CITED BY DIRUTA.

Diruta's ideas on the tonal answer and the "authentic" and "plagal" subject were shared by another organist, theorist, and composer, Adriano Banchieri (1567–1634). Both his organ compositions and his theoretical writings reinforce these views. To the 1614 edition of his *Cartella musicale,* which he published in Venice, Banchieri added new material giving directions for the use of the modes in the new style. By tracing the term "plagal" back to its

Greek root, which meant "contrary," he reinforced the idea that a theme in a plagal mode should by nature go downward and in the authentic, upward.[11] For each of the modes, he gave a fugal duet and a table showing the *modo di fugare* (the way "to fugue"), the *corde del tuono,* the regular cadences, and the final note as they appear in each voice range.[12] (See Ex. 27.) The *fughe* give the fourths and

EXAMPLE 27

(a) BEGINNING OF A DUET ILLUSTRATING THE HYPO-PHRYGIAN MODE (TRANSPOSED TO *A* BY THE USE OF B-FLAT), ADRIANO BANCHIERI.

(b) *Fughe, corde del tuono, et cadenze* LISTED FOR THE BASS AND TENOR IN THIS MODE, ADRIANO BANCHIERI.

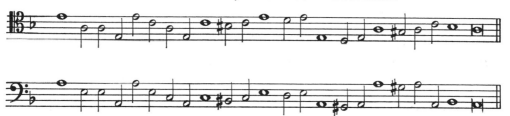

fifths upon which the subjects and answers will be based, the *corde del tuono* include the full triad and the octave of the mode, and the cadence tones also show the proper leading tones. Perhaps most interesting from the point of view of the history of the fugue is Banchieri's terminology, the association of this procedure directly with fugue. The fact that this structure of the subject and the answer was now firmly allied to the structure of the mode shows that, for theorists as well as composers, fugue was finally removed from its dependence on canon and became a technique in its own right.

The emphasis these two theorists placed on projecting the mode is surprisingly dogmatic. It is not just that they felt that, if the subject outlines the fifth of the mode, the answer should outline the fourth and vice versa, but also that they felt that the subject must of itself outline the proper fourth or fifth or both. This was a radical departure from sixteenth-century practice, wherein not only was there a choice of answers, but also the majority of the subjects used did not outline the fifth or fourth of the tone and hence did not even require a tonal answer. The examples given by Diruta and Banchieri, and Banchieri's organ compositions as well, do base their themes on the fifth and fourth of the mode, and they use the tonal form of the answer. (Note their subjects and answers, in Ex. 26 and 27.)

This is likewise true of most of the subjects used by their contemporaries, Giovanni Maria Trabaci (d. 1647) and Girolamo Frescobaldi (1583–1643) but certainly not of all. What is interesting is the fact that most of these subjects fit as a whole into the fifth or fourth of the mode, and the whole of the answer is then adjusted to fit into the appropriate fourth or fifth. (See Ex. 28.) Only

EXAMPLE 28
TRABACI
Subject

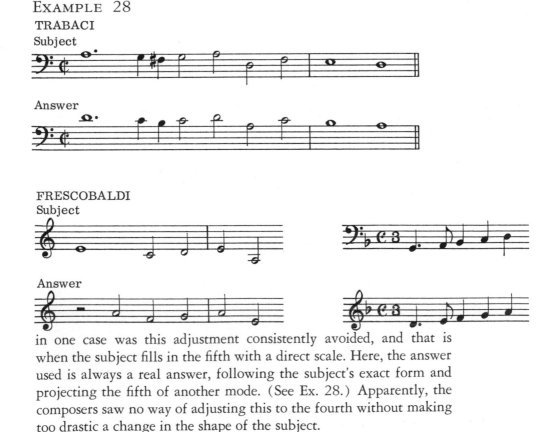

FRESCOBALDI
Subject

Answer

in one case was this adjustment consistently avoided, and that is when the subject fills in the fifth with a direct scale. Here, the answer used is always a real answer, following the subject's exact form and projecting the fifth of another mode. (See Ex. 28.) Apparently, the composers saw no way of adjusting this to the fourth without making too drastic a change in the shape of the subject.

The principle of the tonal answer was accepted by succeeding theorists in Italy—Silverio Picerli (1631),[13] Lorenzo Penna (1672),[14] Giovanni Maria Bononcini (1673),[15] and Angelo Berardi (1687, 1689).[16] It was also used in most fugal works, but there are a few in which the real answer was used where the tonal might be expected; in fact, in the whole history of the fugue, there are always some fugues in which the real answer was used where the subject would normally demand a tonally adjusted answer. The comments by Bononcini and Berardi on the answer forms are worthy of note because they are so much less dogmatic than those of their predecessors. Each of them gave as his example of the real answer (Bononcini used the term "regular") a fugue on a subject that would normally require a tonal answer. Each then followed this with an example of a tonal answer. Bononcini justified his as still deserving to be called a "regular" fugue since, although not precisely imitating the subject, it contains the notes forming the mode. Berardi merely remarked that the answers in the real fugue go out of the mode and gave another version of the answers in the tonal form to show what changes are necessary to make the fugue stay within the mode. In neither case was it claimed that the tonal form is to be preferred.

The history of the theory that the subject in a plagal mode should descend and in an authentic mode should ascend is typical of theories that have no real basis in musical fact. It was repeated by the above theorists, with the exception of Penna. Bononcini subscribed to it at least in his examples but added that its use depends on the arbitrary choice of the composer.[17] Berardi stated the rule but immediately added that it is not given as a *regola fatale*.[18] The terms finally turn up in some eighteenth-century treatises completely divorced from their modal significance. In Marpurg's *Abhandlung von der Fuge, authentica* and *plagalis* were given simply as adjectives applied to subject types, the first meaning ascending and the second, descending.[19] Even during the seventeenth century, the theory was not adopted outside of Italy, and within Italy it gained little acceptance by composers.

THE ADOPTION OF THE TONAL ANSWER
OUTSIDE OF ITALY

The musicians of other nationalities were slower in adopting the tonal answer. In works by German composers, the tonal answer is often found where the subject might demand this type of answer, but it was not used very consistently until the last quarter of the seventeenth century. At the same time, they use more subjects of the kind that would require a tonal answer. German theory follows a like pattern. In the first half of the century, theorists were still very close to Zarlino in their descriptions of fugue. Although, in the last half of the century, German composers were producing more instrumental fugal works than those of any other nation, there are no published works describing fugue, and only two manuscripts discussing the subject have been found—the *Tractatus compositionis augmentatis* of Christoff Bernhard (1627–1692),[20] a pupil of the famous Heinrich Schütz (1585–1672), and the notes of Jan Adams Reinken (1623–1722) dated 1670 and added to a manuscript containing notes by earlier pupils of the Dutch composer and organist Jan Pieter Sweelinck (1562–1621).[21] Both Bernhard and Reinken were well-known composers of their time rather than theorists, and Reinken's music was one of the many influences on the master fugue composer, J. S. Bach.

Bernhard's notes on fugue are somewhat archaic in content, stressing canon rather than fugue, although he mentions that *consociatio modorum* (his term for the tonal answer) is applied to *fuga soluta* (the Latin equivalent of Zarlino's *fuga sciolta*). Significantly, the *consociatio modorum* (uniting of the modes) is defined in the section on the modes and not that on fugue. His rationale for the tonal adjustment of the answer is unique. He attributed this adjustment to the combination of the authentic and plagal modes in adjacent voices, where the fifth is one voice and is answered by the fourth or the fourth by the fifth, a procedure appropriate to the beginning of a work. The rather out-of-date character of this section is emphasized by the inclusion of several examples from Palestrina as illustrations of this technique.

Reinken's notes are closer to the mainstream of theory. He wrote that each fugue must be in one of the twelve modes but did not insist that the subject must define the mode. As this was not a treatise for publication, his discussion of the answer is not complete; he described only the tonally adjusted answers, no doubt because these are the most problematical. But he did take it for granted that, if the subject outlines the fifth or fourth of the mode, the answer will be tonally adjusted, so that the two together will not go out of the octave of the mode. He is the only writer so far mentioned to give examples of wrong and right tonally adjusted answers and the only one to remark that a scale passage filling in the fifth of the mode can be answered exactly even though it moves temporarily out of the octave of the mode.

In England, the tonal answer is also found, but it is not always

used where the subject might imply its use. Only two theorists—
Christopher Simpson in *A Compendium of Practical Musick*
(1667)[22] and the famous English composer Henry Purcell (*ca.*
1659–1695), in his addition to the 1694 edition of John Playford's
An Introduction to the Skill of Musick,[23] described the tonal type of
answer. Both of their descriptions are rather casual and lacking in
detail. Simpson stated that one part in a fugue may rise a fifth instead of a fourth or a fourth instead of a fifth, a change that he felt
is often necessary to maintain the "air"—"air" being used here in the
sense of key. Purcell merely commented on an example in which a
fifth is answered by a fourth, remarking that this is done because it
relates the fugue more to the key—"So all *Fuges* in this nature are to
be managed, if done Masterly." Purcell himself did not, however, always use this form of the answer when he might.

In all the theorists that have been discussed so far, there are no
instructions as to the precise way in which all the notes of a subject
should be adjusted when the fourth of a subject is expanded to a
fifth or the fifth contracted to a fourth. Nor did composers always
make the same changes in the intermediate notes that come between
the notes outlining the fourth and the fifth, although there was an
apparent attempt to keep the intervallic imitation as exact as possible except for the changes in fourth or fifth.

It is the French, with their liking for concrete particulars, that
first gave precise rules for the creation of the entire tonal answer. In
France, the writing of instrumental fugal works in any quantity did
not take place much before the mid-seventeenth century, and theorists before their time did little more than explain the difference
between fugal imitation and canon. But from the time of the publication in Paris in 1650 of Jean Denis' *Traité de l'accord de l'espinette,* the question of the proper form of the answer was discussed
in detail.[24] Denis started by declaring that even those who profess to
understand the problem show little certitude, and among the most
learned there is still a difference of opinions. A subject given to
three different organists would result in three different answers.

The subject and the three answers he gave as an illustration of
this are shown in Example 29. Clearly, the problem here is with
intermediate notes that are so close together in range that the contraction of the whole subject into a fourth is bound to present difficulties. Denis was not satisfied with any of the solutions. According
to him, it is the third one that had been judged the best for this
subject, but Denis himself objected because it passes out of the range

EXAMPLE 29

(a.) Subject   (b.) Answers

of the fourth *d'–a* and because the *e'* that does this gives the effect of
a cadence on the dominant.

But Denis had no better alternative. The difficulty is one that
could not be resolved satisfactorily in the modal system, which required the adjustment of the whole answer within the proper fourth
or fifth without leaving the mode and with as exact an intervallic
reproduction of the subject as could be managed. Many of Denis'
other answers to subjects he proposed are likewise interesting more
for the problems they reveal than for his solutions. The real basis
of the dilemma is the fact that, although seventeenth-century fugal
theory—and most fugal practice—was based on the modal system, at
that time the whole organization of music was going through a stage
of transition between the modal and the major–minor systems.

The Relation of the Subject and Answer in Major–Minor Tonality

The relationship between the subject and answer in the major
and minor keys was continually evolving throughout the eighteenth
and nineteenth centuries, so that a point-by-point description of that
relationship will be misleading if it is taken as representative of the
whole period. Yet, there are certain significant contrasts between the
treatment of the answer in the modes and in major and minor that
must be pointed out before a history of this development will be
meaningful. The following summary should be considered in this
light, as a sketch of tendencies and techniques to be watched for and
noted rather than as a digest of the whole matter.

There is a difference first of all in the structural significance of
the scales. Although the Ionian mode and the C-major scale are identical, their meanings in the modal and major–minor systems are not
the same. The octave range of the Ionian is important in its definition even though it might be surpassed by one or two notes in an
Ionian melody. The plagal form, the same scale notes employed in a
different range, also had a distinct identity, an identity that was lost

in the transition period of the seventeenth century. The octave of the major scale is merely the sum of the notes in a scale that can be repeated in different ranges without losing its identity; the range of a melody in major is not in itself significant in defining the key. In contrast to the modes, major and minor could have the same range, and both were transposed to any pitch level. Because the tonality is defined by harmonic structure, a melody in any key can extend through any range without losing the sense of key.

In Ionian, the fifth *c–g* and the fourth *g–c'* have great melodic significance and, as has been emphasized a number of times, these intervals are enough to imply or establish the Ionian mode. In C-major, *c* and *g* are equally important but less as a melodic interval than as projections of the tonic and dominant harmonies, the two notes being the roots of these two chords that define the key. The other notes of the major scale have similar if less positive harmonic connotations. Rameau expressed this new approach to the scale in his explication of the new harmonically based tonality when he defined the scale as not just the pattern of notes in the octave, but also that which determines a certain order among chords, these chords being made up of the notes of that scale.[25]

The development of the minor scale reinforces this view. The Ionian scale, by its natural construction, fits into or even induces the harmonic order of the major key, but none of the modes with a minor third can provide the complete roster of notes needed to produce all the chords used in the minor key. Rameau needed two forms to procure the chords needed—the Dorian ascending with a raised seventh degree and the Aeolian on *d* with a *b*-flat descending (*d, e, f, g, a, b, c'*-sharp, *d'; d', c', b*-flat, *a, g, f, e, d*)—what has since been called the *melodic* minor scale! As every harmony student knows, the minor key has never been reduced to a single scale form.

The matter of range, of adjusting the whole of the answer within the right fourth or fifth, is no longer significant. It is the tonic and dominant notes themselves that matter. The ending of the third answer cited by Denis (Ex. 29)—which he distrusted because the *e'* moved out of the range of the scale (Dorian) and because the final skip from *e'* to *a* made a cadence on the dominant—would be perfectly acceptable in the minor key. Nor does a cadence on the dominant or even a temporary modulation to the dominant destroy the feeling of the tonic as the basic key, since it takes but one more move harmonically to return to the original tonic. This concentration of tonal functions on the single tones in the key also make it possible for the composer to adjust only the beginning or end of the answer

or both the beginning and end, leaving the rest of the answer to follow more exactly the intervals of the subject.

The old tradition of the tonal answer did not die out. In the majority of the fugues written in the major–minor system, the fifth 1–5
at the beginning of the subject is still answered by the fourth 5–8,
and a subject beginning with 5–8 is given an answer beginning with
1–5. The theoretical rationalization at first followed that given for
the adjustment of subject and answer within the modal system. Later
explanations involved an interchange of the tonic and dominant
functions of the single notes or harmonic usage, the root of the
dominant chord, 5, being answered by the root of the tonic chord, 1,
and so forth.

But under the new tonality, only the beginnings of the subject
and the answer were treated in this way. For the most part, the interrelation of subject and answer became the interrelation of two keys,
the tonic and the dominant. After the beginning of the subject was
adjusted tonally in the answer, those melodic segments of the subject that were in the tonic key would appear transposed in the answer
into the dominant key, and those segments of the subject that were
in the dominant key would appear in the answer in the tonic key. If
the beginning of the subject did not require a tonal adjustment, this
principle of transposition applied to the whole of the subject. These
transpositions were justified theoretically as the balancing-off of the
two keys—a direct contrast to the older idea of arranging the subject–answer pair so that together they projected a single mode.

The new tonal concept created new problems. A special type of
analysis had to be applied in the creation of a proper answer; this
became a limited field where only the dominant and tonic keys were
recognized. What would ordinarily be considered a temporary modulation into another key was ignored, and the accidentals involved
were treated merely as altered notes in the dominant or tonic keys.
Even with the limits of the two keys, decisions had to be made. It
was often hard to decide if a modulation had actually taken place;
if the modulation was obvious, it was sometimes hard to decide the
exact point at which it occurred. Different decisions resulted in different answers. Furthermore, because of the variability of the minor
scales, fugal subjects in the minor keys at times presented special
problems. In many cases, theorists did not agree on the correct
answer for a particular subject and often gave two or three alternate
answers that could be used for a single subject. There was likewise a
certain amount of uncertainty in the practices of fugue composers.
Although the great majority of answers are clearly implied by their
subjects, there are some answers in works of skilled composers that

still engage the speculation of theorists. As with most musical conventions, the subject–answer relationship in fugue is never totally controlled by scientific prescription.

EARLY TREATMENT OF THE ANSWER IN THE NEW TONALITY

During the last quarter of the seventeenth century and the beginning of the eighteenth century, modal tonality yielded to the new key system, and the uncertainties that always attend a period of change are clearly evident in the fugues written at this time. On the one hand, fugue was an old technique, and many fugues, particularly organ and choral fugues, retained modal characteristics in their subjects and answers. But, on the other hand, fugal movements were common in the new *sonate da chiesa* and were found as well in some concertos and suites. It is here that the new tonality was first manifested, and it was not long before the new style of the sonata and concerto along with the tonal system was adapted to the more formal keyboard fugues.

It was in Italy that the major–minor system was first fully established, and we see there the first effects of the new tonality on the subject–answer pair. An examination of Archangelo Corelli's fugal movements shows a strong predominance of real answers where a tonal answer might be expected.[26] This may be partly due to the fact that the style was new, and Corelli did not feel bound by modal conventions. Italian theorists of the time, particularly Bononcini and Berardi, taught the conservative style of counterpoint used in Italian sacred music and derived from sixteenth-century style—a style that was tonally irrelevant to Corelli's music. Even so, they were unique among seventeenth-century theorists in that neither of them insisted that the tonal answer is the only correct form, and Bononcini further remarked, in his section on the church modes, that modal conventions are not used in the concerted style, but only in church music.[27]

A look at Corelli's fugal entries reveals a positive musical cause for these real answers. All of his works have a basso continuo controlling and filling in the harmony and accompanying even the solo entry of the subject. In some, the bass line also takes part in the fugue. In nearly every case, there is a modulation to the dominant reinforced by the continuo either before the end of the subject or in its free continuation preceding or immediately following the entrance of the answer. (See Ex. 30.) A real answer in the dominant is a logical answer in these cases.

In France and Germany, in contrast to Italy, the tonal answer

EXAMPLE 30

BEGINNING OF THE SECOND MOVEMENT, OP. 5, NO. 3, ARCHANGELO CORELLI.

was still considered by theorists to be the normal one. As noted earlier, there was a steady increase in its use by composers as the seventeenth century moved on, and the frequency of its use actually increased as the new major–minor system took hold. The terms "tonal" and "real," used by Italian theorists, did not, however, appear in the writings of French and German theorists. Rules were given for the formation of the answer, and, when these rules were followed, they resulted in a tonal answer where the subject requires it and in an unchanged transposition of the subject to the dominant where no alteration is needed. It was simply taken for granted that the rules are right and that they produce the correct answer when properly applied.

During the time of transition from the modes to the new tonality, composers often invented subjects that presented new problems in the creation of the answer. The subjects and answers of this time (the close of the seventeenth and the early eighteenth centuries) thus provide an interesting study for the musician interested in tonal patterns. The new element perplexing the composers was plainly the use of modulation, or of temporary accidentals, within the subject. The solutions they provided before this new procedure was codified by theorists are often unusual, but they are also logical and make for stimulating analysis.

One interesting subject–answer combination, found in the works of Johann Pachelbel (1653–1706) and Dietrich Buxtehude (*ca.* 1637–1707), has an answer that starts with a proper tonal beginning and ends correctly on the dominant, often with a clear cadence in the dominant that exactly imitates the cadence in the tonic at the end of the subject. The subject is normally a long one, and the tonal adjustment of the head is followed by what is nearly an exact imitation of the subject in the dominant, except that, at some point before reaching the dominant ending, there is an inflection in the subdominant direction—often, as in Example 31, to the subdominant

EXAMPLE 31

FUGUE IN D MAJOR, PACHELBEL.

of the key of the subject (and of the whole fugue). Other intriguing combinations are found as well, usually the result of a temporary accidental inserted in the subject or answer or both. None of these, however, was common enough to become a convention in fugue, and, during the first half of the eighteenth century, the basic conventions of the tonal answer in the major–minor system were formed, leaving these other original solutions far behind.

Theoretical Treatment of the Subject and Answer in the New Tonality

French and English theorists were the first to limit the number of "modes" to two—major and minor, named according to whether the third note of the scale made a major or minor third with the first. The plagal and authentic forms had, of course, disappeared. The French were the first to discuss fugue in these two scales and, continuing their tradition, gave precise and detailed rules for the correct formation of the answer.

Although Guillaume Gabriel Nivers listed the modes in his *Traité de la composition musicale* (1667), the examples he gave for fugal answers are in C major and d minor (Ionian and Dorian provide the first forms of the major and minor scales), and his rules were the basis of those given by succeeding theorists who recognized only the major and minor modes.[28] These rules were given as absolute rules without theoretical rationalization, but they were clearly drawn from practice, and they can still be used for forming answers to short subjects in major and minor containing no incidental accidentals or modulations to other keys in their course.

Much of the material on fugue in Nivers' text was repeated by Charles Masson in *Nouveau traité des règles pour la composition de la musique* (1699).[29] Masson was the first French theorist to recognize only two modes, major and minor, but the rules he gave for making the answer are the same as Nivers'; they are merely spelled out in more detail. These rules, translated into scale degrees, are summarized below. Only the second had been stated by theorists (of all nationalities) before Nivers. The first was derived from the practice of the times. Preceding theorists implied that subjects should start on 1 or 5, but 3 was not mentioned as a possibility, even though it was found at times in works of contemporary composers.

(1) The subject should start on 1 or 5, rarely on 3.

(2) 1 in the subject should be 5 in the answer; 5 in the subject should be 1 in the answer.

(3) 3 in the subject should be 7 in the answer; 7 in the subject should be 3 in the answer. In some cases, though, 3 may be answered by 6.

(4) The skip of 3–5 in the subject should be 7–8 in the answer; 7–8 in the subject should be 3–5 in the answer.

(5) The skip of 1–3 in the subject should be 5–6 or 5–7 in the answer; 5–6 or 5–7 in the subject should be 1–3 in the answer. (The choice was to be left to the musical judgment of the composer.)

A few examples are given in Example 32. The answers in the bottom line can be taken as the subjects, and the top line will then represent the correct answers to these subjects.

The next group of rules pertains to the use of a repeated note to contract a scale passage into a smaller interval. Until this time, ex-

EXAMPLE 32

cept in France, the direct scales filling in the fifth between the tonic and dominant were given a real answer; the scale filling in 1 to 5 was answered by a scale rising from 5 to 2, and the scale falling from 5 to 1 was answered by a scale falling from 8 to 4. The repetition of a note to adjust this and similar scale patterns is found first in French composers and theorists; only gradually did this idea gain ground elsewhere. By the eighteenth century, however, such an answer was avoided more often by not using the type of subject that would require such an answer than by the use of the real answer.

(6) The scale fragment 1, 2, 3 is answered by 5, 5, 6 or 5, 6, 7 (depending on the context and the composer's judgment). Likewise, 5, 5, 6 and 5, 6, 7 are answered by 1, 2, 3.

(7) 3, 4, 5 is answered 7, 7, 8; 7, 7, 8 is answered 3, 4, 5.

(8) 1, 2, 3, 4, 5 is answered by 5, 5, 6, 7, 8 and 8, 8, 7, 6, 5 is answered by 5, 4, 3, 2, 1.

Some of these are shown in Example 33. As in Example 32, the

EXAMPLE 33

answers in the bottom line can be taken as subjects, and then the subjects in the top line will be their correct answers. All the examples in Examples 32 and 33 are given in major, but Masson stated that the same rules hold for minor.

Rameau's *Traité d'harmonie* (1722), which gave the theoretical basis for major–minor tonality, also included a section on fugue.[30] He repeated the basic rules given above, with a few significant additions. He changed the first rule slightly, stating that a subject should by preference begin *and* end on the tonic or dominant notes. He similarly restated the second, ruling that 1 should be answered by 5 and 5 by 1 at both the beginning and end of the answer.

Presumably, he felt that the rest of the rules likewise apply to just the beginning and end, because, after giving these other rules, he stated emphatically that the adjustment of the middle of the answer should be less strict than at the beginning and end where the answering of the tonic with dominant and dominant with tonic are so important. In the middle, it is similarity of line that counts. Normally, aside from the specific cases given in the above rules, the answer will give each note of the subject in the same relation to the dominant as the original note in the subject holds to the tonic—2 in the subject answered by 6, the second degree above the dominant, and so forth. But if this results in a distortion of the original line, one can be more flexible. If it will follow the original subject more exactly, 4 can answer to 1 or 2 to 5. (At the beginning and end only 5 can answer to 1 and 1 to 5.) For example, in the beginning, 5, 4, 3, 2, 1 must be answered by 8, 8, 7, 6, 5, but, in the middle, it should be answered by 2, 1, 7, 6, 5. To sum up (using our terms, not Rameau's), the beginning and end of the subject must be answered tonally, but the middle should be answered exactly, like a real answer. This actually sums up common eighteenth-century practice, but not all earlier answers followed this principle. It is the answer to which we are most accustomed, as the subject–answer pair by J. S. Bach given in Example 34 shows. Here, only those places where

EXAMPLE 34

SUBJECT AND ANSWER FROM THE THIRD FUGUE OF THE *Well-Tempered Clavier,* BOOK I, J. S. BACH.

5 is answered by 2 or by 1 are marked. It can be readily seen that, to answer 5 by 1 at those points where it has been answered by 2, would spoil the effect of the theme.

Rameau also recognized some of the difficulties involved in correctly answering the beginning or end of a subject in minor—difficulties that result from the possible alterations of the sixth and seventh degrees of the scale since these degrees are not fixed as in major. His feeling that harmony is the determining factor led him to give alternate answers where these degrees were involved. The third degree of the scale is normally answered by the seventh degree, but in some cases the sixth is found instead. In major, 3 is always answered by 7 when it is the first or last note of the subject but not always when it comes later, as can be seen in the second subject–answer pair in Example 32. Rameau gave alternate answers in minor using 7 (sometimes raised, sometimes not) and 6 (also in its two possible forms), stating no preferences. These are reproduced in Example 35.

EXAMPLE 35

The last French theorist of the eighteenth century to treat fugue in any detail was Jean Laurent de Béthisy, a follower of Rameau. Consequently, his *Exposition de la théorie et de la pratique* published in Paris in 1754 followed in the direct tradition of Masson and Rameau.[31] He restated much of Rameau's material, sometimes in more detail, adding a few instructions that resulted from growing experience in the key system. He recognized the need for alteration of certain notes in the subject and answer to make their melodic and harmonic relations more accurate—raising 4 to make it parallel to the leading tone or lowering 7 to make it agree more accurately with 4. Example 36, taken from Béthisy's examples, is an interesting side-

EXAMPLE 36

light on French fugal practice of the time. It is the leading tone in the subject that is lowered to agree with the answer (a and a^1), and then the answer raises the fourth degree to reply to the leading tone in the subject (b and b^1). There is a certain amount of freedom in the treatment of both the subject and answer, and the style is unusual to those whose experience of fugue tends to be limited to the works of a serious nature entitled "fugue." Here, and in Béthisy's other examples, fugue is represented by what is really a dance style not unlike the style of J. S. Bach's keyboard suites; it serves as a reminder that "fugue" originally had a much broader meaning than we accord to it today.

It should also be noted that, in all these theorists, the subject and answer were analyzed as though both were completely in the tonic key, despite alterations that seem to us to be temporary modulations to the dominant and subdominant. This probably represents the conservation of seventeenth-century tradition in fugue, when the subject and answer were expected to present a single mode and when temporary accidentals did not have the tonal implications they eventually acquired in the major-minor tradition. These precepts for forming the subject and answer follow fairly accurately French fugal writing in the eighteenth century, when the answer formation was not wholly stereotyped, and a certain leeway was accorded to the taste of the composer.

It was not in France, however, but in Germany that the eighteenth-century fugue reached its height. One of the first reactions of eighteenth-century German theorists to the increasing use of major and minor (which they at first still called Ionian and Dorian) was a sensitivity to the expression of the mode in the subject and answer by accurate reproduction of the correct pattern of whole and half steps.[32] This was important to them in church music, where the chorales used as the basis of many organ and choral works were often in the old modes and the need for expressing these modes properly was felt. The urge to explain the difference between the answers according to whole and half steps in the modes and in major or minor was new and indicates a new sensitivity to scale patterns. It should be noted because of its importance in certain historical investigations, but it was not of primary importance in the development of fugue since major and minor soon dominated this field.

EXAMPLE 37

ANDREAS WERCKMEISTER.

An example from Andreas Werckmeister (1702) is interesting because it relates to the freedom seen in fugal answers dating from the turn of the century.[33] (See Ex. 37.) It shows, first of all, a concern with expressing mode in circumstances in which the mode is not projected by the outlining of the regular fourth or fifth, so that (it seems to us) it must be represented by scale pattern alone. The subject is provided with an answer in Mixolydian (Ex. 37b) and two in Ionian (Ex. 37c). The inclusion of the two Ionian forms indicates the kind of uncertainty felt at times about the proper answer even within the major key. A similar confusion, or perhaps better, freedom, can be found in German fugal writing of this time, a freedom of which the Pachelbel theme and answer in Example 31 is a good indication.

The same rules that were given by Nivers and Masson and that formed the groundwork for Rameau's and Béthisy's treatments of fugue are found in Jean Baptist Samber's *Continuatio ad manuductionem organicum* (1707).[34] Samber's work, however, lacks the detail found in the French theorists; his only addition was one found later in Rameau—that the subject should end as well as begin on 1, 5, or 3.

The manuscript of the unpublished *Praecepta der musicalischen Composition* by J. G. Walther, composer and lexicographer, dates from about 1708.[35] His discussion of the fugal answer was not detailed, but it included a different method for discovering the proper answer, one that was used by later German theorists. The scale of C major and this scale from *G* to *g* are placed alongside each other in the manner shown in Example 38a. (Walther called this the combination of Ionian and Mixolydian, but this was only his terminology,

EXAMPLE 38

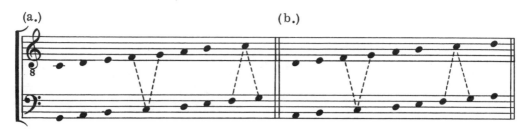

which still depended on the modes. All later writers considered the same scales to be a combination of the tonic and dominant rows.) This was to be used to devise the proper answer. Although handy, it needs rules, examples, and experience to make it truly workable. The accepted tonal beginnings are explained by it. *C* and *G* answer to each other as do *B* and *E; F* and *G* each answered by *C* give the repeated note used in the contraction of the scale descending from 5 to 1 into 8–5, and other similar adjustments can be located by it. But it lacks the flexibility of the alternatives allowed by French theorists for the middle of the answer, a flexibility certainly used in German fugal works. The similar scale alignments for Dorian (called "minor" by later theorists) shown in Example 38b seem less easy to adjust, since the alternative notes *f* and *g* do not fall on the same degrees as in major and because the question of altered notes in minor was often the source of indecision, as Rameau's examples show (Ex. 35).

These same correlating scales were repeated in Johann Mattheson's comprehensive work, *Der vollkommene Kapellmeister,* which appeared in Hamburg in 1739.[36] By this time, the major and minor keys had become the basis of German fugal theory, and Mattheson suggested that these correlating scales could be transposed to every pitch, acting as a guide to forming the answer. He further made a chromatic version with alternate notes on the proper pitches, which could also be transposed. The question of fugal answers in the modes was treated separately, indicative of the complete division that, by this time, was established between the modes and the major–minor tonality.

Mattheson's view of the subject–answer relationship drew fully on contemporary German practice. The use of the correlating scale patterns was not explained, and he did not give lists of rules for the treatment of particular notes, preferring to present the directions for forming the answers in direct reference to specific examples. When summed up, his precepts encompass all those found in Rameau but with two significant additions. He gave special attention to the answer of a chromatic subject and to subjects that modulate to the dominant at the end, requiring a special adjustment in the answer to enable them to end in the tonic. This latter type of subject came into prominence only when the new major–minor tonality was firmly established, injecting a new tonal procedure into the fugal exposition. But, although Mattheson's examples give us valuable insight into the structure of the subject and answer in the first quarter of the eighteenth century in Germany, he did not spell out exactly how the answer is to be formulated in all cases. This was left to Marpurg, whose *Abhandlung von der Fuge* provided a summary of fugue as it was created in the major and minor tonalities.

This work was the first full-fledged treatise primarily devoted to fugue, and it appeared just when the fugue was giving way to the new homophonic style and forms. Not only did it sum up the rules formulated by preceding theorists in the eighteenth century—the influence of Mattheson and Rameau was strong—but it also drew heavily on fugues by composers of the first half of the eighteenth century, with a special emphasis on those of J. S. Bach. At the same time, examples from composers of much earlier times, such as Frescobaldi were cited. The treatise had, in addition, an immeasurably strong influence on late eighteenth-century and nineteenth-century fugue and fugal theory and pedagogy.

It provides us with a comprehensive and detailed procedure for formulating answers to all the types of subjects known to Marpurg. These are illustrated by a good number of examples to which he added pertinent and thoughtful comments.[37] Marpurg included, of course, the general rules found in Masson and Rameau. He also gave the pair of correlated scales used by his German predecessors for calculating the answer. Only the version applied to the major keys was given, however, and this he reduced from letters to numbers that could be applied equally to all keys. But this scale formula was not stressed, being used merely to illustrate the relations between subject and answer indicated by the rules.

It is significant that the old rules were stated in a new context, expressed in a terminology derived from the key relationships inherent in the new tonal concept. The principle of the tonal adjustment at the beginning and end of the answer was couched in the old terms—1 answered by 5 and 5 by 1 in the key of the fugue. But, whenever 7 of the tonic key was mentioned—as when the third degree of the tonic is answered by the seventh degree—Marpurg usually referred to this 7 as the third degree of the dominant key. The same is true when he spoke of the other degrees—2, 4, and 6 of the tonic are represented as being answered by 2, 4 , and 6 of the dominant key. The resulting answer is the same whether these are referred to as 6, 1, and 3 of the tonic or as 2, 4, and 6 of the dominant, but the concept of each in regard to tonal organization is vastly different. To consider the subject as being answered by notes taken from within the tonic scale is to work within the old modal concept where the subject and answer are meant to represent one mode. To consider the answer as being a parallel of the subject in the dominant key is to work in the key system and to consider the answer as providing key contrast to the subject. The tonal adjustments at the beginning and end of the subject then appear necessary in order to avoid too abrupt movement into the new key and to make the return to the tonic smoother. The tonal answer, then, has a less imperative rationale than in the modal system. All of this, of course, was not explicitly stated by Marpurg, but the results of this new orientation are found in later treatises stemming from his work.

Marpurg was the first to analyze and explain the process of creating the answer to a subject that ends in the dominant. This requires, at some point, an adjustment similar to that made when a direct scale between 1 and 5 is made to fit between 5 and 8, and vice versa. At the point where the modulation is apparent in the subject, there is a shift in the interval at which the answer imitates the subject, and, consequently, there is a change in one interval in the midst of the answer analogous to the changes made in the head of a tonal answer. Example 39 shows two of Marpurg's illustrations. In Example 39a, the subject is in the dominant key from the second beat of the second measure, and, in the answer, this must be transposed back to the tonic, down a fifth. The first four notes, however, being in the tonic, are transposed down to the dominant, the interval of a fourth. This

EXAMPLE 39

(a.) Subject

Answer

(b.) Subject

Answer

results in the change of the interval of a second between a' and b' in the subject to the unison e's in the answer. By a parallel process, the third between c'' and e'' in the subject in Example 39b is contracted into the second $g'-a'$ in the answer.

This type of adjustment was not new. It had to be made in the modal system when a subject began on 5 and ended on 1 or when it began on 1 and ended on 5. But the context was different as was the theoretical rationalization. Similar intervallic adjustments were made in the seventeenth century and can be seen in both Example 27 and Example 28. In these examples, the composer was adjusting a subject and answer each of which was to be adapted to the proper fifth or fourth of the mode. In the eighteenth century and later, it was the adjustment of melodic segments in different keys, the tonic and the dominant, that must be re-arranged. In some cases, the answer adjustment would have been the same, but the later one involved a more conscious and regulated use of tonal materials.

Another problem first treated by Marpurg is likewise indicative of the change that the new tonal system wrought in fugue. This is the formulation of the answer to a subject beginning on 2, 4, 6, or 7. The very acceptance by composers and theorists of the possibility of such subject beginnings shows the effect of the major–minor key system.

[97]

The contrast with early modal practice is perhaps greatest in this usage. It will be remembered that the initial notes allowed in fugal beginnings for each mode in the early sixteenth century were subject to little limitation but that, by the middle of the century, beginnings on the final and the fifth above it were accounted the only regular ones. Even in the seventeenth century, these were preferred, although subjects beginning on the mediant of the tonic triad are found at times and were accepted. These limitations were imposed because the melodic projection of mode was not strong enough to make the mode clear in a polyphonic structure and because the various fifths and fourths were associated with particular modes. Thus, if, in a work purporting to be Dorian, the subject began on 2, *e,* and was answered a fifth above by *b,* the opening of the fugue would imply Phrygian. This might be used as a special effect, but it was not "regular" and was rarely used except in vocal works in which the mood of the text called for unusual treatment.

In major and minor, however, a melodic line in which tonic and dominant harmonies are outlined by melodic patterns has an unmistakable tonal center, and the key is obvious no matter what notes the parts begin on. Further, the vertical sonorities serve to reinforce the sense of tonality rather than to obscure it, as in modal polyphony. Hence, a much greater freedom is allowed the composer in the invention of his fugal subject.

Marpurg's answers for subjects beginning on scale degrees other than 1 and 5 were, like his others, mostly derived from the composers of his time. Except for those starting on 4 and 6—which are answered by 4 and 6, respectively, in the dominant—there is a choice of two possible answering notes. For a subject beginning on 3, the answer will start with 3 in the dominant if the subject itself stays in the tonic. (See Ex. 40a.) (Note that in minor it is 3 in the dominant key that answers 3 in the tonic key. Rameau's use of the raised seventh degree of the tonic for the answer to 3 in minor [Ex. 35] was still quoted by Marpurg but in the group of exceptional answers —answers that were unusual and justified by some particular reason. In this case it was the need for that dominant harmony that convinced Marpurg of its correctness.) If the subject moves to the dominant, 2 in the dominant will usually answer to 3 in the subject. (See Ex. 40b.)

When the subject begins with 7 in the tonic, the answer will start with either 6 or 7 of the dominant key. This depends mainly on the musical context. If 7 is treated clearly as the leading tone to the tonic, it must be answered by the leading tone to the dominant (Ex.

EXAMPLE 40

(a.) Subject

Answer

(b.) Subject

Answer

41a), but, under other circumstances, an answer of 6 in the dominant to 7 in the tonic is more appropriate. (See Ex. 41b.)

EXAMPLE 41

(a.) Subject

Answer

(b.) Subject

Answer

If the subject begins with 2 in the tonic, there is likewise a choice of two replies—the dominant itself or 2 in the dominant. Here, the choice depends on which makes the best melody or the closest likeness to the subject. At times, the choice is clear, as in Example 42a, but, for some cases, Marpurg found either answer form acceptable. (See Ex. 42b.)

EXAMPLE 42

(a.) Subject

Answer

(b.) Subject

Answer   or:

Marpurg was likewise the first to give precise instructions for forming the answer to a chromatic subject. The procedure is simple. The subject (Ex. 43a) is reduced to its bare diatonic outline (Ex. 43b), the diatonic answer is made (Ex. 43c), and the chromatic tone is put back (Ex. 43d). Not all chromatic subjects can be so easily adjusted to a tonal answer as this one, but, for Marpurg, the retention of the chromatic movement in the right part of the subject took

EXAMPLE 43

(a.)   (b.)

(c.)   (d.)

precedence over other adjustments.[38] In addition to his intensive treatment of the answer in the new tonal system, Marpurg followed in the footsteps of his German predecessors, including a thorough treatment of the creation of the answer in the modes.

Certain of Marpurg's answers and the answers of other composers that he cited would not be accepted by late nineteenth- or twentieth-century teachers of fugue. The same would be true of some of those included in the works of Mattheson, Rameau, or Béthisy. Likewise, some later theorists disagreed with certain answer forms used by J. S. Bach and his contemporaries. Therefore, it should be strongly emphasized that, at this time, theorists permitted alternative choices, and composers as well felt a certain amount of freedom. This must be kept in mind when looking at the fugues of this period; they should not be expected to conform to more rigid rules invented at a later time. In addition to the allowable freedom of choice shown above, Marpurg picked a number of subject–answer pairs that do not agree with the rules that he had given.[39] But he did not condemn these cases. Rather, there is a feeling of admiration for the unusual and for the good judgment of the composer who did what was musically right even when it did not accord with the rules that Marpurg and other theorists had given.

Terminology: The Use of "Tonal" and "Real" Applied to the Answer

Although one of the main concerns of these eighteenth-century French and German theorists was the definition of what we call the tonal answer in the new tonal system, it must be pointed out that, at this time, the actual terms "tonal" and "real" were not used outside of Italy. It was only during the nineteenth century that the terms were adopted in France, and not until the twentieth century did they become common in German treatises on fugue. The use of the term "tonal answer" is thus anachronistic or historically inappropriate when discussing these earlier theories and compositions (including Bach's fugues!), but it must be used because there is no other available term. Its use cannot, therefore, be abandoned, but, for historical accuracy, one should recognize that it was not used by the composers of most of the works to which we apply it. Nor, since we are well aware of the musical process to which it is applied, is the tracing of the adoption of the term of great significance, but it does provide an interesting sidelight to the development of fugal theory.

In eighteenth-century Italian theory, the terms "real" and "tonal" fugue were carried over from seventeenth-century theory, and thus their meanings differed slightly from later applications of the terms. The *fuga del tuono* still held, in part, a relation with the old modes, since in some cases it seems to have meant the adjustment of the whole answer within the proper fourth or fifth. The *fuga reale* still meant, as in the sixteenth century, an exact intervallic reproduction of the subject, and this was applied to subjects that would, for French and German composers, normally require a tonal answer as well as to those that would not.

Italian theorists of the time followed in the footsteps of the seventeenth-century theorists Berardi and Bononcini. The tonal answer was defined and illustrated but not given precedence over the real answer even where the subjects involved might well imply a tonally adjusted answer. The leading teacher of fugue, Giambattista Martini (1706–1784), still preferred the real answer where a tonal adjustment in the answer would, to his taste, distort the melodic shape of the subject or result in what he considered a monotonous harmonic pattern.[40] Nor did Italian theorists give any detailed rules for forming a tonal answer. Martini's work is not so much a textbook on fugue as a series of examples with penetrating comments. But the preface, which discusses the main conventions of fugue, includes a very brief description of the tonal answer. This shows the adjustment of the head of the subject only, and makes no mention of the problems of modulation. In his comments in the body of the work, moreover, some of the tonal answers he suggested (and condemned as musically unpleasing) would also be wrong according to contemporary French and German practice. One feels that Martini was still concerned with adjusting the whole answer within the proper fifth or fourth of the key and had not considered the harmonic implications and possible adjustments in the middle of the subjects involved.

Other Italian theorists of the time likewise did not consider the tonal answer to be the ideal one when working in the major–minor system, and this attitude plainly reflects the practices followed by Italian composers writing fugues in the eighteenth century. Although the proportion of real to tonal answers (where tonal answers might be expected) is never so great as in the music of Corelli, it is always much larger than in the works of French and German composers of the time. A comparison of the fugues of Italian-trained George Friedrich Handel (1685–1759) with those of his contemporary

J. S. Bach, who followed the German tradition, points up this difference.

An approach similar to that of Padre Martini is found in the pedagogical works of two of his followers—Luigi Antonio Sabbatini's *Trattado sopra le fughe musicali* (Venice, 1802) and Angelo Morigi's *Trattado di contrapunto* (Milan, 1802). In each of these, the real fugue is described using examples whose subjects would, for French or German theorists, require a tonal answer. They likewise gave examples of the tonal fugue with a few simple rules for forming the tonal answer. These are very simple, requiring only an adjustment of the head of the subject, and in none of the subjects is there a modulation to the dominant. There is no insistence on the tonal fugue as the preferred one, and Morigi was careful to state that the real fugue is not subject to the rules of tonal fugue.

Nineteenth-century Italian theory produced little on fugue, since by this time the importance of fugue had declined sharply in Italy, but the Italian influence was felt strongly in France, where Italian composers and teachers were greatly in demand. Here, too, fugue—although losing prestige as a form of personal expression—retained its prestige in church music and as a technical *tour de force* for the composer. As such, it became a necessary part of a composer's training, and it was often considered the halfway stage between exercises and free composition. It was, therefore, discussed in detail in all the major texts on composition, and, in all of these, the formation of the proper answer was considered to be of primary importance.

The Italian attitude was first transmitted to France by H. F. M. Langlé who came from Naples to teach at the Paris Conservatory. In his *Traité de la fugue* (Paris, 1805), he discussed both the real and tonal fugue, and, like his contemporaries Sabbatini and Morigi, his *fugues réelles* are of the type that could be adjusted tonally if desired. (See Ex. 44.) He also included the simple rules for the *fugue du ton* and included fugues written with such subject-answer pairs; but he made no pronouncement as to which is the correct or even the preferred usage.

Marpurg's influence in France had also been felt during this time. His work on fugue was published in French translation in Berlin in 1756 and in Paris in 1801. Despite its title, the *Principes de composition des écoles d'Italie* by Alexandre Choron, published in Paris in 1803 and approved as a text by the French government, depends entirely on Marpurg's treatise for its treatment of fugue.[41] Marpurg's discussion of particular answer types, including chromatic and modal forms and irregular answers is drawn on, and many of his examples

EXAMPLE 44

BEGINNING OF AN EXAMPLE OF A REAL FUGUE, H. F. M.
LANGLÉ.

as well as his comments on them are reproduced. Naturally, the terms
"real" and "tonal" are not used, but it is taken for granted that the
tonal adjustment of the answer is obligatory.

During succeeding years, the teaching of composition—and particularly fugue—in the Paris Conservatory became more conservative
and further removed from contemporary musical practice. The *fugue
d'école,* an academic exercise in "traditional" composition, became a
basic part of the Conservatory curriculum. Since it was considered an
exercise and not a free musical creation, the tendency toward stereotype and pedantry increased and was particularly obvious in the
formation of the fugal answer. Rules became progressively more
dogmatic and inflexible as the century moved on. There was a growing sense of academic absolutism, with most theorists insisting that
there was one correct way to make an answer and that this is found
by reasoning from within the tonal system rather than observing the
practice of composers.

One of the professors who fought a losing battle with the conservative Luigi Cherubini, Professor of Composition at the Conservatory from 1816 and director from 1822, was Anton Reicha (1770–
1836), who was appointed Professor of Counterpoint and Fugue in
1818. A boyhood friend of Beethoven, Reicha shared with Beethoven
a desire to create a new, Romantic type of fugue, and his *Trente-six
fugues d'après un nouveau systême,* published in Vienna in 1805,
was one of the fruits of this youthful enthusiasm. Among other in-

novations, he brought in answers at unusual intervals, often as real answers in keys outside the dominant. The twentieth fugue, for example, has a subject starting in A major, and the answer is an exact transposition starting in E-flat major. The harmonic style, although exceedingly chromatic, fits clearly within the prevailing tonal system. His theoretical works written for pedagogical purposes take a more traditional approach to fugue, and his later fugues tend toward the conventional subject and answer types. But even though he bowed to practicality, his approach as a teacher of composition was justified by the success of three of his students—Hector Berlioz (1803–1869), Franz Liszt (1811–1886), and César Franck (1822–1890)— whereas the names of hundreds of other graduates who distinguished themselves in composition at the Conservatory have long since been forgotten.

Reicha's treatment of conventional fugue is found in the second volume of his *Traité de haute composition musicale* (Paris, 1825). Here, he maintained that any composer who does not know how to make a correct fugal answer cannot be said to know fugue, and his discussion of the answer is thorough and reasoned, including numerous examples and showing how alternate answers can be made to certain subjects.

He followed the normal conventions of tonal adjustment without using the terms "tonal" or "real," but a comment he made in another section of the treatise[42] shows a critical awareness of the increasing use of these terms. Reicha clearly associated the *fugue du ton* with pretonal or modal writing. He further credited Martini with first using the term "real" in an effort to distinguish the "modern" fugue from the older type because, in the newer tonality, the answer "is often made without any change, except for transposition." Neither of these statements is accurate, and they are clearly based on hearsay evidence rather than on a perusal of Martini's writings. But they do show the confusion that attended the use of these terms in the early nineteenth century. Further, Reicha's definition of the real answer, implying that at times some changes might be made, shows that the tonally adjusted answer in which certain notes at the beginning or end might be changed but in which the middle was a straight transposition must have been accounted by some as a real answer, contrasting with the modal *fuga del tuono* in which the whole of the answer had to be adjusted.

The year 1825 also saw the publication in Paris of F. J. Fétis' *Traité de la fugue*—the first text consciously based on a historical approach. Although this historical orientation shows a good understanding of stylistic differences, it also manifests a conviction that the theorists and composers of the past had not completely understood the basis of "modern tonality" and thus propagated errors. In the discussion of the answer, Fétis took it upon himself to correct certain "wrong" answers by composers such as Pachelbel and J. S. Bach. Here, we begin to feel the dogmatism that was to dominate the fugue pedagogy of the later nineteenth century.

Fétis also used the terms "real" and "tonal" in the sense in which we understand them, applying "tonal" both to those fugue subjects that modulate to the dominant key and those in which 5 or 7 of the key used at the beginning or end of the subject requires tonal adjustments in the answer. He also used the adjectival form *tonale* as a synonym for *de ton,* and it is the adjectival form that eventually survived. It is interesting to note, too, that, although Fétis gave detailed rules for the formation of answers to all types of subjects, in his opinion the essential condition of "modern" fugue was that the subject should always end in the dominant key so that the answer will start in the dominant and return to the tonic key. Although this remained solely a personal opinion, it is evidence that the increasing stress on balance of key does have an effect on fugue as well as on homophonic forms.

Succeeding texts on fugue in France continued to use the terms "tonal" and "real" and came to consider the tonal fugue to be the preferred form. Luigi Cherubini's *Cours de contrepoint et de fugue* (1833)[43] draws many elements from Italian tradition, particularly from the followers of Martini, but he also stressed the tonal fugue as being the one most in use. He further defined the real fugue not as Martini and his followers had, but as a fugue in which the subject does not go to the dominant and therefore can be answered by exact transposition to the dominant key. By implication, this reinforced the view that a tonal answer must be given where the subject implies such an answer and the real answer is correct only when there is no need for a tonal adjustment.

Cherubini's rules for the treatment of tonal fugue are limited to a few types, but his explanation of these adjustments have a new rationalization—a rationalization that is significant because it shows the growing emphasis on harmonic rather than purely melodic relationships. Thus, for the subject c'', d'', b', g', the usual answer g', g', e', c' is justified because—in addition to the fact that c'' and g' in the subject will be answered by g' and c'—the intermediate notes d'' and b', the fifth and third of the dominant chord, are answered by g' and e', the fifth and third of the tonic chord.

Hippolyte R. Colet's *La panharmonie musicale* (1837)[44] like-wise stresses the tonal fugue because it is the most used and because it is the only one allowed at the Conservatory. His rules for the answer are not flexible. He criticized Reicha for allowing more than one answer for certain subjects, insisting that there can be only one correct tonal answer for a subject. Like Cherubini, he depended on analysis by means of the tonic and dominant triads for the process of forming the tonal answer.

But Colet himself obviously preferred the real fugue, which he called the free fugue because it is used in free composition in contrast to the *fugue d'école,* in which only the tonal fugue is admitted. To his sense, too, this free fugue admits a real answer to any type of subject rather than, as in academic theory, only to a subject that would not imply a tonal answer. His ideas, however, show no aware-ness of the older Italian tradition but are based on purely musical considerations. This free real fugue is preferred because of the exact similarity of subject and answer, and the problem of key is no prob-lem in the modern style. His example shows a subject that modulates to the dominant at the end; the real answer, of course, ends in the dominant of the dominant. But, as he said, one can get back to the tonic key easily and naturally, so that there is no technical reason why this should not be done. Colet's remarks on the tonal answer likewise hint at the growing conflict between the academic view and the attitude of the would-be composer:

This furor over the answer is so great that some composers spend all their lives searching for the answer to difficult subjects. We counsel the student not to imitate them; this is not real composition.[45]

Despite this attitude, however, Colet seems to have had no objection to the use of the strict conventions of the tonal fugue as a teaching device. He actually considered the academic fugue to be an ideal transition between musical exercises and free composition.

Moreover, the academic approach to the tonal and real answer carried the day. Antoine A. E. Elwart's treatise, *Le contrepoint et la fugue appliqués à la composition idéale* (1840),[46] was meant to avoid the scholastic viewpoint, but it reinforced the emphasis on the prefer-ence for the tonal answer. His reasoning, typical of later nineteenth-century attitudes, was based on the conviction that the purpose of an answer was to sound like an answer to the subject.

At the same time, Elwart was aware of some of the difficulties involved in applying tonal adjustments to certain subject types. One problem that had bothered fugue theorists off and on was the type of answer that resulted when tonal principles were applied to a chromatic subject. Some, like Fétis, felt that a real answer was the only possible solution for a chromatic subject, but exercises in making tonal answers to such subjects continued to be a part of the study of fugue. Example 45a shows what happens when the rules are used

EXAMPLE 45

(a.) Subject

Answer

(b.)

to make a tonal answer to a chromatic subject beginning on the fifth degree (*b'*-flat) and descending. The answer must start on the tonic (*e''*-flat), and the compression of the chromatic scale to fit between the tonic and the second degree of the dominant (*c''*) answering to the second degree of the tonic (*f'*) results in a triply repeated tonic!

He also presented the problem of the answer to a subject in minor beginning with 5 and 7 (*e'* and *g'*-sharp) (Ex. 45b) going to 1 (*a'*). Here, the answer must start on the tonic, *a,* and move to the leading tone of the dominant, *d'*-sharp and then to the dominant, *e'*. In A major, it could be answered *a, c'*-sharp, *e'* (the third of the dominant chord being answered by the third of the tonic chord), but in A minor the third of the tonic chord is a *c'*-natural, so this cannot be used. Elwart deplored this distortion and suggests that, if the composer pleases, he can answer with *a, c'*-sharp, *e'*. (Beethoven's solution, when confronted with this same problem in the first movement of his String Quartet in C-sharp minor, Op. 131, was to use a real answer in the subdominant—to the above subject, *a, c'*-sharp, *d'*.)

Nevertheless, despite problems involved in the tonal fugue, it was taught continuously and with increasing dogmatism in French institutions in the second half of the nineteenth century, and the tradition of the *fugue d'école* reached its climax in two texts published in Paris in 1901—Théodore Dubois' *Traité de contrepoint et de fugue* and André Gedalge's *Traité de la fugue*.

German Fugal Theory in the Late Eighteenth and Nineteenth Centuries

Although no longer a leading form, the fugue was still important to the Classical and Romantic composers of Germany and Austria both as a traditional procedure and as material for musical experiment and development. The experimentation did not, however, mean an abandonment of the tonal adjustment of the answer. Although the terms "tonal" and "real" were not adopted by German theorists during this time, theorists continued in the German tradition that took it for granted that, when a subject implies a tonal adjustment in the answer, this adjustment should be made. However, the use of more altered intervals in subjects made more tonal adjustments necessary, and this new type of subject–answer pair is found much earlier in German music and theory than in other countries because of the German stress on instrumental in contrast to vocal fugue.

The section on fugal answer in Johann George Albrechtsberger's *Gründliche Anweisung zur Composition* (1790)[47] although not detailed or filled with elaborate rationalization, shows some of these subject–answer pairs. As in the simpler adjustments, the intervals involved generally were only expanded or contracted by the interval of a second, but often—as in Example 45—this resulted in a melodic or harmonic distortion of the theme in the answer. Example 46 shows two of Albrechtsberger's subjects and their answers. The first (a) illustrates a subject type that was becoming more common, in which an accidental implies a modulation close to the beginning of the subject. Here, the c''-natural makes it sound as if the subject started in G major and modulated to the dominant at the end. Only with the answer do we become aware of the real key, D, since the first note of the answer, d', is the normal use of 1 in the answer to respond to the dominant, a', that starts the subject, and the rest of the answer is an exact transposition of a melody in D (in the subject) down a fourth into the dominant. If the subject was really in G, the answer would be that added in brackets (by the author) after Albrechtsberger's answer. The first three notes of the subject would then be 2, 4, 3 in G major, to be answered by direct transposition down a fourth into the dominant, D; the remainder of the subject would be analyzed as a modulation into the dominant, to be answered in the tonic, G. In either case, the part accompanying the answer would need to be so composed as to make the key clear by harmonic implications;

EXAMPLE 46

(a.) Subject

(b.) Subject

in Albrechtsberger's answer, g' must be clearly felt as a lowered seventh degree going to 6; in the second, hypothetical answer that presumes the subject to be in G major, the initial notes e' and g' must be heard as 2 and 4 in D.

In Example 46b, a raised fourth degree, g'-sharp, implies a temporary modulation to the dominant, A minor, but the quick return to g'-natural as well as the cadence in the tonic make the key, D minor, clear. The subject, however, is distorted melodically in the answer, since two prominent intervals must be altered in making the required tonal adjustments. Since 1 and 5 at the beginning of the subject must be changed to 5 and 1 at the beginning of the answer, the d'' that begins the subject is a'' in the answer, and the octave $a'–a$ in the subject becomes $d''–d'$ in the answer. The g'-sharp that acts as a leading tone to a' must be answered by c''-sharp, the leading tone to d''. This results in the first interval of the subject, a diminished fifth, being answered by a minor sixth. Moreover, since the last part of the subject (from g' to the end) is clearly in the tonic, it must be transposed directly into the dominant for the answer. This means that the interval of a minor seventh ($a–g'$) in the subject is changed to an octave ($d''–d'$) in the answer.

Both these subject–answer pairs, as well as those in Example 45, show the difficulties involved in making a tonal answer to some types of subject that are normal to the melodic style of the late eighteenth and nineteenth centuries. The tradition of the tonal answer, once rationalized as presenting unity of mode, came to mean balance of key between the subject and answer. At the same time, this was still applied to single notes at the head of the subject, where the root of the tonic triad must be answered by the root of the dominant triad and the third of the tonic triad by the third of the dominant triad (and vice versa). Thus, significant melodic intervals at the head of the subject are often altered in the answer. Likewise, where a subject modulates to the dominant at the end and this melodic segment is transposed to the tonic in the answer, one interval will have to be changed in the midst of the answer (as in Example 46b where the seventh becomes an octave in the answer).

Albrechtsberger did not explain the rationale by which his answers were obtained; he merely gave them as examples of intervals changed in the process of creating the answer. Indeed, evidence has been found that, as a teacher of fugue, Albrechtsberger (who was Beethoven's teacher) was sometimes careless in correcting his pupil's answers.[48] But his type of subject was in keeping with the fugues written by German and Viennese composers in the late eighteenth and early nineteenth centuries, and later German theorists were precise and detailed in giving rules for forming such answers and in developing theoretical justifications for them.

There is no need for a historical treatment of the answer in German nineteenth-century theory because it followed clearly in the footsteps of Marpurg—a thorough treatment of all cases with detailed rules and examples. The tonal principles stated by Marpurg are clearly applicable to more complex subjects, as the examples from Albrechtsberger given here show. It was not a change in the principles, but a change in the subject type that resulted in melodic distortion of their answers. This tonal adjustment of the answer was considered necessary by all German theorists. It is significant that, in their discussions of the free fugue, it was the form that was considered free and not the answer; only French theorists mentioned that the free fugue need not be subject to the rules of the tonal answer.

By the second half of the nineteenth century, German theorists, like their French counterparts, became more dogmatic in their treatment of the answer. Like the French, too, they felt that there was only one correct tonal answer to a subject, but there was more effort put into the theoretical reasoning behind the formation of this answer, and a strong attempt was made to base this theory on actual practice. However, they based their theory on the practice of the past, predominantly on the works of J. S. Bach with Handel as a secondary influence. When exceptions to their rules were found in Bach, these were discussed, and the musical reasons behind these exceptions were sought. In some cases, attempts were made to extend the rules—or create new rules—to adjust to Bach's "exceptions." An interesting case is the rule based on the real answer that Bach gave to the head of the subject of his G Minor Organ Fugue (Ex. 47a). E. F. Richter

EXAMPLE 47

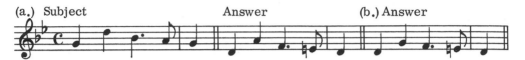

stated that this is no doubt given a real answer because it includes the complete triad, and he and some later theorists would allow a real answer in this case (not mentioning the subject of Bach's *Art of Fugue,* which likewise starts with a complete triad but uses a tonal answer).[49] It is amusing, too, to note that the French theorist Dubois, in his aforementioned treatise published in 1901, gives this same beginning of Bach's G minor theme without mentioning that it is from Bach and uses it as one example of a subject requiring the tonal answer.[50] (See Ex. 47b.)

When we observe the ease with which modulation is accomplished in nineteenth-century music and the distortions that are often made in the answer when tonal adjustments are used, it is hard to see why so much insistence was placed by German theorists on the musical correctness of the tonal answer. The weight of German tradition and the increasing influence of Bach were no doubt important. But there was also a tendency among theorists to agree with the idea expressed by the French theorist Elwart who, as mentioned earlier, wanted the answer to sound like an answer. Similar opinions were expressed by German theorists. Richter justified the answer of the tonic by the dominant by stressing that the dominant is the *antithesis* of the tonic and that the subject and answer should have the effect of antecedent and consequent phrases.[51] It is easy to see that a tonal adjustment would enhance this effect much more than would an exact repetition of the subject in the dominant key.

Many theorists, however, at some time mentioned that there was still disagreement as to the correct fugal answer, and this question was never resolved. The new styles of the twentieth century made the question superfluous, since all the problems in making the answer grew out of tonal conventions—first, of the modes and, later, of the major–minor tonality. Nineteenth-century composers seem to have solved it in their own way. At times, they used the real answer where the tonal answer would bring about mutilation of the subject, but the tonal answer was often used as well. There was, at the same time, a proportional increase in the legitimate use of the real answer; composers apparently learned how to make musically complex and interesting subjects that were so constructed that no tonal adjustment would be required.

NINETEENTH-CENTURY RULES IN SUMMARY

A general summary of nineteenth-century theory concerning the answer is a useful tool even though, as the preceding description makes clear, there was enough divergence to make such a summary slightly misleading. By the last half of the century, the tonal fugue had gained pre-eminence, particularly in the academic texts, and the rules for the creation of the answer thus have a nice clarity. They represent a narrowing-down of the rules bequeathed by eighteenth-century authors—Rameau, Béthisy, Mattheson, Marpurg—from which most alternate versions for answers had been weeded out. Although these rules are rather artificial, being the outgrowth of theoretical speculation, their very limitations provide a conveniently fixed standard from which to judge the fugues of earlier writers; however, it must be realized that they do not provide an absolute musical solution, but merely a solution from a particular theoretical viewpoint. They also can be applied quite successfully to most of the fugues of J. S. Bach and those of the Classical period. Also, those nineteenth-century fugues that use tonal answers will generally be found with answers that concur with these rules. Moreover, these rules are the basis of the rules taught in contemporary courses in fugue (although not courses in contemporary fugue) and thus provide the basis for examinations in fugue writing. A detailed summary of these rules, with exercises and illustrations, can be found in the first section under "Fugue" in the *Workbook,* and direct application of them to particular subjects is as necessary as analysis in gaining a working knowledge of fugue. The following is given mainly to round out the historical development of the treatment of the answer.

The generally accepted theoretical rationalization of the nineteenth century differed from that of earlier periods, since it was based on an opposition of tonic and dominant keys. As a general principle, the answer was conceived as an exact transposition of the subject into the dominant key—a concept that was suggested by some of

Marpurg's statements but that did not form the main basis of his answers. This principle eliminates the subdominant answer, such as those seen in Examples 40b and 42b—an answer form that is found at times in eighteenth-century fugues, including the works of Bach.

Even the principle of direct transposition is, however, subject to a number of modifications. It is applied exactly only when the subject does not modulate to the dominant at any point. If the subject does modulate to the dominant, the part or parts of it that are in the dominant will be transposed directly into the tonic key in the answer. Furthermore, the analysis of "modulation" in the fugue subject is made according to special procedures that differ at times from those applied to tonal music in general.

Modulation to the dominant at the end of the subject is accomplished in two ways. It may be done by the usual means—raising the fourth degree of the tonic to produce a leading tone in the dominant (Ex. 39b); in minor, the raised sixth degree of the tonic is also used to provide the correct second degree in the dominant minor. Or it may be established merely by ending the subject on the fifth or seventh degree of the tonic, these being analyzed respectively as 1 or 3 of the dominant. (See Ex. 39a.) In minor, as usual, this is more complicated. To modulate in this way to the dominant, the subject must end in 5 or in the *lowered* seventh degree, which is the third of the dominant minor key. For this reason, the student was forbidden to end a subject in minor on the leading tone (raised seventh degree), since this could only be treated as the leading tone in the tonic and would have to be answered literally by the leading tone of the dominant minor key—a process that the tonal answer was expressly designed to avoid. It must be emphasized that it is the dominant *key* that is involved and not the dominant *chord*. In major, this makes little difference in most situations, but it is often a source of confusion when the fugue is in a minor key.

When the subject does modulate at the end, the segment that belongs in the dominant is transposed into the tonic in the answer, and this results in a change of interval at the point in which the modulation takes place, as has already been seen in Example 39. The only problem involved in making this type of answer is that of deciding the exact point at which the modulation should take place in the subject, and usually the changeover is made where the alteration will cause the least distortion of the subject when it appears in the answer form.

At the beginning of the subject, this principle of transposition is

applied in a special way. The tonal adjustments that were once explained by the need to stay within the limits of the modal octave by
keeping the subject and answer within the fifth and fourth that belonged to that mode—and that were justified in eighteenth-century
theory by the need to keep within the octave of the key—were now
rationalized by reference to key. In some cases, the change was justified by explaining that one should not move too suddenly from the
tonic of the subject to the dominant of the answer or that the sudden
movement to the dominant of the dominant, which some real answers imply, would be moving to a new key too fast. Others wanted
the opposition of dominant notes in the beginning of the subject
with tonic notes in the beginning of the answer as a basic musical
contrast similar to the antecedent–consequent relationship in a melodic period. But whatever the rationalization involved, the process is
the same, requiring a special type of analysis.

At the beginning of the subject, a "modulation" can take place
on a single note or a pair of notes. Whenever 5 or 7 in the tonic
appear at the head of the subject, as rhythmically prominent notes,
they are counted as 1 and 3 in the dominant key. They are then answered by 1 and 3 in the tonic key. All other notes beside 5 and 7
are counted as being in the tonic key and are answered by exact
transposition in the dominant. This results in the usual type of tonal
answer. A subject beginning *c, e, g* would then be analyzed as 1 and
3 in the tonic followed by 1 in the dominant. This will be answered
by 1 and 3 in the dominant followed by 1 in the tonic, *g, b, c'*. A
similar process gives all the tonal beginnings given in Examples 32
and 33.

But the process in minor, again, is not as simple. The fifth degree again counts as 1 in the dominant minor, but only the lowered
seventh degree can act as the third of the dominant key, to be answered by the third of the tonic key. As a matter of fact, this lowered
seventh degree is rarely found at the beginning of a subject because
it gives an ambiguous, modal effect. Much more common is the use
of the raised leading tone, as seen in Example 45b. Since this counts
as the leading tone in the tonic, it must be answered by the leading
tone in the dominant, resulting in the type of answer given there.
Analyzed by this system, the subject *e', g'*-sharp, *a'* will be 1 in the
dominant followed by 7–1 in the tonic. The answer will then be 1
in the tonic followed by 7–1 in the dominant (*a, d'*-sharp, *e'*)—a
melodic distortion of the subject but one sanctioned by practice as
well as theory. A basic tenet of fugue theory at this time was the
preservation of as much as possible of the exact intervallic shape of

the subject, but, if this is altered by tonal changes, the important minor seconds—7–8 and 3–4 in major and 7–8, 2–3, and 5–6 in minor—must be kept.

As was pointed out earlier in this chapter, the problem of the answer in minor is always more difficult, and this may be why the answers quoted in Examples 32 and 33 were limited to subjects in major. A look at Example 35, which contains some of Rameau's answers to subjects in minor, will point up some of the earlier doubts about the subject–answer relationship in minor. Neither of Rameau's solutions for the answer of the first subject is correct according to later theories. In both, the last note of the subject, *a*, is rightly answered by 1 in the tonic, *d*. But *f'* and *d'*, being 3 and 1 in the tonic, could be answered only by 3 and 1 in the dominant, *c*-natural and *A*. For Rameau's second subject, only the first answer would be allowed.

The ambiguities that are found in minor when applied to the tonal fugue are not the only unsolved problems. The compression of a chromatic subject originally filling a fifth into a fourth by tonal procedure (Ex. 45) is another that many theorists deplore. Even in some simpler combinations, the tonal adjustment of the head of the subject involves complexities resulting in many correlaries and modifications of the given rules. Not the least of the complications that arise is that of deciding where the head of the subject ends, for, once the head is tonally adjusted, the rest of the subject (if it does not modulate again to the dominant at the end) will be transposed exactly to the dominant key in the answer. Even if it should modulate again to the dominant at the end, the middle of the subject will be put into the dominant in the answer.

A last convention applied to the analysis of the subject and answer was the refusal to recognize a modulation to any key other than the dominant and the tonic. All other altered notes were counted simply as altered notes and directly transposed as such into the proper key; a raised first degree in the tonic will be answered by a raised first degree in the dominant, and vice versa.

There are few fields in the study of music in which the complexities of theoretical rationalization and musical logic are so intricate and frustrating as in the study of the fugal answer. Once one has absorbed the main principles involved and learned some of the pitfalls involved, one begins to admire composers of fugue for what they refuse as well as for what they accept—not only in the Romantic attitude that refuses to spoil a subject by using a tonal answer that deforms it, but also in the Classical approach that follows the rules but avoids creating a subject that can be spoiled by a tonal adjustment.

Other Types of Fugal Answers

THE ANSWER BY INVERSION

The practice of answering a fugal subject by its melodic inversion has been used since the sixteenth century. A technique first exploited in canon, it was adapted to fugal writing by the early sixteenth century and appears to first have been consistently exploited in the works of Adrian Willaert. By the second half of the century, it was in common use in secular and sacred polyphony as well as in instrumental music, and it was still in frequent use in the seventeenth century. At the same time, the inverted form of the subject was often used later in the body of an extended fugal work that employed regular answers in the opening exposition—as a varied statement of the subject rather than as an answer. In the eighteenth and nineteenth centuries, when the extended fugal form was the predominant type of fugue, it was this latter use of inversion that was the most common, and the inverted answer in the opening exposition, although still used, declined in importance.

The main problem involved in making the inverted answer is the conflict between intervallic exactness in its (inverted) likeness to the subject and the structure of the scales used together with the need to establish the mode or key. Theorists discussed this type of answer from the mid-sixteenth century on, but a fixed usage never evolved. Willaert's two pupils, Zarlino and Vicentino, pointed out the main problems in their theoretical writings. Zarlino showed that inversions can be made with or without intervallic exactness,[52] but, in actual practice, the inexact inversion—in which the generic intervals are used, but a minor third may be answered by a major third, and so forth—was used in the majority of cases. Vicentino mentioned, in addition, the problem of keeping the inverted answer within the mode by making a tonal adjustment, such as the answering of a subject beginning with the rising skip 1–5 with a falling fourth 8–5. (See p. 75.)

From the early seventeenth century on, theorists gave directions for making an exact inversion, although this was more often done in the section on canon than that on fugue, and the examples of the fugal answer by inversion they gave are more often by inexact inversion. The bare process is quite simple. One merely combines two arrangements of the scale, one rising and the other falling, in such a way that the minor seconds coincide. In the "natural" scales (where no sharps or flats are used), this means that *e–f* must be correlated with *c–b,* as in Example 48. This will result when the Ionian and

EXAMPLE 48

THE ANSWER BY INVERSION.

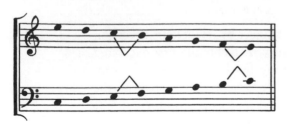

(a.) SWEELINCK   (b.) DENIS

Subject

Answer

(c.) SCHEIDT

Subject

Answer

Phrygian modes are combined, and, in the major–minor system, it results when the major scale is lined up with its form from 3 to 3. Then, one takes the notes of the subject in one line and, finding their correlative notes in the other line, builds the inverted answer.

But to find a subject (and answer) that will work in every mode or scale is not so simple. To get an exact inversion to a subject beginning on *C,* the inverted answer must begin on *E,* and an exact inversion to a subject beginning on *G* must begin on *A.* This is fine for canon, but it means that an exact fugal answer to a subject beginning on 1 or 5 of the major scale (or Ionian mode) cannot be made, since, by fugal tradition, the answer to this subject must begin on the tonic or dominant notes. Only the rising and falling octaves of *d* can coincide, and here an exact answer can be made at the unison, *d'*–*f'*–*a'* being answered by *d'*–*b*–*g*. There is no objection to the answer made at the unison when it is an inverted answer since it will not be a repetition of the subject, so that a Dorian subject starting on 1 and rising or a Mixolydian subject beginning on *d'* and falling can have an exact inverted answer. But at no point can there be an exact answer made at the fifth or fourth, because the scales, by their very nature, will only coincide at the augmented fourth or diminished fifth between *b* and *f*. Nor can any unison answer be made except on *d*. For major and minor and for the other modes, an exact inverted answer to the usual fugal subject is next to impossible.

For the most part, however, composers did not use the exact inversion, nor did theorists ever insist on it in fugue. The ear of the average listener does not readily distinguish the difference between the two types of inversion, so long as the interval types remain the same. Far more important is the shape of the theme and the interval on which the answer enters, and, for most composers, the entrance of the inverted subject at the unison or fifth (or their inversions) established the mode or key and was effectual as an answer whether the intervals precisely mirrored those of the subject or not. (See Ex. 48a.) In some cases, moreover, the use of accidentals in keeping with the prevailing usage could create an exact inverted answer without sacrificing the sense of key. Likewise, by the omission of notes in the subject that would result in an inexact answer in the inversion, the composer might produce an exact answer where one might not usually be expected. The combination of this technique with added accidentals is also fruitful. (See Ex. 48b.)

The tonal adjustment of the inverted answer which was recommended by Vicentino is actually much less common than the other types of inverted answers. Other theorists do not discuss it, and it is rarely found, particularly after the period of modal tonality. When such an adjustment is made the effect of inversion is weakened, as is evident in the answer quoted in Example 48c.

THE *Fuga d'imitazione* AND THE IRREGULAR FUGUE

The *fuga d'imitazione*—a type of fugue in which the answer does not fall into the category of tonal *or* real—was described by Italian theorists of the eighteenth and early nineteenth centuries. In contrast to more conventional fugue types, the answer here is inexact in some way—intervallically, rhythmically, or by curtailment—and it may respond to the subject at any pitch interval as well as at irregular time intervals. Since it is defined negatively by the lack of some strictness that would be found in the answer of a regular fugue, the *fuga d'imitazione* opens up a vast field of possibilities, as the theorist Giuseppe Paolucci said in his *Arte prattica di contrapunto*.[53]

The descriptions of this form of fugue are naturally various, but their source of the term can be clearly traced to Bononcini, who uses it in contrast to the *fuga regolare* or *propria* in which exact intervallic imitation is found.[54] Bononcini evidently took the term from general seventeenth-century usage, where it was often applied to the type of imitation found in madrigals and motets in which the "answers" were changed beyond what was allowed in the tonal answer, differing from the subject rhythmically and intervallically. The eighteenth-century use of *fuga d'imitazione* to describe a type of fugue shows how, by that time, the term fugue had come to be associated not only with the exact imitation of a short theme, but also with the pattern of successive entries that make up the form of the fugal exposition. This freer sort of fugal writing was important not only in sixteenth- and seventeenth-century writing, but was also prominent in the eighteenth and nineteenth centuries, especially in choral works.

As it was used in eighteenth- and nineteenth-century writings, it clearly meant not a "free fugue," but a type of subject–answer relationship either in an opening exposition or in one occurring later in the course of a regular fugue. It was the latter usage that Paolucci and Martini felt to be the most appropriate, but both were common in the literature of the time. Martini's student, Sabbatini, referred to the *fuga d'imitazione* as a type of fugue that can produce a very fine effect if used with taste, although he warned against too much freedom.[55] His use of the term implies that, although, as with the tonal fugue and the real fugue, the term defines a type of answer used in the exposition, it also characterizes an entire fugue based on such an exposition. He was the only one to include examples of actual compositions of this type, and, although with most of them only the first part was included, we find that they all start with an exposition using a free answer.[56]

The examples, seven settings for four-part chorus of various antiphons, are all by one composer, Francesco A. Vallotti (1697–1780). An examination of the answers used shows that deviations from strict fugal procedure are slight. Two have answers starting on the dominant but not transposed into the dominant key as a proper

EXAMPLE 49

EXAMPLES OF *Fuga d'imitazione.*

(a.)

(b.)

answer should be. Thus, in Example 49a, a minor second in the subject is answered by a major second in the answer, which, by using a *g'*-natural instead of the proper *g'*-sharp, stays in the tonic key. Another has an intervallically correct tonal answer at the fifth, but the rhythm is changed. Two have real, rhythmically exact answers in the subdominant, and one, surprisingly, has an answer by inversion that is not intervallically exact—something generally found in conventional fugue. The seventh has a real answer starting on the dominant that does not seem to fit into this category since, for Sabbatini, the real fugue is a perfectly legitimate type even when, as here, a tonal answer might be expected. In all seven examples, however, each answer enters before the subject is finished, and freedom in regard to entrance time is one of the liberties allowed in the fugue by imitation.

Sabbatini's contemporary and compatriot, Morigi, included in his description of this fugue type the usual freedom in the formation of the answer, but his discussion also implies an extended fugue, for he declared that this fugue—as well as the tonal fugue and the real fugue—should end with a stretto.[57] To this, he added that this type of answer will make a stretto more easily than the other types because of the freedom allowed. His examples, unfortunately, include only subject–answer pairs illustrating two types of answers allowed in this fugue.[58] One is an answer made in the key but a third below the subject. The other (Ex. 49b) starts on 5, like a conventional answer, but does not continue with the same intervals as those found in the subject.

In France, Cherubini, like his Italian predecessors, considered the *fugue d'imitation* to be a specific type of fugue but less important than the real and tonal fugues.[59] He also contrasted it to even freer types that he calls *fugues d'imitation irrégulières* or pieces in the *style fugué*. Apparently the main difference between the *fugue d'imitation* and a piece in the *style fugué* was in the form. The former starts with an exposition, although an irregular one, and follows the formal procedure of a regular fugue. The latter is simply a piece in some form other than fugue (such as a scherzo or sonata-form) which uses fugal imitation and perhaps other devices associated with fugue at some point in the form. To this, he added an interesting (and perhaps personal) opinion that a tonal fugue—which, to him, was the correct one—will be changed into a *fugue d'imitation* by making the answer real. Like Paolucci and Martini, he mentioned that a fugue starting as a tonal or real fugue can become a *fugue d'imitation* later if the subject is answered immediately in curtailed form or as a whole with intervallic or rhythmic changes.[60] Later, while discussing fugue form, he again mentioned the *fugue d'imitation* as a type of complete fugue,[61] giving weight to Sabbatini's and Morigi's assumption that this type of answer can characterize a whole fugue as well as part of a work.

Other French theorists in the first quarter of the nineteenth century mentioned this fugue type but briefly and without examples, and even this slight notice was clearly the result of Italian influence. It is not a type listed by eighteenth-century French pedagogues, nor is it included in treatises written later in the nineteenth century, since these stress solely the most conventional of all fugues, the tonal fugue.

German theorists of the early eighteenth century used the Latin term, *fuga irregularis,* to describe a fugal answer that was not made according to the conventional rules. But they gave no examples of it nor any precise descriptions beyond the fact that it differs from the correct answer (which was, for them, the tonal answer). Only in Johann Adolph Scheibe's *Der Critischer Musicus* was a clear definition given.[62] Scheibe considered the irregular fugue to be the middle step between free imitation—short fragments of melody imitated within a piece of any type—and the formal fugue. He clearly described it as beginning with an exposition in which the subject is stated alone and then answered in the second voice at any melodic interval and with allowable rhythmic freedom as long as there is a recognizable similarity to the subject. Once all parts have stated the subject or answer it follows the form of a regular fugue.

Marpurg's treatise made a change in terminology that was kept by later German theorists. Writing shortly after mid-century, he approached fugue as having certain formal characteristics as well as following certain conventions in the treatment of the answer; so, for him, the *fuga irregularis* is a fugue (in the sense of a whole work) in which one or more elements is not handled according to the accepted rules.[63] No doubt an answer in the dominant that is rhythmically or melodically inexact or even a real answer where a tonal one might be expected would fall into this category. At another point in his exposition, Marpurg mentioned the possibility of fugues in which the answer comes at the second, third, sixth, or seventh, but he identified them as extraordinary (*ausserordentliche*) fugues.[64] He felt that neither of these unusual types needed discussion, since what concerned him was the regular, rule-governed fugue, and later German theorists followed him in this regard. Often they mentioned that fugue can be at different intervals and then went on to give a musical justification for the answer at the fifth above (and fourth below) by pointing out the fundamental relationship of the dominant to the tonic in the key system.

Admittedly, this type of answer is but a lesser corollary to the type used in the regular fugue. The use of the terminology, also, is of less importance than the actual composition type. But historically it is significant as an indication that, by the eighteenth century, fugue had come to be associated directly with a subject–answer relationship and particularly with an exposition (either at the beginning or in the middle of a work) in which each part enters in turn with the theme or an answer to it at a different pitch. It is a type of opening that was particularly common in the choral music of the eighteenth and nineteenth centuries. Here, the problem of the range of the different parts is involved, and slight changes in the subject were necessary for effective choral writing. The openings of two choruses from Handel's *Messiah*—"O thou that bringest good tidings" and "His yoke is easy"—are fugal expositions of this freer type. Also, entries at different pitches and freer time intervals can serve to give added harmonic and/or rhythmic tension to a fugal opening, as the beginnings of *Et incarnatus est* and *Qui tollis peccata mundi* from Bach's *Mass in B minor* attest.

Rhythmic Augmentation or Diminution
in the Answer

Augmentation and diminution are used to form variants of the subject when it appears later in the body of a fugal work from the late sixteenth century onward, but they are not applied to the answer in the opening exposition of a work. Bach used both augmentation and diminution applied to the answer in his *Art of Fugue,* and although this work had an important influence—particularly on theorists of the late eighteenth and nineteenth centuries—these procedures never gained general acceptance in the exposition.

Suggested Problems in Analysis

In working with analysis in a field like the fugal subject–answer relationship, which is so deeply involved with theory and conventions, it is well to remember that theory is a statement of an ideal situation but not one that is universally and absolutely true. Knowledge of the rules given and their theoretical justifications is a useful standard and a tool to use in investigating musical situations, but, if a composer departs from them, this does not mean that what he did is musically wrong. If he has done something unusual, investigate the musical effect of what he has done compared to what would have been the musical consequences if he had followed what the theorists prescribe. Because theorists' works are sometimes published after a certain convention has been established and sometimes before, it is wise to take into consideration the theorists writing before and after as well as near the time a work was composed.

Almost any collection of works of a fugal nature can be the basis for an analytical study of the subject–answer relation. The following are suggestions for a few such projects.

1. A valuable study in sixteenth-century music is to take a volume of motets or Masses and check the initial notes on which opening fugal entries are made. Try to ascertain the mode by looking at the tenor, particularly its final note, but also the fifth, fourth, and octave that are most often used in the melodic structure. The melodic dominant, when it differs from the fifth above the final, may also be stressed. Check the final cadence as well, remembering that

it may be on the fifth note of the mode as well as on the regular final. Compare this with the pitches of the entries. If the mode is not clear, this is just one characteristic of the piece, not something to be greatly concerned with or condemned. A study of this kind should show some of the ambiguities involved in the polyphonic use of mode. Works written in the second quarter of the sixteenth century or later will be the best to work with, since it is at this time that the limitation of initial notes and cadences to the final of the mode and to the third and fifth above it began to be made.

2. Another project that can be valuable in working with sixteenth-century music is an analysis of the types of answer used. Any volume of motets, Masses, instrumental music, or secular works of a fugal nature can be interesting, but those published around mid-century and later will have more tonal answers. A survey of the answer forms in works with fugal beginnings found in *HAM,* I makes an interesting study, too.

In addition to the tonal answer, the three types of answer listed by Pietro Pontio will be found, as well as answers by inversion. Other irregular types may be found as well. When there is an irregular answer or even one in which there is rhythmic freedom, seek for the musical reason for this change. It usually can be found in the vertical alignment of the voices, but it may involve other elements as well. When a tonal answer is used, check how the adjustment from the fourth to fifth or fifth to fourth has been made. Take into consideration all the statements of the subject or answer and not just the first entries. If some are made on other pitches—imitations according to the theory of this time—this is something to note. Do not forget the relation of these entry notes to the mode of the work.

3. A similar study of answer forms in the works of seventeenth-century composers can be made. Here, the mode is usually made clear by the form of the subject and answer as well as by the initial notes and final cadence. These may be the only clear guides, since this was a transition period and the tenor cannot in most cases, particularly in instrumental music, be the guide to mode. If there has been a tonal adjustment in the answer, note the position, and, if the answer is tonal, note how the adjustment is made. It may help to number the notes as they appear in the scale. Count the final of a mode as 1, whether the work appears to be in the plagal or authentic form of the mode. Using the rules found in Nivers and Masson may help to elucidate the form of the answer found, and this is a legitimate technique as long as it is used as a tool, and a departure from those rules is not accounted an error on the part of the composer.

A number of irregularities will be found, but this is because the usage is not stereotyped. Seventeenth-century composers, as well as those of later centuries, preferred rhythmic exactness, so note any differences here. The first note of the subject, however, could always be shortened or lengthened and the final note was not assigned a definite time value. One "irregularity" that is often found is that, in the answer, the beginning has been adjusted tonally but the rest of the answer has not. Example 50 shows such an answer. The head has

EXAMPLE 50

OPENING OF A CANZONA, GIROLAMO FRESCOBALDI.

been properly adjusted from the fifth to the fourth, but the passage in the second measure outlining the fourth c''–f'' should, by the standards of Banchieri and Diruta, be answered in measure 4 by the fifth f'–c''. Here it is given a real answer in the "subdominant," outlining the fourth f'–b'-flat, and the answer continues in the subdominant. This illustrates a typical quandary of the time, a conflict between the conventions of tonal adjustment and the natural inclination toward exact intervallic imitation. Since this subject sounds like F major, a good way to investigate this answer would be to work out the answer as it would be made in the major–minor system, and then note how, and why, the composer has departed from these later conventions. The "sub-dominant" answer is very common in the modes and is found at times, especially in the minor keys, even in the eighteenth century.

At times, too, it is difficult to tell just where the subject itself ends. If this is the case, compare the subject with the answers and with other entries on the tonic. In some cases, it will still be unclear. Note, then, how it is joined to the continuing line. Sometimes, this vagueness seems to be used consciously to avoid adjusting the end of a tonal answer.

The keyboard works of Frescobaldi are excellent for the study of early seventeenth-century practices. For experience with the treatment of the answer at a later time, when major and minor were used but not yet clearly separated from the modes, the fugal movements of Purcell's *Ten Sonatas of Four Parts* are recommended. An attempt to decide why, musically, the different answer types are used as they are will be stimulating even if not wholly conclusive.

The fugues of Buxtehude and Pachelbel have already been mentioned as containing some unusual treatments of the tonal answer. When working with these, the rules given by Marpurg and Rameau are good tools. The directions given by Masson and Nivers should also be consulted and, perhaps, the correlated scales given by early eighteenth-century German theorists as well. But none of these will satisfactorily explain all of the answers used by these composers.

4. For fugue in the major and minor tonalities, it is almost a fixed tradition to study the answers of Bach, and, even if no other works are studied, these must be. The two books of the *Well-Tempered Clavier* and the organ fugues can be used for a study of the treatment of the answer in the key system. Bach is almost the only composer of fugues whose works have been the basis of many analytical commentaries on the treatment of the tonal answer. A number of these are listed in Appendix I under "Chapter IV," but it is suggested that the investigation of the works be conducted first, using Marpurg's rules along with those of Masson and Rameau. Then those answers that seem unusual might be looked up in the commentaries.

The very early clavier and organ fugues attributed to Bach have some unusual subjects and answers. They are very interesting from the point of view of the technique of the answer, but the student should be warned against drawing any historical conclusions about them in relation to Bach's other works since most of them have not been positively identified as being by Bach.

An analysis of the answers in Handel's choral fugues from the oratorios presents a good balance to a study of Bach's answers. The student should be warned that, in some cases, Handel used a subject in one of the old modes. Although the rules given by eighteenth-century theorists for modal answers have not been given in this book, these should cause no difficulty. The main thing to watch for is the placement of the whole and half steps that, for this period, were the means by which each mode was identified.

The investigation of the answers used in the nineteenth century presents a different problem because few composers whose music is now in print have written enough fugues to make large generalizations possible. For the convenience of the student, a listing of fugues by selected nineteenth-century composers is included in Appendix I under "Chapter IV." Suggestions of other fugue collections from earlier periods will also be found there along with the editions in which the above-mentioned examples can be found.

WRITING THE ANSWER TO A GIVEN SUBJECT

Going through the process of making an answer to a given subject is the best way to understand the techniques involved and in many cases is an aid to analysis. The difficulty in making such answers lies in the fact that one is working in a musical style that, although familiar, is not instinctive to one who has heard and played so many other styles. Making decisions when there is a choice of possibilities is therefore difficult.

Although the rules for making the answer given for the "school fugue" are sometimes deplored because of their separation from actual practice, some sort of rigidity is necessary as a pedagogical device. A set of such rules, derived from the French and German theorists of the nineteenth century but allowing less freedom of choice, is given in the *Workbook* in the first problem under "Fugue" along with a list of subjects for the student to answer.

This is a necessary preliminary to writing a fugue in the eighteenth-century style. But if these rules are applied retroactively to the analysis of other works, it should constantly be borne in mind that they are rules artificially adjusted for a pedagogical process and not rules that the composer had in mind.

Notes

1. Strangely enough, this is not discussed until the eighteenth century, when the contrast of the modes with major and minor was of interest to church musicians who still used the modes. The main sources are Andreas Werckmeister, *Harmonologia musica* (Frankfurt and Leipzig, 1702), p. 72; Johann Joseph Fux, *Gradus ad Parnassum* (Vienna, 1725), section on fugue translated in Alfred Mann, *The Study of Fugue* (New Brunswick,

N.J.: Rutgers University Press, 1958), pp. 80*ff;* Johann Mattheson, *Der vollkommene Kapellmeister* (Hamburg, 1739), pp. 375*ff;* Meinrad Spiess, *Tractatus musicus* (Augsburg, 1746), pp. 32*ff,* 43*ff.*

2. Zarlino, *op. cit.,* Part IV, chap. XXX.

3. Pietro Pontio, *Dialogo . . . della theorica, e prattica di musica* (Parma, 1595), pp. 49–51.

4. Willaert used both of these forms—G–B–C and G–A–C—in the beginning of his motet *Confitebor tibi Domine,* found in *Opera omnia,* Vol. V: *Musica nova,* eds. Hermann Zenck and Walter Gerstenberg (Rome: American Institute of Musicology, 1957), p. 15.

5. Thomas Morley, *A Plaine and Easie Introduction to Practicall Musick* (London, 1597), p. 77. The modern edition is *A Plain and Easy Introduction to Practical Music,* ed., R. Alec Harman (New York: Norton, 1952), p. 151. Harman, however, transcribes the "fugues" of the original by "imitations"—a common procedure among editors but one that obscures the true meaning.

6. Zarlino, *op. cit.,* pp. 216–7.

7. Nicola Vicentino, *L'antica musica ridotta alla moderna prattica,* [1555], f. 88–9; facs. ed., edited by E. E. Lowinsky (Kassel: Bärenreiter, 1959).

8. Girolamo Diruta, *Seconda parte del Transilvano* [1609] (Venice, 1622), Bk. III, 12.

9. *Ibid.,* p. 11.

10. Seth Calvisius, in his *Exercitationes musicae duae* (Leipzig, 1600), lists works for a large number of voices that encompass both the plagal and authentic ranges of the mode in such a way that they cannot be assigned to either of the two forms.

11. Adriano Banchieri, *Cartella musicale* (Venice, 1614), p. 68.

12. *Ibid.,* pp. 112*ff.*

13. Picerli, *op. cit.,* pp. 90–1.

14. Lorenzo Penna, *Li primi albori musicali* (Monti, 1672), p. 59.

15. Giovanni Maria Bononcini, *Il musico prattico* (Bologna, 1673), pp. 82–3; later eds., 1678, 1688; in German, 1701.

16. Angelo Berardi, *Documenti armoniche* (Bologna, 1687), pp. 36–7; *Miscellanea musicale* (Bologna, 1689), pp. 179–80.

17. Bononcini, *op. cit.,* p. 124.

18. Berardi, *Miscellanea, op. cit.,* p. 180.

19. Friedrich Wilhelm Marpurg, *Abhandlung von der Fuge* (Berlin, 1753–1754), I, 26; second printing, 1806.

20. Josef Maria Müller-Blattau (ed.), *Die Kompositionslehre Heinrich Schützens* (Leipzig: Breitkopf and Härtel, 1926), pp. 98–102.

21. Hermann Gehrmann (ed.), *Jan Pieterson Sweelinck, Werken* Vol. XII: *Compositions-Regeln* (Leipzig: Breitkopf and Härtel, 1901).

22. Christopher Simpson, *A Compendium of Practical Musick* (London, 1667), p. 131.

23. Henry Purcell, in John Playford, *An Introduction to the Skill of Musick* (London, 1694), p. 107.

24. Jean Denis, *Traité de l'accord de l'espinette* (Paris, 1650), pp. 28*ff.*

25. Glossary of terms in *Traité d'harmonie* (Paris, 1722), under "Mode" (which to Rameau meant the major and minor scales).

26. In *Sonate da chiesa a tre,* op. 1 (Rome, 1683); op. 2 (Rome, 1685); op. 3 (Modena, 1689); op. 4 (Bologna, 1694); and *Sonate a violino solo,* op. 5 (Rome, 1700).

27. Bononcini, *op. cit.,* p. 124.

28. Guillaume Gabriel Nivers, *Traité de la composition musicale* (Paris, 1677), pp. 49–52.

29. Charles Masson, *Nouveau traité des règles pour la composition de la musique* (2nd ed.; Paris, 1699). pp. 103*ff.;* 1st ed. (Paris, 1694) is ap-

parently not extant; later eds., (1700, 1705, 1738.)

30. Rameau, *op. cit.,* pp. 332*ff.*

31. Jean Laurent de Béthisy, *Exposition de la théorie et de la pratique* (Paris, 1754), pp. 281*ff.;* 2nd ed. (Paris, 1764), pp. 308*ff.*

32. Sources listed in note 1 above.

33. Werckmeister, *op. cit.,* p. 72.

34. Jean Baptist Samber, *Continuatio ad manuductionem organicum* (Salzburg, 1707), pp. 235*ff.*

35. Johann George Walther, *Praecepta der musicalischen Composition* [1708], ed. Peter Benary (Leipzig: Breitkopf and Härtel, 1955), pp. 180*ff.*

36. Mattheson, *op. cit.,* pp. 370*ff.*

37. Some of this included is in Mann, *op. cit.,* pp. 164*ff.* A large amount of the original is omitted here. See Mann's notes, *op. cit.,* pp. 316–7.

38. *Ibid.,* pp. 170–5.

39. *Ibid.,* pp. 168–70.

40. Giambattista Martini, *Exemplare o sia saggio fondamentale pratico di contrapunto,* Vol. I and II (Bologna, 1775), pp. 35–44.

41. Alexander Choron, *Principes de composition des écoles d'Italie,* (Paris, 1808), Vol. II, Bk. IV.

42. Anton Reicha, *Traité de haute composition musicale,* Vol. II, Bk. IV (Paris, 1825), p. 56.

43. Luigi Cherubini, *Cours de contrepoint et de fugue* (Paris, 1833), pp. 106*ff.*

44. Colet, *op. cit.,* pp. 229*ff.*

45. *Ibid.,* p. 237.

46. Antoine A. E. Elwart, *Le contrepoint et la fugue appliqués à la composition* (Paris, 1840), pp. 76*ff.*

47. Johann George Albrechtsberger, *Gründiche Anweisung zur Composition* (Leipzig, 1790), pp. 171*ff.*

48. Gustav Nottebohm, *Beethovens Studien* (Leipzig and Winterthur, 1873), p. 100.

49. Ernst Friedrich Richter, *A Treatise on Canon and Fugue* [1859], trans. Arthur W. Foote (Boston, 1888) pp. 63, 64; this translation is from the 3rd German ed.

50. Théodore Dubois, *Traité de contrepoint et de fugue* (Paris, 1901), p. 119.

51. Richter, *op. cit.,* p. 53.

52. Zarlino, *op. cit.,* pp. 219*f.*

53. Guiseppe Paolucci, *Arte pratica di contrapunto* (Venice, 1765), II, 61.

54. Bononcini, *op. cit.,* p. 82.

55. Luigi Antonio Sabbatini, *Trattado sopra le fughe musicali* (Venice, 1802), pp. 13–4.

56. *Ibid.,* pp. 313*ff.*

57. Angelo Morigi, *Trattado di contrapunto* (Milan, 1802), pp. 18–9.

58. *Ibid.,* Table 11, No. 32; Table 12, No. 33.

59. Cherubini, *op. cit.,* p. 106.

60. *Ibid.,* p. 117.

61. *Ibid.,* p. 125.

62. Johann Adolphe Scheibe, *Der Critischer Musicus.* Nos. 49–50 (1739), pp. 451–3.

63. Marpurg, *op. cit.,* p. 18.

64. *Ibid.,* pp. 22, 23.

Chapter V

Writing the Subject,

Answer, and Countersubject

The Subject

Once one has become acquainted with the process of making the tonal answer, he is aware of the difficulties attendant upon creating the subject for a tonal fugue if the subject is not to be mutilated in the answer. There are also other limitations caused by the nature of fugue itself that have long been recognized by composers and theorists. Although there is room for invention, it must be kept within strict bounds; otherwise, the composer runs into difficulties not only in making the answer, but also in the continuation of the fugue. For this reason, students learning to write fugues have often been given the subjects to work with, but the experience gained in inventing fugue subjects—even though they are in a style that is no longer used—gives important insight into the nature of fugue itself. The student is therefore urged to write a number of fugue subjects. If, after they are created, he feels a strong aversion against working with his subjects, he may choose some from the list given in the *Workbook* or choose them from the works of other composers.

TECHNICAL REGULATIONS RELATING TO THE SUBJECT

There are a number of purely technical rules that should be kept in mind when making a subject, some of which have already been touched on in Chapter IV. The basic rule, one that has been in force since the mid-sixteenth century, is that the subject should announce the mode or key of the fugue. In the sixteenth century, it was the initial note that did this, and this emphasis on the initial note was reiterated well into the eighteenth century. Throughout this time, the tonic and dominant remained the preferred beginning notes for the subject, and, by the eighteenth century, the third degree was used by composers and permitted by theorists. In the whole history of fugue, these have remained the most common notes with which to begin a subject, and, even in its later development when the subject almost immediately veered off toward a new key (as in Ex. 46a), the initial note was generally a member of the tonic triad. When other notes were used, they generally acted as rhythmically and melodically weak tones leading into an essential note of the key.

Although later theorists did not echo Banchieri and Diruta in their conviction that the subject should outline the fourth or fifth of the mode, one finds that, in most fugues (and particularly instrumental fugues), the subject beginnings do tend to stress the fourth, fifth, or complete triad of the mode or key. This is particularly true of eighteenth-century fugue. An examination of the subjects Bach uses in the two books of his *Well-Tempered Clavier* will show how often the heads of his subjects strongly announce the tonality of the fugue. For the average student, this type of subject opening is likewise the easiest one to handle in writing a fugue in the key system.

A second limitation that is applied to the subject has to do with its final note. The exact point at which the subject ends is not always clear, and the usual advice given to the analyst is that one discovers the extent of the subject by observing how much of it is restated in the answer. This advice generally comes from theorists of the eighteenth century or later, and does not always apply to earlier fugues. In many cases in sixteenth-century choral music and instrumental music as well, the subject appears not to have a distinct end, but moves on freely after a very short beginning or changes from exact fugal imitation to freer imitation after the head of the subject. Example 51a shows the first two entries of a ricercar for lute published in Venice in 1546 by Dominico Bianchini.[1] The first measure sounds like the complete subject, but, when the second part enters, only the first two beats of the subject are imitated exactly, and the rest is a rhythmic variant of the remainder of the first entry.

There was an increase in precision and in demarcation of the subject and answer as time moved on, but, even in the seventeenth

EXAMPLE 51

(a.)

(b.)

century, the precise ending of the subject was at times unclear. An example from Bononcini's text on counterpoint shows a typical case.[2] Example 51b is the beginning of one of his examples of a *fuga sciolta*. Here the subject proper is clearly only the first four notes, but, because the continued movement in both parts follows the same melodic pattern, the ear does not clearly pick out the subject's ending.

It was not until the early eighteenth century that the ending of the subject got the attention of theorists, and this appears to follow on the greater clarity given to the subject as an entity in the fugue by composers of the time. Rameau was the first to give the topic much attention, and his opinions were echoed by most succeeding theorists and became an inherent part of the instructions for the academic or school fugue of the nineteenth century. First of all, he insisted that a fugue subject should end on 1, 5, or 3 of the key; to these, Marpurg added the seventh degree. These, it is obvious, provide for the normal endings found in the tonal fugue, since a subject ending in 5 or 7 of the tonic will have fulfilled the normal modulation to the dominant key (ending on 1 or 3 of the dominant), and one ending on 1 or 3 clearly affirms the tonic. The student learning the rudiments of fugue will be advised to keep his subjects within these bounds, since other endings will cause difficulties in creating the answer and also in the manipulation of keys in the course of the fugue.

Rameau's second rule is practical and typical of fugues of the eighteenth and nineteenth centuries. This is, that, except in a vocal fugue (where the text may make it impossible), the subject should end on a strong beat. This rhythmic precision coupled with limiting the final notes to those carrying strong tonal implications insure that the end as well as the beginning of the subject gives a feeling of the "right" key and makes for easier manipulation of the subject by the composer. To the ear, too, the subject is more clearly delineated since endings of this type give the feeling of a temporary cadence.

Naturally, there are instances in eighteenth- and nineteenth-century fugues where the subject ends before the answer begins, and when this happens there must be a short transition passage filling in and continuing the movement until the answer can enter. But there is rarely any confusion as to where the subject ends because of the rhythmic emphasis and tonal strength of the final note and because the added passage is either clearly transitional or else stylistically differentiated from the subject. These two types are clearly found in Bach's fugues. The time between the end of the subject and the beginning of the answer in the Fugue in F Major from the first book of *The Well-Tempered Clavier* is filled by a simple connecting passage. (See Ex. 52a.) The beginning of the Fugue in E-flat Major

EXAMPLE 52

(a) BEGINNING OF THE FUGUE IN F MAJOR FROM THE *Well-Tempered Clavier*, BOOK I, J. S. BACH.

(b) BEGINNING OF THE FUGUE IN E-FLAT MAJOR FROM THE *Well-Tempered Clavier*, BOOK I, J. S. BACH.

from the same collection is a good example of the use of clearly differentiated material to fill this gap—material that is later used as secondary material in the body of the fugue. (See Ex. 52b.) In both cases, the ending of the subject is clear. Although it is convenient for the analyst to know the exact extent of the subject, it is particularly important for the composer to have a subject that is distinct in extent.

It should be pointed out, too, that the length of the final note of the subject is always variable. It may vary in length in each statement of the subject or answer, and it need never occupy more than a fraction of the beat on which it falls; it is only necessary that the final note begin on a strong beat.

A final restriction made on the subject is that of range. In choral music, it was usually restricted in range because of vocal considerations and a care for its sounding well in the choral range. But there was also, in the period when modal tonality was involved, an insistence that the subject should stay within the characteristic octave of the mode. Even in the eighteenth century, the range was usually limited to the octave for practical reasons, and some pedagogues of the late nineteenth and twentieth centuries would limit it to the compass of a sixth or seventh. Although such limitations seem unreasonable at first hearing, they are really the result of practical experience. When one is using the subject in a three- or four-part texture, a subject that is confined to the octave is much easier to handle without crossing of voices or extremes of range. Subjects of greater ranges were used, but they were always in the minority. It takes great contrapuntal skill to write a fugue on a subject with a wide melodic range.

MUSICAL CHARACTERISTICS OF THE FUGUE SUBJECT

Within the framework set by the above restrictions, there remains ample scope for the invention of an interesting fugue subject. The nature of the subject is particularly important for the fugue, since it is the one dominating feature of the movement and the source of much of the secondary musical material used.

From the sixteenth century through the time of Bach and Handel, fugue was one of the most important procedures used in writing music, and fugue themes represented a living and vital style. At the beginning of the seventeenth century, two main subject types predominated in instrumental music—the slow-moving, serious ricercar theme and the more vivacious canzona subject. The ricercar type is more abstract in character and well fitted for its function of displaying contrapuntal artifice. The canzona, an instrumental outgrowth of the vivacious French chanson, generally kept the ♩ ♪ ♪ | ♩ rhythm of its source (often a repeated note followed by a skip), and although it was generally used in the fugal opening of a work, this opening was often followed by a mixture of homophonic and polyphonic sections, and the theme was rarely used for a show of contrapuntal skill. (See Ex. 53.)

EXAMPLE 53

THEME TYPES FROM FRESCOBALDI.

Canzona

Ricercar

Themes related to these two types appeared in different guises until the late seventeenth century when the new sonata and concerto forms, using fugue in certain movements, opened the way for wider variety of styles. At the same time, the advent of the major–minor tonal system brought into being new ways of writing longer forms, and the eighteenth-century fugue—a long movement based on a single theme—became an important and independent work. A fugue could then become a piece of some length, with the subject setting the movement and mood that dominated the piece. This is particularly apparent in the fugues of Bach; the appeal of his fugues is to a great extent due to the fact that each has a distinct character or mood that differentiates it from the others and for which it is valued. Since it is the form and style of the eighteenth-century fugue that the student will emulate, it is this subject type that should provide the model for the subjects he invents.

The fugue subject should be of a moderate length. Eighteenth-century theorists were very clear about this without being dogmatically precise. Rameau set the minimum length at half a measure but felt that, if it is longer than four measures, the answer should start in the fourth measure.[3] This apparently represented the French view. German theorists gave no precise length but insisted that it should be a complete musical thought. Marpurg warned that too long a subject would be hard for the listener to remember.[4]

Padre Martini designated and defined according to length three subject types used at this time, and his terms are convenient.[5] (See Ex. 54.) The *soggetto* (subject) is of medium length; it is not less than one-half a measure in ordinary tempo nor more than three measures, and it is the one most commonly used. The *andamento* is longer and generally includes more than one idea. Examples of both these types from the fugues of Bach will be familiar to the

EXAMPLE 54

EXAMPLES OF SUBJECT TYPES, G. B. MARTINI.

student. Most of his fugues use the simple subject (*soggetto*), but a number of his organ fugues use the *andamento* type. One of the best-known of his choral fugues, the first Kyrie of the Mass in B Minor, likewise has an *andamento*-type subject. Although either of these two types will make a good fugue, the longer subject naturally should be used in a fugue of large dimensions, so it is advisable to use the *soggetto* type for one's first attempts at fugue. Martini's shortest type, the *attacco,* is, as he admitted, really not much used in a fugue proper, although it is often good for a special effect within a piece. The *attacco* is not bound to the rules of fugue and can enter at any interval. His example of this shows imitations at the sixth and seventh below—a type of *fuga d'imitazione.* Although one finds some fugal sections with as short a subject, it should not ordinarily be used as the basis for a whole fugue. Such subjects are but occasionally used for fugues—the Fugue in C-sharp Major from Book II of Bach's *Well-Tempered Clavier* uses a subject of this type.

The concept of the subject as a complete musical idea usually needs further elucidation for the musician today who is used to the long and complex periods of the Classical and Romantic eras. The fugue theme must not be in a periodic style or form. Nineteenth-century fugue texts reiterated this caution, which was not necessary at an earlier time before periodic structure was the basis of composition. Although the style of fugue subjects (as well as their tonal basis) had changed from the sixteenth century to the time of Bach and Handel, there had been no change in the impetus of their structure. Throughout this period, it was a common procedure for a composition to start with an unaccompanied melody that was its main theme, that moved forward with a firm melodic thrust to its end and still kept on moving after the next part entered and took the lead by stating the theme itself. Even when there were several different

[137]

musical ideas contained in the theme, as in Frescobaldi's theme (Ex. 50) or Martini's *andamento* (Ex. 54), these were part of the continuous melodic flow. In the eighteenth century, this forward movement was made even stronger by implied harmonic progression, and, even though rests were used, the subject with more than one musical idea moved steadily forward to its closing note, and the line still had some melodic impetus after the subject was finished. The subject of the B-flat Minor Fugue from the second book of Bach's *Well-Tempered Clavier* is typical. (See Ex. 55.)

EXAMPLE 55

SUBJECT OF THE FUGUE IN B-FLAT MINOR FROM THE *Well-Tempered Clavier,* BOOK II, J. S. BACH.

The melodic construction found in the homophonic Classical style is entirely different. It is based on the periodic ideal—an ideal that included not only the rhythmic balance or symmetry of phrases, but also the aping of literary structure by using pauses and cadences to imitate the pause or rise and fall of the voice as it makes clear the grammatical divisions of speech.[6] This gives one the feeling that the melody is divided into intelligible segments in the same way that a sentence is made up of intelligible phrases and clauses. Like the sentence, the musical period is not complete until it reaches its end (in a perfect authentic cadence), and the various smaller units are part of a much larger whole. Thus, in a periodic style, a truly complete musical thought is a period, and it is complete in the sense that it can stand alone, requiring no musical continuation. As a part of a longer movement, it is followed by another period that is also a complete and finished musical sentence and may be a complete contrast with the preceding period.

The first period in the first movement of Mozart's Sonata in B-flat, K.333 (Ex. 56) shows this kind of structure. Each of the smaller melodic units is an intelligible idea, just as are the various phrases in a sentence of speech.[7] Also, as phrases are joined together into clauses in speech, so these melodic motives are joined together

EXAMPLE 56

FROM THE SONATA IN B-FLAT, K. 333, MOZART.

to form two longer musical units (phrases)—the first being four measures long and the second, six. But not until the end of the period do we find, as in a spoken sentence, a feeling of completion. Such completeness should never be characteristic of a fugue subject. Neither should there be the sense of inner melodic balance and rhythmic poise that is found in the Mozart melody. A fugue subject should set up a sense of forward-moving melodic energy that may achieve a partial sense of completion at its end but that also calls for further movement after the subject is finished.

It is perhaps better to compare the first four measures of the Mozart melody with the Bach subject, since they both end on the third of the key, and this first phrase of the Mozart period is, like the Bach theme, partially complete although still needing more music to achieve a full sense of finality. There is yet a clear difference between the two. Mozart's phrase pauses heavily on the cadence tone, whereas Bach's subject pauses only briefly, moving on steadily after the d'-flat. But even if Mozart's phrase were to end on a short d'' on the first beat of the measure, from which the composer could move on quickly, it would not make a good fugue subject. The inner divisions are too balanced, and it gives the effect of a musical phrase requiring not a continuation, but another, consequent, phrase to round it off musically. The Bach subject, although similarly divided into small, intelligible segments, does not have this sense of inner equilibrium. The motives are, like those in the Mozart melody, set off by stops in the rhythmic motion, and, also like those in Mozart's phrase, they start on the up-beat. But the rhythmic and melodic movement of Bach's subject is such that the rhythmic motion increases as the melody rises, working up to a kinetic climax in the first part of the fourth measure and then releasing some of the energy at the end, but one still feels the need for continued forward movement. In contrast to this, the rhythmic and melodic energies of the melodic motives in the Mozart theme are balanced—the second giving balance to the first and the fourth to the third. Moreover, the third and fourth combine into a unit that acts as a balance to the combination of the first and second, and the two larger units are similar enough in musical content to make the last two measures act as a consequent to the first two measures. Because of this, the entire four-measure phrase sets up a demand for a second phrase with a logical musical relationship to the first, which will provide a balance and bring the period to a logical and final close. In contrast to this, the melodic units in Bach's subject seem to grow logically out of one another in direct forward progression, spinning out from the head of the theme. This creates a demand for more forward movement generated out of the theme, continued movement instead of the stabilizing effect of a balancing phrase that comes to a complete close.

Bach's subject represents the kind of theme that should be used for a fugue, although it need not be as long; in fact, a theme of medium length is more practical for a study fugue since it will result in a shorter fugue. The subject is best that starts with a distinctive head that announces the beginning of the subject and that clearly establishes the key of the fugue. It may begin on any beat or part of a beat. The rest of the subject should appear to spin forward from this head, developing a sense of forward movement that is not entirely dispelled by the time the subject ends. The final note should be the first or third degree of either the tonic or dominant key and should fall on a strong beat. Repetition or even varied repetition is rarely used, but sequences—exact or varied—are good.

Although there are limitations in structure, various styles can be used. The fugue may be diatonic, chromatic, or a mixture of the two, but the tonic key (or the tonic and dominant keys) should be clearly projected. It is also a practical help for the subject to have more than one musical motive, since this provides extra material for subsidiary parts of the fugue. The exact formation of the Bach theme in Example 55 need not be followed, but only the basic principle of its construction. Several shorter subjects are given in Example 57, and those given earlier in the book as well as those available in the

EXAMPLE 57

BAROQUE SUBJECTS OF MODERATE LENGTH.

NIKOLAUS BRUHNS

A. CORELLI

G.F. HANDEL

GEORG BÖHM

J.S. BACH

VINCENT LÜBECK

published works of Bach, Handel, Telemann, Buxtehude, and their contemporaries can serve as models.

LATER USES OF THE SUBJECT AS A DETERMINANT OF SUBJECT TYPE

At times, it is important to take into consideration in what forms the subject will appear when writing the subject for a particular fugue. The answer form should always be taken into consideration so that the subject will not be too greatly deformed when tonally adjusted to form the answer. The subject will be stated somewhere in a fugue transposed to another key or in another mode (generally the relative major or minor of the key of the fugue), but this needs to be considered only on those rare occasions when the change from major to minor or from minor to major is awkward. Usually, this is accomplished with good effect, but sometimes, when a subject is very chromatic or includes a number of altered tones, the change of mode may be difficult. A case in point would be the use of the raised second degree as a lower auxiliary to the third degree in a major key —*e, d*-sharp, *e* in *C* major. This would have to become 3, 2, 3 in minor—*c', b, c'* in A minor (because there is already a minor second between 2 and 3 in minor)—and might make other changes necessary in contiguous parts of the subject.

The subject may also appear in melodic inversion, and, if this is planned, the subject should have a distinctive melodic shape so that the inversion can be recognized by the ear. Large skips or scale passages moving directly up or down are a help. Rhythmic augmentation or diminution does not generally create particular problems for the subject, nor does melodic or rhythmic variation, and none of these are common in the study fugue so they can be disregarded when the subject is being invented.

Stretto, however, is a fugal device that is important and necessary for the student of fugue to understand and one that must be planned in advance if it is to be used in a fugue. This is the overlapping entry of two or more statements of the subject, forming a type of canon. (See Ex. 58.) If one is planning a stretto, the subject must

EXAMPLE 58

STRETTO (FREE ACCOMPANYING PARTS OMITTED) FROM J. S. BACH.

be made in advance with this in mind, since not all subjects will make a stretto. The time interval at which the succeeding entries come should be decided in advance as well as the pitch interval at which the imitation will take place. Then, the stretto should be composed in the same way as a canon, measure by measure, and the subject arrived at by this method. This process, however, should be deferred until later, when the basic elements of fugue writing have been mastered. The stretto is discussed in more detail in Chapter VIII.

SUGGESTED PROBLEMS IN INVENTING FUGUE SUBJECTS

It is a good idea to write a number of fugue subjects, each with a particular problem in mind, and to make the answer (using the procedures followed in Section 1 under "Fugue" in the *Workbook*) for each as soon as it is written. You may want to alter the subject once you find what its answer will be like. If so, be sure the answer is changed to conform with the new shape of the subject.

There are four main types of subjects that should be included among those invented: (1) those that can have a real answer; (2) those that require no tonal alteration in the beginning but modulate to the dominant at the end; (3) those that require a tonal adjustment at the beginning but do not leave the tonic key thereafter; and (4) those that require a tonal adjustment at the beginning and modulate to the dominant at the end. Each of these presents a different problem in forming the answer, and one should keep clearly in mind the type of subject one is attempting to formulate. Try each of these four types in major and in minor.

If it seems difficult to write a fugue subject, it often helps to make a definite plan in advance—deciding the key, style, meter, relative rhythmic motion, points of melodic and rhythmic climax, initial and final notes, and the like. Should the subject in its final form deviate from the projected pattern, this does not matter. If it helps to get the subject started, it will have served its purpose.

Before starting to make the subject, it may be helpful to look at the examples of "unsuccessful" subjects (with suggested improvements) listed in the *Workbook* in Section 2 under "Fugue."

When the subjects (with their answers) have been completed and approved, add them to the list of subjects and answers completed in "Fugue," Section 1. They will be used in later exercises.

THE SUBJECT IN THE LATE EIGHTEENTH AND NINETEENTH CENTURIES

The changes that took place in the nature of the fugue subject in the Classical and Romantic periods are interesting mainly from the points of view of historical development and the analytical study of music literature. They are not recommended as models for use in the study of fugue; indeed, the most interesting ones are successful only because of their use in unusual or experimental fugues. Although certain elements of the generally accepted styles of the times crept in, the subjects shown in the academic text (for the study fugues of the eighteenth and nineteenth centuries) were of a conservative nature, leaning heavily on earlier practices and, particularly in the last half of the nineteenth century, on the styles of Bach and Handel. A number of the subjects used in composition of free fugues also remained conservative in style, especially in choral fugues intended for use in the church.

By the second half of the eighteenth century, the fugue had become associated in composers' minds with abstract formality, with the learned style inherited from the past. It was no longer a leading form, and the idea of personal expression was allied to the *galant* style and *Empfindsamkeit,* with the new symphony and sonata and the types of themes they required. Fugues were still written, but the fugue theme, being nonperiodic and objective, was no longer in the most progressive style, and composers like Haydn and Mozart used an entirely different type of theme when they wrote fugues or fugal movements than when they wrote their other works. Nevertheless, there are certain changes found in the fugue subjects at this time.

One of the most interesting from the point of view of the effect of theory on practice (or, more precisely, the effect of pedagogical processes on practice) is the influence of Johann Joseph Fux's (1660–1741) new system of teaching counterpoint on composers of the Classical period. This was presented in his *Gradus ad Parnassum,* which was published first in Vienna in 1725 and was translated, republished, and borrowed from by theorists who followed him.[8] Its influence is still felt in contrapuntal pedagogy today.

Fux taught a neo-Palestrina style of strict counterpoint, and, although composers rarely wrote in the precise contrapuntal style he taught, most composers of succeeding generations learned the basis of counterpoint from it and then went on to write in the free style, using freer dissonance and writing in major and minor rather than in the modes. But his exercises still had an evident effect on their contrapuntal style. He taught counterpoint by using a cantus firmus in whole notes against which students learned to solve contrapuntal problems one at a time, writing two notes against one, four against one, a series of suspensions against the given cantus, and so forth, before they were allowed to write counterpoint without a cantus firmus and with free rhythms in all parts.

It is a system that is admirable for its clarity, solving one contrapuntal technique at a time. But, for a time, it tended to make composers write counterpoint in this way in their free compositions. In the works of the Classical composers, one often finds one line in long notes accompanied by others in one of Fux's fixed "species" patterns—two notes against one, four against one, and the like. Among Viennese composers of the generation following Fux, fugue composers sometimes used fugue themes in whole notes against which were put countermelodies in faster notes in one of Fux's species. The first theme of the finale of Mozart's *Jupiter Symphony* is perhaps the best-known example of this type of contrapuntal subject. Another more obvious example is the fugue subject at the beginning of the finale of his Quartet in G Major, K. 387. (See Ex. 59.) Here, the

EXAMPLE 59

(a) BEGINNING OF THE FINALE FROM THE QUARTET IN G MAJOR, K. 387, MOZART.

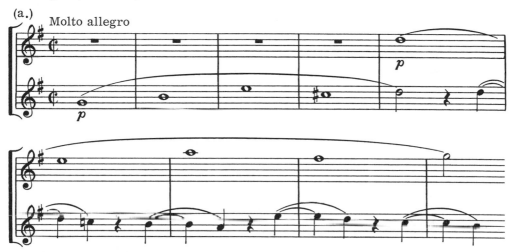

(b) SUBJECT OF FUGUE NO. 8 FROM *School of Fugue Playing*, CZERNY.

countermelody appearing against the answer uses a variant of Fux's fourth species of counterpoint, syncopation against a whole-note cantus firmus. The syncopations here are shorter rhythmically than would be found in Fux's exercises, but the basic pattern is the same.

Other, more "progressive" trends in the formation of the fugue subject are found at this time. One that is first noticeable in the fugues of Bach's sons, his pupils, and their followers is the steady increase in the length of the fugue theme. This continued in the nineteenth century and is particularly characteristic of fugues for piano. One of the longest is Beethoven's subject for the fugue finale of his *Hammerklavier Sonata,* Op. 106, but most subjects for keyboard fugues of the nineteenth century tend to be of the *andamento* type, often very extended. The fugue subject by Carl Czerny (1791–1857) shown in Example 59b is typical. It also shows another innovation found in the post-Baroque fugue—the inclusion of markings for phrasing, dynamics, and touch, which are treated as an integral part of the fugue theme.

The greater freedom in the treatment of key within the subject and the use of initial and final notes that do not project the key as clearly as do the first and third degrees of the tonic and dominant have been discussed in Chapter IV, along with the problem of movement to the dominant or subdominant keys immediately after the first note of the subject. This latter, illustrated in Example 46, not only results in a necessary distortion of the melodic line at the beginning of the tonal answer, but also makes the key uncertain to the ear. However, this is in keeping with the style of the times, which was an attempt to adapt new patterns to the old structure of the subject.

Also mentioned in Chapter IV are the early nineteenth-century experiments in fugue made by Anton Reicha. These include a conviction on his part that the fugue should use any type of subject.[9] Among the subjects used for his experimental fugues illustrating his theories are the first theme of the first movement of Haydn's Quartet in F Minor, Op. 20, No. 5 and the first phrase of the first theme from the first movement of Mozart's *Haffner Symphony.*[10] Both of these are in periodic form. Reicha avoided coming to a final close in the Haydn by putting a rest where the final tonic note would fall (on the first beat of measure 5 of the Haydn). The first four measures of the theme from Mozart's symphony end in a half cadence, so the sense of ending is not a problem, but the theme has a range of two octaves plus a fourth that leads to all sorts of difficulties. Two other very experimental themes of Reicha's own invention are given in Example 60a. None of these is successful in producing a fugue in the normal sense of the term, and Reicha's experiments were not accepted by his contemporaries. As stated earlier, his later fugues were quite conventional. But the experimental fervor he inspired in some of his pupils resulted in fugue themes like that Liszt used for the

EXAMPLE 60

(a) FUGUE NO. 12 AND FUGUE NO. 18 FROM *Trente-six fugues,* ANTON REICHA.

(b) THEME OF THE FUGATO IN THE THIRD MOVEMENT OF THE *Faust Symphony,* LISZT.

fugato in the third movement of his *Faust Symphony.* (See Ex. 60b.) These experimental themes were never successful in the working-out of a larger form, since the fugue form of the time depended so heavily on tonality in its structure. Themes of this type demand a kind of structure that could only be developed in the twentieth century, when tonality no longer depended on the major–minor system.

The Countersubject

After the first part of a fugue has finished stating the subject and the second part has entered with the answer, the first part sometimes moves on freely, merely as accompaniment to the answer. In fugues of the late Baroque period and after, this free part is normally organized rationally, made up of definite motives and their variants and introducing in this way subsidiary musical ideas that can be used in the free parts (parts not engaged in stating the subject) throughout the fugue. If, however, instead of accompanying the answer with a free countermelody, the first part states a definite melodic subject against it and this appears in conjunction with the subject and answer in most of their appearances throughout the fugue, this second subject is called a "countersubject."

This term is used rather freely at times by theorists and historians, and this reflects a free usage in the music itself. At times, the countersubject appears with only a few entries of the subject and answer, and, at other times, it is present with every statement except the first, unaccompanied entrance of the subject. In some cases, it keeps a fixed form, undergoing only the minor alterations necessary to make it fit with both the tonally adjusted answer and the subject. In other fugues, it is varied considerably from one appearance to another. It also has varying degrees of independence, and in some fugues it is used alone as well as in conjunction with the subject and answer.

The historian and the analyst must use this one term for all these cases, since it is the only one available. The term itself was given by Marpurg in the Latin forms, *contrathema* and *contrasubjectum,* as the name for the second theme in the double fugue, but nineteenth- and twentieth-century usage is less strict.[11] As used in fugue pedagogy, especially in relation to the academic or school fugue, countersubject generally means a counter-theme that remains practically unchanged and that appears with nearly every statement of the subject or answer. This is in keeping with one type of double fugue found from the late sixteenth century on, and many of the conventions involved in this use of the countersubject derive from the double fugue. (Since this is but one type of double fugue and the only one involving written assignments, it will be treated separately here; a more thorough treatment of fugues with more than one subject can be found in Chapter IX.)

It is this use of the countersubject that is recommended here for the study fugue. At first thought, this may seem to introduce extra complications into the writing of fugue, but in actual practice it will save time and trouble when the complete fugue is being written. Once a countersubject has been made that will work with the subject, this will be used to accompany every statement of the subject and answer; thus, there is one less free part to write. For the person not

skilled in composition, it takes much more time to write good, intelligible free parts that are motivically united to the whole than to
transpose and copy in a preformulated countersubject. Furthermore,
the countersubject is written in invertible counterpoint with the
subject, and the student thereby gains a little practical experience in
this important device.

Invertible counterpoint is counterpoint in which one line may be
transposed up or down a certain interval and still make correct
counterpoint with the other part. Example 61 illustrates how this is

EXAMPLE 61

done in invertible counterpoint at the octave. In the first version,
melody *a* is above melody *b,* but, in the second, inverted form,
melody *b* is transposed up an octave, appearing above melody *a.* The
interval by which the melody is transposed is the interval by which
each type of invertible counterpoint is designated—double counterpoint at the tenth and at the twelfth being the transposition of the
lower part up a tenth or twelfth, respectively.

For each type of contrapuntal inversion, a certain list of rules
exists that, if followed, will automatically make that specific type of
transposition possible. These rules are based on the general rules
used for writing counterpoint with the added prohibition of certain
intervals that will, when the counterpoint is inverted, result in contrapuntal mistakes. Although countersubjects have been written in
invertible counterpoint at various intervals, most of them are
written in invertible counterpoint at the octave or the fifteenth, and
it is invertible counterpoint at the octave that is used in the school
fugue and will be used here.

In invertible counterpoint at the octave, the two lines must at no
point be more than an octave apart, since an octave inverted makes a
unison, and a greater interval will result in a crossing of parts. In
fugue, it is not advisable to have the subject and countersubject cross

over each other, since this makes it less easy to identify the two by ear. This limitation poses the greatest difficulty to be overcome in writing the countersubject, since it sometimes takes imagination to create a countermelody within this limit that does not closely parallel the movement of the subject.

When all the intervals of the octave are given, along with the intervals that will be formed by their inversion, it is easy to see what intervals must be avoided in writing invertible counterpoint at the octave. The unison becomes an octave and the octave a unison; the second becomes a seventh and the seventh a second; the third becomes a sixth and the sixth a third; and the fourth becomes a fifth and the fifth a fourth. The augmented fourth becomes a diminished fifth and vice versa. Only in the case of the fifth will a consonance become a dissonance (since the fourth is a dissonance in two-part counterpoint). Elsewhere, the consonances will invert to other consonances (the sixth and third, the unison and octave) and the dissonances to other dissonances (the second and seventh). So in this species of invertible counterpoint, the fifth must always be treated as a dissonance; then the inversion will work. Although the prohibitions are simple, sometimes the inversions will not sound well for other reasons, so it is wise to make the inverted form at the same time that the original contrapuntal phrase is being created. (Invertible counterpoint can be made with various numbers of voices, not being limited to two, but, since only the countersubject and subject are involved here, there is no need to discuss the problems of invertible counterpoint in more than two parts.)

Like many of the elements and devices used in fugue, invertible counterpoint was first consistently exploited in the music of Willaert, and it was again his two pupils Vicentino[12] and Zarlino[13] who described the technique. Although it was not used primarily for fugue, one outgrowth of invertible counterpoint was the development of fugues using two (or more) subjects, since with this device it became possible to have the second subject appear above or below the first. This type of double fugue in which the second subject does not enter with the first, but comes in as the continuation of the first voice when the second voice enters with the answer, was well established by the end of the sixteenth century and continued in use through the nineteenth century, although by then it was usually called a fugue with a countersubject rather than a double fugue.

From the beginning, we find certain characteristics associated with this type, and these remained characteristic of the countersubject. The first is, of course, that the subject and countersubject are written in invertible counterpoint with each other and that, in the course of the fugue, the countersubject is used both above and below the subject. The second is that the countersubject has a distinct character of its own; it is a subject in its own right. The third is that, since the countersubject comes in as a continuation of the first part, the beginning of the countersubject is set off from the subject (or the free continuation of the line after the subject is finished) so that the countersubject is clearly delineated as a unit. This may be done by the use of a skip or a rest just before the countersubject begins or by a clear change in melodic direction or rhythmic movement. The important thing is that it should stand out to the ear. (See Ex. 62.)

EXAMPLE 62

G.M. TRABACI

J.S. BACH

The adoption of the tonal answer created another problem—the adjustment of the countersubject to the differing forms of the subject and answer. If the subject has a real answer, there is naturally no difficulty. If the tonal adjustment takes place only at the beginning of the subject, either the countersubject must be written in such a way that it will fit with both forms (as in Ex. 63a) or else it must be adjusted at the beginning (as in Ex. 63b). The first solution is the more common one, since by use of passing tones a line can often be created that will fit with both forms. The second is less common and not as pleasing. The rules for school fugue often recommend a third way—delaying the beginning of the countersubject until after the tonal adjustment of the head. This is recommended here for the study fugue if the first solution cannot be obtained. It has the added

EXAMPLE 63

J. S. BACH.

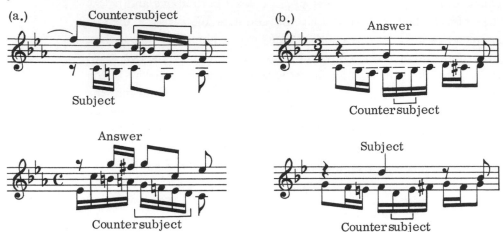

advantage of making the countersubject stand out more clearly, since its beginning does not coincide with that of the subject. (See Ex. 64.)

EXAMPLE 64

J. S. BACH.

[Transposed down an octave]

A modulation to the dominant at the end of the subject that results in a change of interval at some point in the middle of the answer requires a similar change at this point in the countersubject when it is adjusted to the answer and the subject. This happens at

[152]

points *a* and *a'* in Example 64. This adjustment in the countersubject, like the adjustment in making the tonal answer, should be made so that it is not too obvious to the ear.

With regard to the character of the countersubject, it should be in contrast to the subject but not so drastic a contrast as to contradict the basic aesthetic effect of the subject. It should contain its own melodic and rhythmic ideas and should not imitate those of the subject. The countersubject is also a good source of musical ideas to be used later in the fugue, so the ideas used should be clearly defined. Furthermore, it should, like the subject, be able to stand on its own as an intelligible and logical musical idea.

WRITING THE COUNTERSUBJECT

Before starting to write the countersubject, go through the preliminary examples and exercises in the *Workbook* in the section on the countersubject. Then choose from the list of subjects and answers (including those you have written) some that you would like to work with, including at least one of each of the subject types given in the preceding assignment in this chapter.

Since the countersubject appears first against the answer, it should be composed against the answer. At the same time, it is a good idea to see how it works with the subject, transposing it to the tonic key and copying it down with the subject as it is written. Try it also both above and below the answer and subject to be sure it sounds well in both cases. If it is to coincide with a tonal change at the head of the answer and subject or if there is a modulation at the end of the answer and subject, it must be worked out at this point with both the answer and subject simultaneously. If an alteration has to be made when the projected countersubject is adjusted to fit with the subject and this alteration results in an awkward or distorted version, change it (in both forms).

The countersubject should also make good harmony with the answer and with the subject—harmony that clearly reinforces the tonic or dominant keys, not "original" harmony that disguises the key. The ending of the two will be less final if the subject and countersubject do not end on the octave or unison of the tonic note, but the latter is not forbidden if one of the parts moves on at once. It is more common, however, to end with the third or sixth made by the root and third of the final chord. (A fifth is not allowed in invertible counterpoint.) It is helpful to sketch out the harmonic plan to be followed by the answer and subject in their separate combinations with the countersubject before working out the counter-subject itself.

It is usually not a good idea to create both the subject and countersubject at once, since this often results in trying to make up for deficiencies in the subject by adding movement in the counter-subject. The countersubject should provide movement when the subject pauses, and vice versa, but, if the two are composed at once, there is often less individuality in the two subjects. It is far better to work out a good subject—which will be, after all, the main theme of the fugue—and then invent a countersubject to go with it. Make more than one countersubject for each subject, choosing the most successful one. These countersubjects should be kept, along with their correlative subjects and answers, for use in future exercises. Do not worry at this time about the melodic connection of the subject with the countersubject that follows in the same part. This will be done after the study of the exposition of the fugue.

Notes

1. Dominico Bianchini, *Intabulatura de lauto libro primo* (Venice, 1546), p. A2ᵥ.

2. Bononcini, *op. cit.,* p. 82.

3. Rameau, *op. cit.,* p. 336.

4. Marpurg, *op. cit.,* p. 27.

5. Martini, *op. cit.,* II, viii, ix.

6. Leonard G. Ratner, "Eighteenth-Century Theories of Period Structure," *Musical Quarterly,* XLII (1956) 439–54.

7. The word "period" comes from a Greek word meaning "sentence," and this is the primary sense in which it was used in eighteenth-century treatises on periodic structure. In Baroque opera, the setting of the text uses cadences, rests, and so forth, to make the grammatical structure clear, and it is the transfer of this style to instrumental music that was the source of the periodic structure found in eighteenth-century homophonic music. For a treatment of the operatic usage in the late Baroque, see Mattheson, *op. cit.* An English translation of the relevant material by Hans Lenneberg can be found in "Johann Mattheson on Affect and Rhetoric in Music," *Journal of Music Theory,* II (1958) pp. 47–84; 193–236. pp. 206*ff.*

8. The English translation is *Steps to Parnassus,* trans. Alfred Mann (New York: Norton, 1943).

9. Anton Reicha, *Über das neue Fugensystem* (Vienna 1804–1805). Fugue examples from this are found in Anton Reicha, *Trente-six fugues d'aprés un nouveau systême* (Vienna, 1805).

10. *Ibid.,* Nos. 3 and 7, respectively.

11. Marpurg, *op. cit.,* p. 21.

12. Vicentino, *op. cit.,* pp. 90ᵥff.

13. Zarlino, *op. cit.,* pp. 229*ff.*

Chapter VI

The Exposition,

Counterexposition, and

Later Statements of the

Subject

The Exposition

The exposition of a fugue comprises the successive statements of subject or answer made by each part as it enters at the beginning, and the continuation of each part until the last to enter has completed the theme. The use of the term "exposition" to specify the opening of a fugue is a rather recent innovation. It was first used in the nineteenth century, when the various sections of a musical form were called after the parts of a formal rhetorical discourse that they seemed to parallel; the exposition, in both the fugue and in sonata form, is that section where the main musical subjects to be developed in the remainder of the movement are first presented. Reicha applied the term to the beginning part of a fugue in his *Traité de haute composition musicale,* 1825[1] and, with the exception of Cherubini, succeeding French treatises on fugue adopted

it. By the second half of the century, it was in common use in England and America as well.

The term is slightly misleading when used in the analysis of
fugues because its association with sonata form and literary discourse
lead one to expect a clearly defined section. By definition, the exposition in a fugue is complete once the last voice to enter has finished
stating the subject (or answer), but in some fugues an extra entry
(in a voice that has already stated the subject or answer) is found.
Also, by associating the word "exposition" with a definite section of a
work, we tend to look for some clear-cut ending made by a cadence
or a definite change in texture or musical material. A clear cadence
is often found at the end of the subject or answer as stated in the
last entering voice if the subject is constructed so that a cadence
is implied, and one feels that a section has been brought to a close.
But, at times, a strong cadence clearly defining the end of a section
is not found until several measures after the last entering voice has
finished its statement (as in the G Minor Fugue in the first book of
the *Well-Tempered Clavier*); in other fugues (such as that by
Handel given in Ex. 65), there is neither a cadence nor a break in
the musical treatment, but only a continuation of the material used
and an immediate statement of the subject transposed to another
key. In this latter case one certainly cannot say that there is a
definite section that can be specified as "exposition."

The term was, furthermore, first adopted for the French *fugue
d'école,* where the exposition was meant to present all the musical
ideas to be used later in the fugue. This is a fine idea for an exercise
in composition, but it must not lead the analyst to feel that a fugue
that introduces and uses new material after the exposition is irregular. Nevertheless, "exposition" is an apt term because the section
does expose the main subject of the fugue, and it must be used since
it is the only term we have for the opening part of a fugue. Earlier
terms such as the Latin *repercussio* (translated by the German
Wiederschlag by Marpurg) refer simply to the order of the entrances
of the different parts with the subject and answer. Marpurg also
used the term *Durchfürung* (the bringing in of the subject and answer in the different voices) for this but in a less specific sense since
it was applied to entries throughout the fugue, the opening entries
being referred to as the first *Durchführung.*[2] These two terms were
used by late eighteenth- and nineteenth-century German theorists,
but, by the twentieth century, "exposition" supplanted them, and it
is in common use today, even retrospectively, in fugal analysis.

EXAMPLE 65

BEGINNING OF THE FUGUE IN C MINOR, HANDEL.

The fact that theorists (and, presumably, composers) had no real term for the exposition during the times when most fugues were being written is not a particularly significant point, although it is one that historical analysts should keep in mind when looking at these fugues. From the point of view of the composer, the important decisions to be made in beginning a fugue had nothing to do with terminology, and they remain the same from the late fifteenth-century beginnings of *fuga sciolta* through the academic fugues written by today's music students. Once the subject and the proper form of the answer have been decided on, these questions must be answered: (1) In what order will the subject and answer be stated, in which voices will they appear, and in what order will these voices enter? (2) How will the succeeding entries be spaced? (3) What other material beside the subject and answer will be used?

THE HISTORICAL DEVELOPMENT OF THE EXPOSITION

When these three aspects of the exposition are investigated historically, one finds a steady movement from great variety and freedom in the early sixteenth century to what is almost a stereotyped pattern in the eighteenth and nineteenth centuries. One of the most important musical forces bringing about this narrowing-down of possible choices was the steady movement to the major–minor tonal system that took place during this time. The effects of this on the subject–answer relationship have been outlined in Chapter IV.

Another important factor was the development of the long fugal piece based on a single subject. Especially in the eighteenth-century fugue, where the subject was first presented clearly in its simple form and the exercise of contrapuntal ingenuity and invention was saved until later in the piece, do we find the beginning of a fugue taking on the function and character of a simple exposition of the subject. In the sixteenth century, when choral and many instrumental works using fugue were built on several subjects—or, more precisely, a series of fugal sections each based on a different subject—we often find that composers wanted to make the opening itself display their skill and ingenuity, so a rigid formula did not develop. Bach's use of inversion, augmentation, diminution, and stretto in certain expositions in his *Art of Fugue* is unusual for his time, and this is because it, too, involved a display of skill and invention. Even here, he used subjects in those forms that had already been heard in earlier fugues in the work and had therefore been subject to clear exposition.

Before discussing the first of the questions listed above, it may be helpful to recapitulate briefly the points in the development of the subject–answer relationship that have a bearing on the exposition. During the sixteenth century, there was a gradual limiting of the possible initial notes allowed in each mode, so that, by the beginning of the seventeenth century, the regular initial notes were the tonic and dominant notes in each mode.[3] During the seventeenth century, subjects began to start on the third degree of the scale answered by the sixth or seventh degree of the same scale, and, at the same time, the movement toward the major–minor tonal system forced other changes in the subject–answer pair. Once the tonic and dominant keys were established as the basis of subject and answer, the subject could begin (or end) on any note of the scale without losing the feeling of the key, and, by the eighteenth century, the exposition was conceived as contrasting the subject and answer forms rather than as establishing mode by proper entry notes.

When we begin to examine solutions made by composers to the problems posed in the first question, it is clear that the changing relation of the subject and answer had a direct influence on the order in which they were used. In the last part of the sixteenth century and the early seventeenth century, the order was not stereotyped since the idea was to insure the projection of a single mode. Subject and answer might appear in regular alternation, two subjects might be followed by two answers, or they might appear as subject–answer–answer– subject. And even though the theorist Vicentino complained in 1555 that fugal imitation at the octave and unison gave too little variety and should be replaced by imitation at the fourth and fifth,[4] a combination of three subjects followed by an answer or even four subjects without an answer are found. But as the century moved on, the regular alternation of subject and answer became more common, and it is this order that is found most often in examples of fugue in theory books. The use of the term *seconde partie* by seventeenth-century French theorists to describe what eighteenth-century writers called the *réponse*[5] is indicative of this growing convention. By the eighteenth century, the order subject–answer–subject–answer was considered to be the regular one for a four-voiced fugue. Others were found but were no longer considered regular. At the same time, the subdominant answer along with melodic variants was relegated to the category of irregular fugues or *fughe d'imitazione*. Although some experimentation is found in the nineteenth century, the regular alternation of subject and answer was obligatory in the academic fugue, and its correctness was reinforced by the feeling that it was natural for the tonally adjusted answer to follow the subject since this gave the effect of antecedent–consequent phrases.

The assignment of subject and answer to particular parts derives mainly from the fact that, because of their formation, they will naturally be in different ranges; if the subject is in the tenor, the answer will fall most easily into the bass or alto range, whereas the subject will recur most naturally in the soprano part. Although limitations of range are not so important in instrumental music, the analogy still holds because of its naturalness and practicality in polyphonic writing. Even though the instrumental fugue does not limit the range of each part to that of the vocal part for which it is named, the assignment of the subject and answer to adjacent ranges became the norm. In unaccompanied vocal fugues, the announcement of the subject in one voice meant that the answer would be in a voice adjacent to it; if the subject began in the soprano, for example, the answer would have to be in the alto; if the subject was in the alto, the answer might be in either the tenor or the soprano. This, of course, was because too widely spaced entries made good intonation difficult. In instrumental fugues, this was not necessary—the subject could start in the bass followed by the answer in the soprano—but even in instrumental works, this pairing was much less common than the pairing of adjacent voices.

By the eighteenth century, the consistent alternation of subject and answer in the exposition was accounted the only correct order, and there were then only eight possible arrangements for a *regular* four-voice fugue.

1. Soprano, alto, tenor, bass
2. Tenor, bass, soprano, alto
3. Bass, tenor, alto, soprano
4. Alto, soprano, bass, tenor
5. Tenor, alto, soprano, bass
6. Alto, tenor, bass, soprano
7. Soprano, bass, tenor, alto
8. Bass, soprano, alto, tenor

Numbers 7 and 8 are the least used, even in instrumental music, because of the great distance between the two beginning voices. Otherwise, those with like pairs—numbers 1, 2, 3, and 4—are most often used. A few studies have been made as to which patterns were most followed by certain composers, but an exact tally of large numbers of fugues so that particular trends can be picked out must await the future labors of musicologists. Only one strong historical trend can now be identified—the rigid formula for the exposition of the four-part choral fugue in the Viennese Catholic tradition. Based on Italian convention and established in Vienna by the composers Antonio Caldara (1670–1736), Johann Joseph Fux, and Johann Adolph Hasse (1699–1783), the stereotype beginning for a four-voice fugue (soprano, alto, tenor, bass plus an extra statement of the subject in the soprano; or bass, tenor, alto, soprano with an additional statement of the subject in the bass) was commonly used by later Viennese composers in their choral fugues, particularly by Joseph Haydn and his brother Michael (1737–1806), Mozart, Schubert, and Carl Maria von Weber (1786–1826).

In general, the four-voice fugue was most often used, but the alternation of subject and answer was also characteristic of fugues of more or fewer voices. In a five-voice fugue, the fifth entry would be another statement of the subject; in a six-part fugue, the sixth entry would be another answer, and so forth. For the fugue with only three voices, eighteenth-century theorists only insisted that the first entry be a subject and the second an answer. The third could be either of the two. It is notable, however, that Bach clearly preferred the subject for the third entry and often added a fourth entry with another answer in a part that had already entered.

In fugal works of the sixteenth and seventeenth centuries, where the order of entry might be subject–subject–answer–answer, subject–answer–answer–subject, or other such combinations, the order of the entering parts would be altered, producing such voice orders as soprano, tenor, alto, bass and soprano, alto, bass, tenor. For Marpurg, these orderings of the subject and answer entries were "irregular" but still possible, and he included these as well as the regular ones in his listings of possible voice-entry orders. In the nineteenth-century school fugue, only the regular alternation of subject and answer with its correlated patterns of voice entries was permitted. In those cases— mostly found in the sixteenth century—where three subjects are followed by an answer or where each entry repeats the subject at the octave or unison, the ranges are alike, so that no regular pattern of entering voices could be established.

Composers' answers to the second of the stated questions are of greater interest to the historically oriented theorist, since the spacing of the entries involves consideration of composition techniques and changing attitudes toward the purpose of the opening set of entries. In opening entries of the early *fuga sciolta,* we often see a close relation to the *fuga legata* or canon. This is very evident in certain fugal works by Obrecht and Des Près, which begin with two adjacent parts in close canonic imitation at the fourth or fifth that is carried on for several measures, these two parts then dropping out when the other two voices enter. (See Ex. 66.) As the *fuga sciolta* gained in importance, fugal beginnings in complex stretto arrangements were used as well as widely spaced entries, and, in many cases, there are exposi-

EXAMPLE 66

THE FIRST TWO ENTRIES OF SECTION *Adhaerat lingua*
FROM THE FOUR-PART MOTET *Si oblitus fuero,* JACOB
OBRECHT. [TEXT OMITTED]

tions that seem to stress variety, each part entering to fit in a different
place against the thematic statement that precedes it. (See Ex. 67.)

The differing usages in spacing entries were reflected in the
opinions of contemporary theory. Tomàs de Sancta Maria's book on
the technique of improvising fugal fantasias, *Arte de tañer fantasía*

EXAMPLE 67

OPENING OF FIRST KYRIE FROM *Missa Media vita à 5,*
NICOLAI GOMBERT. [TEXT OMITTED]

(1565), included a long discussion on the placing of the entrances,
and the author considered this an intricate and important part of
fugue.[6] Zarlino complained that the use of very close entries, although helping the ear to recognize the theme, limited the types of
themes that could be used (because of the stretto overlap) and made
for a tiresome lack of variety in fugues. He pleaded for entrances at
greater distances, with a resulting increase in the variety of fugal
points.[7] A few decades later, Pietro Pontio described long, well-
spaced entries as an important requisite of the instrumental ricercare,[8]
but, at the close of the century, Thomas Morley still recommended

the narrow spacing of entries because it was easier for the listener to follow the theme.[9] These differing opinions show a lack of theoretical conviction as to what constituted a proper beginning, and an examination of the compositions of the sixteenth century seems to indicate that composers worked for variety in treatment rather than the single, perfect solution that is so evident in the compositions of the late eighteenth and nineteenth centuries.

During the seventeenth century, there was a movement toward regularity in exposition, a tendency felt most strongly in works for keyboard. In many cases, an overlap of only one note between the first and second entries is found—an elision rather than a stretto; this type of overlap was well-liked in the eighteenth century and even in the conventionalized school fugue of the nineteenth century. At the same time, however, stretto openings remained popular. One of the most common spacings used, with either stretto or elision between entries, is the paired-entry pattern that was used in the preceding century. Here the subject and answer pair come in with some measure of overlap, the two entries move on to the end of the subject and answer, and then the other two voices enter with the same stretto overlap as the first pair. (See Ex. 68.) In some cases, when the stretto overlap between subject and answer is only two or three notes, there

EXAMPLE 68

BEGINNING OF THE *Ricercar Sesto Tono* (Hypolydian), ANDREA GABRIELI.

may also be some free material interpolated between the end of the first two entries and the beginning of the second pair.

If we are to believe the theorists of the time, the removal of stretto from the beginning of the fugue was motivated by a growing formal sense and a desire to have the listener well acquainted with the subject before the stretto appeared. In the late seventeenth century, both Berardi and Bononcini recommended saving the stretto until rather late in the fugal movement—Bononcini because he wanted the listener to know the subject well before the stretto came[10] and Berardi because he felt the most exciting part should come at the end of the fugue.[11] In the first part of the eighteenth century, the German theorist Mattheson likewise instructed the composer to save stretto entries for later in the fugue, and his Viennese contemporary Fux also conceived of stretto as an artifice to be employed in the latter sections of a fugue.

There is evidence, though, that in many cases this was taken to mean that the closer strettos were to be saved until later, since an overlap of two or three notes is often found in the expositions of the first half of the eighteenth century as well as in the fugue examples given by several theorists.[12] The French theorists Rameau[13] and Béthisy[14] still recommended the overlapping of entries when the subject was long. By mid-eighteenth century, however, the overlap of entries in the exposition by more than one note had all but disappeared. Certainly, it was not characteristic of the instrumental fugues of J. S. Bach nor of the fugues of the Classical period, and, by the nineteenth century, a clear separation of the entries in the exposition was taken for granted.

This separation of the opening entries, in combination with the more complex relationship between subject and answer found in the major–minor key system, led to a new use of free material (material that is not the subject, answer, or countersubject) in the exposition of the eighteenth-century fugue. Naturally, there had always been free material in an exposition. When the first part has finished with the subject or answer, it must move on freely in counterpoint against the subject or answer as it is stated in the next part, and so on. Even if there is a regular countersubject, this accounts for only two parts of the contrapuntal texture. Furthermore, there are often places in an exposition when a short transition is needed between entries, and these are freely composed as well.

In early fugal works, these free parts served a variety of uses. In Example 67, they are important in defining a polyphonic texture of interest; in the second measure, the free part combines with the answer and subject to produce parallel motion; in the third measure, they provide the most active rhythmic element in the texture. In Example 68, they fill a less obvious role. Because of the pairing of the entries, there is less room for free parts. Only in measure 6, after the tenor has entered with the subject, do we find both upper parts moving freely. Here they are subordinate polyphonically, merely making the harmony and the rhythmic movement more complete.

In Example 65, a fugue from the second quarter of the eighteenth century, we see an entirely different relationship. The free accompanying parts are also important in establishing the key harmonically, and, although they help to maintain polyphonic interest, they are likewise related to the theme, being based on short motives derived from it. They serve a minor thematic function but never in such a way as to confuse the ear about the extent and identity of the subject. Because of its rhythmic distinctness and the strength of the cadence that ends it, it is clear that the subject ends on the c' on the first beat of the third measure and that, even though the answer does not enter until the next beat, the continuation of the first voice is free, no longer part of the subject.

Usually, this transition between the end of the subject and the entrance of the answer is not more than a measure, and most of the time it is much shorter. At times, it has a modulatory function, moving to the dominant when the answer begins in that key. This transition was first pointed out by German theorists of the early eighteenth century, who called it a *conciliatio*[15] since it filled in the space between the end of the subject and the beginning of the answer and often connected the tonic and dominant keys as well. Later German theorists dropped the term and developed no special name for it, although they recognized it as free material in the fugues they analyzed.

Padre Martini and the Italian theorists who followed him gave it a special name, "coda," which, in the nineteenth century, was eventually changed to "codetta." Along with the name, it acquired a definite function in the exposition as it was discussed in fugue pedagogy. It was a short musical phrase added after the subject proper was finished, usually with a certain degree of thematic independence (Ex. 69). In the French *fugue d'école,* it gained an importance out of proportion to its use in fugue literature. Here, it became a natural ending for the fugue subject, leading from the end of the subject proper to the beginning of the countersubject. Its use was not strictly obligatory, but it was sometimes used even when it would be possible to bring in the answer on the last note of the subject and was often

EXAMPLE 69

EXAMPLES OF CODETTA BETWEEN SUBJECT AND COUN-
TERSUBJECT FROM *Cours de contrepoint et de fugue,* LUIGI
CHERUBINI. (a) DIVISION MADE BETWEEN CODETTA AND
COUNTERSUBJECT. (b) CODETTA CONNECTED TO COUN-
TERSUBJECT WITHOUT CLEAR DIFFERENTIATION.

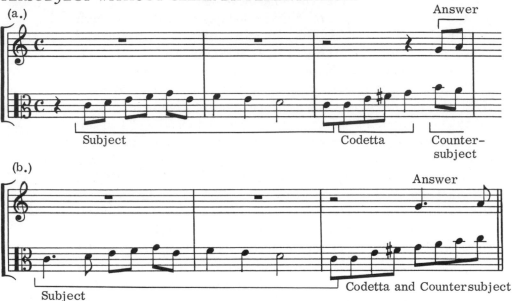

introduced with the idea of providing extra thematic material that
could be used later in the body of the fugue.

In analyzing earlier fugues, it is not a good idea to use this term
unless the transitional phrase covering the space between the end of
the subject and the beginning of the answer has a rather definite and
independent shape. As such, it is rare in the fugues of Bach, although
certain fugues of his do have passages that merit this distinction. The
Fugue in E-flat Major from the first book of his *Well-Tempered
Clavier,* given in Example 52b, has what might well be called a
codetta. Here, after the end of the subject, a broken-chord figure in
sixteenths is used to span the space before the entrance of the answer. This is a distinct musical idea that he uses again in the exposition at the end of the answer and the second entry of the subject and
that is also thematically important in the fugue, being the basis of
most of the modulatory episodes.

It must be admitted, however, that, in many smoothly written
fugues, the use of the term "codetta" seems to place more emphasis
than is deserved on what is merely transitional material. Further-

more, at some times, this codetta is used so consistently in the exposition that it seems like a part of the subject, and it is only later in
the fugue that the subject's true extent is made clear. Its connection
with the countersubject is also of interest, since it is often used in
an exposition as a lead in to each statement of the countersubject.
Again, it is only later in the fugue that the exact extent of the
countersubject is made clear. In analysis, therefore, one finds that
terminology is not always useful descriptively, although it may at
times help one's perception of the musical structure.

A more essential section of free material in the exposition is the
transitional passage that is often found between the end of the answer in the second voice to enter and the entry of the third part with
the subject. This is sometimes found in earlier fugues with paired
entries, but, in fugues in the major–minor system, it is often a necessity. In Example 65, the subject begins and ends in c minor, and the
answer ends in g minor, so that some sort of harmonic transition
must lead back to c minor before the subject can enter smoothly on
the second beat of measure 6. This is done by a short, modulating
sequence moving from c to g in measure 5. Here, this sequence uses
a motive from the subject, but new material is often used instead. At
times, this transition passage may be formed by a prolongation of a
codetta that follows the answer. This modulatory section is often
needed in fugues, and, early in the eighteenth century, German theorists recognized its importance and gave to it an equality with later
modulatory episodes in the body of the fugue.[16] Like the codetta, it
gained prominence in the French *fugue d'école,* some theorists recom-
mending it even when it was not needed, as a means of introducing
further material for use later in the fugue. Occasionally, it was called
codetta, but the accepted term used in the majority of textbooks is
that which was also used for later episodes in the fugue—German,
Zwischensatz; French, *divertissement;* Italian, *divertimento.* Although this episode in the exposition is often sequential in nature
and in most academic fugues it is sequentially organized, there are
a number of fugues—especially eighteenth-century fugues, including
those of J. S. Bach—in which a short, nonsequential transition is
used to effect the necessary modulation. It had a much more important role than did the codetta in fugue, being found in a great
many eighteenth- and nineteenth-century fugues. At times, such an
episode is found between the third and fourth entries, but the musical
need for it at this point is seldom very strong, and its use at any other
place than between the second and third entries is not common.

SUGGESTED PROBLEMS IN ANALYSIS

The analysis of several expositions of fugues written in the eighteenth century is a good preliminary to writing a fugue exposition, and the fugues in Bach's *Well-Tempered Clavier* provide interesting material for such analyses. Check the relation of the subject and answer first (the keys in which they begin and end), noting any particular problems that may arise in connecting them harmonically in the key system. Then note whether or not there is a regular countersubject and, if it is a three-voice fugue, if there is an immediate extra entry of the answer before the exposition of the theme is completed. Bach's expositions often end with a cadence, but the cadence is not accompanied by any pause in the rhythmic motion; at any rate, for purposes of analysis, the exposition may be said to be completed when the final entry is finished. When the entries of the subjects and answers (and countersubjects if the fugue uses them) are located, observe the free material—the use of a transition or codetta between the end of the subject and the beginning of the answer in the next part to enter, the connection of the countersubject with this, or the use of a modulatory episode between the second and third entries. Note the keys used in the subject and answer and the rhythmic positions of the beginning and ending notes of the subject and answer; see how these relate to the presence or absence of transitions and modulatory episodes. Also identify the musical ideas found in the free material, locating their sources in the subject or countersubject and labeling any new ideas that are found.

Although Bach's expositions reveal a masterly solution of the problems that arise in writing the exposition, they are not based on a fixed prototype, and many of them present some "exception" from the exposition as found in later fugues and especially in the academic fugues taught in nineteenth- and twentieth-century textbooks. Each of these "exceptions" is the result of musical logic, and although exceptions are not admitted in the exercises in writing fugue that follow, the perception of these and a search for the musical reasons motivating them are essential to an understanding of fugue. After the student has written two or three stereotyped expositions, he will find that a second look at Bach's expositions will be even more meaningful to him; the restrictions he has applied in writing serve to bring the procedures used by Bach into clearer focus.

Example 70 shows the exposition of the Fugue in C-sharp Major from the first book of Bach's *Well-Tempered Clavier*. It was chosen because, like the exposition stereotype that the student will write in

EXAMPLE 70

OPENING MEASURES OF THE FUGUE IN C-SHARP MAJOR
FROM THE *Well-Tempered Clavier*, BOOK I, J. S. BACH.

a study fugue, it uses a regular countersubject. The entries of the
subject and answer are marked off in brackets. The subject has a beginning that needs a tonal adjustment in the answer, but it does not
modulate thereafter, ending on 1 in the scale of C-sharp. The answer,
with its tonally adjusted head, has a beginning that can belong to
either C-sharp or G-sharp, but it ends very definitely with a cadence
on 1 in the scale of G-sharp.

Since the subject begins on the second half of the second beat of
the measure but ends on the first beat of the measure, there will
necessarily be a gap between the end of the subject and the beginning
of the answer. This is filled in by what a later theorist would call a
codetta. Clearly, Bach started this with an octave skip because he had

to get that voice into the higher range so that the part entering with the answer would have enough space in the middle range to state the answer. The codetta, moving in sixteenth notes, clearly anticipates the faster movement of the countersubject (which begins with the g″-sharp at the beginning of measure 3 and is enclosed in dotted brackets). The countersubject here is written in invertible counterpoint at the fifteenth with the answer, since the big skips in the subject would make it impossible to create a good countersubject within the limits of an octave from the theme. The codetta does not modulate to the dominant because the answer begins by outlining the root and third of the C-sharp major triad, and this can enter against a melody still in the tonic key.

The answer and countersubject end on a strongly established tonic in G-sharp major. Since the subject starts on g-sharp (5 in the key of C-sharp) and there is, by nature of the rhythmic structure of the subject, a natural gap between the end of the answer and the beginning of the subject, Bach easily makes possible the smooth entry of the third part by changing the tonic chord in G-sharp to the dominant seventh in C-sharp by the addition of f″-sharp. A modulatory episode is not needed. The part that has finished the answer uses a variant of the codetta at the end of the subject, with the last note altered because an exact transposition of the original codetta would make a repeated c″-sharp with the beginning of the countersubject— an awkward movement at this spot.

Although the middle voice has the codetta and countersubject, the top part is now free. At the beginning of measure 5, it skips up to the half note f″-sharp, which is the essential tone bringing the exposition back to C-sharp major. After this, the soprano moves down the scale in slow syncopation, interrupted only by the eighths at the end of measure 6. This free part is clearly subordinate thematically, but both the falling scale and the turn figure in eighth notes at the end of measure 6 can be distinctly related to material already used in the exposition; the falling scale is found in sixteenth notes in the countersubject (soprano, measure 3, fourth beat) and the turn, also in sixteenth notes, in the countersubject as well (soprano, measure 4, third beat). Despite the subordinate nature of this free part, it has a clear rhythmic and melodic shape and is obviously more than just random filler.

The exposition finishes on the first beat of measure 7, with the last note of the subject in the bass. The subject clearly delineates a strong cadence, but Bach minimizes it and keeps the movement going by a suspension with an ornamental resolution in the free soprano.

There are no "irregularities" in this exposition, but the use of analysis by terminology does involve some ambiguity in the relation of the "codetta" and the countersubject. The identity of the countersubject as marked in Example 70 does seem established, because it is identical in its appearances against the answer and the subject. Yet, in both cases, the "codetta," because of its range and melodic and rhythmic character, attaches itself naturally to the countersubject, and the octave skip between the end of the subject and the beginning of the "codetta" detaches it from the subject. The fact that it is not exact in its appearance against the answer and the subject beginnings would keep it, by some definitions, from being a part of the countersubject. This can, on the other hand, be rationalized as a necessary adjustment made so that it would fit with the heads of the answer and the subject; thus, it could be included as part of the countersubject, beginning ahead of the answer and subject. Such an adjustment is not unusual in eighteenth-century fugues. An examination of the rest of the fugue will not resolve the question, since the "codetta" is attached to the "countersubject" in several later statements of the subject and answer—and in both of its forms—but it is not attached to all. This is a case, not too rare in music, in which the use of terms with fixed definitions is not helpful in explaining musical structure.

In general, the analysis of expositions from earlier or later periods may wait until the form of the whole fugue has been examined in the next chapter. However, the analysis of expositions for the purpose of discovering a composer's habits or procedural techniques is an interesting historical or theoretical study. It is wise to stick to the expositions of a single composer or even a particular collection of the works of one composer. Any detailed historical conclusions covering a period of time must wait until a great many smaller studies of individual composers have been completed. Enough published works of composers from the sixteenth to the early twentieth centuries are available to provide material for many such studies.

WRITING THE EXPOSITION

In writing an exposition for a study fugue, it is best to stick to a simple prototype. Since this is to be used as an exercise in working out the structure of a fugue exposition, the rather fixed conventions of the nineteenth-century academic fugue will be used, but it is well to remember that this is a theoretical abstraction that does not represent the particulars of each single fugue composed by the masters of

fugue writing. Since the purpose is to gain experience in putting together an exposition, the student is advised to write expositions in
three voices only, using his time to write more than one exposition
rather than in the writing of a single exposition in four or more
voices.

For each exposition, choose the subjects, answers, and countersubjects worked out in previous exercises. First of all, examine the
subject and answer to observe what order of entries would be the
best for the exposition. Check the notes on which the subject and
answer end, their rhythmic placement, and the keys involved and see
if the answer can begin on the last note of the subject (above or
below) or if they must be separated. If they will fit with an elision,
copy them out in the correct positions; if not, copy them out in the
proper voices leaving a blank space between the end of the subject
and the beginning of the answer. The answer should not enter on a
unison with the end of the subject, but any other consonant note may
be used. The answer need not enter on the exact beat on which the
subject started if the fugue is in 4/4 time, but it should enter in an
equivalent position; if the subject starts on a strong beat, the answer
may start on either the first or third beat, and so forth. A wait of
more than a measure between the end of the subject and the entry
of the answer should be avoided.

When the placement of the subject and answer has been made,
copy in the countersubject against the answer in the voice that has
just finished stating the subject, and, if there is a blank space between
the end of the subject and the beginning of the countersubject, leave
it until the rest of the entries have been written.

The next thing to do is to note the ending of the answer and the
countersubject to see if the subject can enter immediately in the third
voice or if there must be a modulatory passage back to the right key
before it can enter. If there needs to be a short episode, leave a space
on the manuscript and then copy the subject in in the third part,
adding the countersubject in the voice that has just stated the answer,
remembering to use it in the form in which it is transposed (and
adjusted if necessary) to fit with the subject. If a four-part exposition
is to be written, the fourth part must now enter with the answer. If
possible, this should be in the same rhythmic position in relation to
the subject ending that was used in the first statement of the subject
and answer. The countersubject fitting with the answer should then
be copied in in the third voice to enter, which voice has just finished
stating the subject.

When all the entries of the subject and countersubject have been copied in, it is time to compose the free parts. Usually, there needs to be some connection between the end of the subject and the beginning of the countersubject, even if the answer begins on the last note of the subject. Before inventing this passage, remember that the countersubject should stand out, and this is best done by using a short rest or a definite skip before it begins. It is, however, not advisable to stop a melody on the weak part of a beat. Thus, a certain amount of calculation must take place before either a short transition or a regular codetta to the subject is created. Also, if the subject ends in the vicinity in which the answer is going to enter, the free part should move quickly out of this range so that the part bringing in the answer can enter clearly and the two parts can be clearly differentiated. This free part should likewise sound like a logical continuation of the first part and should keep moving until after the answer has entered. When this has been sketched in, see if it will work at the end of the answer and, if the fugue is in four parts, after the second entry of the subject. The use of the same material at these points is not necessary, but the same or similar extension of the subject and answer will give a sense of unity and at the same time save time in the invention of more free material.

If a modulatory section between the answer and the entry of the subject in the third voice is needed, note the harmony (and key) on which the answer and countersubject end and that with which the subject begins. This short episode is not always sequential in fugue literature, but it is a good idea to make it so in a study fugue. Calculate, first, how to get from the end of the answer to the subject by harmonic sequence, and translate these chords into a two-part polyphonic sequence of which at least the first two statements are exact. Material derived from the subject and countersubject may be used here, or new material (in keeping with the ideas in the subject and countersubject) may be used. Be sure to calculate the spacing and range of this episode so that the subject entry can be heard clearly and each part keeps its distinct place. The entry of the countersubject, which will come in the part that has just stated the subject, must also be planned, and this voice in the episode must continue so that a logical approach as well as an obvious entrance of the countersubject can be made. This third entry need not enter on a simple consonance. Any properly treated contrapuntal dissonance may be used. A suspension in one of the other parts against which the subject enters, and which is then properly resolved, can be used here to good effect.

When all these "joints" have been filled in, the other free parts may be written. In a three-voice fugue, all that will be left is the continuation of the third part (the first part to enter) against the second statement of the subject and countersubject. This will be subordinate polyphonically and related to the general style of material used in the exposition thus far. It may use material already stated, material derived from it, or new material. The choice rests with the composer. But there should be no sudden changes in the general rhythmic or melodic movement at this point. In the study fugue, once all parts have entered, they should be kept moving (except for very short rests) until the end of the exposition. Although this is certainly not characteristic of all fugues—and even a few fugues of J. S. Bach do not always follow this rule—it is good and necessary experience for the student of fugue to do this. If the subject allows, the exposition should end with a cadence on the last note of the subject (or answer, in a four-voice fugue). The endings of the expositions written here should be sketched as tentative endings that may be altered later when the rest of the fugue is written.

Before starting the exposition, it will be helpful to do the preliminary exercises and note the examples given in the *Workbook* in the section on the "Exposition."

When the expositions are finished, copy them into the *Workbook* for future use.

The Counterexposition

The counterexposition is a section either directly after the exposition or following the first episodic digression after the exposition, where the voices that originally stated the subject now state the answer and those that stated the answer now state the subject, still in the key of the first exposition. Ideally, the entries also follow the order of entries in the exposition, so that the part that first stated the subject will begin the counterexposition with the answer, and so forth. This type of counterexposition is most characteristic of Italian and Italian-influenced fugues of the eighteenth century. The model that Martini gives in the preface to his treatise on fugue has this type of counterexposition,[17] and the fugue by Luigi Battiferi that is the first of the examples of complete fugues that Marpurg gives in his work on fugue[18] (and that Alfred Mann includes in his published translation of excerpts from Marpurg's text[19]) are readily available examples of this type. This is by no means characteristic of all fugues, and it is certainly not characteristic of the German fugue of this period, although some examples of its use are found. The F Major Fugue from the first book of Bach's *Well-Tempered Clavier* has a counterexposition.

This procedure was not named in German texts of the eighteenth or early nineteenth centuries as a necessary part of the fugue, and Marpurg made no special comment about its use in the Battiferi fugue, merely describing what was done with no further comment. Neither did French theorists name it or point it out until, in the nineteenth century, the influence of Italian theory was felt. The prominence given to it in the school fugue and in German texts in the last part of the nineteenth century seems to be due as much to its rational appeal as a theoretical conception as to its musical logic, but, even in the *fugue d'école,* it was never considered an essential part of a fugue. A great deal of the emphasis placed on this device in late nineteenth- and twentieth-century theory was no doubt due to the term "counterexposition," which, by association with the all-important exposition, sounds more official and important than it is in actual musical practice.

Naturally, the term "counterexposition" did not come into being until after the term "exposition" was adopted for the opening entries of the fugue in the second quarter of the nineteenth century in France. Martini called it the *rovesciamento,* the reversing of the order of the subject and answer,[20] and later Italian theorists use a similar term, the *rivolto.*[21] Fétis, in his treatise of 1825, noted that German fugue writers often omitted this *renversement* but, although he saw it as an "old" Italian technique, he—a dogmatic theorist, if an objective observer—thought it should be included as part of a fugue.[22] Reicha, who first used the term "exposition" as the proper term for the opening of the fugue, also established the term "counterexposition" to designate this *renversement.*[23] But neither he nor his successors claimed that it is necessary to the fugue. Reicha also moderated it in his definition, declaring that one statement each of the answer and subject is sufficient to form a counterexposition.[24] This is the sense in which the term was generally taken thereafter.

Thus the counterexposition is something that may be found in a fugue, but not something that can be expected. Its presence should be noted in analysis, but there is never any need to remark upon its absence, and in historical studies one should be aware that the use of the term is convenient, but often anachronistic.

Statements of the Theme after the Exposition

From the early sixteenth century on, it has been common practice to make further statements of the theme of a fugue after the exposition is finished. This is, in fact, the basic means for extending a fugal section or for building up an entire movement from a fugal exposition. No single term for these later statements has ever been adopted, although a number have been used. Most of these, such as "reprise" and "repercussion," have the disadvantage of being used for other procedures, so in this book the term "restatement" will be used to indicate any complete statement of the theme after the opening exposition.

From the beginning, these restatements have included both the subject and answer forms as well as variants of these, and these have appeared both on the original pitch levels and transposed to other levels. In many cases, particularly in instrumental fugue, restatements on other pitch levels have been the most important device in building up an extended form. Certain rather rigid changes of the subject found in fugue—augmentation, diminution, inversion, and the like—are especially associated with fugue throughout its whole development, although they first originated in strict canon. For the sake of clarity the different ways of treating the theme will be discussed separately, but several of these can be used at once in a single restatement of the subject. A subject may be found in augmentation transposed to another pitch, or it may be found inverted, in diminution, and transposed at the same time. Stretto, a special device often used in restatements, will be discussed in later chapters since it involves different techniques. Like stretto, some of these changes made in restatements may also be found in expositions of the sixteenth and early seventeenth centuries, but, from the late seventeenth century on, they are usually reserved for the portion of the fugue that follows the exposition.

TRANSPOSITION

Transposition can be used in either the subject or answer form and may be made either on a degree of the scale where the intervallic pattern is exactly like the original, on one where the generic (but not exact) intervals are found, or transposed to a degree where exact intervallic imitation would not take place naturally but altered by the use of accidentals to make exact imitation. (See Ex. 71a.)

EXAMPLE 71

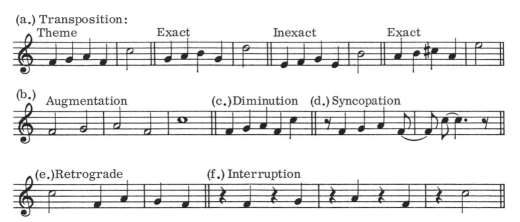

All of these are found in all periods, but a certain historical pattern can be seen. In the sixteenth and seventeenth centuries, exact imitation seems to have been preferred, and it is found most often at those points where it can occur without added accidentals or with the addition of only one or two added accidentals. At the same time, transpositions are found to degrees where exact intervallic imitation does not take place—a procedure that is very rare (outside of stretto) in fugues of the eighteenth and nineteenth centuries written in the major and minor keys. In this case, it may have been considered a restatement of the subject in another mode, but no explicit descriptions of this have yet been found. Camillo Angleria in *La regola de contraponto e della compositione* (1622) suggested that, after the subject has been heard on the regular notes of the mode, it could be answered at other intervals (or in inverted form), and his examples show transpositions of the subject starting on each note of the mode. The only alterations made are those necessary to avoid outlining the tritone. No attempt was made to make the imitation exact by making a major second answer to a major second, a minor second to a minor second, and so forth. Angleria commented that, of these intervals, the restatement of the subject at the seventh, sixth, and second are the newest.[25] By the mid-seventeenth century, some theorists began to recommend the use of chromatic alterations to make restatements exactly like the original. Giovanni d'Avella, whose text *Regole di musica* (1657), was not concerned with fugue as such, described in one section the growing use of accidentals.[26] One of their practical uses was in "multiplying the *fughe*" (increasing the number of exact imitations), and the examples he gave use a great many accidentals to obtain this exactness. Lorenzo Penna described this same technique as part of the formal extension of a fugue in *Li primi albori musicali* (1672). After the opening entries, he recommended that, in the progress of a piece, the theme should appear on different pitches, such as a step above or below the original statement of the subject, but with the addition of proper accidentals to make it like the subject.[27]

These descriptions point to the coming of the major–minor tonal system, where the major and minor modes are found beginning on each semitone within the octave; exact transposition is the same as repeating the theme in another key, and this repetition of material in a new key is a primary element in creating a long form. The fugues of the eighteenth and nineteenth centuries were for the most part constructed according to this principle. As there are only two modes in this system, the contrast of mode is obvious when a subject in major is heard in minor, or vice versa, and, within this limited field, this change of mode is more exploited than in the earlier system with its multiplicity of modes. In these fugues, transposition of the subject to other keys is the accepted procedure.

MECHANICAL CHANGES OF THE THEME
IN RESTATEMENT

This category—one invented here merely for convenience in organization—includes a number of changes that are applied mechanically to a subject without altering its original form. In augmentation, the length of each note is increased by some simple multiple, each note becoming two, three, or four times its original value. (See Ex. 71b.) Diminution is the opposite, each note being shortened according to a simple divisor. (See Ex. 71c.) Inversion, which has been discussed earlier (p. 117), may be according to exact intervals or generic intervals, but, in restatement in fugue, it is the key or mode and harmonic considerations that prevail, and the generic intervals are used with the accidentals necessary to keep it within the proper scale and harmony.

These three means of treating a theme are common throughout the whole history of fugue but were originally worked out for canon. Their use in canon involved a great deal of disciplined technique, and the prestige associated with them in canon has also been associated with them in fugue but with less reason. Making a pleasing canon in which a melody will fit with itself in its augmented, diminuted, or inverted form (and combinations of these) takes a great deal of skill, but merely restating a subject in augmentation, diminution, or inversion requires a merely mechanical alteration of the original; there is neither invention, imagination, nor compositional skill involved. But their use in restatements does serve the interest of form, providing unity in variety and a useful means of extension in a work. In many cases, moreover, they are still used in stretto, which requires the skill of canonic writing.

Three other mechanical techniques first developed for canon were used in fugue in the restatement of the subject only during the eighteenth and nineteenth centuries. These are syncopation, retrograde motion, and interruption. (See Ex. 71d, e, and f.) Syncopation or imitation by *arsin et thesin* came from the old Renaissance canon *ad miniman* where the imitation was so close that, when the theme started on the strong beat, the following part started on the weak beat. In fugue, this device was first introduced in stretto, which is a canonic treatment of the subject. The influence of Fux, who suggested that a stretto this close be saved for the end of a fugue, resulted in a conscious use of this type of stretto from the mid-eighteenth century on. Bach used it, for example, in *Contrapunctus IV* of *The Art of Fugue* and Mozart used it in the coda of the fugal finale of his Quartet in G Major, K. 387. Its use as applied to a theme restated, but not in stretto, came later. Marpurg claimed that its only use in a fugue is in stretto since he could find no examples of its being used in a simple restatement in fugues,[28] but Albrechtsberger listed it as one of the ways of treating a theme in restatement[29] and used it as a variant technique in the restatement of the subject in certain of his fugues.[30]

It was apparently through the influence of Albrechtsberger that Beethoven used this technique in restatements of the subject in the first fugue of his *Grosse Fuge* (m. 111*ff.*).[31] In all of these cases, the subject is in rather long notes and involves no rhythmic complications, so that the effect is that of simple syncopation. The term *arsin et thesin* is sometimes applied as well to the restatement of a theme with a more complex rhythm that appears in a rhythmic position where the accents are changed; that is, if the subject begins on a strong beat, it will start on a weak beat, and vice versa, and no actual syncopation of notes need be involved. In the Baroque period and earlier, this rarely happened outside of stretto, and when it did occur, it probably was not a consciously used device. Beethoven, however, used it with good effect in the fugue in the finale of the *Hammerklavier Sonata,* Op. 106.

Evidently, the techniques of retrograde motion and interruption that Beethoven used in restatements in his fugues also came to him directly from the theoretical treatises of Marpurg and Albrechts-berger.[32] Retrograde motion or *Cancrizans* had been used in canon in the sixteenth century and came into prominence in canons of the seventeenth and early eighteenth centuries. Interruption, in which the imitating part is broken up by rests, first appeared in canons in the seventeenth century, and in the late seventeenth and eighteenth centuries we find this type of imitation described in pedagogical treatises (p. 29). Marpurg listed both retrograde and interrupted motion as techniques to be used in restatements in fugue,[33] and Albrechtsberger included interruption as one of the artifices to be used in a fugue.[34] Beethoven uses them both; retrograde motion is emphasized in the fugue finale of the *Hammerklavier Sonata* and interruption in the *Grosse Fuge*. It may not be technically correct to speak of Beethoven's use of interruption in the *Grosse Fuge* as re-statement since it appears in this form at the beginning of the first fugue of the work; but, in the introductory section just preceding (measures 1–25), the subject has already been stated in a simple form and in two rhythmic variants, so this is, in effect, a varied restatement of the subject. Its use here and the use of retrograde motion in the *Hammerklavier Sonata* are particularly interesting as examples of the direct influence of theory on a composer. By this time, fugue was no longer a dominant form, and, although fugues were still being written, there was not a strong, living tradition of fugue writing. Beethoven was forced to go to written authority for his information on erudite techniques. These ways of treating a fugal theme, rare in fugue literature, might have had more effect on later composers, but the Romantic composers were more influenced by Bach, whose works underwent the great revival begun by Felix Mendelssohn (1809–1847), than by the fugues in the last works of Beethoven. The *fugue d'école* and the German academic fugue like-wise looked back to Bach and ignored Beethoven's fugues. These three ways of treating a fugue theme—syncopation, retrograde mo-tion, and interruption—were never accorded the stress given to augmentation, diminution, and inversion.

VARIATION AND TRANSFORMATION

As in nearly every form of music, fugue incorporated the tech-nique of variation in the treatment of the theme. It, along with thematic transformation, is most often found in the fugues of the sixteenth, early seventeenth, and nineteenth centuries. Fugues of the late seventeenth and eighteenth centuries use it less often, and, since these are the fugues that are most often heard, it has been accorded less emphasis than the more rigid techniques discussed above. But it was never entirely absent from fugue, and certain fugues of the eighteenth century, especially some by J. S. Bach, use it to good and apparently calculated effect.

Like many of the devices listed above, it sometimes appears in the expositions of sixteenth- and early seventeenth-century fugues. In addition to these variants found in composed works, it must be remembered that the sixteenth-century practice of adding ornamental passages in performance meant that entrances of the subject left untouched by the composer were often subject to ornamental variation in performance. Many arrangements of vocal polyphony for lute and keyboard published in the sixteenth century show this treatment of fugal subjects, in which some entries are extensively ornamented (even in the exposition) and others not at all. Likewise, some independent instrumental works of a fugal type show similar freedom of treatment.[35] By the seventeenth century, this attitude was reversed, and performers who made arrangements of fugal works were warned not to ornament *fugae* or, if they did, to use the same ornaments each time they appeared.[36] From the seventeenth century on, ornaments to be used were generally written in or indicated by signs in every simple statement of the subject. In fugue, at least, variation of the subject lay in the province of the composer.

Variation as one of the main processes in melodic development has been discussed by music theorists throughout the whole history of music, but it has scarcely been mentioned in regard to fugue. This is no doubt because theorists were concerned primarily with the required or conventional techniques used in fugue and with the precise and relatively fixed usages involved. Fugue was, of course, primarily concerned with exact imitation and restatement, so that variation was gratuitous in a fugal work rather than structurally necessary.

The means of variation vary from slight rhythmic variants in the midst of the theme (the first or last note of a subject could always be shortened or lengthened) to changes in meter and rhythmic distortion of the subject and from such minor melodic changes as the adding of passing tones or the changing of one or two notes to rather free developments. In fugues of the sixteenth and early seventeenth centuries, there are passages where it is difficult to say whether one is looking at a variant of the subject or a new theme. One of the most obscure variants that was popular in the late sixteenth and early seventeenth centuries is the *inganno*—a statement of the subject that retains the basic rhythm and the *sol-fa* syllables on which it is based but changes the melodic pattern. The *sol-fa* syllables in use then were based on the hexachord rather than the octave scales as today, so that the repetition of the same syllable pattern occurred more often. To locate the *inganni* in these early fugal works, it is then necessary to learn the old hexachord syllable system.[37] Fortunately, Trabaci indicated his uses of *inganni* in the ricercares he published in 1615,[38] so we have some examples of this. (See Ex. 72a.)

EXAMPLE 72

(a) SUBJECT WITH TWO *inganni* VERSIONS, G. M. TRABACI. [SYLLABLES ADDED BY AUTHOR]

(b) SUBJECT AND VARIANT FROM *Contrapunctus IV, Art of Fugue*, J. S. BACH.

They illustrate clearly the love of obscure devices and techniques that do not primarily appeal to the ear.

Thematic transformation is most often used as a device for creating an expanded form based on a series of different fugues without sacrificing a sense of unity. During the sixteenth and early seventeenth centuries, this was used in single ricercars and canzonas that were built up from several short fugues—sometimes expositions with added restatements and sometimes only expositions—and these were unified by using subjects that are variants of the subject of the first exposition. Today these are often called "variation ricercars" and "variation canzonas." Willaert and Frescobaldi, particularly, exploited this type of structure. In the eighteenth century, this was still found in the works of composers like Buxtehude, but the most important use of it is in Bach's *Art of Fugue*. Here, a whole cycle of separate and complete fugues is given unity by using one main theme that appears in many simple variants and transformations (as well as in augmentation, diminution, inversion, and combinations thereof) as subject or countersubject of the different fugues. Beethoven likewise used this device to unify the various fugues and fugal sections in his *Grosse Fuge*. In the nineteenth century, this type of thematic development became a commonplace in all forms, and, as such, it found its way into the free fugues of the time, often used as a basis for a short section within a single fugal movement.

The use of variations of the subject within a fugue was at its lowest point during the eighteenth century, and the variations used then are generally simple and easily heard by the listener. J. S. Bach showed wise planning in his rare uses of variations, bringing them in at the exact moment where they would be most effective in the over-all form. Generally, these are simple variants—the addition of a few passing tones or the displacement of one or several notes in the theme. In the latter case, the change was often made for harmonic reasons, and this changed form of the theme makes a small harmonic climax in addition to giving variety. A good example of this is the change of one note (g'-natural to g'-flat) in the final statement of the answer in measure 34 of the E-flat Major Fugue from Book I of the *Well-Tempered Clavier*. Another such displacement is found in *Contrapunctus IV* of the *Art of Fugue*. (See Ex. 72b.) Here, the displacement was clearly used for effect, since the ending of the variant is so arranged that it still ends on the same note as the subject does. In Bach's writing, one can see the virtue, from the point of view of the listener, of using few variants; when they are used, it is with great effect in the over-all plan of the fugue.

ANALYSIS OF AND WRITING RESTATEMENTS

Work in analysis in the forms of restatements used can be deferred until Chapter VII, since the real meaning of these restatements is only discovered in relation to the form of a fugal work. Likewise, exercises in writing will be kept for Chapter VIII, when exercises in writing a formal fugue are given.

Notes

1. Reicha, *Traité* . . . , *op. cit.,* Vol. II, Bk. IV, 26.

2. Alfred Mann, in his translation of excerpts from Marpurg's treatise in *The Study of Fugue* (*op. cit.*), translates both *Wiederschlag* and *Durchführung* as "exposition."

3. In some cases there is used a "subdominant" answer, but this is not always a clear description of the case. For instance, the answer on *a* in Phrygian might have been called the result of a mixture of Phrygian and Hypoaeolian or a work in Aeolian ending with a dominant cadence. In these cases, the answer would have been considered normal. (See p. 68f.)

4. Vicentino, *op. cit.,* f. 88ᵥ.

5. Denis, *op. cit.,* pp. 28*ff.;* Nivers, *op. cit.,* pp. 50*ff.;* Masson, *op. cit.,* pp. 104*f.*

6. Tomàs de Sancta Maria, *Arte de tañer fantasía* (Valladolid, 1565), Pt. II, f. 64ᵥ*ff.,* f. 120ᵥ.

7. Zarlino, *op. cit.,* p. 214. However, one contemporary, Vicentino (*op. cit.,* f. 88ᵥ) impartially lists the intervals of entry from a half rest through a four-measure wait as good intervals for beginning a fugue; another contemporary, Thomàs de Sancta Maria (*op. cit.,* Pt. II, f. 64ᵥ) also lists two types of entries on an equal footing—those where the second part enters before the subject is finished and those where it enters after the subject is finished.

8. Pietro Pontio, *Ragionamente di musica* (Parma, 1588), p. 159. Pedro Cerone (*El Melopeo y maestro* [Naples, 1613]) gives the same opinion, but his book depends heavily on sixteenth-century sources.

9. Morley, *op. cit.,* p. 158, Harman ed., p. 264.

10. Bononcini, *op. cit.,* p. 86.

11. Berardi, *Documenti armoniche,* p. 40. Lorenzo Penna (*op. cit.,* p. 59) likewise suggests a close stretto as a good way of ending a fugue.

12. Mattheson, *op. cit.,* pp. 380*f.;* Spiess, *op. cit.,* pp. 138*f.;* Martini, *op. cit.,* Vol. II, p. xxxv.

13. Rameau, *op. cit.,* pp. 338, 340.

14. Béthisy, *op. cit.,* p. 320.

15. Mattheson, *op. cit.,* p. 383; Spiess, *op. cit.,* p. 153.

16. Mattheson, *op. cit.,* p. 388.

17. Martini, *op. cit.,* Vol. II, p. xxxv.

18. Marpurg, *op. cit.,* p. 124; Tables 24 and 25.

19. Mann, *op. cit.,* pp. 181*f.*

20. Martini, *op. cit.,* Vol. II, xxxvi.

21. Francesco Galeazzi, *Elementi teorico-pratici di musica* Vol. II (Rome, 1796), 220; Morigi, *op. cit.,* p. 29.

22. F. J. Fétis, *Traité de la fugue* (Paris, 1825), Pt. II, 48. Thus, although Fétis, like Reicha, used "exposition," he had not yet thought of the *renversement* as the counterexposition.

23. Reicha, *Traité* . . . , *op. cit.,* II, Bk. IV, 25.

24. *Ibid.,* Vol. II, Pt. IV, p. 35.

25. Camillo Angleria, *La regola de contraponto e della compositione* (Milan, 1622), p. 78.

26. Giovanni, d'Avella, *Regole di musica* (Rome, 1657), p. 72.

27. Penna, *op. cit.,* pp. 58, 59.

28. Marpurg, *op. cit.,* p. 189.

29. Albrechtsberger, *op. cit.,* p. 194; see also Mann, *op. cit.,* p. 160.

30. Albrechtsberger, *Douze fugues pour le clavecin ou d'orgue,* Op. 1 (Berlin, *c.* 1778), and *Six fugues en form de quattuors* [1781] (Offenbach, *c.* 1830).

31. See Warren Kirkendale, "The 'Great Fugue,' Op. 133; Beethoven's 'Art of Fugue'" *Acta Musicologica,* XXXV (1963) 14–29.

32. *Ibid.,* p. 17; see also Gustav Nottebohm, "Ein Skizzenbuch aus dem Jahre 1817," *Zweite Beethoveniana* (Leipzig: Peters, 1887 and 1925) p. 350.

33. Marpurg, *op. cit.,* p. 25; see also Mann, *op. cit.,* p. 160.

34. Albrechtsberger, *op. cit.,* p. 195.

35. Imogene Horsley, "The Diminutions in Composition and Theory of Composition," *Acta Musicologica,* XXXV (1963) 130, 131, 144, 145.

36. Diruta, *op. cit.,* Pt. I, p. 10.

37. See Reese, *Music in the Middle Ages* (New York: Norton, 1940) p. 151, and Donald J. Grout, *A History of Western Music* (New York: Norton, 1960) p. 56.

38. Trabaci, *Il secondo libro de ricercate.* Berardi (*Documenti armoniche, op. cit.,* p. 41) also defined *fuga d'inganno.*

Chapter VII

Fugue and Form: History

Note: In this chapter the following works are referred to in detail. When they are available in collections of works for historical study, these are given in parentheses. Palestrina: *Sitivit anima mea* (second part of the motet, *Sicut servus*) (HAM I); Sweelinck; *Fantasia cromatica* (GMB, MSO I); Corelli; *Op. 3, No. 7* (MM) and Op. 5, No. 3 (HAM II); Bach: Fugue in F-sharp Major from book one of the *Well-Tempered Clavier;* Schubert, *Cum Sancto Spiritu* from the *Mass in E-flat Major,* D. 950; Brahms: Fugue from *Variations and Fugue on a Theme by Handel.*

*F*rom the late fifteenth into the early twentieth century, fugue has been closely associated with the development of musical form because it involves two elements intrinsic to the formal procedures of this period—a melodic subject and the means of clearly projecting a tonality. But its relation to form varies from one period to another. During the sixteenth century, it was one of the primary form-building elements. By the eighteenth century, "a fugue" was a complete and often extensive musical unit—a form in itself, although not a rigidly prescribed form, but one that combined the basic procedures of fugue with the newly emerging principles of tonal form in the major–minor system. Only during the nineteenth century, when the problem of musical form had become a subject for theoretical rationalization and speculation, do we find outlined an abstract "fugue form"—and this when fugues were no longer produced in any quantity outside of the classroom. Nor did the use of fugue as a structural element in a larger form cease at the end of the sixteenth century. By its very nature, it could be used as a part of most large forms, and it was found in combination with a great many musical forms in the seventeenth, eighteenth, and nineteenth centuries. Fugue was, in fact, one of the most important primary and secondary formal elements used in the sixteenth through the nineteenth centuries, and, because it was in active use over such a long period of time, the investigation of its relation to form makes an absorbing study—one that could easily fill several volumes the size of this one.

Fugue and Form in the Sixteenth Century

An examination of the choral polyphony of the late fifteenth and early sixteenth centuries shows the *fuga sciolta* rapidly gaining precedence over the *fuga legata* or canon. Its advantages for the creation of a polyphonic setting of a text are obvious. Like the canon, its use of exact imitation was directly related to the projection of the text; the opening, where the voices enter one after the other stating the same text in the same or closely similar melodic setting, exhibits the same identity of text and music that the canon does. But the *fuga sciolta,* in which each part may continue freely after its entering statement of the theme, can do what the canon cannot do—restate the theme in one part while the others move on freely. Thus, by restating the theme (and its associated text) in different parts at different times, a more or less extended polyphonic section based on a single theme and a single fragment of text can be created. This freedom gives the composer much scope for musical extension, whereas in canon the repetition of the opening theme in one part automatically brings about its repetition in all parts at a fixed rhythmic and melodic interval, an extension that is not necessarily musically interesting.

With Gombert, the *fuga sciolta* became the main building-block of the polyphonic structures used during the sixteenth century. It was, of course, first established in choral music, where the polyphonic setting of a text could follow the form of the text by using a series of *fughe sciolte* each of which was based upon a different fragment of text. In some of these, only one statement of the theme in each voice is found; in others, a section may have a long extension with numerous restatements of the theme. The proportionate length of these various sections was one way of molding the form of the whole movement. Naturally, all of these sections are not necessarily fugal. Sections in familiar style, sections based on imitation rather than fugue, sections in quasifamiliar style, sections only partially fugal, sections based on the play with invertible counterpoint—all are found in the motet, in Mass movements, and in the madrigal and chanson. But the *fuga sciolta* remained the most important and the most prestigious element in the form. Even in those pieces where canon was used as the basis, the canon was arranged so as to give the effect of a series of *fughe sciolte* (see p. 14), and, if there were free parts added, these imitated the thematic points in the canon in such a way as to give the effect of a series of fugal sections (p. 15).

Apparently, this type of formal structure was also closer than canon to the humanistic ideal of the time, which stressed the subordination of musical structure to that of the text. Although the most avid humanists did not approve of polyphony as the ideal vehicle for presenting a text, the monodic ideal did not have much hold over sixteenth-century composers, and the humanistic ideals that did influence the composers and theorists of the time were first consistently applied in polyphonic text settings. Several of these produced fixed musical conventions that were to remain a part of musical language for several centuries to come. The one that concerns us here is the one that had an important effect on the articulation of musical form —the restriction of cadences and rests to the function of musical punctuation.

Cadences and rests had long been used to distinguish the ends of musical sections and phrases, but they also appeared elsewhere in a work, and it was not until the second quarter of the sixteenth century that they began to be limited to the function of punctuation. This usage was firmly established in the works of Gombert, Willaert, and their followers; the writings of theorists of the time show that it was a consciously used procedure—a "modern" usage that replaced an older and more "barbaric" practice. Once accepted, this limitation led to the development of conventions that were to be important in the articulation of vocal and instrumental forms until the musical revolutions of the early twentieth century.

Restricting the use of cadences to the act of musical punctuation was first discussed by theorists as a general principle, but, as is usually the case with successful theories, this general principle underwent steady refinement as to the particularity of its usage as time moved on. Vanneo in 1533[1] and Picitono in 1547[2] defined the cadence as the *punctum* or punctuation mark of music and insisted that it should therefore be used only when an appropriate point in the text had been reached. Zarlino, in his *Istitutione harmoniche,* reiterated this rule but was more precise in prescribing its application.[3] The cadence should only be used at the end of a sentence (in verse or prose) or at the end of one of the members of the sentence (a clause or a phrase in our terminology).

Zarlino went on to define the types of cadences in two-part writing—the perfect cadence that ends on a unison or octave and the imperfect cadence that ends on the third, fifth, or other consonances. These latter he described as not absolutely cadences and thus they should not be called cadences without adding the modifier "imperfect." Later in the same chapter, he again referred to these as appropriate for marking some lesser division within a sentence (of the text) but not for the ending of a sentence, which demands a complete close and therefore should be marked by a perfect cadence ending on the unison or octave.

At the same time, Zarlino added that musicians of his day called the use of the cadence ending on the third, fifth, or sixth "fleeing the cadence" (*fuggir la cadenza*). He pointed out that many times the composer finds himself writing a passage that seems to work best in a cadence but has not yet arrived at a place in the text where a cadence would be appropriate. In this case, the composer must avoid the true cadence or perfect ending, and he can do this by ending on the third, fifth, or sixth, or by a number of other ways that Zarlino showed in his next chapter.[4]

Here we find articulated a principle of construction that, even though first applied as a means of making clear in musical terms the grammatical divisions of the text, became by analogy the basis for the organization of instrumental forms as well. Limiting the use of cadences to the definition of musical sections and starting to assign to different types of cadences different functions so that major as well as minor divisions could be clearly defined was an important step toward the development of larger forms. The terminology used suggests the type of cadence description that is found in the homophonic forms of the eighteenth and nineteenth centuries. But, although the source of the terms may be Zarlino, their meanings and uses in his time were not the same as those in later periods, and Zarlino's instructions require some explanation.

The main confusion is due to the fact that Zarlino discussed cadence types in detail only in the section on two-part counterpoint, and it is only in this section that any number of examples were given. His perfect cadences here are achieved by approaching the unison in contrary motion from a minor third or by approaching the octave in contrary motion from a major sixth, either in note-against-note counterpoint (Ex. 73a) or using a suspension (Ex. 73b). The sus-

EXAMPLE 73

SIXTEENTH-CENTURY CADENCES FROM ZARLINO (a AND b) AND VICENTINO (c AND d.)

(a.)

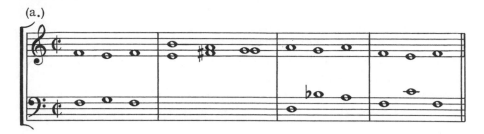

(b.)

(c.)   (d.)

pension cadence in its simple or ornamented versions was at this time so much in use as the cadence formula that the suspension was almost synonymous with cadence. Most of the cadences given by Zarlino, his contemporaries, and his immediate successors use the suspension pattern; the few cadences given in Zarlino's sections on three- and four-part writing are of this type.

When the implied "harmonic" patterns of Zarlino's cadence type are observed, one finds that his two-part cadences include what we would call authentic cadences (V–I; vii$^0_6$–I) as well as the Phrygian cadence, where the leading tone is in the lowest part a half tone above the final of the mode (the second cadence in Ex. 73b). These same types are found in his section on three- and four-part writing,[5] and, here, those that follow the "authentic" formula also use the downward skip of a fifth or the upward skip of a fourth—a movement that was also approved in Zarlino's original section on cadences in two-part writing. However, he gave no example in these sections of the cadence in which the bass falls a fourth or rises a fifth—the cadence that we now call plagal (IV–I) or half cadence (I–V). This cadence pattern had long been in use and appears in the lists of cadences given by other theorists of Zarlino's time. (See Ex. 73c.)

It must be emphasized that the cadence formulas were not yet fixed. Theorists gave a vast number of examples of cadences but did not categorize them into types. The fact that, in some cadence examples, they made an effort to point out and correct errors that might appear in students' works show that they were, however, well aware that the patterns were relatively fixed.[6] The basic principle cited by these theorists is contrapuntal, not harmonic, and involves the simple two-part formulas given by Zarlino (Ex. 73a and b), the approach to the unison or octave by contrary, stepwise motion. The plagal cadence (Ex. 73c), which does not involve stepwise, contrary motion to a unison or octave, may perhaps have been omitted by some theorists for this very reason. The skip of a fourth or fifth (up or down) in the lowest part was not the result of contrapuntal or modal-melodic principles, but of composition practice involving a sense of *harmonic* progression, which principle was not to be theoretically formulated for about two centuries, despite the fact that theorists continually listed such cadences in their texts. It should also be pointed out that these sixteenth-century cadence formulas, unlike those of the major–minor system, were not associated with particular tones in the scale (or the chords built on those tones), but could be applied to any tone. This also made precise definition and nomenclature difficult to achieve.

This difficulty in nomenclature is obvious in the case of Zarlino's definition of perfect, imperfect, and avoided cadences. In addition to defining these cadence types and prescribing a new use for them, it will be remembered that Zarlino also proclaimed that only the cadences made on the tones of the tonic triad of a mode could be considered regular cadences in that mode. This was based on mathematical reasoning (see p. 61), and, although this rule was reiterated by his followers in Italy, Germany, and France, it was a ruling that never completely dominated actual composition practice. Cadences on I and V were always the most frequently used. In these modes in which the third degree was a minor third above the final (Dorian, Phrygian, Aeolian), cadences on the third degree were common; even in the common practice period of the eighteenth and nineteenth centuries, the relative major was considered much closer to a minor key than its dominant (minor) key. In Ionian and Mixolydian, on the other hand, cadences on III were used with less frequency. As for the other degrees of the scale, cadences on these tones were used and allowed, but, for Zarlino and those who accepted his theories, these were to be accounted as irregular—as *peregrinae*—which did not serve to establish the basic mode of a piece.

Another confusion found in regard to these regulations is apparently due to the fact that cadences were associated with the suspension pattern, a melodic formula. In some cases, a suspension pattern in the tenor or soprano will resolve to a note that is the proper one in a mode, for example, b' as 5 in Phrygian or 3 in Mixolydian, but this b' will not be treated as the "root" of a "chord." Often it will be found treated as the fifth (twelfth) above the bass note e or the third (tenth) above the bass note g following a plagal cadence. (See Ex. 73c.) These examples are taken from cadences listed by Zarlino's contemporary Vicentino, also a pupil of Willaert, from a context where these b's are clearly used as the fifth above e' in Hypophrygian or the third above g' in Hypomixolydian, so that the intention is clear and their use in similar situations in actual compositions can be so analyzed by analogy.[7] At the same time, there are innumerable compositions where the first of the two cadences in Example 73c is found as a final cadence in a work that is obviously in Phrygian. And b' is likewise found in the soprano above a bass G at the end of works in Mixolydian, although in most cases the cadence would use the suspension on g' and follow an "authentic" rather than a "plagal" cadence formula. (See Ex. 73d.)

This flexibility in treatment is one indication of the transitional aspect of the music of the late sixteenth century. In the area of tonality there was not only experimentation in chromatic and enharmonic writing, but also, in those works written in the diatonic modes, which were considered particularly appropriate for sacred works, there is clear evidence of movement toward the vertical rather than the horizontal statement of mode. This is particularly evident in the treatment of cadences; they have a genuine harmonic basis but also include at this time melodic stereotypes, the most prominent of which is the suspension. While rigid classification of cadences came only with the major–minor system, important cadences are almost always clear in the music of the sixteenth century, and the relative flexibility of treatment only makes the music more interesting. Zarlino himself recommended at the close of his article on the cadence that the composer strive to invent new cadential patterns.

Since Zarlino's rules and terms were accepted by later generations of composers and developed by seventeenth-century theorists (particularly in Germany), his meanings should be understood as an aid to the understanding of the music of the sixteenth century. But Zarlino's terms did not have the same meaning for him that they had for later writers; moreover, his examples are not always clear because they are given mainly in two-part writing, and his explanations are at times ambiguous. A book published in Venice in 1588 by one of his followers, Orazio Tigrini,[8] makes his meanings clearer, and the following summary is based on the writings of both Zarlino and Tigrini.

Zarlino's description of the perfect and imperfect cadences is clear only in two-part writing. Here the perfect cadences end on the unison and the octave, and the imperfect cadences end on the fifth, sixth, and third. These imperfect cadences, however, include examples of regular cadences that are properly resolved to the correct "tonic" chord— the root and third, the root and fifth, or the sixth, which represents to us a first inversion of the tonic; there are also cadences that are not resolved properly and that we would call deceptive cadences. (See the third and fourth cadences in Ex. 74a.) Zarlino suggested that their use is proper for lesser divisions of the text but not for final endings. His few cadence examples in more than two parts and the many cadences in more than two parts listed by Tigrini, as well as usage in the compositions of the time, indicate that the official cadences that are used for final endings and signify a perfect close are cadences that end on the expected chord and that have the "root" in the bass. That is, cadences that can be represented by V–I, vii°$_6$–I, IV–I and the Phrygian cadence ending on a root position chord represent a "perfect" cadence in writing in three or more parts, and it does not matter what member of the chord is on top. Thus, a perfect cadence in several parts would include some of Zarlino's two-part imperfect cadences, those with a third or fifth above the "root" of the proper chord of resolution, as well as those ending on the octave or unison.

Those cadences that are distinctly labeled as avoided cadences are easier to identify because the two-part examples given by Zarlino,

EXAMPLE 74

CADENCES FROM ZARLINO AND TIGRINI.
(a.) Imperfect cadences

(b.) "Avoided" cadences

Tigrini, and Vicentino[9] use only suspension–cadence patterns. These would normally resolve to the unison or octave, but this normal resolution is avoided by moving one of the parts on by a step or skip or by using a rest in one part, thus clearly evading the proper resolution of the cadence prepared. (See Ex. 74b.) In most cases, this is what we call a deceptive resolution, the movement to the wrong chord of resolution; in others, it moves to an (implied) first inversion of the proper chord of resolution. There are also occasions when the avoidance is purely melodic, a skip away from the proper resolution of the suspension but only to a different member of the chord of resolution than that which is expected melodically.

To sum up, one can find avoided cadences that are deceptive cadences as conceived in today's terms, avoided cadences that are less strong versions of regular cadence types that we would call imperfect because they end on a first inversion triad, and various other types that do not fit into later categories in which the proper resolution of the suspension is evaded by skipping away or using a rest. In practice, we find that nearly all of these occur in the midst of a phrase where the suspension formula is melodically appropriate, but, because it is in the middle of a section of the text, the composer must avoid coming to a close. Since there is no break in the rhythmic movement, these should not considered in analysis to be cadences—not even deceptive cadences—but to be merely "avoided" cadences. They may be re-

marked on, but have no structural importance. In a few cases, there are deceptive or imperfect cadences involving a definite rhythmic break, and here it will be clearest to use our terms, "deceptive" or "imperfect," in defining them. The most common cadence used in three or more parts is the authentic cadence moving to its normal resolution with the root in the bass, and in actual practice it is used to point up minor as well as major divisions in the text. The definition of the relative importance of these lesser divisions is achieved primarily by the rhythmic treatment of these cadences.

A break in the rhythmic motion brought about by a rest is another way of emphasizing articulation points in a work, and it is under the influence of humanism that the use of rests became limited to appropriate places in the text. Zarlino was the first to describe this new usage as a fixed law. He said very emphatically that, when rests are used, they may only be used at appropriate places in the text, at the ends of grammatical divisions as were the cadences. He further declared that the longest breaks are made at the ends of sentences, the shorter ones being reserved for lesser divisions within the sentence.[10] Musical practice shows another use of the rest, as a break where a pause could be used for dramatic effect in formal oratory or dramatic declamation. Zarlino's rules—which were accepted and refined throughout the next two centuries—need to be modified by a look at the musical practice of the time. A clearly heard break—one in which all parts stop at once—is generally found only at the end of a very complete unit of text, marked by a colon or period, and where a pause would be effective in emphasizing the meaning of the text. In sacred works of a polyphonic style, it is not often found, and, when it is, it usually follows a cadence made in long notes so that there is already a pause in the rhythmic movement. Several theorists actually list cadences of short, medium, and long note values to mark out breaks of different importance,[11] and Zarlino's instructions should be expanded to include pauses in the motion made by held chords as well as by actual rests.

The most common use of rests in all parts for clear and dramatic presentation of the text is in familiar or quasifamiliar style, such as the four-part madrigals of Cipriano de Rore who was, like Zarlino, a pupil of Willaert.[12] Such articulation by rests can be readily seen in certain examples reproduced in *HAM*, I, such as de Rore's *Da le belle contrade* (No. 131), *O vos omnes* (No. 149) by Tomas Luis de Victoria (*ca.* 1540–1611), and *Io pur respiro* (No. 161) by Carlo Gesualdo (*ca.* 1560–1614). It is a usage that increases in importance in the late sixteenth century and one that is exploited in the

operatic recitative of the seventeenth century. In polyphony, a rest in all parts is found much less frequently and only to mark off an important break in the text. It is usually the slowing down of rhythmic motion at the cadence that emphasizes lesser divisions.

The importance of rests in fugue is great because it is necessary for the entries and restatements of the subject and answer to stand out, and the most obvious way to make them do so is to have each entry of the theme preceded by a rest in the part in which it is to be stated. Nearly all sixteenth-century instruction books describe a basic use of rests as that of separating the entrances of *fugae,* but the contexts in which the rules are given would make it appear that this refers to the beginning of a canon or perhaps the fugal opening of a movement using *fughe sciolte.* The more important function of using rests before the entries of later restatements of a theme or the opening entries of a new *fuga sciolta* is perhaps meant as well. This usage is first seen consistently in sixteenth-century polyphonic vocal works, and it may well have been in part the result of the rule Zarlino gave—a rule that was clearly in force in the music of many composers of the Gombert-Willaert generation. In a way, it is a negative rule, for it states that rests are not to be used except where appropriate in the text; but its result is that, when a rest is used, it will then be at the end of a melodic phrase. Since rests are necessary for breathing, they occur quite frequently, and, if they occur at the end of a phrase in one part, their use will emphasize the re-entry of that part. If that re-entry is on the theme of a fugal section—and, in Gombert's music and that of most composers of the last half of the century, the writing tends to be more thematic with less free melisma —the theme will stand out more clearly. The relative lengths of rests in relation to the importance of the phrase or sentence articulated in a single section, which Zarlino describes, is not observed in each separate voice of a polyphonic work. Here, naturally, it is the placement of rests that were observed and not their length. In each part, if a rest is introduced, it will come at the end of a phrase of text; but there may be a long or short wait before that part re-enters, and, as the other parts are still moving, the length of the rest is not noticed.

The conventions that reserved the use of cadences and breaks in rhythmic movement to musical punctuation, audibly marking off sections within a piece, grew up at the same time that modal usage was being more precisely defined. By the second half of the century, tonal patterns for the over-all form of a work that had become more evident in the works of composers were being described by theorists.

Unity of mode was becoming more important, especially in church music where the ideal was to begin and end in the basic mode of the piece. In the middle of the work, it was permissible and even preferable to move out of the mode for a while.[13] In church music, it was judged appropriate to leave and return to the basic mode smoothly; but, in secular music with texts having strong emotional contrasts, a sudden change of mode was an important device. Each mode was associated with a particular mood, and a text with a dramatic change in mood would naturally demand a drastic change from one mode to another or even a change from the diatonic to the chromatic genus. Certain texts might also be appropriately set with a beginning in one mode and an ending in a different mode, so that the basic mode might be unclear.

It was the individual melodic lines, the cadences, and the initial notes that projected a mode, and of these three the cadences and the initial notes of the different entries were the strongest ways of establishing the mode. The regular initial notes and cadence tones for each mode, as we have seen, were the final note of each mode and the fifth and third above it. The others were out of the mode, *peregrinae,* belonging to other modes. In practice, some of these *peregrinae* were more often used as cadence tones than were certain regular ones. A cadence ending on B in the bass was less common in the pure modal system because the fifth above it was *f,* which makes a diminished fifth. For this reason cadences on *c* were common in both the Phrygian and Mixolydian pairs, as well as cadences on A in the Phrygian pair, both of these being substituted for the adjacent B. Further, the regular cadence on the third of the mode, although supported by mathematical justification, was never as common in Mixolydian and Ionian (the major modes) as it was in the minor modes (Dorian, Phrygian, and Aeolian) where its frequent use anticipated the close relationship that the relative major has to a minor key in the major–minor system. In fact, early seventeenth-century German theorists, who based their ideas mainly on the works of Lasso and his generation, considered the cadence on the third degree as the musical equivalent of cadences on the irregular degrees of the scale; cadences on the first degree were classified as primary, those on the fifth degree as secondary, and tertiary cadences included those on the third degree along with the *peregrinae.* Those cadences on degrees other than 1, 3, and 5 were, however, considered to be out of the mode, and the classification of cadences as regular on 1, 3, and 5, which establish the mode, and as *peregrinae,* those that belong to other modes, continued until the eighteenth century. Even though many cadences, such as those on the fourth degree, seem to anticipate common practice in the major–minor system, this modal categorization should be held to in analyzing works written in the modes.

Fugue joined with cadence as one of the main ways of establishing a mode. The initial notes usually outlined a fifth or a fourth, often with the octave of one or both of the initial notes, and these are the notes that clearly establish a mode. In sixteenth-century vocal polyphony, where a series of *fughe sciolte* were used to build up a single movement, not only the opening exposition, but also the later expositions of new themes present in this way the main notes of a mode. These fugal expositions combine with the cadences in establishing a mode, in moving to other modes, and in returning to the original mode; thus, they are one of the primary elements in the establishment of the tonal pattern of the movement. Often restatements of a theme will follow its exposition, and these may serve to further emphasize a mode or to act as a bridge between one mode and another. Although the fugues so precisely suggest the main notes that, according to modal theory, define a mode, there are at times ambiguous situations that are only satisfactorily resolved (as far as terminology is concerned) when the major–minor system is in force. But these ambiguities, which derive from the conflict between the melodic and the vertical establishment of mode, only make the music more interesting to the theorist.

Fugue is also important in these works because of its thematic nature. Each fugue theme represents an intelligible segment of the text but serves as well to give the aural effect of a series of sections, each based on a theme that is stated at least once by each part and therefore gives thematic shape to the work.

ANALYSIS OF A SIXTEENTH-CENTURY MOTET

A diagram of the structure of a motet will bring these points into focus. Example 75 shows an analysis of the *secunda pars, Sitivit anima mea* from Palestrina's motet *à 4, Sicut servus* (reproduced in *HAM,* I, No. 141). This has been chosen not only because it is readily available in most music libraries, but also because it is a good example of a motet in Ionian (transposed to F) and thus will be useful later in showing the structural difference between a work in Ionian and one in the major in the major–minor system. The themes (with the texts to which they are set) are given in the upper staff and are represented by letters. At times a theme appears in more than one form. Those variants that are the result of very slight changes in

EXAMPLE 75

FUGAL ENTRIES AND CADENCES IN *Sitivit anima mea*, SEC-
OND PART OF *Sicut servus*, GIOVANNI DA PALESTRINA.

melody or rhythm, are not noted in the analysis here. Only where the
variant is a tonally adjusted answer—as in the case of *a* and *a¹*—are
the two forms given. For clarity, cadences are represented as if the
final chord were the tonic of the key of the chord on which they end.

It must be remembered that contemporary theory thought of them as being on a particular degree of the over-all mode of the work, and the Roman numeral in parenthesis after each cadence shows the relation of this tone to the mode (i.e., B♭ is IV in F-Ionian).

The pitches of the initial notes of each entry of a theme are indicated in the two-staff score. The letter representing the theme used appears directly below the staff under the initial pitch of its entry, and the numbers above indicate the measures in which these entries occur. The numbers represent the barring used in *HAM,* and the numbering used here starts with measure 1 at the beginning of the *secunda pars.* Pitches in parenthesis indicate free entries that are not restatements of themes or obvious variants of them, but which follow a rest and therefore stand out so that their initial notes are emphasized. The first entries of the *b* theme, which are circled, indicate a theme that first appears in the continuation of *a* but that is used later (not circled) as a separate theme (still associated with the same text) appearing in a fugal exposition with each entry preceded by a rest (m. 12 and 13). This is a common usage of the time. The majority of entries are preceded by a rest or are emphasized by entering after a large skip or immediately after a cadence or a long note indicating the end of a phrase.

MAJOR DIVISIONS OF THE FORM

The motet is in transposed Ionian with the final F. The main cadences are on *C* (m. 12–13), *F* (m. 16–17), *B*-flat (m. 30–31), *C* (m. 41–42), and the final cadence is on the tonic, *F.* These are on the first, fifth, and fourth degree of the mode. Only the cadence on IV, *B*-flat, would be irregular according to sixteenth-century theory.

All of these cadences come at appropriate places in the text, and the inner cadences all give the feeling of intermediate articulations since the movement does not come to a full stop in all voices at the same time. Here the timing of the entries of a new fugal exposition is important in defining the relative importance of cadences and in weaving together the different sections of the work. In measures 17, 21, and 42, all the voices taking part in the cadence arrive at the final chord with the final notes of their phrases, and these cadences represent major divisions within the text, indicated here by a colon, a question mark, and a comma. At times, one finds major divisions of the text within a motet (generally indicated by a period or colon in the text), and in these cases a break occurs in all parts, indicated by long notes in all parts, by rests in all parts, or by a combination of both. The continuity is maintained in measures 17 and 31 by holding the last note in one or two of the voices and by immediately bringing in the first entry of a new fugue. In measure 42, the next section is in familiar style, and all four parts start immediately on the next beat.

In measure 13, a lesser division of the text is found, also indicated by a comma, but it anticipates merely an emphasized repetition in a fugal exposition of a fragment of text already heard, *ad Deum fortem vivum,* and uses theme *b,* which also has already been used. Here, the effect of the cadence is made less strong by the continuation of the alto line beyond the cadence and the entry in the soprano of *b* before the alto stops. The member of the cadence chord, which is in the alto, *e′,* is not the last note of that phrase, and the alto moves on to *d′* before the rest that indicates the phrase-ending.

Instances of avoided cadences in the midst of sections also occur. In measure 24, the suspension pattern, which is a common cadence formula, is found in the tenor, which voice also cadences on the *c′.* Although the editors of *HAM* have not indicated a raised leading tone (*b*-natural) here, it might well have been used in singing according to the rules of *musica ficta.*[14] A new point, *d,* also enters here to form another fugal section. But the bass moves steadily on, negating any effect of cadence. In measure 48–49, a cadence that seems about to occur because of the usual ornamented suspension formula in the soprano and the strong harmonic implications of the bass is averted by the bass moving up to *d,* creating what we now call a deceptive cadence. Both of these come under Zarlino's category of avoided cadences. In measures 20–21, a cadence is found on F that evades finality by the *a* in the lowest part, which makes it an imperfect cadence. It is worth noting that both coincide with a cadence ending a phrase in one voice but not where a significant division of the text is found.

THE TONAL FORM

The structural relation between the text and the music has been stressed because text was the basis of the formal structure of the polyphonic works of the time and because these important means of creating a longer musical form were first used in the polyphonic setting of texts. But the abstracted formal elements are what most concern us. The foremost of these is the element of tonality in the form, since this is the element that was the basis of most forms until the late nineteenth century. Here, the tonality is expressed most strongly by the cadences and by the beginnings of the various fugal sections. The opening fugue clearly states the mode by the initial notes c', f', c and f, and this mode is even more emphasized by the melodic outlining of both the fourth and fifth of the mode, which is the result of the tonally adjusted answer.

The fugues likewise focus on the chords on which the cadences are made and, in some instances, help the movement toward these cadence centers. This can be seen more clearly in the diagram than in the work itself, since it is the initial notes of the fugue entries that, at this period, emphasize the main notes of the mode. After the opening exposition, the entry of theme b on the pitch g after a rest in the tenor in measure 9 and a belated restatement of theme a^1 on c' in the alto in measure 11 indicate a movement toward C, on which the work cadences in measure 13. The entries in the fugue on theme b in measures 13 and 14 likewise stress the pitches C and G. This fugue, being based on a theme that, with its associated text, has already been heard several times, is not extended, coming quickly to the strong cadence on F in measures 16 and 17.

This fugue on theme b in itself is not a modulation to C, but is, rather, a fugue that is clearly *on* the "dominant" in F in association with the cadence on C that it ornaments. A look at the theme as it is used in the fugue shows how this is done melodically. The first two entries of the fugue in the soprano and tenor in measure 13 outline the fourth of Mixolydian on C (the "relative Mixolydian" of F-Ionian)—G, A, B-flat, C—but this is not a modulation to the dominant key in the eighteenth-century sense. A modulation to the dominant key would necessitate the use of B-natural in the theme instead of B-flat. The "relative" Mixolydian on C used here in theme b is much closer to F-Ionian than is C major to F major in the major–minor system because of the B-flat that is common to F-Ionian and C-Mixolydian. The answers in measure 14, which outline the F-Ionian fourth—C, D, E, F—merely re-emphasize the basic mode and lead naturally to the strong cadence on F in measures 16 and 17.

The next section, which ends in measure 31, includes two fugal expositions and is an interesting one. It begins in measure 17, stating the subject c in the alto starting on b-flat, and the initial notes of the four entries of the exposition emphasize the fifth B-flat to F. A free part in the bass in measure 17 starts at the same time as the alto, entering on the B-flat an octave below the alto and giving further emphasis to this note. The use of a free part in this way is often found in fugues at this time, in the opening fugues as well as in later expositions. The last entry of the subject (in the bass in measure 21) is doubled at the tenth by the soprano. This use of an "imitation" to double a fugal entry was also a common sixteenth-century device.

The second fugue in this section, based on theme *d,* starts in measure 24 on *g′* in the soprano, and this series of entries follows a pattern that, by the time of Palestrina, was characteristic only of the middle of a movement—down by two successive fifths, from *g′* to *c′* to *f* with the last entry of the exposition (in the bass in measure 27) on *c* doubled at the tenth above in the soprano. These entries appear to serve a function not unlike that of a bridge in eighteenth-century music, leading back to the basic mode on F that is emphasized by re-statements of the subject on *f* in the tenor in measure 28 and on *c′* in the alto in measure 29. However, it moves on to cadence, in measures 30 and 31, on *b′*-flat, and the initial notes of the fugue on subject *e* (which appears in a close stretto exposition in measures 31 and 32) reaffirms the fifth, *B*-flat to *F.*

This movement to B-flat, the "subdominant," would be considered a movement out of the mode by sixteenth-century theorists, since the fourth degree was one of the *peregrinae* and not one of the cadence points affirming the mode. It is not a modulation in the eighteenth-century sense, however, for this section is at no time in the key of B-flat major (or Ionian on B-flat), E-natural being used throughout. Like the entries of theme *b* on *G* (in measures 13 and 14) discussed above, this would probably be considered to be in a "relative" mode, the "relative Lydian" of F-Ionian. The theme *c,* which clearly outlines melodically the characteristic fifth of Lydian on *B*-flat has, like subject *b,* an answer that reaffirms the basic mode, F-Ionian—in this case, by moving scalewise through the character-istic fifth *f′, g′, a′, b′*-flat, *c″.*

F-IONIAN CONTRASTED TO F MAJOR

Since this usage is not characteristic of fugue in the major–minor system and its replacement by the later usage is important as an in-dication of a departure from modal procedure and a movement toward major–minor, it may be wise to emphasize in more detail the difference between the two. If we consider the cadences on C and B-flat so far discussed, they are cadences *on* the fifth and fourth de-grees of F-Ionian. Even if we think of this motet as being in F major in the eighteenth-century sense, these are still cadences within the key—cadences on the dominant and on the subdominant—rather than cadences *in* the subdominant and dominant keys. In F-Ionian, the fugues on themes *b* and *c* might be called, in later terms, fugues *on* the dominant and subdominant.

There is no equivalent concept in the major–minor system. Theme *b*—*g′, a′, b′*-flat, *c″*—would still be in the key of F, but it would not be a good fugue subject because, moving by the scale notes 2, 3, 4, 5, it does not express the key strongly. It would be difficult to make an answer to it. (See Ex. 76a.) A real answer would be in

EXAMPLE 76

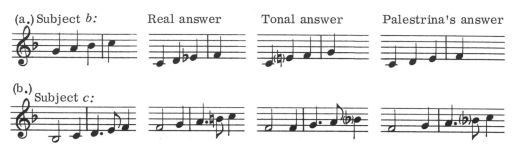

(a.) Subject *b*: Real answer Tonal answer Palestrina's answer

(b.) Subject *c*:

the subdominant, *c′, d′, e′*-flat, *f′*. Nor would a tonal answer be feasible, since the subject goes from 2 to 5 in the scale of F. In F major this would be an irregular subject, one to which a proper answer could not be made. The normal usage in a work in F major would have been to use a real modulation to C major at this point. Theme *b* would then have been *g′, a′, b′*-natural, *c″*.

The type of subject which Palestrina uses here is successful only in the modal system. Outlining the fourth *g′–c″*, using a *b′*-flat, it emphasizes the fourth of the Mixolydian mode on C (the "relative" Mixolydian of F-Ionian) and, according to modal theory, the tonal answer would outline the fifth of C-Mixolydian, giving the tonal answer *c′, e′, f′, g′* shown in Example 76a. Palestrina's answer is, however, the last one shown, *c′, d′, e′, f′*. He has decided not to establish C-Mixolydian melodically in his answer but to return to the main mode, F-Ionian, by outlining the fourth of that mode.

A similar analysis of the use of theme *c* shows again the difference between the modal and the major–minor system. The subject *c*, shown in Example 76b, would be a highly irregular one in F major because it goes by scale from 4 up to 8 in that key. The real answer is impossible because, as shown in Example 76b, it goes by scale from 4 up to 8 in the key of C. In the modal system, however, this subject strongly established B-flat-Lydian, and a tonal answer would fit the theme into the fourth of that mode, probably in the form seen in Example 76b. Here, again, Palestrina avoids moving completely into

Lydian, and answers the subject as shown in the last answer in Example 76b, reaffirming the tonic mode, F-Ionian. If this had been in the major key, theme *c* would have used an *e'*-flat, establishing clearly the key of B-flat major, and used the tonal answer which would have affirmed the modulation to that key.

There is in major–minor fugal theory or practice no direct equivalent of Palestrina's subject-answer pairs. This is because in this system there is only one "relative" pair of modal scales, that is, only two different modes that use the same signature: C major and A minor, D major and B minor, and so forth. The "relative" modes on the other degrees of the scales, such as the "relative Mixolydian" of C major (which would be on *G* using, like C major, no sharps or flats in the signature) or the "relative Lydian" of C major (which would be on *F* with no sharps or flats) have disappeared. The difference between the major-minor and the modal system is even more evident in the remaining fugues of the Palestrina motet.

The second fugue on *B*-flat, using theme *e* and starting in measure 31, comes closer to a modulation to B-flat-Ionian, since there is an *e'*-flat in measure 33 indicated by the composer (the entrance of theme *f*) and there are no E-naturals in measures 31–34 to counteract it. But the entry of theme *f* on the *e'*-flat in measure 33 is the beginning of a further digression from the basic mode of the work. Here, the entries come in imitation—starting on *e'*-flat, *g, b*-flat, and *d″*—not in fugue and thus do not establish fugally the fourth or fifth that would define a particular mode. Nor do they establish a mode melodically, for each statement of the theme moves down by scale a sixth or seventh before turning upward again, so that no characteristic fourth, fifth, or octave is outlined. After this, the work moves smoothly back to a cadence on *C* in measures 41–42, a regular cadence on the fifth of the mode. This is followed by a section in familiar style centering around the tonic, *F,* but ending with a rather weak cadence on *B*-flat in measure 46.

The last section, which starts in measure 46 and is based on theme *g,* is a very interesting one. As the diagram shows, all the main entries of this theme are on *D,* and these would come under the category of fugue at the unison and octave. The only entries on other pitches are in measure 46 and 55, and both are "imitations" that parallel an entry starting on *D* in another part. The initial notes of all entrances of theme *g* are tonally obscure since they do not outline a fourth or fifth of a mode, and the single *D* that is reiterated is an irregular initial note in F-Ionian. The theme itself is ambiguous since it does not clearly outline a fifth, fourth, or octave that would make its mode obvious. Because the *B*-flat chord dominates measure 46 and this chord is a resolution of a cadence, the first statements of the theme give the effect of starting on 3 in B-flat (Lydian), and a single *e*-flat in the bass in measure 51 gives weight to a "subdominant" feeling, as does the free entry on *B*-flat in the bass in measure 48. A second concentration of entries of theme *g* is found in measures 55 and 56. These again follow a less important cadence on *B*-flat. The doubling of the soprano entrance at a tenth below in the bass and the *f*-sharp moving to *g* in the bass part in measure 56 reinforce what sounds to our ears like a movement through the subdominant and supertonic and leads to a well-prepared final cadence on the tonic.

Fugue subjects beginning on the third of the scale were rare during the late sixteenth and early seventeenth centuries, and they appear more frequently in the seventeenth century only when the melodic-rhythmic style of the subjects made the tonality so clear by stressing the other tones of the tonic triad that the mode or key of the subject was clear. In most sixteenth-century fugues, a subject beginning on the third of the mode does not do this, and, moreover, when the subject does start on 3, the answer starts on 7, the fifth above, or on 6, the fifth below. This would imply a mode other than the basic mode of the piece, either an irregular beginning of a movement or else a digression in the midst of it. A subject beginning on the sixth degree (as theme *g* would be if counted in F-Ionian) would of itself be irregular. Thus, whether it is related to B-flat or F, this theme is tonally ambiguous and constitutes a subtle and skillful play within the modal conventions. Palestrina's sensitivity to the problem involved is shown by the fact that here he does not answer the *g* theme at the fifth above or below—which would positively state another mode—but uses it only to suggest.

To our ears, which are harmonically oriented, this last section is simply a movement toward the subdominant in preparation for the final cadence. Except for the cadences, the harmony of this motet has not been discussed because, although there is a definite sense of chordal movement, at the time the work was written harmony was not consciously used as the basis of polyphonic form. The tonal structure is established melodically and polyphonically through the shape of the themes and the initial notes of fugues and imitations; only at the cadence points does harmony have a formal function. Nor, according to the teaching of the time, is the mode established harmonically, except by the chords to which the cadences resolve. Yet, to our ears, the choice of chords used and the emphasis on chords built on 1, 4, and 5 make it sound like major.

It is indeed major, but it is modal major—Ionian. It is not in the major–minor system, for, if it were, the fugue on theme *b* would be in C major and those on themes *c* and *e* would be in B-flat major. This point is emphasized here again because few students have had practice in detailed analysis of modal works and thus tend to judge only those works to be in a mode in which the melody and harmony are distinctly different from that found in simple major or minor.

THE DIFFICULTIES OF ANALYSIS IN SIXTEENTH-CENTURY FUGAL WORKS

Theory by its very nature tends to be more absolute than musical practice because, for the most part, theory is the result of abstracting logical patterns from musical practice and rationalizing them. Only within the last few years, when the composer has set up a series of criteria and then made a work that follows them, has theory preceded practice, and, even then, it is only in pieces in which every element is serialized or prescribed in advance that the music precisely follows a pre-ordained pattern. In most earlier styles, we find that only one or two of the musical elements adhere closely to a set of formulated rules, and one will naturally base his analysis primarily on those rules as a guide to understanding a composition in a certain style.

Sixteenth-century composers had two sets of theoretically formalized principles that were the basis of their musical education—the rules of counterpoint and the conventions involved in the modes. Neither of these was applied with absolute strictness at all times, and such other forces as chromaticism and dissonance for expression worked counter to the conventionalized rules; still, these contrapuntal and modal rules provide the most accurate basis for the analysis of this music. Chromaticism and freer dissonance usage, which were not ordered into a fixed system, can then be described as elements working against the stricter organization implied by the conventional contrapuntal and modal rules. Another element of secondary importance found in the music of this time is the growing sense of harmonic order, which culminated in the harmonic rules of the major–minor system in which the polyphonic and melodic aspects come under strict vertical control. A good many sixteenth-century works contain elements of this system even though it was not yet a conscious technique. The harmonic rules formulated by eighteenth-century theorists can at times be a useful tool in the analysis of this music, but they should be used with caution and should not take precedence over modal conventions.

The above analysis illustrates some of the problems. Since the aspect of the music that concerns us here is tonal form and the part that fugue plays in delineating that form, contrapuntal style has been ignored. The modal system has been the primary basis of the analysis, and the major–minor system has been referred to only when some musical occurrence could not be explained by the modes alone. In many instances, a difference of opinion can be expected, and this is particularly true when the composition involved does not adhere as closely to modal conventions as this motet does.

Much of our confusion is due to the fact that we tend to think in the modal system in the same way that we have been trained to think in the major–minor system. When working with major, for example, we tend to associate the half steps with the tonal functions allotted to 3–4 and 7–8 and to fit various melodic fragments we hear within the major scale. Thus, in C major, the passage *d, e, f, a, g, a* is automatically felt on first hearing to be a theme starting on the second degree of the C-major scale and centering on *a,* the sixth degree, and we expect it to move on through passages growing out of the dominant chord and cadence in C. To modulate to D minor, we would need the leading tone *c*-sharp or a strong melodic implication of the dominant or dominant-seventh chords. To those trained from childhood in the modes, this would not have been the case. They learned at least four primary modes (eight including the plagal forms)—after mid-century, they may have learned six (twelve including the "hypo-" forms)—each of which was organized around a particular octave and the fourth and fifth into which it was divided.[15] The placement of the half steps within each fourth and fifth were important in defining the mode and in projecting its emotional flavor, but they did not have the harmonically based need for resolution associated with the half steps in major and minor. This same passage—*d, e, f, a, g, a*—in the Ionian mode is a temporary modulation to Dorian, and one should not feel a need to move on to a cadence in C. A modulation in the modal sense is thus much weaker and seems less obvious to us, but it is nevertheless clear if one understands the conventions of modal structure.

Understanding the difference between modal and major–minor tonality is essential to the understanding of early fugal works, and for most of us it requires a conscious effort to think in the modes. Playing through this motet, which sounds so "major" to us, our ears tend to hear themes *b* (*g, a, b*-flat, *c′*) and *e* (*b*-flat, *c′ d′, e′ f′*) as, respectively, 2, 3, 4, 5 and 4, 5, 6, 7, 8 in F major. Yet, as has been pointed out above, these are, according to modal practice, 5–8 in Mixolydian on C and 1–5 in Phrygian on B-flat. The fact that each definitely outlines the fourth and fifth of the mode in question makes this clear, and the fact that the initial notes in each exposition also outline the fourth and fifth in question reaffirms it. To miss this would be to lose much of the significance of fugue in its function of forwarding the tonal movements within the form.

Once these modal formations are recognized, we can perceive the subtleties of the style; in fugue, this is evident in the choice of the type of answers used and in the order of entries in the expositions and restatements of the themes. For example, in this Palestrina motet, the first theme has a tonal answer, and this means that the basic mode is established not only polyphonically by the initial notes of the entries, but also melodically in each part. Themes *b* and *c* do not have tonal answers, so that the modes implied by the subjects and by the initial notes of the entries are not reinforced melodically in the answers. The answer to theme *b*—*c'*, *d'*, *e'*, *f'*—is the F-Ionian fourth, and the answer to theme *c*—*f'*, *g'*, *a'*, *b'*-flat, *c''*—is the F-Ionian fifth. Thus, the new modes established by the initial notes are not affirmed melodically by all parts, and the relation to the mode of the motet is made clear.

The exposition of each of these themes also has a different order of entries. Subject *b* comes as subject–subject–answer–answer. Here, the modulation to C-Mixolydian is first emphasized by stating it melodically two times, and the return to F-Ionian is strengthened by stating the answer twice. The exposition of theme *c,* which follows the order of subject–answer–answer–subject, provides more of a digression because it begins and ends with a melodic theme in the new mode.

We have also seen that the modal references of the other themes are less clear. Theme *e,* which outlines the B-flat triad, seems to have less relation to B-flat Lydian, because no *E*-naturals appear during its exposition, and the *e*-flat in measure 33 adds to the impression of B-flat major—or, rather, B-flat Ionian. Modal theory does not include the concept of a single mode appearing on two different pitch levels in the same melody or movement. Yet, examples of this are found in sixteenth-century music—examples that are sometimes quite obvious.

Only one theorist of the time seems to have been concerned with this, and his explanation is intriguing because it shows an effort to explain it within the rational framework of the modal system. This extension of modal theory was expounded by Illuminato Aijguino in his treatise *Il tesoro illuminato,* published in Venice in 1581. In each mode (he recognizes only eight, not accepting the Aeolian and Ionian pairs), he found what he called an "extraordinary" fifth or fourth, often both a fifth and a fourth, that has the same scale pattern as the basic fifth or fourth of the mode in question and that has as one of its outer notes an outer note of either the regular fifth or fourth of that mode. In Dorian, in which the regular fifth is *d–a* and the regular fourth is *a–d'*, the extraordinary fourth *d–g* starts on the bottom note of the regular fifth, *d,* and has the same pattern of half and whole steps as the regular fourth, *a–d'*. The extraordinary fifth *a–e'* starts on the top note of the regular fifth and has the same scale pattern as the regular fifth. This is obviously an early rationalization of the use of a mode along with its transposition by a fourth or fifth up or down. Illuminato considered these "extraordinary" fifths and fourths to be subordinate to the true fifths and fourths of the mode, but a strengthening influence and an aid to intensifying the effect of the mode. However, his theory seems to have had no subsequent influence, and the idea of a single mode in close conjunction with its transposed form—such as Dorian on *d* and Dorian on *a* (with an *f*-sharp)—must be associated with the trend toward the major–minor rather than the pure modal system. When this practice is found in sixteenth- or early seventeenth-century music, it is helpful to recognize this as an anticipation of eighteenth-century tonality.

Themes that do not clearly outline a fourth, fifth, or octave—such as themes *f* and *g* in the Palestrina motet—are difficult to assign to a particular mode. If they appear in a fugal exposition, the fifth or fourth outlined by the initial notes of the entries will suggest a mode. If not, as is the case with the treatment of themes *f* and *g,* then the mode may remain ambiguous. In some cases, an investigation of the harmony by analogy with major or minor or of longer sections of each melodic line according to modal conventions may help to elucidate the musical function. But tonal ambiguity may be the true characteristic of a theme or section—perhaps purposely or perhaps through ignorance or willful disregard of rules. Sections of this type show the importance of fugue as a stable tonal element because, by its very nature, a fugal exposition suggests a particular mode. Even in such intensely chromatic music as that of Carlo Gesualdo, a fugal exposition represents a stable modal structure. His madrigal *Io pur respiro* (*HAM,* I, No. 161) is a nice example. The regular fugal exposition at the beginning establishes the Phrygian fifth, and, although the rest of the work cannot be analyzed according to mode, the final chord is on *e,* the regular final of the Phrygian mode.

Not all sixteenth-century works are as clear as the Palestrina motet just analyzed, and the detailed discussion of this one is given to point up the problems and characteristics of the early fugue. The style and structure of sixteenth-century music is exceedingly subtle and complex, worked out in fine detail; analysis of this music requires a good deal of experience with this style. Because the study of fugal form in the choral works of this period is basically the analysis of choral forms in which fugue is but one of the elements, no suggested analysis projects are listed here. The general understanding of fugue in this music is important for a historical study of fugue because it was in this choral music that the *fuga sciolta* was first exploited. It was, however, in instrumental music, which was not subordinate to a text, that the fugal process became the impetus for the growth of abstract forms.

Instrumental Fugue in the Sixteenth and Early Seventeenth Centuries

During the first half of the sixteenth century, instrumental music lagged behind choral music in the development of polyphonic forms based on fugue. Instrumental ensembles performed works written for choral performance, and these were also available in transcription and parody arrangements for lute and keyboard instruments; but it was not until the third decade that fugal imitation became a common technique in the composition of abstract instrumental works.[16] Even then, it was the style of an older generation—that of Des Près and his followers—that was used. Only in the mid-forties do we find instrumental works published that use the *fuga sciolta* in the way that Gombert used it to build up longer forms and incorporate the modal practices, cadence usage, and contrapuntal techniques used by the generation of Willaert and Gombert.[17]

Once this formal procedure was adopted, instrumental fugue started on a path of its own, and, by the end of the century, long movements based on the *fuga sciolta* are found that, using the same materials and techniques as the motet and the Mass, are far more advanced as integrated and extended movements. From this time on, it was the instrumental use of fugue, free of the domination of the text and depending on the need for a logical, yet abstract, form, that led the way in the development of fugue. Only in the early, mid-century ricercars and fantasias do we find a series of short, interlocking fugal sections similar to that found in vocal polyphony. These fugal sections soon became longer and fewer; they ceased to be convenient building blocks, and their inner structure and extension became the center of attention. Instrumental forms based on fugue were soon much longer than their vocal prototypes, and with this expansion a number of new problems arose.

Tonal Conventions before the Full Establishment of Major–Minor Tonality

The principles of form used in the motet were likewise the basis of these instrumental forms. The tonal conventions of the modal system remained in force until the major–minor system became dominant, and, even when the new system was used in practice, it was generally described in modal terms until rationalized by Rameau. The period in which these forms were developing was the time of transition from the modes to the key system, and, although these early fugal forms reached their height in the first half of the seventeenth century, many of the procedures they used lasted until a new fugal form based in major–minority tonality took over.

During the seventeenth century, theorists reported certain refinements in the usages of modal tonality, and a short summary of these will be helpful in looking at the tonal structure of these forms. The emphasis placed by late sixteenth-century Italian theorists on unity of mode—beginning and ending a piece in a single mode—was aimed primarily at sacred music, but, by the early seventeenth century, this unity was felt to be proper for all music, including instrumental music. Although in some cases the assignment of a single mode to an instrumental piece seems impossible, in most cases the mode is clear; in fact, many instrumental composers included the mode as part of the identification of a piece. *Ricercar terzo tuono* (Phrygian) is a typical title for this time.

As the seventeenth century moves on, the assignment of mode often becomes clearer, for the movement toward major and minor consisted in part of the cutting down of variety in scale and harmonic materials. Only in the case of a mixture of two modes does this seem difficult. By this time, the most common "mixtures" are those in which the two modes combined have an embryonic tonic–dominant relationship—two modes a fifth apart in which the tonic triads of each are similar (both major or both minor) but with different scale patterns. These pairs are surely symptoms of the gradual amalgamation of similar modes into what was eventually to be a single, fixed major scale and a relatively fixed minor scale. A work seeming to us to be in C major but ending with a cadence in G and starting with a fugue in which the answer is in the subdominant (such as the subject G, B, d answered by c, e, g) can be analyzed modally as a mixture of Mixolydian and Hypoionian. To us, it is an example of the coming merger of the two to form C major, but it will not analyze satisfactorily within a single mode or in C major. A similar combination is the mixture of Phrygian with Hypoaeolian, which anticipates A minor.

The two main ways in which mode was clearly projected in the seventeenth century were melodically by the themes and harmonically by the cadences. Both theory and practice acted to make the fugal exposition less ambiguous. Theorists began to state positively that the subject of a fugue should establish the mode of the fugue by emphasizing the fourth, fifth, or octave of the mode or, preferably, the tonic triad of the mode. This means that the subject itself rather than the initial notes of the exposition establishes the mode and that the subject can start on 3 and be answered by 7 without destroying the sense of the mode; the initial notes of the entries were no longer the sole determining factor. The beginning of a fantasia by Jan Pieterson Sweelinck illustrates this.[18] It is in Dorian, and the subject begin on the fifth of the triad—a', f', d'—and moves on to end with a direct scale from d' to a'. Sweelinck used a real answer—e', c', a', etc., but, even though this answer outlines the Aeolian triad and despite the fact that the initial notes of the subject and answer outline the Aeolian fourth, the subject (which is four and a half measures long and is finished before the answer enters) has firmly established the Dorian mode. The tonally adjusted answer that was gradually adopted as the correct answer in this same century made any confusion impossible, for with it both the subject and the answer establish the mode melodically and beyond any question.

The Italian Diruta felt that the tonal answer ought also to be used at the end of a piece where the basic mode was to be re-established,[19] but other theorists and composers did not treat this as an infallible rule. The normal way to establish the mode at the end is with a well-prepared tonic cadence, and in practice this was often reinforced by a pedal point. Cadences also remained important in cutting off the inner divisions of a work. If the work is divided into several sections differing musically, these sections are often brought to a close by a cadence that comes to a stop rhythmically, and, in many cases, particularly in keyboard works, these cadences are approached with cadenza-like ornamentation on the dominant chord. Even in cadences that do not come to a full stop, the degree of importance may be shown by the amount of ornamentation in the antecedent measure and the amount of time the motion is suspended on the chord of resolution.

Only after those cadences that indicate a very important break in the form is there a long wait before the entry of a fugue theme. The length of this wait before the entry of the subject often helps to define the importance of the cadence. When the break is to be minimized, the new entry may begin before the final chord of the cadence is reached. This treatment of the inner cadences, which was taken over from the choral style of the second quarter of the sixteenth century, became an important part of instrumental fugue. Tomàs de Sancta Maria discussed the bringing in of fugal entries at cadence points in great detail, and, from this time on, it remained a regular practice in fugue.[20] Likewise, the use of rests before a new entry of the theme became a common practice in instrumental fugue in the mid-sixteenth century, and, although even in the fugues of J. S. Bach an entry is not always preceded by a rest, this practice remained the norm; from the seventeenth century on, pedagogical works on fugue gave instructions that each entry should be preceded by a rest or made obvious by a melodic skip before its first note.

Inner cadences on notes other than the tonic are clearly the historical antecedent of the later practice of modulation to a new key. But, in the modal system, these cadences rarely establish a new mode except momentarily; they act as brief resting points, and, unless the entering fugue subject or exposition partakes of the mode implied by the cadence, there is no polyphonic or melodic affirmation of that mode. It is enough that the entering part be consonant with the cadence chord.

One often finds very clever modal relations between cadence and subject. Example 77 shows the second main cadence of a piece in G-Dorian,[21] an anonymous *Canzona per l'epistola* from the early seventeenth century. (The canzona is reproduced in *MM*, No. 26.) The cadence is on B-flat, the third degree, a regular cadence tone for the mode. A new fugue subject enters on the third beat of the measure on f' in the alto, and the next two entries are answers, coming in on b-flat and b'-flat in the tenor and soprano. The initial notes of these entries outline the fifth B-flat–F of the cadence chord, but the

EXAMPLE 77

Canzona per l'epistola (ANONYMOUS).

[M. 36]

subject and answer forms do not outline a fifth or fourth melodically. The subject might be thought of as outlining the B-flat triad starting on the fifth, but, since the *b′*-flat turns back to *a′* it can equally be read as an outlined minor triad on *d*. The first answer (in the tenor) emphasizes by a slight rhythmic change the E-flat triad, but the second answer, by another rhythmic change (reinforced by the harmonies of the other parts) emphasizes the G-minor triad, and it is clear in the succeeding measures that this triad, the tonic triad, of the basic mode is the important one. With a harmonic pattern that anticipates to a degree the later minor key, the B-flat, d, E-flat and G triadic aspects of this theme are utilized, and the piece ends firmly with a cadence on *G*. Here again is an example of the good use to which modal ambiguity in a theme can be put.

But there is also ambiguity in the cadence usage when considered as a whole, and the cadences that anticipate the technique of modulation in the major–minor system do not have clear tonal implications until the music is dominated by major–minor tonality. Seventeenth-century theorists continued to list the regular cadences for the modes as occurring on 1, 3, and 5 of the scale, with 1 as the final cadence point and 5 and 3 as the intermediate cadences. Italian theory remained conservative on this point, but by mid-century theorists in England, France, and Germany show that a change was occurring in cadence usage.

[215]

English theorists, whose knowledge of the modes had never been very technical or doctrinaire, were the first to speak of the modes or keys as being limited to two—one having a minor third above the tonic and the other a major third. Their instruction books, based on practice rather than theoretical reasoning and tradition, began at the same time to list cadences according to what they observed in practice. As yet, their music was not wholly in the major–minor system, being, rather, a nice intermingling of modal and major–minor practices, and the customs they observed are those characteristic of the period of transition. Christopher Simpson, whose *Compendium of Practical Musick* was published in London in 1667, listed the cadences on 1 and 5 as the most common in all modes.[22] For cadences in the middle of a piece, he recommended those on 3 as proper for a minor key and those on 2 or 4 as characteristic of major. The cadence on the subdominant loses out as the new tonality becomes stronger. The material added by the composer Henry Purcell to the twelfth edition of John Playford's *Introduction to the Skill of Musick* (1694) shows a closer relation to the relative keys attendant to a key in the major–minor system. In addition to the common cadences on 1 and 5, he gave for minor the subordinate cadences on 3 and 7 and for major those on 6 and 2.[23]

Another rather obscure element in the modal use of cadences is the weight given to cadences on 5 and 3 as belonging to the main mode and to cadences on other tones as belonging to other modes. Since all of them are treated equally—that is, all are temporary cadences that do not imply a modulation in the eighteenth-century sense—it is hard for our ears to differentiate between their tonal implications. The cadences on 5 and 3 seem to be as much a temporary movement to another mode as do the cadences on 2, 4, 6, and 7—more so, really, since the cadences on 5 and 3 are used to end larger sections and are therefore given more rhythmic weight and stronger preparation. But, to a musician schooled in the modes, these served to reinforce the mode while the other cadences on 2, 4, 6, or 7, which received much less emphasis musically, were thought of as departures from the mode. This points up one of the main differences between modal and major–minor tonal thought.

One important aspect of the full use of the key system is the development of a series of cadences ending on the dominant and tonic chords that serve only to reinforce the key in contrast to cadences that belong to other keys, and it was the French and German theorists of the last half of the seventeenth century who began working in that direction. The French developed a terminology that is the basis of that which we use today. Early in the century, Solomon de Caus had christened the fifth degree of the scale as the dominant, and this was accepted by his compatriots along with the term "mediant" for the third degree.[24] Marin Mersenne, in his comprehensive treatise *L'harmonie universelle,* (1636–37) defined the two main cadence types by bass progression—those in which the bass rises a fifth or falls a fourth and those in which the bass rises a fourth or falls a fifth. In general, his definitions followed those of Zarlino, but he recorded a tendency on the part of French musicians to feel the different psychological effect of certain cadences. There was a growing tendency, he stated, for musicians to call the imperfect cadences *cadences attendantes,* because they make one wait for a final resolution to a perfect consonance. But Mersenne gave no musical examples and his descriptions show that his concept of the imperfect cadence was still rather broad.[25]

Mignot de la Voye's *Traité de musique,* published in Paris in 1656, gives a clearer view of the subject.[26] His examples of the perfect cadence are in our terms either a V–I or a vii^{0}₆–I cadence. The *cadence attendante* is a cadence that remains on the penultimate chord—in our terms, a half cadence, I going to V. The term "imperfect cadence" is abandoned and for it is substituted the term deceptive cadence (*cadence rompuë*), a cadence without its normal resolution in which the bass rises a second or falls a third including both what we would call deceptive cadences and imperfect resolutions of the authentic cadence.

Charles Masson, at the close of the century, was the French theorist who first recognized only two modes, major and minor; he discussed the cadence in terms that seem logical to those who have been trained in eighteenth-century harmonic practice.[27] The natural cadences of major—the ones that define the key—are those on the tonic and the dominant. The cadence on the tonic is some form of V–I and that on the dominant has the second degree of the scale for its bass and raises the fourth degree—in other words, a V–I cadence in the key of the dominant. The half cadence is I–V, ending on the dominant (and now called the *cadence irrégulière*). These cadences are formed the same way in both the major and minor keys.

For minor keys, the cadence on the mediant is still considered a regular one in the key, and this is formed with the seventh degree (the lowered seventh in our terms) as the bass of the penultimate chord; in other words, the cadence here is V–I in the relative major. The cadence practice is the same as that described in modal theory, but here the cadences are defined as made within the key, using altered scale tones, and the half cadence is clearly differentiated as a special type of cadence ending on the dominant chord. Their formal functions were also defined. Normally, the cadence ending on the dominant is used to end the first section of a piece, but the half cadence may be used here as well; in minor, the cadence on the mediant may also be used. The relation of these cadences to what happens immediately after was also defined. A cadence on the dominant must not be followed by a melody based on the tonic triad but by one using the notes of the dominant triad. If it is a work in minor and the section ends with a cadence on the mediant, the melody following should be based on the notes of the mediant triad. Although these instructions apply to all sorts of forms, they are particularly apt for fugue where a cadence is so often associated with a statement of a subject—in some cases, the statement of a new subject and, in others, the restatement of a subject already used. In analysis of both sixteenth- and seventeenth-century fugues, the relation between the subject and cadence is one to watch. Masson added, also, that a cadence may be made on any note of the scale of a piece as long as it is made properly, with the correct leading tone.

The musical conventions expressed in the rules given by French and English theorists reflect rather clearly their musical practice in the seventeenth century. Especially in major, their music was often close to eighteenth-century tonal practice, but the more elaborate key organization and modulations of the full major—minor system were rarely used. Minor, of course, retained the remnants of the different minor modes for a much longer time and, as we still know today, never did settle down into a system that could be expressed in a single scale form. Although these theorists implied in their rules the proper cadence system for the minor mode, the lack of examples for particular modes leaves us unsure as to what the writers had in mind. This would not have been the case with their contemporaries who were trained in the modal system, but it is confusing for us who have been trained in the conventions of a later and more closed system.

CADENCE TYPES IN SEVENTEENTH-CENTURY MODAL THEORY

German theory of the seventeenth century, which lacks a detailed discussion of fugue, gave the most extensive summary of the cadence system followed in the modes. Although it would be a mistake to attribute to composers of other nations as detailed and precise a knowledge of cadential treatment as we find in the German texts, the conclusions of these German theorists were obviously the result of the direct observation of the music of their time, and they provide a most useful tool for the examination of the fugal forms of the late sixteenth and seventeenth centuries.

German theory and practice during the first half of the seventeenth century was derived primarily from that of Italy. But, from the beginning, there was a tendency toward clarity of nomenclature and precise definition of function, and this continued to grow until, at the close of the century, all the main cadence types found in the modal system were categorized and listed. The very name by which the cadences were known—the "formal cadences"—show the emphasis placed on the fixed harmonic and melodic formulas that are characteristic of cadences and that make them so useful in the formal articulation of a musical composition. At the same time, the theorists attempted to define more exactly the psychological effects of the different cadences and their placement within a mode. The emphasis that the Germans placed on the relation between musical and rhetorical structure led them to take Zarlino's ideas on the use of cadences for punctuation and refine them. The most obvious use of the conventions they recorded is in opera and church music—particularly in the recitatives—but by analogy these associations can be used to assess the relative importance and formal functions of these cadences in instrumental forms.

As long as the modes remained the tonal basis of music, 1, 3, and 5 of the scale were considered to be the proper places for the cadences in each mode, and, by the seventeenth century, this meant (in our terms) the cadences ending on chords of which the roots were 1, 5, or 3. Cadences on 1 were called the primary cadences; those ending on 5, secondary; and those on the mediant were called tertiary, but these latter were usually equated functionally with the *peregrinae*— those on other degrees of the scale that were considered to be out of the mode.[28] Furthermore, the primary cadences were meant to function as the period does in punctuation, to end a complete section; those ending on the dominant, the secondary cadences, were made equivalent to the colon or interrogation mark; and the tertiary and *peregrinae* were both associated with the comma and used to cut off smaller sections of music.[29]

In the analysis of instrumental fugue, we can translate this into simple formal functions. Cadences on the tonic will end a work and mark off with finality lesser divisions of a work; those on the dominant can mark off important divisions but cannot end a work; and those on the mediant and other degrees will be used only for lesser divisions. At times, we find two other cadence types used for these lesser divisions—those ending on a first-inversion chord (imperfect) and those that we today call deceptive cadences. In analysis, the question of relative rhythmic weight, length of cadence preparation, and the degree to which the rhythmic motion is arrested must be taken into consideration as well. It must also be emphasized that these cadences were points of arrival in the mode (or another mode) but, unless accompanied by melodic confirmation (expressed in the fugue theme itself), they do not imply actual modulation to another mode. If they are clearly accompanied by an exact transposition of the theme to another pitch level along with the harmonic establishment of a major or minor key other than the tonic of the piece, this can be accounted a modulation to a new key in the eighteenth-century sense and analyzed in those terms.

During the second half of the century, these theorists adopted precise names for all cadence types and recorded examples of these cadence types as found within each mode. (The cadences used in both the authentic and plagal forms of a mode were the same; only in melodic range and in melodic [chanting] dominants did the two forms of a single mode differ.) The first complete listing is given in W. C. Printz's *Satyrischer Componist,* which was published in 1695, at about the same time as the works by Masson and Purcell mentioned above.[30] The value of Printz's work is great, for his precise examples act as an explication of the general rules given by Purcell and Masson. In addition, the fact that he gave a listing for each mode makes his work a great help in the analysis of earlier modal works.

The precise and minutely detailed terminology given by Printz was used by eighteenth-century German theorists until the influence of Rameau became dominant. But it is not the terminology used today, so that, except in cases where there is no convenient equivalent, these terms will not be used here. The one important cadence type that our terms do not sufficiently describe is that in which the bass moves up a fifth or down a fourth—a pattern used in our plagal and half cadences but one that also appears on other degrees in the modes. The term used by these theorists, *dissecta,* is more useful because it signifies a particular root movement rather than a cadence on a particular scale degree, and it will be adopted here. The cadences given by Printz for the Ionian and Aeolian modes are listed in Example 78 because they will help to clarify major and minor usage as described by French and English theorists as well as earlier modal usage, and, by analogy, they indicate the cadence types found in other modes. Phrygian, being an exceptional mode, is also included.

The cadences are of two main types, *dissecta* and authentic, and they include variants of these two types as well. For Printz, however, each is a fixed cadence form with specific characteristics, characterized by the melodic movement in each part. The first column shows the totally perfect cadences, those that give a complete final ending based on the authentic cadence. Because in Phrygian there is a diminished fifth, f, above the dominant, B, there is no cadence in this column, and the cadence in the second column, a form of the *dissecta* ending on the tonic, is used instead. The third column gives cadences in which the bass rises by step to the root of the final chord. In all modes but Phrygian, this gives a V_6–I cadence. The cadences in the fourth column, where the root of the final chord is approached in the bass by the downward motion of a step, a vii^0_6–I cadence, is likewise the same in all modes but Phrygian. In Phrygian, the cadences included in these columns are both variants of the regular Phrygian cadence, as it is called today.

Nor does Phrygian have any cadences in the remaining columns, since these all involve the use of the dominant chord that Phrygian lacks. The fifth and sixth columns give for the other modes two forms of the *dissecta* that are types of the half cadence, ending on V. Those in the seventh and eighth columns show the two kinds of cadences that were still described by French and English theorists as belonging to one category, a type that we generally translate as the deceptive cadence—those in which the bass rises a step or falls a third. Here we can see, perhaps, why the cadences falling in this category—cadences that we would call deceptive or imperfect and that were lumped together as weaker cadences by Zarlino—might still have been thought of as being similar in function. There are so many different types that, when cadence types were still being differentiated and categorized, these may not have seemed so obviously different in type as they do today. Clearly, they all had the same function, the avoidance of a strong close. The forms that we would call deceptive are even different in different modes. While the imperfect cadences in the eighth column are the same, the cadence in the seventh column in Ionian is a V–vi deceptive cadence in our terms, and the parallel cadence in Aeolian is a V–IV_6.

These cadences are concerned only with the dominant and tonic chords or with deceptive resolutions of the dominant. Those cadences ending with the dominant chord (the cadences in the fifth and sixth columns) can be counted as secondary cadences—cadences on the dominant—in these modes. But other cadence forms on the dominant are more often used as secondary cadences, as Printz made clear in a table (Table I) showing the relationship between the primary, secondary, and tertiary cadences in all the modes. The primary cadence forms in one mode act as secondary cadences in another and as tertiary cadences in still another mode.

In Example 78, the primary cadences (cadences on the tonic) appear in the first through fourth columns. These primary cadences in Ionian can then be used for secondary cadences in Lydian (where *C* is the fifth degree) and as tertiary cadences in Aeolian (where *C* is the third degree); in other modes, they will be *peregrinae* and counted as cadences borrowed temporarily from the Ionian. Conversely, to find the secondary cadences for Ionian, one will take the

EXAMPLE 78

PRIMARY CADENCES AS LISTED BY W. C. PRINTZ.

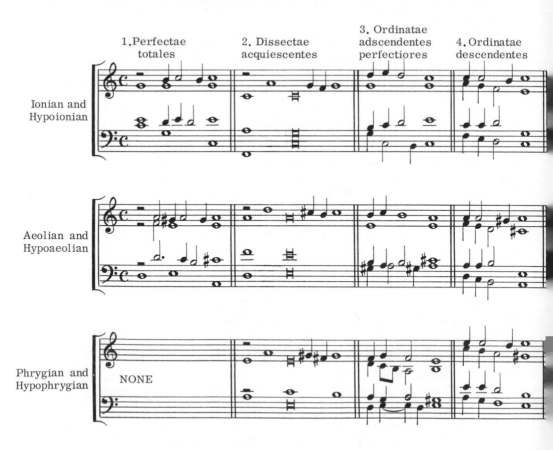

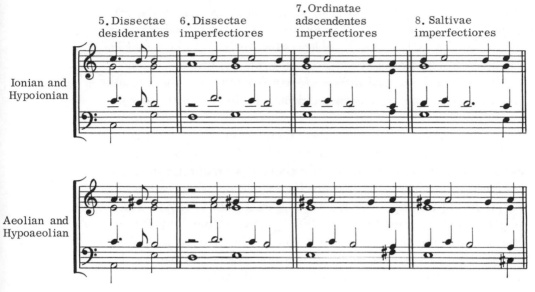

Phrygian, none

TABLE I
Interrelation of Cadences in the Modes
as Given by W. C. Printz

PRIMARY CADENCES IN THESE MODES	ARE SECONDARY CADENCES IN THESE MODES*
Phrygian and Hypophrygian	Aeolian and Hypoaeolian
Mixolydian and Hypomixolydian	Ionian and Hypoionian
Aeolian and Hypoaeolian	Dorian and Hypodorian
Ionian and Hypoionian	Lydian and Hypolydian
Dorian and Hypodorian	Mixolydian and Hypomixolydian

PRIMARY CADENCES IN THESE MODES	ARE TERTIARY CADENCES IN THESE MODES*
Ionian and Hypoionian	Aeolian and Hypoaeolian
Phrygian and Hypophrygian	Ionian and Hypoionian
Lydian and Hypolydian	Dorian and Hypodorian
Mixolydian and Hypomixolydian	Phrygian and Hypophrygian
Aeolian and Hypoaeolian	Lydian and Hypolydian

* There are no secondary cadences in Phrygian and Hypophrygian nor tertiary cadences in Mixolydian and Hypomixolydian.

primary cadences from Mixolydian (which are not given in Example 78, but which are an exact transposition up a fifth of the Ionian cadences). The tertiary cadences in Ionian, on *E,* are simply the primary Phrygian cadences found in Example 78 in the second through fourth columns. All the regular cadences for Aeolian can be found in Example 78. The secondary cadences, on E, are the primary cadences in Phrygian in the second through fourth columns, and the tertiary cadences, on C, are the primary cadences in Ionian, first through fourth columns.

As in many musical systems, there is one point at which the rules do not work. This is where a major chord on B would be required. Because, in the modal system, the fifth above B is *f*-natural, which is a diminished fifth, it was felt that no chord could be made there without producing a transposition to another system—the system in which all the modes are transposed up a fifth or down a fourth by the use of *F*-sharp in the signature (Dorian on *a,* Phrygian on *b,* and so forth). Thus the major triad on B was not accepted as part of the untransposed modal system (Dorian on *d,* Phrygian on *e,* and so forth), and this meant that certain cadences were missing from the system. We have already seen that the authentic cadence in Phrygian is not found for this reason. Printz added that there are also no secondary cadences (ending on the chord on B) in Phrygian and no tertiary cadences (likewise ending on the chord on B) in Mixolydian. This is one obvious aspect of the conflict between harmonic and melodic expression of tonality found in the music of the period. The modes originally were purely melodic in character, and the grafting of such vertical patterns as harmonic cadences onto this system that began in the sixteenth century was never wholly consistent. As we have seen earlier, the result of the increasing dependence on harmonic order finally resulted in the cutting down of the modal scale system and the adoption of the major–minor system, and the works of the late sixteenth and seventeenth centuries are thus written in a period of tonal transition.

In the works of the early part of this period, we find at times a melodic cadence on B used as the secondary cadence in Phrygian and the tertiary in Mixolydian, but this melodic B is then harmonized as the fifth of an E-major chord or the third of a G-major chord. (See p. 192.) The composer's usual practice—actually noted by several theorists—was to use the Primary Ionian cadence in these cases, and cadences on C are common in both Mixolydian and Phrygian for this reason. A cadence on *A,* the Primary Aeolian cadence, is likewise common in Phrygian. Modal terminology labeled them *peregrinae,* accounting for their frequent use in these modes by observing that the Mixolydian and Ionian pairs had an affinity for each other and that both the Ionian and Aeolian pairs were commonly intermixed with works in Phrygian.

While the cadences in Example 78 are a good basis for the harmonic forms of cadences for the purposes of our analyses, the particular melodic forms—the use of suspensions and the melodic ornamentation of them—that are shown are more localized German forms for the late seventeenth century. Various melodic and rhythmic variants can be found. In early seventeenth-century keyboard works, elaborate trill patterns are usually attached to important cadences, and many works written throughout the period use the simple harmonic form without the suspension. Variations in the melodic and rhythmic forms appear in cadence listings throughout the period.[31] Also in this period, it was thought that a cadence ending on a major triad (regardless of mode) gave the most satisfying sense of finality.

INTIMATIONS OF MAJOR–MINOR TONALITY

It should be pointed out again that, during the seventeenth century, transposition of the modes became increasingly common and, by the end of the seventeenth century when the major–minor system had become the dominant form practiced, instructions were given for transposing to all different pitches.[32] But transposition from one modal "system" to another in the same piece was not a part of regular modal practice. Temporary use of melodic accidentals did not constitute such transposition, nor did the raised leading tone in the first chord of a cadence; but the *consistent* use of an accidental that changed the normal position of the tritone in the scale, such as B-flat or F-sharp, did constitute such a transposition, because it changed the significant arrangement of the minor seconds in the octave. This is why the use of a B-major triad was not accepted in Phrygian on e, the f-sharp changes the mode into Aeolian on e. Regular modulations in the modes occurred within a particular modal system; in the natural system (using no sharps or flats in the signature), one could expect to find a modulation to any mode in that system. In a piece in C-Ionian, one could expect to find cadences and melodic modulations to such modes as Dorian on d and Aeolian on a but not to Dorian on g (with a b-flat and an e-flat) or Aeolian on e (with an f-sharp).

At times, however, these or similar modulations to another system are found. It was the cadences that establish such modulations, and they apparently were accounted for as cadences on *peregrinae.* A cadence on a regular cadence tone of a mode that used tones going out of its modal system was not considered a regular cadence by seventeenth-century theory, but a *peregrina* cadence.[33] Thus, a cadence on *e* in Aeolian or Ionian using a V–I formula, the first chord made up of *B, D*-sharp, *F*-sharp, would be irregular, a *peregrina,* out of the mode, in contrast to the usual Phrygian or plagal cadence on the same note. The admission of such cadences and of clear and frequent movement from one modal system to another (such as a piece in C-Ionian moving to G-Ionian or A-Aeolian moving to E-Aeolian) is a sure indication of the replacement of the modal system by the major–minor system. Such signs are found in the sixteenth century, but only in the last half of the seventeenth century do they appear consistently in diatonic music (as opposed to experiments with the chromatic genera). This conflict between the two systems of tonality makes the works of this time particularly interesting.

The regular cadences of a mode, on 5 and 3, should be analyzed in modal terms as secondary and tertiary cadences in the mode (or dominant and mediant cadences) rather than as modulations to another mode. Thus, a cadence on *G* in Ionian would be a secondary cadence in Ionian rather than a modulation to Mixolydian, and a cadence on *E* would be called a tertiary cadence in Ionian rather than a modulation to Phrygian. If, on the other hand, at the same time, there is a clear modulation melodically to the mode in which the cadence is a primary cadence (such as a transposition of a fugue theme to that mode) or polyphonically (as by a new fugal exposition in that mode), there certainly exists a temporary modulation. This is part of the ambiguity of the rules of modal tonality, and, to make the analysis clear, one must certainly count it as a modulation.

Theme as a Determinant of Form

As we have seen, the over-all tonal form during this period was achieved by cadences in the modes expressed by the fugal themes and their expositions, and by the modes implied in transpositions in restatements of these themes. But, aside from this tonal function, the themes (or theme) used play an important part in making a form clear to the listener because they are the most evident material of a piece. As in most forms, what the listener follows is the thematic structure, the statements of themes, departure from and return to these themes, the bringing in of new themes, the combination of themes, the variation of a theme, and the like.

Analysis of these early fugal works from the point of view of the patterns presented by the themes and their use is interesting, for the thematic structure does not always coincide with the tonal structure as outlined by cadences. In fact, one of the main characteristics of fugal forms in all periods is the use of an entrance of the theme across an important cadence point, so that a cadence does not necessarily mean the termination of a theme or a section of the form as it does in homophonic music. Nor does a cadence necessarily coincide with the introduction of a new theme or a new treatment of an old theme. For these reasons, it is a good plan to first make an analysis of the cadences in a work and to follow this by a tonal analysis made solely of the modes implied by the themes with their expositions and restatements before marking out the abstract pattern made by the themes themselves. The procedures to be followed are those that have already been illustrated in the analysis of the Palestrina motet, and in instrumental fugue this is often easier because, particularly in seventeenth-century works, the themes project the mode more clearly. In instrumental forms of this time, there are often episodic sections that are based on fragments of themes. These may be saved until after the purely thematic analysis has been made.

Instrumental works of this period are generally categorized as monothematic and polythematic—monothematic meaning a work in which one main theme is presented at the beginning in an exposition and polythematic meaning that several themes appear in the course of a work, each being presented first in an exposition. The two types are clearly differentiated only by their use of expositions and not in the number of themes used. In a great many cases, both types use one or more secondary countersubjects, and, in some polythematic works, the later themes may be variants of the first. Also, during the late sixteenth and early seventeenth centuries, there was often such extreme variation in restatements of the subject that it is hard to be sure that it *is* the same subject. It is often difficult to make a clear analysis thematically because, at this time, subtlety and complexity were more prized than obvious clarity, and the instrumental piece was considered an ideal vehicle for showing off compositional skills.

Although the tonal elements of form are the same for both types of fugue, each presents a different problem in thematic organization. The composer of a monothematic fugue was concerned with extension and avoidance of monotony. The composer of the polythematic fugue extended his work by adding a series of fugal expositions on different themes but sacrificed thematic unity, and, as this instrumental form developed, we find the single fugues from which it was built becoming more extended and fewer in number, until the polythematic form became what was, in effect, a stringing together of several monothematic fugues. Unity was at times achieved by using subjects that could later be combined contrapuntally, and these became, then, a type of double or triple fugue—a fugue type that will be discussed in Chapter IX. In a few cases, a later repetition of the first fugue gives a sense of unified form as in the *Ricercar 12° Tono* (*HAM*, I, No. 136) by Andrea Gabrielli (1510–1586).[34] Those in which each section is a self-contained fugue on one subject appeared less often as the seventeenth century moved on, for the monothematic fugue became the dominant type in the major–minor system. The monothematic fugue is actually the most interesting one formally because it is the one that could first be called "a fugue"—a form created by the extension of a single fugue rather than a form in which several fugues were used as building blocks.

In many of these fugal forms, sections of thematic contrast are found. The polythematic forms often include noncontrapuntal sections for contrast; the second section of the work by Andrea Gabrieli mentioned above, which is antiphonal in nature, is a good example. Toccata-like sections were often used in the approach to the cadence of a section or of a complete piece. By far the most interesting sections of thematic relief are episodes that appear at times in the midst of a monothematic fugue or a long fugal section in a polythematic work. These are sections of a measure or more in which the theme itself does not appear as a whole. They range from rather aimless interludes to highly organized sequential or imitative developments of short thematic fragments, and these latter are of great interest to us because of the importance they assume in the eighteenth- and nineteenth-century fugue.

Another element that enters into the formal effect of these works is one derived from an aesthetic ideal of the sixteenth century—the feeling that the end of a work should be the most interesting and exciting part. This was justified by quotations from textbooks on rhetoric, which insist that the end of a speech or a sentence should be the most important part. Sixteenth-century choral forms generally have a quickening of motion near the end, and this was carried over into the instrumental fugue. Sometimes stretto is used and sometimes diminution of the subject. Often it is just the introduction of active rhythmic figuration in the countermelodies to the theme. But this intensification at the end of a work or at the endings of the main sections within a work, plays an important part in the articulation of these fugal movements.

ANALYSIS OF A MONOTHEMATIC FUGUE OF THE
EARLY SEVENTEENTH CENTURY

Although we often find one composer preferring a particular formal procedure, there is no fixed fugue form that predominates at this time, and the analysis of these works is best approached without prejudiced anticipations. The general principles have been touched on above, but their application in particular cases varies widely. This was a time when there was much concentration on small detail—in craftsmanship, in skill in variation, and in contrapuntal combination and manipulation. In some works, one feels that only the small detail is important, but, in others, one finds a tremendous feeling for the building-up of large and satisfying forms.

The monothematic forms present some of the most interesting formal solutions because the problems they present force some ingenious and aesthetically satisfying solutions. A very satisfying procedure is found in the fugal fantasias of Sweelinck (and later in the works of his pupil, Scheidt). Sweelinck's *Fantasia cromatica*[35] (In GMB, No. 158; MSO I, p. 98f. note values reduced by half through m. 36) in addition to being a successfully extended monothematic fugue, is based on a chromatic subject often used in the modal fugues of the time—a subject form that keeps the chromatic passage within the fourth of the mode so that its tonality is not in question.[36] (See Ex. 79.) The mode is clearly Dorian, although the

EXAMPLE 79

Fantasia cromatica, J. P. SWEELINCK.

use of B-flats in some sections betrays a tendency toward Aeolian on *d*. As is usual with Sweelinck, the answer is a real answer, outlining the Aeolian fourth, but the countersubject emphasizes the Dorian fourth against the head of the answer (measure 3), and this same countersubject in a tonally adjusted form emphasizes the Dorian fifth when the subject appears in measure 5.

TABLE II

Cadences in Sweelinck's Fantasia cromatica
(*Dorian Mode*)

MEASURE	SUBORDINATE CADENCES	MAIN CADENCES	SCALE DEGREE OF FINAL CHORD	PLACEMENT IN MODE
18	g: vii°–i		4	*peregrina*
25	a: V–i		5	secondary
37		d: V–I	1	primary
54	F: V–I		3	tertiary
65	a: V–VI		3	tertiary
86		a: V–iv	1	primary
107	d: V–i		1	primary
116	d: iv₆–V		5	secondary
128	d: vii°₆–i		1	primary
138	d: iv₆–V		5	secondary
156		d: V–I	1	primary
161		d: iv–I	1	primary

The cadence structure of the fantasia is shown in Table II. As in the diagram of the Palestrina motet, these are for convenience listed as if they were in the key of the final chord of each cadence. The listings of the scale degrees in Dorian on which they fall along with the type of cadence they make in the mode, show their modal functions. The two inner cadences accounted the most important are so chosen because they have the strongest preparation and because the resolution of each is followed by a sudden slowing-down of the rhythmic movement and a cutting-down of the polyphonic texture to two parts. In neither case is there a complete stop, the entry of a restatement of the theme beginning in the measure of resolution. The cadence in measure 86 is weaker than the first, being a deceptive cadence, but it appears at a much stronger rhythmic and textural break than any of those listed as lesser cadences. All of the cadences listed

are clearly "formal cadences," having the type of ornamentation associated with cadences of the early seventeenth century.

As Table II shows, these cadences follow a pattern characteristic
of modal tonality. The first section has a strongly established tonic
in the exposition and ends with a strong tonic cadence in measure 37,
but, within this section, there is a *peregrina* cadence and a secondary
cadence on the dominant. The two inner cadences of the second
section (m. 37–86) are tertiary cadences, but, at no point in this section, is F established as a tonal center as it would be were the piece in
D minor. It remains centered around Dorian, although less strongly
than in the beginning as the use of tertiary cadences indicates, one
rather weak tertiary cadence (m. 65) being a deceptive cadence. The
third section (starting in m. 86) comes closer to the tonic, with the
cadences either on the tonic or dominant, and ends with a strong
cadential section extending from measure 151 to measure 164.

The melodically based tonal pattern is similar to that established
by the cadences. Because of the chromatic nature of the subject, there
are measures that are in no mode, but, in the beginning of each of
the three main sections, Dorian is clearly established. In the first
section, the first departure from the mode appears in measure 11
where the countersubject combines with the answer to outline the
main notes of Aeolian, and, although it returns to Dorian in measure
15, the *peregrina* cadence on *g* in measure 18 moves out of the mode
again. The secondary cadence on *a* in measure 25 is surrounded by
melodic modulations to Aeolian in measures 22 and 26 and an emphasis on the Phrygian fifth and octave in measure 27, and it is in
this area that the only transpositions of the subject in this section
are found, transpositions beginning on *e*. A stretto of the subject and
answer (beginning on *d* and *a*) makes the return to Dorian that ends
this section.

The second section contains no transpositions of the subject (except for the answer form starting on *A*), but the subject appears in
augmentation so that the chromatic portions of the subject last for
a long time, making for stronger digressions from the mode. There
are also, in this section, three clearly defined episodes, each starting
out of the mode and each ending with one of the cadences in this
section, in measures 54, 65, and 86.

The third section also starts in the tonic and stays closer to it in
the cadences used but provides between cadences strong departures
from the mode. The three statements of the theme in augmentation
provide a good deal of chromatic movement, but the sequential treatment of the theme now in rhythmic diminution that starts in measure 116 provides an even stronger sense of continuing modulation.

Although it moves rapidly through a number of transpositions, a careful analysis shows that the seven different initial pitches on which it appears all belong to the tonic scale, here in its Aeolian form— d', e', f', g', a', b'-flat, c'', (d''). Another stretto of the subject and answer beginning in measure 138 signals the return to the tonic, which is firmly re-established in the closing measures.

As for thematic structure, only the first section is a unit, treating just the subject and countersubject. With its inner modulation, and its stretto at the end with the return to the tonic and the strong final cadence on the tonic, it is a self-contained form that could be a unit in a polythematic movement or could stand alone as an independent *fuga*. Many seventeenth- and early eighteenth-century fugues are about this length, follow the same general tonal pattern, and get their extension by an almost continuous restatement of the subject and countersubject like that seen here.

The rest of the Fantasia has a different structure, a series of different treatments of the theme marked off by cadences. The cadence in measure 86, which marks a major division because it is associated with a rhythmic pause and a marked change in texture, does not set off a new treatment of the theme, for, from measure 71 through measure 115, the subject is used in augmentation with sizable episodes inserted. Sweelinck's use of augmentation was typical of his time. The augmented theme was treated as a cantus firmus and was accompanied, as in his chorale variations, by changing figurations. It is these figurations that stand out to the ear. They are not countersubjects, but are short motives used in sequence and imitation against the theme, and most of them attain importance because they are used as subjects for the episodes.

Superb craftsmanship is shown in the writing of these episodes and in their integration into the movement. The first of these begins in measure 49, but it uses a motive that has accompanied the first two statements of the theme and is connected smoothly with the last measure of the theme in measure 48. (See Ex 80.) The episode itself is sequential, and each unit of the sequence is a tight little stretto of the motive. The episode moves on to the cadence on F ending in measure 55, but the same motive is used to surround the next statement of the theme (starting in the alto in m. 55), and the connection here is also made very smoothly.

Another interesting use of episode can be seen starting in measure 65. Here, in the tenor, a new motive is introduced that is first used in the episode and then continues to appear sequentially against the augmentation of the theme starting in measure 71. After the theme is complete, the motive is developed further in another episode

EXAMPLE 80

Fantasia cromatica, J. P. SWEELINCK.

[M. 47]

end of subject

leading to the cadence in measure 86. Two more statements of the augmented theme lead to the last episode (m. 101–106), which is based on a motive first used against the theme in measure 96. This episode leads to the cadence in measure 107, which introduces the final statement of the augmented theme. With this, the treatment of the theme in augmentation is concluded; from this point on, the subject in its original form is used continuously in some way until the final diminution occurs.

Thus, thematically, there is a section from measure 71 through measure 115 that uses the theme in augmentation accompanied by a series of new secondary motives interspersed with well-developed episodes. This does not coincide with the rhythmic and polyphonic structuring because, from measure 107 through measure 137, the rhythmic figuration is consistently faster and the texture is reduced. Nor is it reinforced by the cadence pattern for, although the lesser cadences tend to articulate the smaller groupings of theme statements, the bigger cadence in measure 86 marks only a rhythmic and textural change.

SUGGESTIONS FOR ANALYSIS

It must be clear from the above that a formal picture of these works can be gained only by first analyzing one element at a time. The order of analysis used above seems practical in most cases, but it need not be adhered to in all. With some works, it may seem logical to start with the element that sets off the sections most obviously, whether it be tonality, theme usage, cadence, rhythm, or some other factor. Some of the most interesting details in the fugal works of this period are still to be found after the form has been thoroughly brought into focus—the treatment and recurrence of subordinate motives, the variations in the themes and fragmentary developments thereof, small-scale harmonic patterns, and the like.

Because these works were created in small detail, a single diagram of a piece is usually as complex as the piece itself. A diagram of entrances such as that given for the Palestrina motet may be used, but the initial notes alone are not always so indicative of tonality in the seventeenth as in the sixteenth century. The entire head of the theme may be needed to make the mode clear. Even if cadences are included in such a diagram, the relative importance of these cadences and their relation to the main mode should be shown in a diagram such as Table II. Diagrams of other sectional elements may be used where feasible. The main problem in fugal analysis is that it is polyphonic, and the form is never as clearly outlined as are the homophonic forms.

In a polythematic work, each section can be analyzed separately. Often, the cadences point up the expositions of new themes but not always. Variants of the opening theme should be watched for as well as the reuse of themes from earlier sections. In all of these works, extreme variants of the theme should be watched for and, in Italian works particularly, the *inganni* (p. 181), which often can be located by their close adherence to the original rhythm of the theme.

Aside from the Sweelinck Fantasia just analyzed, there are no really extensive fugal works from this period reproduced in the collections of miscellaneous works available to students. A great many are available in collected editions of the composers themselves, and a list of suggested works is included in Appendix I.

Toward the Eighteenth-Century Fugue

During the whole of the Baroque period, fugue remained a primary element in many forms. In the early Baroque, it was the basic element in such instrumental pieces as the ricercar, canzona, fantasia, tiento, and capriccio, which were often made up of several fugues combined at times with sections based on invertible counterpoint, on toccata-like figuration, or on simple chordal structure. Fugue was also an element in large concertato and choral works, in vocal ensembles, in the overture, the ensemble sonata, the chorale prelude, and the toccata. In all of these, it performed a strong tonal function as well as being a useful means of polyphonic organization. The monothematic fugal work, however, pointed in a new direction, toward the piece in which the fugue on a single theme was extended to create a work that existed as an entity complete in itself.

Sweelinck's monothematic Fantasia illustrates some of the ways in which this extension could be achieved. The first section of the *Fantasia cromatica* achieves its extension by an almost continual restatement of the subject and answer in company with the countersubject. As in sixteenth-century choral works, there is no break between what we call the exposition and the successive entries of the theme. This is an older usage derived from the time when fugue was still associated with canon, and it seems more realistic to think of this continuation as a single fugue growing continuously from the opening entries rather than as an exposition followed by a fugal extension. Works of about the length of this first section with similar construction appeared early in the seventeenth century, each called simply a *fuga*.[37] In some cases, there is a stretto at the end, as there is here; in others, there is continual overlap of entries from the beginning, but they are all made up of continual entries of the theme, and any episodes used are short and incidental. Like this section of the Sweelinck work, they have a clear tonal pattern beginning and ending in the tonic mode with perhaps a modulation or two in the middle brought about by transposition of the theme. Cadences provide short points of arrival on regular tones of the mode or on *peregrinae,* but the continuous rhythmic and polyphonic motion does not stop until the end of the piece.

The rest of the *Fantasia cromatica* is extended by means that do not belong necessarily to fugue; the theme is not treated imitatively again until the closing stretto. It appears in augmentation and diminution, which admittedly have their origin in canon, but here they are simply mechanical ways of altering the theme. They remain associated with fugue throughout its history but are often merely ways of changing the theme in restatement—a means of extension aside from direct fugal imitation. The treatment of theme in sequence, giving a sense of modal modulation, is also not primarily a fugal technique but was a common developmental device of the period. The sequential episodes are imitative and fugal; they develop not the main theme, but new motives introduced as secondary material to accompany the augmented forms of this theme. They are also a typically Baroque feature. Here, they give momentary relief from the main theme and are integrated into the whole, but they are not primarily fugal devices.

All of these devices—the fugal devices in the first section and the techniques of formal extension by varied restatement and episode found in the rest of the work—were combined in the eighteenth-century extension of a fugal exposition that is called "a fugue," and thus they became, by tradition, elements of the form that, in the eighteenth and nineteenth centuries, was called "the fugue." They do not have the same functions or relationships that we find in Sweelinck's work, however, because, by that time, the tonal organization was based on the major–minor system, and this brought about a different ordering of form. Nor should Sweelinck necessarily be considered the source of these later uses. The devices that we find concentrated here are found to some degree in many fugal and nonfugal works of the time; his work is used here as an illustration because it includes so many of these devices and because it is an aesthetically satisfying ordering of them in an earlier tradition. His influence on the German musicians whom he taught and their followers was undoubtedly strong, but other important influences were at work as well.

Effects of the New Tonality on Form

The first effect that the major–minor system had on the fugue was to remove tonal ambiguities. Like all forms of this period, the fugue began and ended in one key. There was no question of being in two keys at once (like the modal mixture of Hypoaeolian and Phrygian) or of ending on the dominant chord (like Hypoionian ending with a cadence on G).[38]

Secondly, instead of inner cadences on regular tones of the mode (5 or 3) or cadences in other modes (on the *peregrinae*), an authentic cadence ending on a note other than the tonic of the main key accomplished a modulation to another key. Nor was a major chord the preferred final chord for the cadence. If the modulation was to a minor key, the cadence ended on a minor chord. In the Baroque period, a major chord was still preferred as a final ending to a piece, but after mid-century even the final chord was meant to be minor if the main key was minor.

Thirdly, the key of the subject and of the answer (or keys, in the case of a subject that modulated at the end) was clear. If the subject was transposed, it was transposed to another key. On the rare occasions when it was not transposed exactly, it could still be accurately located in the key. A subject in C,—*g, f, e, d, c, B, c*—might appear in the form *b, a, g, f, e, d, e.* This would be the subject in C but starting on the seventh degree. It would not be considered to be in a mode (in this case, Phrygian); if *e* were to be the tonic, both *f* and *d* would need to be sharped to put it into E minor.

The prescribed tonal pattern for a fugue was the same in the major–minor system as in the modes—an establishment of the overall key at the beginning and end with some movement out of the key in the middle. The keys into which a fugue modulated were generally those close to the main key, and, for the theorists of the time, the keys that were close to the main key were found on those notes in the scale of the main key on which a perfect triad (one with a perfect fifth) occurred naturally. In major, this included 2, 3, 4, 5, 6 and in minor, 3, 4, 5, 6, and lowered 7. Each of these keys was major or minor according to the type of triad that was found on the corresponding scale degree in the main key. In C major, the key formed on 3 would be E minor; in C minor, the key formed on 3 would be E-flat major.

The degree of closeness to the original key that was associated with each of these related keys varied with different theorists. For Rameau, the closest keys were those in which the tonic chord of the main key could also be found—in later terms, those keys in which this tonic triad could become a pivot. These would be, in major, the keys on 3, 4, 5, and 6; in C major, these were E minor (C: I = e: VI), G major (C: I = G: IV), F major (C: I = F: V), and A minor (C: I = A: III). Rameau did not detail this in minor, only remarking that it is better to go to the key on 6 in major (our relative minor) and to the key on 3 in minor (our relative major).[39]

In mid-century Rameau's follower Béthisy gave a more definite ordering.[40] If the main key was major, one ordinarily went first to the dominant key, but one could also go to the subdominant at once or after having gone first to the dominant. After these came the keys on 6 and 2 (in C, a and d); Béthisy considered it rare in major to go to the mediant key (in C, to e). In a minor key, the dominant minor (in c, g) and the mediant (in c, E-flat) were equally good for the first modulation, and after this the subdominant was good (in c, f), but modulations to the keys of the sixth and lowered seventh degrees should occur only if a piece is long. He and Rameau mentioned a few other possibilities, such as the dominant minor in a major key (in C, g) or the lowered seventh or the major supertonic (in C, B-flat and D), but these were considered more distant. Neither Béthisy nor Rameau insisted that a fixed order was obligatory but left the choice to the cultivated taste of the good composer.

German theory of the same period shows a preference for a slightly different order. Scheibe, in 1739, considered the keys formed on 5, 3, and 6 of the basic key (major *or* minor) to be the closest keys; next in order came those on 4 and 2 in major and those on 4 and 7 in minor.[41] Other keys were *peregrinae,* which Scheibe felt one might pass through, but they should not be established by a strong cadence.

Two later theoretical works are important because of their connection with German fugues of the first half of the century. J. P. Kirnberger (1721–1783), a pupil of J. S. Bach known both as composer and theorist, gave as the proper order for modulation from the opening tonic a movement to the dominant key, then to the keys on 3 or 6, and then modulation to some of the more distant keys before returning to the tonic by way of the dominant.[42] In a short outline, he gave the following as a good order of modulation in C major:[43]

C, G, a, e, d, C, F, C.

Earlier, Marpurg in his treatise on fugue, which is also based in part on the works of J. S. Bach, gave a similar order—5, 6, and 3 as the closest keys for both major and minor, then 2 and 4 for major, and 4 and lowered 7 for minor.[44] This German stress on the mediant key in major as well as minor contrasts with the preferences of Rameau's followers, and it clearly originated in earlier modal theory, which stressed the cadences on 5 and 3 as those that strengthened a mode.

Both Kirnberger and Marpurg paid much attention to the more distant keys, but only Marpurg related them to fugue. Keys such as 7 in major (in C, b), 2 in minor (in c, d), and lowered 2 in minor (in c, D-flat) are the closer of the nonrelated keys, but these—as well as the more distant ones—should not be used in restatements of the subject, but only as passing modulations in episodes.

The cadences used in the new key system were those still learned today in traditional harmony, and the functions assigned to them are similar. The strongest cadence is the authentic cadence, V–I or V^7–I, in which the bass skips from 5 to 1 and the top voice moves by step from either 2 or 7 to 1. The half cadence, I–V or I–V^7, which demands more harmonic movement, is always found within the key and is strongest when the bass skips from 1 to 5. These cadences keep their identities and functions when one or both of the chords involved is inverted or the top voice has a different melody note, but the effect is weakened. A like weakening is felt when vii⁰ is substituted for V.

An important distinction between this and earlier conventions is that now an imperfect authentic cadence (V–I₆) is no longer in the same class with the deceptive cadence but has a clear function within the key. The deceptive cadence is now one that starts out to be an authentic cadence but moves to some chord other than the tonic. It does not affirm the key, but leads to an extension within the key or to a modulation to another key. The plagal and Phrygian cadences are still used but are much less important. The use of the Phrygian cadence is restricted to the function of a half cadence in minor, iv₆–V. The plagal cadence is considered to be much weaker in effect than the authentic cadence, and, when it is used, it normally follows a strong authentic cadence and serves only to add weight to the finality of the authentic cadence.

In fugue, the theme also defines key melodically. In the modal fugue, the melodic definition of tonality is the way this was done; only at the cadences was mode expressed harmonically. But the way of expressing major and minor is by both melodic and harmonic progression, and at times there was a conflict in fugue between the key expressed melodically by the theme and that projected by the harmonic progression of the entire texture. In the exposition, the melodic key is normally reinforced by the harmony, and this is often true in later restatements of the subject. Reharmonization of a melody, however, is one of the composition techniques exploited in the new tonal system, and it is used at times in restatements of the theme. If the theme is transposed in restatement—and this is one of the ways in which modulation is accomplished in a fugue—it may as well be reharmonized in such a way that the harmony implies one key whereas the theme considered as a single melodic line implies another.

Furthermore, the subject and answer forms of the theme may differ, and, in a fugue in major or minor, these two forms of the theme differ more than in a modal fugue. If the subject is nonmodulating and has a real answer (an exact transposition of the subject to the dominant key), this problem does not arise. In analyzing a fugue of this type, all of the entries after the exposition may be considered as simple transpositions of the subject. Some analysts, however, prefer to call this theme the answer whenever it appears in the dominant, and, in those fugues where there are no transpositions of the theme except to the dominant, this gives a good picture of the whole. It is usually clearer in other cases to consider all transposed entries of the theme after the exposition as simple transpositions of the subject.

When the answer has a tonal adjustment, there are two distinct forms of the theme used in the fugue, and this can play an important part in modulations in the body of the fugue. In some cases, where the head of the answer is adjusted tonally, the beginning of the answer outlines the I chord of the tonic key whereas the remainder of the answer is in the dominant. This answer form melodically implies the tonic and dominant keys, whereas the subject implies only the tonic. This does not necessarily mean that the answer must express the two keys, since the I chord in the tonic key can be accounted IV in the dominant, but the possibility is there, and this can be exploited by the composer. Example 81a, from the second fugue in the first book of Bach's *Well-Tempered Clavier,* shows how Bach used such an answer form as a further means to modulation. The answer is used, untransposed, in the alto starting in measure 15. In measures

EXAMPLE 81

(a) FUGUE IN C MINOR FROM THE *Well-Tempered Clavier,* BOOK I, J. S. BACH.
(b) FUGUE No. 1 IN G MAJOR FROM *Wohlklingende Fingersprache* BY JOHANN MATTHESON.

13 and 14, a sequential episode has moved through E-flat, B-flat, and f to c, and the answer in measure 15 starts in c as though this were the final goal of the modulation. But, by the end of measure 15, both the answer and the accompanying harmony of the other parts are in g, and it cadences strongly in g at the beginning of measure 17.

When reharmonization is involved, there may be a change in key without transposition of the theme. Example 81b, taken from a fugue by Johann Mattheson, illustrates this. The answer, untransposed, appears in the bass, starting in G and ending in D in a purely melodic analysis. The harmony, on the other hand, places it in the key of E minor. Both quotations in Example 81 show an untransposed answer centering on the dominant key. The same processes are also found in transposed restatements.

Subjects that begin in the tonic and modulate to the dominant at the end have answer forms that differ even more from the subject in their tonal pattern. In these cases, the answer has a modulation opposite to that of the subject, starting in the dominant and modulating to the tonic. If, in addition to this, the answer also has a tonal adjustment at the beginning, the answer will differ even more strikingly from the subject. Depending on the particularities involved, a number of key relationships become possible that are limited only by the ingenuity and taste of the composer.

It is important in analysis to note which form of the theme—the subject or answer—is being used and to record for each entry the keys involved. In recording the *melodic* key of the statement, it is usually enough to indicate the key in which it begins and the one in which it ends. This can be written in above the designation of the theme. For the harmony, however, the chords as well as the key, at the beginning and end should be shown.

The Expanded Fugue Form

A great many fugal works are found in the late seventeenth and early eighteenth centuries that differ from earlier fugues only in being written clearly in a major or minor key. Here the short piece called a *fuga,* which was a simple extension of a fugal exposition, differed only from its predecessors in that it was in a major or minor key. Several such fugues are reprinted in *HAM,* II. The fugues of Buxtehude (No. 234), Johann Christoph Bach (1642–1703) (No. 237), and Johann Krieger (1649–1725) (No. 249) are typical. (It should be noted that the answer forms do not always coincide with the forms approved by later generations.)

The real culmination of the combination of fugue with the new formal procedures developed in the major–minor system is what is often referred to as "the Bach fugue." Although this form did not originate with J. S. Bach and its use was not limited to him, the formal procedures involved are found in most of his fugues, and, since more of his fugues are performed today than those of any other composer, it is not surprising that the form should be associated with his name. The term "expanded fugue" is used here only to associate it with a type of formal principle rather than with one composer.

This expanded fugue differs from its immediate predecessors in the reduction of the number of restatements given to the theme and in the emphasized use of longer episodes between these restatements. These episodes are often modulatory, serving a clear tonal function in the form. They also have a formal function, giving relief from continual restatement of the theme, and, in some fugues, the re-use of the same material in several episodes gives further coherence to the whole. At the same time, they often provide a relaxed developmental play with fragments of the subject or countersubject, welding the movement together thematically and giving pleasure to the listener.

THE EARLY EXPANDED FUGUE

The works of Archangelo Corelli are the first that exploit the formal possibilities inherent in the new tonal system. Significantly, it is in his fugal movements that their use is first ordered, for they are based on a single short theme, and some means of expansion must be found if they are not to consist of continual restatements of the theme. Two distinct ways of extension are evident—the episodes mentioned above and the extension of a fugal exposition or statement of the theme by a combination of a melodic and polyphonic spinning-out of the parts and harmonic movement and sequence.

The second of these appeared first. The idea of continual movement was not new, but, in earlier music, it was achieved by a combination of avoided cadences and continual polyphonic movement. It was the forward harmonic motion of the new tonality, spurred on by deceptive cadences, dissonances (such as suspensions and seventh chords), sequences, and modulations, that gave these extensions a new effect. In these tonal forms, as in the modal ones, cadences are still the main points of articulation, but they become points of arrival as well—temporary stops of harmonic motion that are felt more strongly because of the continual harmonic drive leading up to them.

The second movement of Corelli's *Sonata da chiesa à 3* in E minor, Op. 3, No. 7[44] (reproduced in *MM*, No. 39) shows this formal principle applied in fugue. The movement has four sections, each starting with a fugal statement of the subject, beginning in measures 1, 14, 21, and 25. The first section, which includes a regular exposition, ends with a half cadence in measure 14. All the others end in a perfect authentic cadence in a different key from that in which they began. The cadences function as arrival points but do not control the keys in which the next sections begin, so that the movement (thirty-five measures long) has the following tonal pattern:

$$e\text{–}V; \ b\text{–}G; \ e\text{–}a; \ a\text{–}e.$$

Although each section begins fugally with the theme in at least two parts, only in the exposition does the theme appear as a whole. The other sections start with truncated versions that spin on melodically in new extensions. The tonal form and the thematic form coincide. With x indicating the theme, the thematic form can be expressed as x–ext., x'–ext., and so on, each new section beginning with some form of x.

This movement shows, in embryo, one of the main ways of expanding a fugue in the late Baroque period. It is particularly characteristic of those movements of sonatas, concertos, suites, and choral works that start with fugal expositions. Few of these exploit such scholarly contrapuntal devices as stretto, augmentation, diminution, inversion, and the like, and most of them use more variants and truncated forms of the theme than the more self-conscious keyboard fugues. Fugue is used as a formal device rather than for its own sake. In later works, the extensions are much longer than are those in the Corelli sonata, often including fragments of the theme in imitation and extra entries of the theme itself. The second movement of the Trio Sonata, Op. 3, No. 2 (*HAM*, II, No. 269) by Evaristo Felice dall'Abaco (1675–1742) is a nice example of this type of fugue.

This type of extension is often found in the expanded type of fugue that stresses interpolated episodes, the extension being used to round off an exposition or a restatement of the theme. But it is the episodes that give these fugues their particular character. Corelli first used episodes in this way in fugue in his *Sonate da chiesa* Op. 5 for Violin and Continuo; and the second movement of the sonata Op.

5, No. 3[45] (*HAM,* II, No. 252) is a fine example of this. The fugue has three voices, the solo violin playing two of them and the continuo bass, the third. The tonal outline is similar to that of the trio sonata (see p. 243), but the thematic structure differs:

$$\text{C–G*–a; a–C*–e; C–G*–(C: V}^7 \text{ dominant pedal) C.}$$

As in the tonal outline of the trio sonata, those sections that begin with a statement of the theme following a cadence are preceded by a semicolon. The key indicated before the semicolon shows the key in which the preceding section ends and the key shown after the semicolon indicates the key in which the theme is restated. The asterisks indicate episodes, sections that do not start with the theme. Only one key is given at these places because the episodes are taken as starting in the key on which the cadence ends. (The dominant-seventh chord and the dominant pedal are in parenthesis because they appear in the midst of an episode, not being preceded by a cadence.)

Here, each section, whether it is the continuation of the exposition, the continuation of a restatement, or an episode, fulfills a similar tonal function—starting in one key and ending in another. Both this movement and the movement from the trio sonata return to the tonic briefly in the midst of the movement—a common practice in the Baroque fugue—and both stick to related keys. In contrast to the trio sonata, however, the tonal and cadence structure of this sonata does not coincide with the thematic structure. Beside the opening exposition, only two sections start with the theme, and otherwise it appears only in the bass in the middle of the final episode (m. 35) and in a truncated form in the bass at the end of the other episodes. The episodes have a different thematic use. The first and third (in the outline, the two G*'s, starting in m. 10 and 31) are developmental and diversionary, using fragments of the theme. The middle episode (in the outline, C*, starting in m. 21) is a complete contrast, using free figuration designed as technical display for the soloist.

The use of harmonic sequence in these episodes and extensions is twofold. The modulating sequence and the tonal sequence (which stays within a key) each have a special function in a tonal form. The modulating sequence, by continually changing key, gives a feeling of tonal unrest and forward movement that must be resolved by settling into a key. The tonal sequence serves to establish a key, although it is not fully established until it arrives at an authentic cadence.

Example 82 shows measures 10–20 of the Corelli violin sonata, starting with the first cadence in the key outline, in G, which formalizes the end of the exposition. Immediately following this cadence

EXAMPLE 82

SECOND MOVEMENT OF THE SONATA FOR VIOLIN AND
CONTINUO, OP. 5, No. 3, ARCHANGELO CORELLI.

comes a modulating sequence, the progression V–I in F, G and a.
Arriving at a, and using a chromatically descending tetrachord in the
bass (over which the top has only two sequences), Corelli arrives at
the authentic cadence in a in measure 14. The next section starts with

a restatement of the subject in a, but, by measure 16, Corelli has returned to C and an extension by a tonal sequence in C using seventh chords settles firmly in C with the strong cadence in measure 20.

During the eighteenth century, the sequential episode came into common use. One of its most practical applications was found in the solo concerto and the concerto grosso, where long episodes made up of chains of sequences function as modulatory passages between statements of the main theme by the orchestra, serving at the same time as a vehicle for the exhibition of technical skill in virtuoso passages and as a development of musical ideas. The last movement of the Solo Concerto, Op. 8, No. 8 by Giuseppe Torelli (*ca.* 1650–1708) illustrates an early use of this formal device (*HAM*, II, No. 246). This movement also illustrates a rather relaxed use of fugal imitation in the two upper parts. The first movement of the Concerto Grosso, Op. 3, No. 8 of Antonio Vivaldi (*ca.* 1680–1743) shows a later, more sophisticated usage (*HAM*, II, No. 270).[47] Sequential episodes are found at times in such other media and forms as sonata and suite movements—they are, in fact, a typical late-Baroque device—and their use in the expanded fugue simply corresponds to their use in other expanded tonal forms.

The developmental character of these episodes is one of their most interesting aspects. It is not the type of development found in the late eighteenth- and nineteenth-century homophonic forms, but a more static type. The developmental process usually comes into play in the choice of material to be used for an episode and in its contrapuntal combination. This material comes most often from the subject and countersubject. Short motives from these are selected, often altered slightly in their melodic or rhythmic contours, and combined contrapuntally so that they fit into a strong harmonic progression. Example 83 shows how Handel derived the material for the episodes in the Fugue in G Major from *Six Fugues or Voluntarys* published in London in 1735. The sources of his material are the subject and countersubject (shown here as they appear in the second entry in the exposition, answer with countersubject). Excerpts (a), (b), and (c) are taken from different episodes in the fugue where they act as a basic unit used in sequence. Brackets in the answer and countersubject show the motives used.

Although this type of development does not have the intellectual or dramatic interest of that of a Classical sonata form, it acts as a pleasant diversion, and the extraction of motives from the exposition for these episodes results in an integrated, expanded form for the fugue. At times, composers used these episodes for a lesser display of

EXAMPLE 83

THEME AND COUNTERSUBJECT, WITH EPISODIC MATE-
RIAL DERIVED FROM THEM, FROM THE FUGUE IN G MA-
JOR, *Six Fugues or Voluntarys,* G. F. HANDEL.

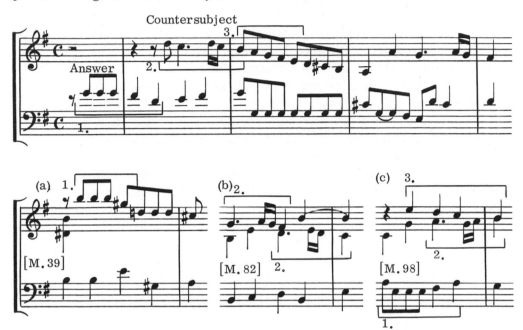

contrapuntal technique, using imitation or invertible counterpoint as
well as sequence in their construction.

ANALYSIS OF THE EXPANDED FUGUE

The only formal pattern rigidly prescribed for these fugues is the
tonal one—beginning and ending clearly in the tonic key and modulating in the middle to related keys. No fixed order was given for the
appearance of these related keys, and, in fugues more than in other
forms of this time, there is often a return to the tonic key between
modulations, expressed by the restatement of the subject in the tonic
key rather than by a cadence. In addition to the tonal structure, there
are certain conventional restrictions on the contrapuntal placement
of the statements of the theme. By the eighteenth century, the exposition was conventionalized, and a special rule governed the placement of subsequent entries of the theme as well; no entry should come
in in the voice that carries the immediately preceding statement of
the theme. It was also considered appropriate to spread out the entries

among the parts so that each part would have approximately the same number of entries.

There was thus much freedom allowed the composer in the area of form—in the number of restatements, the keys used, the placement and relative strength of cadences, the number and make-up of episodes—in fact, in the aspects of form that are most obvious to the average listener. There could be a single restatement of the theme in one key or a whole series of entries in that key, and scholarly devices such as stretto, canon, inversion, augmentation, and diminution could be used in any of these restatements as well as freer techniques of variation. There was as yet no conventional ordering of the placement of these devices when they were used. Another formal technique, the repetition of sections later in a movement, was also used without any regulation other than the composer's taste.

Most fugues of the eighteenth century and much more sophisticated and complex in detail than those by Corelli. The Corelli fugues discussed above have real answers, and the tonal complications involved in the restatement of various answer forms do not arise. His movements are relatively short and involve few key changes and not many restatements or long episodes. His cadences are nearly all perfect authentic cadences, easily picked out. But the expanded fugues of J. S. Bach, Handel, and their contemporaries are much more complex and require analysis on several different levels.

Aside from their inherent musical worth—something that has not yet been defined by analytical techniques—the fugues of J. S. Bach have always been valued for their individuality. One of the most striking ways in which his fugues differ one from another is in the details of form. Table III attempts to show the patterns made by the different formal elements in one of his fugues, the F-sharp Major Fugue from the first volume of the *Well-Tempered Clavier*. Although the answer in this fugue has a tonally adjusted beginning, only the subject form of the theme is used in the restatements, so that one complication is avoided. Other formal devices, however, make it an interesting work to study.

The top line of the table indicates the measures. The second line shows the most important cadences and, thus, the keys established at the major points of arrival in the form. These cadences are clearly the most important ones, being perfect authentic cadences with some type of melodic ornamentation, a suspension or trill, to make them noticeable. Each is also further emphasized by dropping out one part after the cadence is accomplished.

In the third line, three half cadences are indicated. These are not

TABLE III

Structure of Fugue in F-sharp Major from Bach's
Well-Tempered Clavier, Book I

	1	3	5	7	11	15	17	20	23	28	31	35
Measures	1	3	5	7	11	15	17	20	23	28	31	35
Strongest Cadences					C#;F#							F#
Less Strong Cadences						C#;#C (½)		d#;d# (½)			F#;F# (½)	
Weak Cadences				F#*			C#*		d#*	F#;B		
Keys of Subject Entries	F#	C#	F#		F#	C#		d#		B	F#	
Polyphonic Structure	S	Cs	A		Cs Ep	Cs Ep S	Ep	Cs	Ep	S	S Ep	(Coda)
			Cs Ep	X	(Cs)	(Cs)		(Cs)		(Cs)	Cs	
	S		S		S	S		S		S	S	
Repeated Sections				X	Y		Z′			Y′	X	
				Z								

Cadences authentic except where "½" indicates half-cadence.
S = Subject
A = Answer
Cs = Countersubject 1
(Cs) = Countersubject 2
Ep = Episode
* = cadences followed by episode

strong arrival points like the cadences in the second line, but they have strong preparation, are emphasized by dropping out one part directly after the cadence, and each precedes a restatement of the subject. On the fourth line, there are two weaker authentic cadences with the root of the final chord in the bass, but the third of the chord is in the top voice, and there is no dropping-out of parts or rhythmic break at these points. Each, however, articulates an important point in the thematic structure. The first signals the end of the exposition and the second the entrance of a restatement of the subject.

The main cadences outline the tonal form of the fugue, and, in analyzing a fugue, the relative significance of cadences must be taken into consideration. There are often many places in a fugue of this period where the dominant chord is followed by a tonic chord, so that rhythmic placement and pauses, changes of texture, melodic ornamentation, and the like, must be taken into consideration. Generally, a perfect authentic cadence is clearly placed and prepared and is the most important cadence form in articulating the key scheme. It is the lesser cadences that are difficult to categorize at times, and there may well be a difference of opinion in these cases. Many fugue subjects end with a clear melodic cadence (as does this one), and this gives the effect of a cadence at the end of each melodic statement, but these are not necessarily important formally. Only the first cadence in the fourth line of this diagram is one that ends a section as well as a theme statement. As in fugues of earlier periods, a complete break after a cadence is not found unless there is a complete end to a part of a sectional fugue, such as the C minor Fugue from the second book of the *Well-Tempered Clavier*. In most cases, however, important cadences are marked by some rhythmic break in the movement combined with melodic ornamentation, as seen in this fugue.

As in earlier diagrams, those cadences that are followed by an entry of the subject are indicated by a semicolon following the designation of the cadence. The key listed after a semicolon is the key in which this restatement of the subject occurs and the keys in which they stand melodically are shown in the fifth line of the diagram. Here, as in the Corelli fugues, these entries are not necessarily in the key that the cadence establishes before their entries, and, in one case, the key of the next cadence following the entry also differs from the key in which the restatement of the subject appears. Thus, the key scheme of the over-all form indicated by cadences is not the same as the order of keys in which the restatements appear melodically. In this fugue, the subjects are always harmonized in the key in which they appear melodically, so there is no further complexity involved.

One of the particular details in the construction of this fugue is the introduction of new thematic material after the exposition (m. 7) that is used later in the episodes and also forms the basis of a second countersubject. This fugue has a regular countersubject, and, on the sixth line of the table, countersubject 1 and countersubject 2 are shown as they appear in the three voices of the fugue. Example 84a shows the regular countersubject against the subject in the last entry of the exposition (accompanied by a free part) and the new episodic material that immediately follows it. Example 84b shows the subject and the first countersubject with the addition of the second countersubject as it appears in the first restatement section in measures 11–13. As the diagram shows, this second countersubject re-enters later against the entries of the subject in D-sharp minor (m. 20) and B major (m. 28).

Widely separated repetition of sections also give this fugue its particular formal shape. The new material introduced in measure 7 reappears at the end of the fugue, starting on the third beat in measure 33, to make a short codetta. This is shown in the seventh line of the table, this section being labeled X. Bach's re-use of this new material is characteristic of his formal procedure; new ideas are never abandoned, but are re-used significantly in the form. This economy of ideas was one of the things that later generations so admired in his work.

Another section of the fugue, a longer one, is repeated later with only slight variations. This is shown in the table on the seventh line, indicated by the letters Y and Y'. It includes the entire section from the restatement of the subject in F-sharp starting in measure 11 through the cadence in C-sharp in measure 17, a section that also includes a second restatement of the subject in C-sharp starting in measure 15. The same material recurs in measures 28–33 but transposed down a fifth (in some parts, up a fourth) so that the entry in measure 28 is now in B and the entry in measure 31 is in F-sharp, the tonic key.

There is some contrapuntal rearrangement of the material, although the section is not inverted strictly in the manner of conventional invertible counterpoint. What was in the top part in Y is in the middle in Y'. The regular countersubject that appears in the middle voice in Y is omitted in Y'. A free part with a subdominant pedal is substituted for it in the bass in measures 28 and 29, and then the soprano in measures 30–33 carries what the middle voice had carried in measures 14–16. A similar split is found in the treatment of the bass part from Y. The material from the second beat of meas-

EXAMPLE 84

FUGUE IN F-SHARP MAJOR FROM *The Well-Tempered Clavier,* Book I, J. S. BACH.

(a.)

[M.5]

Countersubject I.

Subject

(b.)

Subject

[M.11]

Counter-subject I.

Countersubject II

[252]

ure 12 to the first beat in measure 13 (the second countersubject) appears in the soprano in Y′, from the fourth beat of measure 28 to the beginning of measure 30. From this point on, the bass in Y′ is the same as the bass in Y.

A third re-use of material is the transposition of the episode starting in measure 8; this is found starting in measure 18, Z and Z′ at the bottom of the table. This type of re-use of episodes is quite common in fugues of this period and is often found coupled with the use of invertible counterpoint, so that the later uses of the episode may be contrapuntally rearranged in the manner of Y′. The material for episode Y combines a figure based on the material introduced in measure 7 and the head of the subject of the fugue. Although the other episodes are not exactly the same as Z, they derive their material from the same two motives, providing further unity to the fugue. The other episodes, by using new forms of this material, also provide further development of these two motives to please the listener.

The asterisks in the second and fourth lines of Table III show that, after these cadences, an episode begins. The episode that starts on the D-sharp minor cadence (m. 23; see Ex. 85b below) has two distinct parts, each based on a different figuration but without a cadence break between them. If one is analyzing by musical content he may prefer to count this as two episodes, but, since there is no cadence between them, there is no structural break separating the two sequences. Similar changes of figuration within an episode are common in pieces with extended episodes like the Baroque concerto.

The section beginning in measure 7 has likewise been treated as a single episode since it is found between two cadences. Within it are found several small divisions. Measure 7 serves to introduce new material, the sequential pattern does not start until the third beat of measure 8, and, from measure 10 on, there is a simple extension leading to the cadence in measure 11. Certainly, in studying and analyzing such a fugue, one should be aware of these differences in material, and they may well be indicated in further diagrams if the student feels these to be a help in visualizing the structure of the fugue. Yet, the whole section does stand as an episode between two entries of the subject.

The question of terminology arises in regard to very short episodes like those found in the exposition of a fugue, which may be as short as one measure and may not even be sequential. These are normally called episodes because they do not state the subject and are transitional in character. There is one of these in the exposition of the Corelli violin sonata that was not shown on the diagram of the tonal sections of the form because it was such a small detail within the exposition.

There is no such episode in the exposition of this F-sharp Major Fugue, but there is a short episode from the third beat of measure 13 to the beginning of measure 15 that serves as a transition between the restatements of the subject beginning in measures 11 and 15, modulating from F-sharp to C-sharp. It reappears, beginning in measure 30, in the transposed repetition of this section. This again is not shown in the table because it comes within a clear formal division of the fugue. This type of transitional episode is often used within a section that includes more than one restatement of the theme, and its presence should be noted.

When the analysis gets down to small details, the diagrams involved may be so complex that they are no aid in visualizing the over-all form of the fugue, although the process of making them is certainly an aid to perceiving these details. Once the large sections of a fugue have been picked out, the best way to discover and record the smaller details is to mark them on the score of the fugue using different colors to make the patterns visible. This should include a complete analysis of the harmony, the temporary key changes, and the motives used in the free parts, as well as the sources of the material used in the episodes.

HARMONIC STRUCTURE OF THE EPISODE

The analysis of the large episodes that constitute a section in themselves requires some discussion. These episodes should not be confused functionally with the sonata-form bridge. In some cases, they do start in one key and move to another in which the next restatement will occur. But in other cases, as we have seen, they may cadence in a firmly established new key only to be followed by an entry of the subject in the original key or in some other key related to the one in which the episode ends. Very often, the episode will arrive at the new key at the beginning of or even before the sequence starts. Then the sequence may be a tonal one, serving only to further establish the key. On the other hand, the sequence may start in the new key, move away from it, and return to it again at the end of the episode. Sometimes, it is only the short one- or two-measure transitional episodes between entries that move directly from one key to another. These latter are the kind of episodes that occur in the short fugues that were written earlier than the expanded fugue. The larger episodes in the expanded fugue are often more diversionary and developmental than they are modulatory in function.

The technical process involved in making a sequential episode will be described in the next chapter, but in a study fugue the structure of the episode is often simplified and more directed than the episodes in a Baroque fugue, and the examination of a few episodes from the fugues of Bach will be an aid to the analysis of Baroque episodes. The melodic and polyphonic construction of these episodes shows much variety, but harmonically they fit into three main types of sequence. There are those that move through a series of keys in a modulating sequence (sometimes called a "real" sequence; see Ex. 85a); there are those in which the new key appears at the beginning so that the sequence is wholly tonal (Ex. 85b); and those that combine the modulating and tonal sequence (Ex. 85c).

Example 85a (from the C Minor Fugue of Book I of the *Well-Tempered Clavier*) is a very simple type of episode in that it starts at the close of the subject and modulates steadily, leading directly into an entry of the theme in a new key. The inner construction of this sequence is, however, on two levels. An exact sequence in all parts is found only in one-measure units (shown above the example), but the harmonic sequence goes by half-measure units (indicated below the example). When a few notes are removed (the notes circled in the example), a unit of a half measure coincident with the harmony is revealed in the bass. The upper parts fit into this second pattern as well, although this is partly disguised by the fact that the melodic unit is put into overlapping imitation. The upper parts are shortened at the beginning and end of the episode because they must fit into the material preceding and following the sequence.

Example 85b is from the F-sharp Major Fugue. It immediately follows the cadence in D-sharp minor that ends the preceding section, where the tonic triad in D-sharp minor is taken as a pivot chord, becoming vi in F-sharp major, and a tonal sequence in F-sharp follows. Its structure appears to be like that of the sequence in 85a, but it is not. The full measure is the unit in the sequence because, although the harmonic pattern fits into a half-measure unit, the melodic patterns do not.

In measure 25, a half-cadence is approached, but an ending is evaded by a suspended D-sharp and an unusual deceptive resolution, so that the last chord in the measure is ii^7 in B major. This leads into a new sequence with a different figuration of half-measure units. The harmonic movement from one unit of the sequence to the next differs also; harmonically it moves downward by fifths (as does the sequence

EXAMPLE 85

EPISODES FROM THE *Well-Tempered Clavier,* Book I,
J. S. BACH.

in Ex. 85a), but the melodic unit moves down by step. It starts on V^7 in B, but, by the third beat of measure 26, the sequence is already back in F-sharp; a tonal sequence follows cadencing in F-sharp in measure 28, only to be followed immediately by an entry of the subject in the key of B major! (See Table III).

Example 85c, from the D Minor Fugue, is an episode in which the sequence is in part modulating and in part tonal, as the harmonic analysis shows. Here the unit is a measure long, crossing over the bar line. The harmony within the unit is strong, including the downward movement of a fifth over the bar. The entire unit, like the second sequence in 85b, moves down by step. By measure 33, when the sequence is over, it has just reached vii^0 in F major, which must be treated as a pivot chord—ii^0 in the key of D minor—to get to this key which is finally established by a cadence in the next measure.

Both Examples 85b and 85c show episodes that are used primarily for development and for a relief from continual statement of the theme. The modulation in Example 85b could have been accomplished in a very short time. That in Example 85c is scarcely necessary for, although it arrives at D minor in measure 34 (not shown in Ex. 85c), by the second beat of that same measure, the V^7 in G minor has appeared, and this is the same chord that appears in measure 30, at the beginning of the sequence.

OTHER FORMAL PROCEDURES USED IN
FUGUES OF THIS TIME

The F-sharp Major Fugue was chosen as an illustration because it shows so many aspects of the structure of the expanded fugue, but no single fugue includes all the procedures found in the late Baroque fugue. Each has its peculiar problems, and, although this means that no rigid analytical process can be applied to all fugues, it also provides an impetus to analysis, for each fugue becomes a special problem in itself. There is also plenty of room for disagreement among analysts.[48]

Formal procedures not shown in the above fugue can be readily found in the other fugues of the first book of the *Well-Tempered Clavier.* One already pointed out in the Corelli sonatas is the extension of a section after its main structural purpose has been achieved. In the F-sharp Major fugue of Bach, this happens in the first episode where, after the sequence is finished in measure 10, there is a free extension leading to the cadence in measure 11. The Fugue in G Minor has such an extension in the exposition section where the cadence following the end of the last entry in measure 8 is not resolved, and an extension follows that finally cadences on the third beat of measure 10.

Some fugues have no strongly marked cadences but have a series of less final cadences coinciding exactly with the thematic form. This is true of the C Minor Fugue. Here, a listing of cadences on different levels like that given in Table III cannot be made, and the form may well be analyzed as a series of alternating thematic statements and episodes each ending with a cadence in some key. The same is true of the B Minor Fugue. Here, the cadences are clearly approached but weakened in effect by the use of suspensions with delayed ornamental resolutions. Yet, the thematic character of the sections, as well as the key pattern, is clear. In both of these fugues, however, even though a simple diagram of sections and keys will outline the basic structure, there is re-use and varied repetition of episodes, and this imposes important secondary thematic patterns on the fugue.

The B Minor Fugue has the added complication of strettos in the restatements, and when strettos are used they should be shown in the analysis—not only their occurrence, but also the time and pitch intervals at which they take place. This can best be done by a graphic representation like that showing the arrangement of the entries as they occur in the different voices in Table IV. In some fugues, there is stretto in almost every restatement of the subject, and these often do not have any large episodes, the free material used being found in extensions spinning out from the strettos. In the C Major Fugue, there is almost continual stretto, and the modulations take place within the strettos themselves. Clear cadences make the points of tonal arrival clear, but the inner modulations—taking place within the stretto rather than in sequential episodes—should be analyzed.

Modulations taking place within a modulating subject or answer should likewise be included in the diagram or description of a tonal pattern. The C Minor, E-flat Major, and G-sharp Minor Fugues provide nice examples of this. A fugue like the D-sharp Minor Fugue (some editions give it in E-flat minor) has—in addition to complex strettos involving inversions, augmentations, and modulations—a great many melodic variations of the subject. In analyzing a fugue like this one, a diagram complete enough to show details beyond the basic tonal form implied by the cadences would be so complex as to defeat its purpose. The best way to map an analysis of such a fugue is to make the analysis directly on the score.

The problem that comes up most often in fugal analysis, deciding how to define sections, has no ready answer. Contemporaneous theorists give little help in this. German theorists mentioned the presence of episodes but did not describe them in detail since they were only concerned with such formal elements as key scheme and apportioning of the entries among the parts. Nor, as a matter of fact, were the episodic sections discussed in relation to the concerto or the sonata. The consideration of form by theorists came into prominence only in the second half of the century.

Only two theorists of the next generation depended at all on J. S. Bach in their discussion of fugue—Marpurg and A. F. C. Kollman. Kollman, a German organist, composer, and teacher who settled in London, was schooled in the conservative German musical tradition and was one of the first to suggest bringing out an edition of Bach's *Well-Tempered Clavier* there. His book, *An Essay in Practical Musical Composition,* which appeared in 1799, shows a definite dependence on Marpurg in the discussion of fugue,[49] but it is clearer and more precise in its approach and is a help in clarifying Marpurg's ideas.

Both considered the fugue to be built of a series of sections. The main element in each section is what Marpurg called the *Durch-führung*[50] and what Kollman described as "a *connected introduction* of the Subject and Answer in different parts; with the Intermediate Harmony that belongs to it."[51] This intermediate harmony is what Marpurg calls *Zwischenharmonie* or *Zwischensatz,* German terms already used by other theorists to describe what we call episodes. Kollman made explicit what Marpurg indicated in his examples and their analyses—that the episodes are short, that they are normally the continuation of a *Durchführung* (an extension in our terms) and not the independent kind of episode found in the expanded fugue of Bach and his contemporaries, and that the two together constitute one inclusive section of the fugue, although the possibility of starting a section with an episode is mentioned.[52] The examples that they chose[53] are fugues of this type—a series of sections each including entries of the theme and an extension moving to a cadence in a new key. In our analysis of these expanded fugues, we must then rely on such things as cadences and the musical character of the sections in our decisions. In many fugues of Bach and his contemporaries, the episodes are not only stressed as part of the form, but also they sometimes provide climactic effects not found in sections restating the theme.

SUGGESTED ANALYSES

If the student has had no experience in analyzing the tonal structure of Baroque music, it may be to his advantage to make a few such analyses—the key scheme plus the cadence points of arrival—of some nonfugal works of the early eighteenth century, such as concerto movements, suite movements, or arias. Here, he can learn to follow the tonal structure of Baroque forms without the added complications of fugal structure. The analysis of fugues from the *Well-Tempered Clavier* is traditional in the study of fugue and for good reason. Those in the first book are recommended, particularly the ones mentioned above for the study of specific structural procedures. The D Minor Fugue in this book is suggested as a good exercise in formal analysis, since it combines most of the complications picked out singly in other fugues mentioned above. Once several of these Bach fugues have been mastered, any fugue of his period should provide food for thought. A list is given in Appendix I.

In working with accompanied vocal fugues, the student should first of all discover if the instrumental accompaniment merely doubles the vocal parts, adds another real part to the fugue, or merely provides free accompaniment to it.

Italian keyboard fugues of the period using the expanded form make a nice foil for the fugues of Bach and of his German contemporaries. Often, they lack the clear voice-leading and scholarly devices found in German fugues, leaning strongly toward the concerto in style and formal procedures. Nevertheless, they were considered legitimate fugues in their time, and the analysis of one or two of them is a broadening experience for those who have been brought up on fugues written in the German tradition. The fugues of Francesco Durante (1684–1755) are recommended for this purpose.[54]

The Classical and Romantic Periods: Theory

After the mid-eighteenth century, theory assumed more importance in the development of fugue form even though the relation of theory and practice in the realm of fugue became more artificial. During the later years of Bach and Handel, polyphony gave way to the new homophonic style. Of all the old polyphonic ways of composing, only fugue survived as an important composition technique. Most genres, such as the concerto and sonata, took on the new style, abandoning old forms. Fugue, being inherently polyphonic, could not do this, and many techniques that were basically Baroque survived thereafter only in fugue. At the same time, the number of fugues produced by major composers was very small compared to their total output; and these composers were not such masters of fugue that they could teach it. Also, although the fugues written by Baroque composers were available, they were not a part of the concert repertoire before the self-conscious restorations of mid-nineteenth century. Composers who wanted to write fugues had to learn the technique from textbooks or from pedagogues. There was no longer a wide musical background of frequently heard fugues to help them to musically assimilate this knowledge. Thus, although the examples of fugue given by the theorists are rarely related to those found in contemporary practice, a knowledge of the formal principles the composers imbibed in their study is a helpful background for an understanding of the fugue forms found in these periods.

Historians complain that fugue form was discussed by theorists only after most of the fugues had been written, but this statement, although true, is misleading. It must be qualified by adding that form was not the subject of much theoretical rationalization before the late eighteenth and nineteenth centuries. Theories of melodic construction in relation to form had barely gotten their start by the late seventeenth century,[55] but, as we have seen, what fixed principles of tonal form existed—first in the modes and then in major–minor—had been discussed by theorists from the mid-sixteenth century.

[261]

Fugue actually received more attention during this time because of its relation to tonal form, and, when in the early eighteenth century the expansion of a fugue exposition into a long movement became important, fugue certainly received more theoretical notice than did other forms such as the suite, concerto, and variation. Those elements of fugal structure that were subject to theoretical scrutiny—the subject and the form of the answer, the order and spacing of the opening entries, the transposition of the theme in restatements, and the construction of inversions, strettos, and the like—were discussed in most books concerned with the art of composition. Formal devices characteristic of all tonal forms—cadences, modulations, and order of and establishment of keys—were also described. Elements that were not yet fixed—the structure of episodes, the exact placement of such devices as stretto, and the best order of modulation—were naturally not yet subject to theoretical pronouncements. Theorists of the late eighteenth century succeeded in fixing the place of the stretto, but fixed forms for the fugue were not formulated until the second quarter of the nineteenth century when fugue writing became a part of the conservatory curriculum. It is interesting to note that the same pedantic approach to form is first found in the teaching of homophonic forms around this same time.

When Marpurg wrote his treatise on fugue in mid-eighteenth century, he did not define a "regular" fugue by its form, but by the proper use of what he considered the five essentials of fugue: (1) the subject, (2) the answer, (3) the order of their entrances, (4) the free countermelodies in the other parts against the subject and answer, and (5) the intermediate harmonies (episodes).[56] At the end of the century, Kollman added two more essential elements—sections, which included restatements of the theme, and modulations.[57] Marpurg certainly described these sections and modulations, but as the extension, the *Verfolg,* of the fugue.[58] German theorists and lexicographers of the nineteenth century followed Marpurg in listing five fundamental elements that excluded form, but, although the list of essential ingredients varied, a common variant omitted Marpurg's third item (since by then the order of the exposition was taken for granted) and gave instead: (3) countersubject, (4) episodes, and (5) stretto; they also gave more dogmatic instructions with regard to form.

Kollman not only insisted on sections as a necessary part of form, but also prescribed their ideal content.[59] For him, a "proper" fugue should have no less than three and no more than six sections. The first, of course, is what we call the exposition. The second may stay in the tonic or dominant keys or be divided between the closest related keys and should end in one of the nearest related keys. The final section should be in the main key, in some cases beginning in the subdominant, and it is in this section that the closest stretto appears as well as canonic treatment of the subject or skilled imitations of fragments of the subject. If there are more than three sections, the others should follow a well-ordered progression of keys, and the stretto section should come last, followed by a free coda or cadenza. Only at the end would there be a full cadence.

THE INFLUENCE OF JOHANN JOSEPH FUX

Although Kollman's treatment of fugue shows familiarity with the fugues of Bach and Handel and was primarily based upon Marpurg's work, it also shows the indirect influence of Fux. It is Fux who was the dominant influence on fugal theory of the Classical period. His *Gradus ad Parnassum* is not only a practical pedagogical method for the teaching of counterpoint (see p. 144), but it also proceeds step by step from the simplest contrapuntal exercises to the writing of a four-part fugue. This was doubtless the cause of its success. It was soon translated from the original Latin (1725) into German (1742), Italian (1761), French (1773), and English (1791), and it went through many editions.

The contrapuntal style that Fux taught was archaic—neo-Palestrina—and the fugue forms that he gave were incredibly simple in construction.[60] Most probably, it was this simplicity of form that made them such a pedagogical success, since, until this time, no method had ever been published showing exactly how to construct a simple study fugue, that is, how to solve the elementary problems of fugal form.

Based on the sixteenth-century ideal, each fugue is in a mode; it does not modulate from that mode, uses no transpositions, and the inner cadences are on the regular cadence tones allowed within that mode. All of the fugues are in three sections, each of which begins with a full exposition of the subject and answer involving all the voices of the fugue. The second and third sections involve stretto, the closest stretto starting the third section.[61] The whole is closely knit. There are no further restatements of the theme beyond those that begin each section, and, once the full exposition is accomplished, the parts move on to a cadence. The inner cadences (which appeared at the end of the first and second sections) are treated as avoided cadences or deceptive cadences, and their effect is further minimized because the entries of the next section overlap the cadence in the manner of inner cadences in sixteenth-century motets; but, in Fux's fugue, it is the same theme and not a new one that enters. A pause of at least half a measure anticipates each entry of the theme.

FORM IN NINETEENTH-CENTURY GERMAN THEORY

It was this three-section form, adjusted to the major–minor system, that became the basis of the exercises in fugal form given in nineteenth-century German composition texts. This three-section fugue should not be confused with the three-*part* fugue that gained ascendancy in German theory in the latter part of the century. In the miniature three-section fugue, each section is a simple *Durchführung,* a leading of the theme through the different parts. It is unfortunate that this term has no English equivalent, for it emphasizes the main fugal function of the "sections" of a fugue. To add to the confusion, the term *Durchführung,* which was used in German writings on fugue in the eighteenth and nineteenth centuries to denote what Kollman first called "sections," acquired another meaning in the nineteenth century when it was applied by German theorists to the development section of sonata form, a meaning that is still used. This further contributes to the misleading character of some translations of German writings on fugue, wherein the fugal use of *Durchführung* is translated by "development," a term that is misleading when applied to fugue.[62]

A series of German theorists—including J. G. Albrechtsberger (*Gründliche Anweisung zur Komposition,* 1790);[63] Joseph Preindl (*Weiner Tonschule,* 1827);[64] E. F. Richter (*Lehrbuch der Fuge,* 1859);[65] Ludwig Bussler (*Kontrapunkt und Fuge im freien (modernen) Tonsatz,* 1878);[66] and Solomon Jadassohn (*Kanon und Fuge,* 1884)[67]—used this short three-section form as the basis of academic fugue writing. For all of them, this constituted a basic minimum that had to be greatly extended if the fugue was to become a serious work of art.

Certain changes appear in the inner make-up of this school fugue. After Fux, it was calculated within the key system rather than in a mode. The first section is still what we call the exposition. The tonal function of the second varies from one teacher to another. For the students' first fugues, Richter did not allow any transposition of the subject and answer within the fugue, and this second section is also a counterexposition; the examples given by Albrechtsberger and Preindl also show this type of second section. (See Ex. 97.) By

Jadassohn's time, the second section was in the form of a counter-exposition if it was in the dominant, but, if in a minor fugue it was in the relative major, the subject started and was followed by the answer. He also allowed freer alternatives for entries of the theme. For all of them, the third section was the stretto.

The basic structure remained the same; each section begins with a full exposition of the theme in all parts and moves on to a cadence. This cadence is rarely given strong preparation and is further weakened by the use of inverted chords or a delayed resolution in one part. Albrechtsberger and Preindl, like Fux, included no formal episode in the section but cadenced soon after all parts had stated the theme. Richter and those who followed him had a short episode at the end of each of the first two sections, and these sections modulate to cadence in a new key. The first section normally cadences in the dominant, preparing for the statement of the answer that begins the second section. The second section may end in a closely related key, but theorists from Albrechtsberger on also suggested ending with a half cadence and a hold, so that the final section can start like an exposition of the theme, only now in stretto, thus giving emphasis to the stretto.

All of these theorists gave suggestions for expanding this simple fugue—suggestions that include extra entries of the theme in other keys—involving the theme in augmentation, diminution, inversion, retrograde, or perhaps a varied or curtailed version of the theme. Richter also described a free and fully developed fugue—the type he recommended for an actual composition—and gave as characteristic of this form a more developed order of modulations, long and independent interludes, and long, free codas. The latter two, he admitted are not characteristic of Bach (although long episodes do appear in some of the organ fugues), but he recommended the instrumental fugues of Mendelssohn and Schumann as good examples of fully developed fugues.

None of these teachers were dogmatically specific about the form of the larger fugue that they considered an art form. They were well aware that nonacademic fugues do not fall into any fixed pattern, an awareness that was due in part to the growing influence of the fugues of J. S. Bach, which began in the second quarter of the century. They recognized that Bach's fugues are remarkably varied in form, and they were therefore hesitant about prescribing a particular pattern for fugue. In the field of form, the German school fugue had a comfortable, unconfining connection with the fugue as used in actual practice. As Richter said, beyond the basic elements and techniques taught in the school fugue, the pedagogue could only give hints and suggestions to the young composer.

THE THREE-PART FUGUE FORM

During this same period, there was also a tendency among the Germans to consider musical form as a subject of theoretical rationalization and aesthetic judgment; this rested on the conviction that there exist ideal forms or prototypes that underly all satisfactory musical works. Fugue was admittedly more difficult than the homophonic forms to classify because its rhythmic continuity and the absence of pauses, strong cadences, and symmetrical phrase and period structure made it hard to justify a clear pattern of formal divisions. Only the conclusion of A. B. Marx (in the second volume of *Die Lehre von den musikalischen Komposition* published in 1842)— that all fugues could be divided into three distinct parts according to key—gained much acceptance.[68] Marx, starting with actual fugues rather than pedagogical methods, reasoned that, as the important moments in a fugue are the *Durchführungen* and as these appear so frequently, there can be no thematic basis for a formal pattern any more than there can be clear formal divisions according to rhythmic stops. The only pattern that he could find that fit all fugues was the one that is the basis of all forms based on key. This is a three-part action—the establishment of a key, the departure from that key, and the return to it.

The first part of his fugue form is the exposition of the fugue, the first *Durchführung* of the three-section school fugue. This exposition may at times include extra entries of the subject and answer, and the first part may also include a counterexposition. The second part is not the second *Durchführung* of the school fugue, but rather the whole series of *Durchführungen* and episodes that begin with the departure from the tonic key and end with the return to that key. The last part is, of course, the part of the fugue that follows the return to the tonic.

This makes a nice general pattern within which to arrange a fugue, but it raises questions when one gets down to precise analysis, the main question being the exact point at which one part ends and the next begins. According to Marx, the first section ends when the fugue starts to leave the main key, that is, with the last statement of the theme or with an episode following this that modulates to cadence in the dominant or the relative-major key. When the modulation starts, either before or after the cadence, the second part begins.

The third part begins with the return to the tonic key, perhaps with the dominant chord or a dominant pedal point. This part may also have more than one *Durchführung* that is normally in the tonic key but may also move temporarily into the subdominant key. This last part is likewise the best place for strettos, although they may also be used in the second part.

This three-part form appears to have had some effect on the school fugue, mainly in permitting the second section to be in relative keys such as Jadassohn suggests. Several theorists such as Edward Krüger (*System der Tonkunst,* 1866),[69] Hugo Riemann (*Grosse Kompositionslehre,* 1902)[70] and the English theorist Ebenezer Prout (*Fugue,* 1891)[71] made this ternary form the basis of their teaching.

Like many theoretical ideas that have a logical and aesthetic appeal, the three-part fugue form affected many fugues written in the last half of the century. Its influence is most obvious in those fugues where the three sections delineated by key are set off clearly by audible means such as strong cadences or clear changes in texture, dynamics, or register or are separated by long episodes. Such fugues can be found among the works of J. G. Rheinberger (1839–1901) and Max Reger (1873–1916). The final fugue from the *Variations and Fugue on a Theme by Handel* of Johannes Brahms is a successful fugue in this form. These fugues, with their three parts so clearly articulated, may differ from the form Marx described, wherein the exact points of division between the parts are hard to pin down, but this only presents another illustration of the generative power of theory when it stimulates the imagination of the composer.

The idea that all fugues are in ternary form had a very different effect when used as the basis for analysis, particularly the analysis of fugues written before Marx. Marx himself admitted that these sections were not always clear in the fugues of Bach, but later theorists who accepted the idea of ternary fugue form went to great effort to fit Bach's fugues into the form. Many nineteenth-century fugues do leave the tonic key after the exposition, modulate through a series of related keys, and then return emphatically to the tonic. But not all of them avoid returning to the tonic in the midst of these speculations. Many Baroque fugues—especially the short fugues written in the major–minor system—leave the tonic key rarely if at all. Some of them modulate to other keys in the episodes but always restate the subject and answer on the pitches on which they were first stated, and this, furthermore, is characteristic of the German school fugue. Even in the expanded fugue form of the late Baroque period, there may be one or more returns to the tonic key in the midst of sections restating the theme in different keys. A number of fugues by Bach and Handel return to the tonic key in the midst of modulating sections, and the same is true of many late eighteenth- and early nineteenth-century fugues. Mozart and Albrechtsberger both tended to return to the tonic several times in the midst of their instrumental fugues; in fact, early training in fugue following the procedures of Fux would tend to induce such a practice.

Because of this, analysts and historians working with the ternary fugue form as the basis of their analyses often have great difficulty making fugues fit within this pattern.[72] Ludwig Czackzkes lists four different analyses by theorists who have tried to fit the C Minor Fugue from the first book of Bach's *Well-Tempered Clavier* into this form.[73] Hugo Riemann divides it as follows (numbers indicate the number of measures in a section): 8, 13, 10; F. B. Busoni gives 8, 17, 6; W. Werker, 8, 17½, 5½; and Luigi Perrachio, 8, 11, 12.

The concept of ternary form can be useful in looking over some fugues written before it was articulated by Marx, but it is misleading to say, as some historians do, that a fugue is written in three-part form because it follows the tonal pattern outlined by Marx. For example, a fugue that several analysts have described as being in ternary form is the finale of the String Quartet, Op. 20, No. 5 by Joseph Haydn. In this fugue, once the composer leaves the tonic key, he does modulate through a series of other keys without return to the tonic until he settles firmly into it near the end. But the actual point of return comes in the midst of a continuous series of strettos. Some would say that the third section begins in measure 81 because measures 80–81 present a cadence in the tonic, F minor. However, in measure 81, the answer returns in the first violin, and this, naturally, modulates to the dominant, C minor. Others, therefore, prefer measure 89 as the start of the third section because here the subject enters (cello) in F minor.

Both of these analyses ignore the formal conventions of the fugue taught by Fux within which this fugue was written. According to this school, the final section starts with an exposition of the subject and answer in close stretto. This occurs in measure 112 and is emphasized by a half-cadence ending (over a dominant pedal) in measure 111. No matter how one analyzes the sections between the exposition and this half cadence, the *final* section begins here, and it is followed by a coda that begins in measure 161. This half-cadence, final stretto section and coda are conventional for this period; it was described by Albrechtsberger and Kollman and perpetuated by those German theorists who followed in the Fux tradition. Even if this traditional background is ignored, it must be admitted that the break in measure 111, reinforced by cadence, rhythmic pause, change in texture, and the start of a new stretto exposition, is as strong a formal articulation as one could find in a fugue, and it cannot be ignored.

ITALIAN THEORY AND THE FRENCH *Fugue d'École*

Beginning in the second quarter of the nineteenth century, the French also had a school fugue, but it differed strikingly from its German counterpart. It was not an embryo fugue intended to form the basis for a freer, expanded art fugue, but it was a complex and finished form meant to give the student his first introduction to the techniques of composition. Nor was there any theoretical concern about the existence of an ideal fugue form. According to Reicha, the fugue form is merely a convention and is not interesting in itself; it is the thematic material used that gives a fugue its character, and one could have fugal writing without the form.[74] The school fugue soon became a rigid form within which the student practiced definite composition techniques.

In regard to fugue form, nineteenth-century French theory was shaped by the Italian tradition that stemmed from the teaching of Padre Martini. Although Martini was an enthusiastic disciple of Fux, believing that the old modal style of vocal counterpoint is the true basis for polyphonic writing, his works are in the key system, and the one fugue that he gave as an example for the beginning composer is quite different in form from those given by Fux and his German followers.

Martini's fugal prototype is a tightly knit series of sections—each a full exposition in all parts of the subject and answer—articulated by passing cadences.[75] The example he gave is in a minor key, and it has an exposition, a counterexposition, and a full statement of subject and answer in the subdominant before he inserts an episode modulating to the submediant key. This episode was included partly to accomplish the modulation but also, according to Martini, to avoid the tedium of continual statements of the theme.

The subject and answer forms used in this new key were analyzed by Martini in a way that differs from later practice. Here, the subject is described as being on the sixth degree and the answer form on the third since they start on these notes in the scale of the tonic key. But to us they are simply the subject and answer forms as they both appear in the *key* of the sixth degree (in this case, in E-flat major, the fugue being in G minor). Later theorists who followed

Martini—Francesco Galeazzi (*Elementi Teorico-Pratici di Musica* 1796) and Angelo Morigi (*Trattado di Contrappunto Fugato* 1802) —did instruct the composer to go, at this point, into the *key* of the third *or* sixth degrees and to give the subject and answer forms in that key. This tendency to give equal stress to the keys of the sixth and third degrees in both major and minor shows a dependency on the old modal tradition as does also the use of the subdominant key at an early point in the fugue. By Morigi's time, a change was seen, and he suggested that it was preferable to keep the subdominant key until later in the fugue.[76]

After these modulations into the relative keys, Martini returned to the tonic, pausing on a half cadence. Then follows a close stretto exposition of the subject and answer in the tonic key. A short coda with a dominant pedal brings it to a close. Both Galeazzi and Morigi prescribed this same form, their only addition being the insertion of episodes between each series of entries. All use a regular counter-subject that appears throughout the fugue.

This same fugue form became the norm in French instruction books by the beginning of the nineteenth century and was the basis for the later *fugue d'école*. The first hints of the designation of this particular fugue form for pedagogical use come with Reicha's *Traité de haute composition* in 1824–1825 and Fétis' *Traité de la fugue* in 1824; with Reicha's pupil Colet, in 1837, the form became fixed, and the separation between the school fugue and free composition was recognized and accepted. Even Elwart, whose *Le contre-point et la fugue* (1840) attempted a more pratical approach, followed the structure of the school fugue in his examples, and Gedalge's expert *Traité de la fugue,* published at the beginning of the twentieth century, is merely a masterly and detailed exposition of this same form.

The fugue begins with a regular exposition followed by an episode and a counterexposition. In some cases, the counterexposition was considered optional; at any rate, from the time of Reicha, one statement each of answer and subject was considered sufficient for the counterexposition and for the restatements of the theme in other keys as well. After this, there came a series of alternating episodes and restatements of the theme in a fixed order of keys. This practice in modulation, without the necessity of inventing new and beautiful melodies, was considered one of the main purposes of the study of academic fugue.

The order of keys did not remain the same. Colet, who was the first to prescribe a fixed order, gave the following:

In a major key—the relative minor, the subdominant, then the supertonic or mediant;

In a minor key—the relative major, the dominant (minor), the subdominant or supertonic.

The order given by Gédalge reflects a general change in the priority of keys found in theory of the time. He also did not allow the use of the answer in the subdominant key, since this answer would be in the tonic key of the fugue making a return to that key before the proper time. His order is:

In a major key—the relative minor, the subject in the subdominant followed by a short transition, and the subject or answer in the supertonic;

In a minor key—the relative major, the subdominant followed by a short transition, and the subject or answer in the submediant key.

In both Colet and Gédalge, the restatements are followed by an episode leading up to a climactic dominant pedal, a pause, and a stretto exposition (in which each part must state the subject or answer preferably in the order of the opening exposition) in the tonic, and a final coda. This last section often includes more than one stretto, and may include strettos using inverted, augmented, or diminuted forms of the subject or answer. These fugues all use one or more countersubjects that appear in conjunction with the theme throughout the fugue, and these countersubjects may also be used in stretto in this section.

Form in Practical Composition in the Classical and Romantic Fugue

Fugal theory and practice during the late eighteenth and nineteenth centuries did not retain the simple interrelationship of the earlier periods, since at this time fugue was considered a traditional form with established rules. Composers either accepted the rules (with theory texts or pedagogues as their source) or rebelled against them as unrelated to "modern" music, the aesthetic of which stressed expression, imagination, and inspiration rather than musical erudition. Form was a new concern in the theory of fugue, but too few composers were actively interested in creating new forms based on fugue. What strongly based growth in fugue there was was concentrated in the Viennese composers of the late eighteenth and early nineteenth centuries, but the new and exciting ventures of Mozart, Beethoven, and Reicha in this direction did not find followers among the composers of the Romantic era. The rediscovery and romanticizing of J. S. Bach that took place in the second quarter of the century turned the attention of fugue composers like Felix Mendelssohn and Robert Schumann to the past, and movement toward an integration of fugue and nineteenth-century form lost its momentum. Theory and pedantry, consolidated in conservatory curricula, took as their task the preservation of fugal tradition.

The acknowledged separation between the school fugue and free composition meant that freely composed fugues are rarely found that follow the prescribed pattern of the school fugue. Nevertheless, the patterns of the school fugue present us with a better prototype for analyzing fugues of the Classical and Romantic periods than does a knowledge of the fugues of Bach. Even those composers who strove most earnestly to reconstitute the fugue of Bach produced fugues that are better understood by recourse to contemporary textbooks. Although the exact formal outlines given in these textbooks were rarely followed, a number of general characteristics involving form that are inherent in both the French and German school fugues are found in composed fugues of the time.

Stretto, for example, came to be considered an essential part of the fugue form, and its form and placement in the fugue was conventionalized. It was usually reserved for the end of the fugue, and if more strettos were used earlier these would appear in order of increasing closeness with the closest reserved for the final sections. The best stretto was considered to be a close one between the subject and answer. If this was not possible, other combinations such as two subjects at such other intervals as the second, third, or sixth could be used; but these latter were referred to by theorists such as Kollmann and Reicha as imitations rather than proper strettos. Distinction was also made between a stretto for effect—the subject being slightly changed in order to make the entries fit—and the canonic stretto in which the subject and answer remain unchanged.

Another element that became associated with the fugue was pedal, usually a long, sustained note in the bass that has its place near the end of the fugue; fragments of the theme in close imitation, canons, augmentation, diminution, and inversion of the theme are added above it, and freer dissonance treatment increases the excitement. In piano fugues, free virtuoso figuration and activation of the pedal tone add tension by noncontrapuntal means. (See Ex. 86.) Sometimes, as in the *fugue d'école,* the pedal on the dominant leads

EXAMPLE 86

PEDAL POINT WITH PIANO FIGURATION FROM THE FUGUE
IN D MAJOR, OP. 400, NO. 5, CARL CZERNY.

to the return to the tonic and the final stretto. At other times, the
tonic pedal is part of the final section or of the coda.

Not only in the stretto, but also in the various sections restating
the subject in different keys, there was a tendency to include both the
subject and answer forms in each *Durchführung*. There was also a
notable increase in the number of entries in each section. The use of
a counterexposition of at least two entries (answer and subject) became more general, as well as the inclusion of an extra entry of
subject or answer in the exposition itself.

The over-all key scheme likewise underwent certain changes, and
these are parallel to the growing freedom of key in the homophonic

forms. In general, fugue tended to be conservative compared to the other forms. In the last half of the eighteenth century, most composers stayed with the closely related keys, as did the composers of the Baroque period. Only C. P. E. Bach (1714–1782) was really adventurous in the use of distant keys for restatements of the theme; Beethoven was the first major composer to go to distant keys in his fugues. Those composers who followed him were freer and apparently chose their key spectrum according to their inclinations; the school fugue always remained conservative but theorists never sought to control the key schemes of long and involved fugues. Two main changes in the over-all key scheme that took place in the nineteenth century are the moving of the subdominant entries to the latter part of the fugue and the tendency to avoid returning to the tonic key in the sections between the exposition (or counterexposition) and the final return to the tonic. This tendency was strengthened in the second quarter of the century by the key pattern of the *fugue d'école* and by the proposed ternary fugue form of Marx, which was predicated on a middle part that modulated away from the tonic.

Despite the lack of episodes in the academic prototype of the Fux school, episodes were an accepted part of the fugue by this time. These episodes, however, differed from those of Bach, Handel, and their contemporaries, which were predominantly sequential even when they involved invertible counterpoint and imitation. Sequential episodes, when used in the Classical fugue, usually consisted of several different sequences loosely strung together. (See Ex. 87a.) Episodes were developmental in a less static way than those of the Baroque period; they were unified by imitation and sometimes by melodic sequences but without necessarily having all parts organized in a rigid sequence. (See Ex. 87b.) Complex episodes based on canon or invertible counterpoint were also taught in academic counterpoint, but these appear infrequently in actual practice. In some cases, the episodes were much less contrapuntal than the rest of the fugue (Ex. 87c), and, in all cases, their importance as developments or diversions (as the French and Italians named them) giving temporary relief from complete statements of the theme gave them an important place in the fugue form. These episodes served a definite tonal function as well, acting as a modulatory bridge between entry sections in different keys. This was not always the case in eighteenth-century fugues.

One of the main structural differences between the Classical-Romantic fugue and the Baroque expanded fugue was in the use of cadences. The importance of cadences and rhythmic pauses in the

EXAMPLE 87

FUGAL EPISODES FROM LATE EIGHTEENTH AND NINE-
TEENTH CENTURIES.
(a) FUGUE IN B MINOR, No. 25 FROM *Gradus ad Parnassum* BY MUZIO CLEMENTI.

(b) FUGUE IN B MINOR BY G. B. MARTINI; FUGUE FROM
Variations and Fugue on a Theme by Handel, JOHANNES
BRAHMS.

(c) FUGUE IN B-FLAT MAJOR, OP. 35, NO. 6 BY FELIX MENDELSSOHN.

articulation of Classical and Romantic homophonic forms was in direct contrast to the polyphonic Baroque forms, where the cadence was a definite point of harmonic arrival but rarely a break in the rhythmic motion. Marpurg and later theorists emphasized the contrast between homophonic forms and fugue (the one Baroque survival), stressing and idealizing the continuous motion that characterizes a fugue. The derivation of the term "fugue" from the Latin *fuga* or flight was constantly cited, and, except for a possible hold on a half cadence preceding a final stretto in the tonic, no pause was admitted in the ideal fugue. Perhaps because of this idealized concept of continual movement, there was a predilection for fugues in a fast tempo. Among Beethoven's published fugues, for example, only the fugue that opens his String Quartet in C-sharp Minor is in a slow tempo.

Continual rhythmic motion—at whatever tempo—is characteristic of most expanded Baroque fugues, but these usually also have clear cadences that were well prepared. Often, these are strong cadences with the bass skipping from 5 to 1 and the tonic note in the top part, and important cadences are generally signaled by suspensions or by such stylized melodic ornaments as the trill or appoggiatura. Even if the cadence is avoided or the resolution delayed in one part, the approach to the cadence is felt and the key is made clear.

Fux stressed the avoidance of cadence resolution by a deceptive harmonic resolution and by bringing in the theme starting the next section before the cadence occurs, but, in the archaic style he professed, the suspension formula makes these cadence attempts clear. As the ideal of weak or avoided cadences was perpetuated in Classical and Romantic fugues, the cadences became less frequent and less clear. Cadence types were less clearly defined, less strongly prepared, and usually involved chord inversions so that they did not stand out as articulation points. Other devices became more important in articulating form.

Two other means of articulating sections gained importance in this period. Contrast in tone color—between instruments and voices or between solo and tutti—was inherent in the Baroque concertato style, but such contrast was rarely used to differentiate formal sections in what Marpurg called the regular fugue because, in this, each contrapuntal voice maintains its identity throughout the fugue. Such contrasts are found mainly in concertos and choral-orchestral movements that use fugue but do not maintain it throughout the movement. Nineteenth-century practice was much freer. So long as the number of contrapuntal voices and their identity remain clear, changes in tone color were used to good effect. Often, it was used to indicate a division between sections, to contrast an episode with a restatement of the theme, or to reinforce a climactic pedal point or stretto. Although it is most obvious in orchestral fugues, in fugues that combine orchestra, choir, and soloists or in organ fugues where registration is indicated, a change of color effected by a change of range in the piano or string quartet is also used to differentiate sections.

The second element, dynamics, is clearly a part of fugue in the Classical period, and its use as a formal device (as well as a means of expression) became more important during the nineteenth century. In a number of late nineteenth-century fugues, the dynamic pattern must be included as an integral part of the form and indicated on the diagram that outlines this form.

Some older techniques also help to make audible the formal divisions within a fugue. One is a stronger contrast in style between the *Durchführungen* that remain contrapuntal and the episodes that become more homophonic. Another is the habit of dropping out a voice before it re-enters to state the theme. The parts are dropped out for a longer period, so that the re-entry stands out more; often, more than one part is dropped out, particularly at the beginning of a stretto, so that this is clear to the listener. All in all, despite infrequent and weak cadences and, in the nineteenth century, a rapidly fluctuating sense of key due to chromaticism, the forms of these fugues are usually clearer than the forms of Baroque fugues. This is because, whatever methods of formal articulation are used, they reinforce each other. There is not the complexity resulting from different and conflicting means of division or from re-use of earlier material that is found in Baroque fugues.

PROBLEMS IN ANALYSIS

It is not necessary to give detailed analyses of fugues written in this period since, except for the possible need to include dynamics or tone color, the same analytical techniques used for earlier fugues are found here. Needless to say, not all fugues of this time exhibit all the formal characteristics discussed above, but, by reference to these and to the known techniques found in earlier fugues, the main questions regarding form in a particular instance will be answered. A brief description of two nineteenth-century fugues that are clear examples of the two main ideal forms of the period and that are readily available in several editions may be of help.

The *Cum sancto spiritu* from the Gloria of the E-flat Major Mass (D. 950) by Franz Schubert (1797–1828) is typical of the fugue type cultivated in Vienna in the eighteenth and early nineteenth centuries, a form that derived from the Italian tradition and especially from the teachings of Fux. Consisting of a series of *Durchführungen* alternating with episodes, it inculcates the type of form toward which the three-section German school fugue was meant to be the first step and foreshadows many of the features of the French *fugue d'école*.

As is the case with Viennese fugues, the exposition starts in the bass, moves to the soprano, and ends with an extra statement of the subject in the tonic (B-flat major) in the bass. This exposition, which includes two short episodes, is marked off only by a very weak cadence in c, the succeeding episode beginning before the final statement of the subject is finished. Example 88a shows this place in the fugue. Before the subject is finished in the bass, the succeeding episode starts in the tenor (m. 310).[77] The two upper parts drop out in measure 311, soon to re-enter imitatively with the head of the subject that starts off the episode. The beginning of the episode is emphasized by the dropping-out and re-entry of parts, and the preceding section ends when the statement of the subject is finished. The form is clear to the listener, but the analyst cannot pick a particular measure as the point of division except by some arbitrary definition of his own.

The ending of the episode is marked by a cadence in F, the dominant, and a restatement of the subject in F starts in the alto on the final chord of the cadence (m. 328). (See Ex. 88b.) This point of articulation is also emphasized by the dropping-out of the bass and the fact that the episodic material is finished on the final chord of the cadence. But the cadence here is a weak one and would pass unnoticed were it not for the thematic entry that starts at this point, and the dropping out of the bass.

This next section includes a restatement of the theme in G minor (in the bass) and moves on without a discernible break into the second long episode. This episode likewise comes to a weak cadence in E-flat major (m. 354) that is emphasized by an entry of the theme in the bass on the final chord of the cadence and the dropping-out of the three upper parts.

The same formal pattern is maintained throughout the rest of the fugue; each section starts with a statement of the theme, merges into an episode that acts as an extension within the section, and finally cadences, the final chord of the cadence coinciding with the first note of the restatement of the theme that starts the next section. The cadences are not particularly strong, and the entrances of the theme plus the dropping-out of other parts really mark the division points. The construction is such that the fugue divides audibly into sections, each of which contains a *Durchführung* and a long episode. (See Table IV.) The clear sectional divisions come only at the end of each episode.

The third and fourth sections start with strettos; here, the sectional division is more obvious because all parts except that which starts the stretto drops out, and the nature of the theme, beginning on a whole note, results in a cessation of rhythmic movement. Example 88c, the end of the third section and the beginning of the fourth, shows how definite a break is made in the texture—also how weak the cadence is tonally; it is not a well-prepared point of arrival, but part of a series of continuous modulations.

The strettos beginning each succeeding section become progressively closer. That starting the third section is at the distance of three measures; that at the end of the fourth is at a distance of two measures. Both of these are two-part strettos, but, as the diagram shows, each pair of voices states each stretto. The fourth section ends with the conventional cadence-ending on the dominant chord with a hold. Then follows the "real" stretto section, with all four voices taking part, entering at the distance of one measure. This happens in two different arrangements. The first is listed as a separate section (5) because, although short and without an episodic extension, it leads by a strong cadence to the next stretto and is stated by the orchestra

EXAMPLE 88

MASS IN E-FLAT MAJOR, FRANZ SCHUBERT.
(VOCAL PARTS; TEXT OMITTED)

alone. The return of the chorus at the beginning of the sixth section states the stretto in a different version and moves on to a final extension, or coda, that is quasihomophonic in style and provides a final grand climax.

(c.)

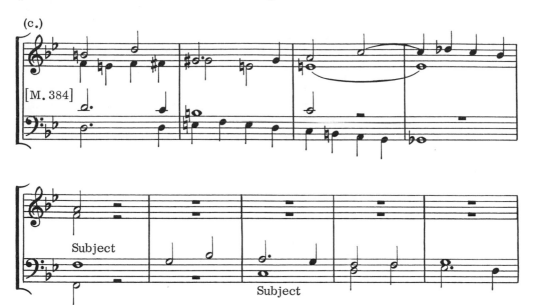

[M. 384]

Subject

Subject

Only at the end do dynamics and tone color enter into the projection of the formal design. An orchestral build-up and crescendo
gives emphasis to the ending of the fourth section, and the *piano*,
orchestral section that follows provides sharp contrast. When the
chorus re-enters *forte* in the sixth section, there is another clear contrast that points up the final stretto, and the orchestra adds to the
climactic effect of the coda.

The clarity of the section endings seen in this fugue is not always
found in fugues of this type, but a familiarity with the structural
points of this fugue will help in the analysis of similar fugues of
lesser clarity—for example, the instrumental fugues of Mozart and
Albrechtsberger. The key scheme of this fugue is interesting, too.
There is not the continual return to the tonic that one finds in some
eighteenth-century fugues, but the use of the subdominant key so
close to the beginning (the opening of the third section) shows that
this is still a relatively early fugue. By mid-nineteenth century, the
subdominant key is avoided until later in the fugue. The use of key
here is worthy of study. The keys in which the theme is restated are
quite conservative, as is characteristic of fugue, but this is because
they are arrived at by melodic analysis. The accompanying harmonies
are not so much in one key, but in a series of different keys (or in
greatly altered harmonies within the key of the theme they accompany). The harmonic progressions in the episodes are also interesting, especially in comparison with those of the fugues of Bach and
Handel, and the conservative key centers in which they end are not
indicative of their tonal content.

TABLE IV

Structure of the Fugue Cum Sancto Spiritu from Schubert's Mass in E-flat Major-(D.950)

Measures	260	270	282	292	304	310,312,314	328	334
Cadences						c	F	g
Keys of Subject Entrances	Bb	F	Bb	F	Bb	d, a	F	g
Polyphonic Structure				A		(S)⁺		
			S			(S)	S	
		A						S
	S			S				
Sections	. . . . (Exposition)						 2	

[282]

Measures	354,357	365,368	388,390	396,398	422,423,424,425,426	433,434,436	464
Cadences	E♭		F	F	F (𝄐)	B♭	B♭
Keys of Subject Entrances	E♭, c	E♭, c	F, c	F, c	B♭, E♭ d, g	B♭, E♭, c, d	
Polyphonic Structure	S / S / S+	S+	S	S / S	S / S+ / S+	S / (S) / S / (S)	
Sections	3 · · ·		4 · · ·		5 · · ·	6 · · ·	(Coda)

S = Subject
(S) = Head of Subject plus free continuation
S+ = Altered subject
A = Answer

Not scaled evenly by measures.

Blanks in lines indicate dropping-out of a part for one measure or more (after the Exposition and excluding Coda). In section 5, chorus drops out, orchestra takes S; chorus enters one voice at a time in section 6. Countersubject material not indicated.

The continuous use of stretto to start the later sections and the planned, progressive arrangements of these strettos show the Fux influence. Reicha, writing in 1825, described this use of stretto as characteristic of fugue, and German manuals through the first quarter of the century used progressively closer strettos in the three sections of their fugue exercises. But, by the 1830's and 40's, this had changed, doubtless because of the influence of the rediscovered J. S. Bach. Both the academic fugues and the art fugues of the later period use more simple restatements of the subject and answer in different keys, usually saving the stretto for the ending of the fugue. It is worth noting, also, that only the stretto that starts the fourth section in the above fugue is in the preferable stretto relation of subject and answer and that the final stretto uses only the beginning of the theme; it is used for effect rather than a display of technique.

A FUGUE IN TERNARY FUGUE FORM

The fugue from Brahms's *Variations and Fugue on a Theme by Handel* is a fugue in ternary form and in a much clearer ternary form than that described by Marx, for the three parts are made audible by formal devices and not simply by the key scheme. Although Brahms's use of a ternary form for his fugue seems to be due to the German theorists' insistence on the ternary basis of all fugues, this fugue is a more obvious ternary form than that expounded by Marx and his followers. As Table V shows, the three sections of the fugue that include complete statements of the theme are clearly set off from one another by two long episodes—episodes that are much longer than those appearing between statements of the theme within the three parts.

The character of each of the three main parts, however, adheres to that prescribed by theorists for the ternary fugue. The first part is the exposition, which includes a short episode and an extra statement of the subject in the tonic key of B-flat major. The middle part begins in measure 25 with the restatement of the subject in the tonic minor (which is not a closely related key) and ends with the augmented subject in F minor. This part includes restatements of the theme in several distant keys, in the inverted and augmented forms as well as in the original form, and these restatements are usually separated by short, modulatory episodes. The third section, which would normally open with a stretto on the tonic, starts in measure 75 with a simultaneous mirror combination of the subject—in the right hand, in the tonic doubled in sixths, and inverted and doubled in thirds in the left

TABLE V
Structure of Fugue from Brahms's
Variations and Fugue on a Theme by Handel

Measures	3 5 7	11 13	18	25			49 53 55		75 77 82	95	108
Keys of Subject Entries	B♭,F,B♭,F	B♭		b♭ f D♭ D♭ G♭	a b	b♭ f f		B♭ c*		
Polyphonic Structure	A	S	S SI SI	SI	S	SA	S S			
	S	A	S		S		SI SI			
	S		S	SI	SA		SI SI			
							S S Dom.			
							SI SI Pedal			
Section	Exposition	Epis.		Middle Entries			Epis.	Final Section	Coda		
Dynamics	f	p	f	p	f	p	f	p	f	ff	

* = S altered to fit in c.
S = Subject
I = Inverted
A = Augmented
Measure numbers omitted for entries in the middle section. Countersubject material omitted.
Short episodes within Exposition and middle section omitted.
Crescendos and short changes in dynamics omitted.
Blank spaces in tenor and alto represent drop-out of those parts (after the exposition). Real answer used; pairs of entries such as those in b♭ and f at the beginning and end of the middle section might be called subject and answer.

hand—providing as dynamic a beginning as would a stretto and doubtless used because the subject itself does not provide good strettos. (See Ex. 89a.) This mirror is repeated in C minor, and then, after a short episode, begins a long dominant pedal followed by the coda.

The division into three parts is reinforced by the dynamic pattern, and dynamics also emphasize the transitional character of the episodes that separate them. The exposition begins and ends *forte* and, except for measures 8–10, is loud throughout. The sudden

EXAMPLE 89

FUGUE FROM *Variations and Fugue on a Theme by Handel,* JOHANNES BRAHMS

change to *piano* in measure 13 marks the beginning of the first long episode, which remains quiet until the crescendo in measures 23 and 24 that leads to the *forte* beginning of the second part in measure 25. This second part changes from *forte* to *piano* frequently, in keeping with the changes of key and different treatments of the theme and with the short episodes that separate them. A sudden *piano* in measure 57 ushers in the second large episode and this, like the first, remains quiet until the crescendo (starting in measure 72) that leads to the *forte* beginning of the last part in measure 75. This last part— the climax of the fugue and of the whole set of variations—stays on a high dynamic level until the end.

Since there are no strong cadences or rhythmic pauses to mark divisions, the coinciding patterns set up by dynamics, tonality, and musical character act to project the form. Although the pattern outlined above seems to be the most obvious division of the fugue to this author, there are two other ways, equally logical, in which the major divisions could be made. According to the basic outline of the ternary fugue form given by Marx and Riemann, in which key is the decisive factor, the middle section would include both of the long episodes that flank it since they are not in the tonic key. A third division into three parts can also be made. Each of the two long episodes is made up of two sections that distinctly differ as to thematic material and texture. In each, the first section is thematically an extension of the statement of the theme that closes the part preceding the episode. Likewise, the second section of each starts up with a fragment that is derived from the head of the subject and that leads into the statement of the subject that follows the episode. Thus, two main breaks at measure 20 and measure 66 could be made; the first part of each episode before these points would be thematically an extension of the preceding *Durchführung,* and the portion of each episode following these points would be thematically an anticipation of the beginning of the following *Durchführung.*

The fact is that this fugue is a remarkably unified work, and the "joins" are so smoothly made that the exact point at which one section merges into another is not obvious; we are only sure once the new section is well under way. This is in keeping with the concept of fugue as continual movement that was stressed by theorists and aestheticians of the time. The rhythmic continuity is strong. From the third measure until the beginning of the pedal in measure 82, there is constant sixteenth-note motion in at least one part. There is also frequent modulation, and, by changing harmonizations of the theme, modulation often takes place within thematic statements.

One factor that helps to conceal the "joins" between sections is this use of the subject as a means of modulation. The connection between the exposition and the first big episode is a case in point. Example 89b shows measures 11–13, where the subject in the tonic in the soprano in measures 11 and 12 is doubled at the sixth in such a way that, in measure 12, the key implied is no longer the tonic, B-flat major, but is E-flat minor. The modulation has begun before the subject is finished. The imitation of the subject in measure 13 connects the episode very smoothly to the subject ending, and the dynamic change is the most overt sign that a new section has begun.

The connection between the end of the middle section and the episode that follows it shows a real overlap between the end of a statement of the theme and the beginning of an episode. (See Ex. 89c.) The subject appears in augmentation in the soprano, starting in measure 55, in F minor. (Brahms uses the raised third degree whenever the theme is changed to minor, treating it as a leading tone to 4, but the rest of the theme is always clearly in the minor key.) The octaves in the right hand in measures 57 and 58 are still the theme in augmentation, but they are treated as the beginning of the episode. A change in texture and dynamics makes it sound like a new section, and the material in these two measures becomes the basis for the episode.

This same spinning-out from the theme is often found in fugues of the Classical and Romantic periods. In many ways, this fugue of Brahms is a continuation—and a rather conservative one—of the piano fugue of this time. The style of the fugue is in the direct tradition—the quasipolyphonic style with much doubling in octaves, thirds, and sixths—and the use of accompaniment figures that are simply broken chords are as much a part of the tradition as is the pianistic figuration of the pedal and coda. Typical of fugues of all media is the strong harmonic basis, the change of chord on the smallest rhythmic value, and the tendency to minimize linear texture and cut down the amount of contrapuntal dissonance heard. Probably the most typical of all is the rather self-conscious awareness of form that is so evident in fugues written in the nineteenth century.

Strict and Free Fugue, Ricercare

The preoccupation with form in relation to fugue which is characteristic of this time is nowhere so obvious as in the attempt made during this period to codify different subtypes of fugue. During the Baroque period, the type of irregularity ascribed to fugue by theorists was limited to the improper answer—the answer at some interval other than the dominant or made with intervallic or rhythmic freedom. (See p. 122.) Beginning with Marpurg's treatise, the regular or proper fugue included, in addition to the correct form of subject and answer and their proper order in the exposition, good countermelodies and episodes. If any of these were not present or were improperly used, the piece could no longer be called a regular fugue.[78] Later theorists added other elements to this list, such as countersubject, transposed entries, stretto, and pedal. Although the exact number of elements varied, they were elements that defined formal content, and a certain order in their formal arrangement was also taken for granted.

Within the category of regular fugue, Marpurg created two

further categories according to content—the strict fugue and the free fugue. A strict fugue uses no thematic material except that derived from the subject and counterparts (or countersubject, if one is used). This definition dominated only German theory in the later eighteenth century, but, by the nineteenth century, it was found in theory books and musical dictionaries of Europe and the Americas. The strict fugue was also the ideal for the French and German school fugue and the academic fugue in other countries that derived their theory from France and Germany. The ideal of craftsmanship, of creating a form from a limited amount of thematic material, was associated with fugue, and the teaching of craftsmanship became one of the main functions of fugue in musical pedagogy. In the school fugue, the exposition is the only legitimate source for the material used in the rest of the fugue.

The free fugue, as defined by Marpurg[79] differs from the strict fugue only in the introduction of thematic material not derived from the subject or its counterparts. It retains the formal elements of the regular fugue. For Marpurg and Kollman,[80] the strict fugue was characteristic of the fugues of Bach and the free fugue of the fugues of Handel. It is thus far removed from the "irregular fugue" which lacked some essential element of fugue, such as the correct answer, or a proper exposition. Marpurg gave no examples of an irregular fugue, but Kollman cited Bach's *Inventions* and Handel's choral fugues as typical irregular fugues.

Free fugue kept its special meaning through the second quarter of the nineteenth century: a fugue with all the conventional formal elements but with new and usually contrasting material added, normally in episodes and codas. The term was used in this same sense by German pedagogues throughout the nineteenth century. As Bussler put it, the difference between strict and free fugue is not a question of form but of the musical materials used in that form.[81] Thus, the fugue by Brahms just analyzed would be accounted a strict fugue, but the fugue from César Franck's *Prelude, Chorale and Fugue,* conventional in form but using material in the episodes and coda that is not derived from the exposition, would be called a free fugue.

The free fugue was not necessarily considered inferior to the strict fugue, either by theorists or composers, although the strict fugue was preferred for academic exercises. In collections of fugues such as Mendelssohn's *Six Preludes and Fugues,* Op. 35 and Schumann's *Six Fugues on BACH,* Op. 60, strict and free fugues appear side by side, simply entitled "fugues." Only by analysis do we find out which of them would be called strict and which free. And the analytical process does not differ: it is only necessary to make note of the addition of new material when it appears in a free fugue. In some cases, it may be hard to decide whether the material is new or not, especially in nineteenth-century fugues when the process of thematic transformation is applied to the fugue theme.

The specific term applied by Marpurg to a strict fugue that is extensive and that uses a number of scholastic devices (such as augmentation, canon, stretto, inversion, and the like) is "ricercare" or "ricercata"[82] (in French, *recherchée*). By this time, the old meaning of ricercare had been lost, and, for the eighteenth and most of the nineteenth centuries—until musicology focused attention on the ricercar of the sixteenth and seventeenth centuries—it indicated a master fugue in which all the material was derived from the subject and countersubjects and in which the composer showed off his contrapuntal skill.

It is in the above meaning of the term that Beethoven used the words *tantôt libre tantôt recherchée* on the title page of the first edition of his *Grosse Fuge*, Op. 133. It is exceptionally long and uses almost all of the technical devices listed by Albrechtsberger in his instructions on fugue,[83] hence *recherchée;* at the same time, new material is introduced in the course of the fugue, so it is also free. The fugue in the finale of the *Hammerklavier Sonata,* Op. 106 might well have had the same designation, since it also uses most of the devices known for the treatment of a fugal theme and introduces new material in the body of the fugue. The *alcune licenze* that Beethoven put in the heading of the *Hammerklavier* fugue is most probably used in the sense in which Albrechtsberger used it in teaching Beethoven and in his own fugues and the examples in his composition text, as an indication that slight changes in the theme—the alteration of an interval or of the time value of a note or the omission of the end of the theme—are made or that some unusually free treatment of contrapuntal dissonance has taken place. Such "liberties" occur constantly in the fugues of Bach and Handel, and freedom in the treatment of the theme (but rarely in dissonance treatment) is characteristic of most fugues written in the last two-thirds of the nineteenth century. But, during Beethoven's time, the strict pedantry of the Fux school, particularly of Albrechtsberger, was still dominant. It was only when the school fugue became consciously divorced from the realities of free composition that such pedantry was reserved for academic discipline.

Beethoven stands alone as a fugue writer. Most of the fugues that he wrote are unusual in some way, from the irregular answer in the fugue that opens the String Quartet, Op. 131 to the formal experimentation of the *Grosse Fuge.* Since Beethoven shows a conscious knowledge of the conventions of the strict Classical fugue of the Fux school as exemplified by Albrechtsberger in his textbook and his compositions, as well as the fugues of his predecessors Mozart and Haydn, his fugues must be approached with a knowledge of this tradition. Although he was acquainted with many fugues of Bach, there is no clear evidence of Bach's influence on his fugal writing.

Once the conventional features have been picked out by the analyst, the new features that are singularly Beethoven's may be clearly seen. The analysis of the fugues of Beethoven is still an adventure, and, despite the many discussions available in critical and analytical writings, there is no consensus of opinion as to their correct analysis or evaluation. A knowledge of Beethoven's usage in homophonic forms is also a help in the study of his fugues, and analogies with these works can be useful.

Beethoven was the last major composer to think of fugue as capable and worthy of further formal development. Whatever evaluation is made of his experiments in fugue form, it must be regretted that his fugues had no effect on the generation of composers that followed him. His fugues are scarcely mentioned in the textbooks devoted to teaching the school fugue. In the realm of fugue, it was Bach who influenced the theorists and composers for the rest of the century. If "contemporary" fugues were mentioned in German fugue texts, it was Mendelssohn and Schumann and not Beethoven whose fugues were cited.

SUGGESTIONS FOR ANALYSIS

A thorough acquaintance with the two nineteenth-century fugues analyzed above plus one or two each of the fugues of Haydn, Mozart, and Beethoven—strict or free—is as necessary to the understanding of the problems of fugue form as a knowledge of the fugues of Bach. In contrast to earlier periods, however, the Classical and Romantic periods provide relatively few fugues for analysis; fewer fugues were written during that time, and of these only a small proportion remain in print today. Most of the fugues in print are those written by composers such as Haydn, Mozart, Beethoven, Schubert, Mendelssohn, Schumann, Brahms, and Reger; the fact that they are still published is mainly due to the reputation these composers have gained for works in other forms. Their fugues provide enough material to give an insight into the formal procedures of the time, but they do not provide sufficient or typical material for broader evaluations. Fugues by other composers of the time are beginning to appear in historical editions and dissertations, but a broader spread of composers and of nationalities represented must be available before any conclusive studies can be made. A list in Appendix I includes some useful collections now available in historical editions as well as some fugues by minor composers of the time now out of print that are to be found in some American libraries. Because of the scarcity of nineteenth-century piano fugues available in print, two fugues—one by Muzio Clementi, and one by Felix Mendelssohn—are given at the end of the Workbook. Instrumental fugues have been stressed because, in these, the problem of formal construction is usually more pressing than in fugues with texts and because a greater freedom of style results in many new ways of using old techniques.

Fugue in Homophonic Forms

The combination of contrapuntal and fugal elements with the homophonic *style galant* was an important and consciously used technique with the Viennese Classical composers. In many cases, this resulted in a simple confrontation of sections in different styles—a simple accompanied melody followed by a section in imitative style, for example—and the main problem, that of moving smoothly from one style to the other, was solved in the mature works of Haydn and Mozart. There was also, on the part of some of these composers, an interest in combining fugue with homophonic forms, and certain compositions present a special problem in form resulting from the conflict between the conventions associated with fugue form and the homophonic forms. What concern us here are the various ways in which a fugal exposition or an exposition plus a few restatements of the theme was used in a homophonic form.

FUGUE INSERTED IN A HOMOPHONIC FORM

The use of a fugue as the contrasting section (complete in itself) in a simple three-part song form or variant thereof (as in the second movement of Beethoven's String Quartet, Op. 95) does not necessarily present a formal problem since it is a separate part starting after the full close of the preceding part. Beethoven here connects the fugue thematically to the final section by bringing in the fugue theme in that section but the fugue is formally distinct from the rest of the movement.

The insertion of a fugal exposition or a short fugue as a developmental device applied to a theme first stated in a homophonic milieu is often found in sonata form. Two familiar examples are the last movement of Mozart's Symphony No. 41, where the first theme of the movement is presented in a fugal exposition in the bridge (m. 36), and, in the development of the first movement of Beethoven's *Eroica Symphony,* the use of a developed form of the theme first presented in measure 45 as the subject of a fugue exposition. (m. 236). But here again there is no formal difficulty beyond the connection of the fugal section with the sections that precede and follow it.

HOMOPHONIC FORMS STARTING WITH A
FUGUE EXPOSITION

It is those works in which the fugal exposition is the opening theme of a primarily homophonic form that are the most interesting formally since they involve a conflict between two formal procedures as well as between two styles. Starting off a scherzo or the trio of a scherzo movement with a fugal exposition is a gambit that Beethoven used to good effect. The scherzo from his Ninth Symphony and the trio of the scherzo from his Fifth Symphony start with fugal expositions and provide a good study in the problems involved in this type of combination. The primary problem is that of continuation, a stylistic problem still; the fugal beginning implies a polyphonic continuation, and the shift from polyphony to homophony must be skillfully made. There is also the question of which elements of fugue form and which of homophonic form will be used. In both of these examples, the over-all form follows the basic divisions of the homophonic form, with clear cadences and repeats attended by definite breaks in rhythmic movement, rather than the sectional form of the strict fugue. On the other hand, each of these has also later *Durchführungen* of the subject in which all voices take part, and these follow the formal tradition of the Fux-Albrechtsberger fugue in which the entries in the later *Durchführungen* come in successively closer strettos. In the trio of the scherzo from the Fifth Symphony, the second section opens with such a stretto, and the same stretto is used for the varied reprise of this section. In the scherzo from the Ninth Symphony, successively closer strettos appear at the beginning of the sections marked *Ritmo di tre battute* and *Ritmo di quattro battute.*

FUGUE COMBINED WITH SONATA FORM

The combination of fugue with sonata form is even more interesting because the sonata form is more complex and because sonata form and fugue embody strong formal conventions. Both Mozart and Beethoven wrote sonata forms beginning with a fugal exposition that are well-thought-out works of artistic maturity. Each of their works in this combination is also a different solution to the problem. In all of those mentioned here, the sonata form is the basic framework for the movement, and all of them embody, as well, certain characteristics of strict fugue form.

One of the main problems to be solved concerns the recapitulation of the first theme. The exact recapitulation that would be expected in sonata form is not used in Classic fugue where the exact repetition of a passage is never made, particularly not an exact repetition of the exposition. Mozart's *Magic Flute Overture* and the finale of his String Quartet, K. 387 are both sonata forms in which the first theme is a fugue and neither has an exact repetition of this fugal exposition in the recapitulation. The first has a developmental statement of the theme in the tonic key. The finale of K. 387 provides a most logical combination of the procedures of fugue and sonata form. Here, the opening theme of the second theme group is another fugal exposition stating a new theme in the dominant key— a theme that fits in double counterpoint with the first theme. In the recapitulation, the two are then combined as the exposition of a double fugue (in the tonic key), and this acts as the recapitulation of both themes and is followed directly by the closing material of the exposition.

Beethoven, in both the second movement of his First Symphony and the fugal finale of his String Quartet, Op. 59, No. 3, movements that also use fugal expositions as first themes, repeats exactly the opening fugal expositions, but adds a countersubject to each entry of each theme. This resembles Mozart's solution, but the analogy to double fugue is less integrated with the sonata form since the countersubject appears for the first time in the recapitulation; it is not, as in the Mozart, a recapitulation of another exposition theme.

Another variable is the amount of homophonic material included; each of the above-mentioned movements includes at least one major homophonic theme and includes other, less important homophonic material. Whether the development of the fugue theme is done in the fugal way—restatements, stretto, inversion, augmentation, and the like—or whether it is subject to motivic treatment and other homophonic developmental procedures is another question to be considered. Procedures that are not in accord with the conventions of strict fugue may often be found in purely fugal sections; strictness in the form of the answer in the fugal exposition, alterations in the subject in later statements, and especially strettos are often found, since it is the total effect that matters rather than traditional rules.

Composers of this time did not discuss the amalgamation of fugue with homophonic forms, and it was rarely mentioned by contemporary theorists. Only Beethoven's pupil Carl Czerny made reference to a freer fugue type that "approximates to sonata form," and this is but a brief notice at the end of his discussion of fugue.[84] Reicha, who, as a composer, was actively concerned with adapting fugue to the new style, articulated the way in which he felt such adaptation should be made in his *Traité de haute composition* and this only after a full section on the strict academic fugue.[85]

REICHA'S *Fugue Phrasée*

The solution Reicha gave is not a homophonic form in which fugue plays a part, but a strict fugue with structural elements derived from homophonic procedure. His reasons for the projected change show how far from "modern" tastes the strict fugue was felt to be before the Bach revival took hold, and make clear to today's scholar one of the reasons why fugue form has always been so difficult to define. For Reicha, as for all Classical and Romantic theorists and composers, the most mature and expressive music was based on periodic structure. Reicha felt that the fugue form had been invented too early, before the true language of music had been discovered. For him, the basic fault of fugue is that it lacks coherent structure, does not move by clear phrases within musical periods that end with intelligible perfect cadences, and that its continual rhythmic movement precludes any clear delineation of phrases and periods. In other words, it is polyphonic, and formal clarity is to be found only in homophonic style.

The solution he proposed was a *fugue phrasée,* which he outlined in his text and illustrated with a movement for string quartet. The exposition is a regular fugue exposition except that it ends as a homophonic period with a strong perfect authentic cadence and a rhythmic caesura. Each episode is *bien rhythmé et bien phrasé*—that is, clearly homophonic with clearly delineated motives and phrases, and each episode is a single period ending with a strong perfect cadence. The material for these episodes, as in the strict fugue, is drawn from the exposition. Between these episodes, following in the usual fugue key scheme, are the counterexposition and strettos. These, while polyphonic, also end with strongly marked cadences. The whole ends like a regular fugue with a series of imitations or with a stretto, followed by a pedal point and canon of the subject and a coda.

Reicha's attempt to introduce a more "modern" fugue form into conservatory curricula met with no success. Cherubini, then director of the Paris Conservatory, was horrified by the *fugue phrasée,* and his faction, which wanted to perpetuate the traditional strict fugue, won out. Later attempts to liberalize the *fugue d'école* were also quelled. Likewise, in Germany, the rediscovery and idealization of Bach turned composers away from such experimental fugue forms as Beethoven's *Grosse Fuge.* Attempts at combining fugue with "modern" elements concentrated on fitting fugal elements into homophonic forms rather than injecting new elements into traditional fugue.

While an analysis of these combined forms is no aid to the writing of strict fugue, a thoughtful study of such combinations as sonata form and fugue will provide an insight into the general principles of polyphonic and homophonic form as nothing else can. To the examples from Mozart and Beethoven given above may be added the scherzo from Beethoven's String Quartet, Op. 18, No. 4, the finale of the Fifth Symphony of Anton Bruckner (1824–1896), and the fourth movement of the String Quartet, Op. 54, No. 1 by Max Reger. No fixed conventions for analyzing such forms have been established, and a detailed analysis has been avoided here so that the student will feel free to work out his own conclusions. Needless to say, a good deal of experience in working with conventional sonata forms and fugues of the late eighteenth and nineteenth centuries is a prerequisite for such a study.

FUGAL STYLE, *Genre Fugué,* FUGATO, FUGHETTA

During the late eighteenth and nineteenth centuries, the term "fugue" was directly associated with a form, the form described as strict fugue in German and French theory and with free fugue in German theory (in which only the source of the material used and not the form itself set it off from strict fugue). A regular exposition with the proper answer and correct order of presentation of subject and answer was taken for granted. This was followed by a series of episodes and restatements of the theme—not a fixed number but usually three or more. The exact order of keys used (outside of academic exercises) was not fixed, but, by the nineteenth century, the fugue was expected to leave the tonic key after the exposition (or counterexposition) and to return to it only at the closing section of the fugue. A regular countersubject, counterexposition, stretto, pedal, and such devices as augmentation and diminution could be included but were not insisted on. No pause in the rhythmic motion was allowed except immediately before a final stretto section.

In France, fugues that departed from the current pattern of the *fugue d'école* were called free fugues whether the departure was in the form of the answer or order of exposition or in more radical departures from the conventional form, and this is the sense in which "free fugue" is used today. Fugal works that differ greatly from the norm were rarely called fugues by composers. If fugal matter—an exposition, a stretto, an imitative development, and the like—was used in homophonic forms, this was included in the broad category of *genre fugué*. For many pedagogues, one purpose of the *fugue d'école* was to prepare the composer to use fugal material in choral works, operas, symphonies, sonatas, and other nonfugal forms.

A similar term was used in German, Italian, English, and other languages, the general terms "fugued style" or "fugal style" standing for material that originates in fugue but is used in other forms. Two more precise terms were used extensively by German theorists in the nineteenth century that, by the close of the century, were used in a specific sense by most theorists—*fughetta* and *fugato*. Both had Italian origins but gained their particular meanings from their use by nineteenth-century German theorists.

Fughetta, from the Italian diminutive of *fuga,* was used in both the eighteenth and nineteenth centuries as a title given by composers to a correct but short fugue that exists as a separate piece. It is normally used in this sense today. *Fugato* was originally used in Italian as an adjective (as in *contrapunto fugato,* fugued counterpoint or fugued style), but the term soon gained independent existence as a noun that meant, in the usage of German theorists, a short fugue or fugue exposition inserted in some other form. This was the primary meaning, and the one generally in force today. However, some theorists, such as Solomon Jadassohn, used it in the sense of "fugued counterpoint" to stand for what would earlier have been considered a *fuga d'imitazione* or *fuga irregolare,* the sort of fugal choruses found in the oratorios of Handel where the answer and exposition are irregular and the strict contrapuntal style is not kept throughout.[86] This is equivalent to the nineteenth-century use of "free fugue" in France. In many contemporary musical dictionaries, this is listed as a secondary meaning of fugato. To compound the difficulty involved in using fugato and fughetta, some nineteenth-century theorists were undecided as to their exact meanings. A. B. Marx, for example, merely considered fughetta to be a fugato of a less serious nature.[87] The terms "fugued style," *genre fugué,* "fugato," and "fughetta" are theorists' terms, not composers', and any doubts as to their meaning in a specific case can immediately be resolved by recourse to the composition discussed.

Notes

1. Vanneo, *op. cit.,* f. 93ᵥ.

2. Picitono, *op. cit.,* Bk. II, chap. xxxix.

3. Zarlino, *op. cit.,* Bk. III, chap. liii.

4. *Ibid.,* Bk. III, chap. liv; chap. lii in later editions. Vicentino also showed ways of avoiding the cadence (*op. cit.,* f. 53ᵥ), but he did not discuss this in relation to text setting.

5. *Ibid.,* Bk. III, chap. lxvi.

6. See, for example, Vanneo, *op. cit.,* f. 86ᵥ*ff.*

7. The difficulty is clearly due to the fact that to make a perfect fifth above *b* by adding an *f*-sharp was considered to be what we would call a modulation, moving out of the "natural" modal system to the system where all modes use an *f*-sharp—a practice forbidden in strict modal writing in a piece in the natural system (although it is found in works using the chromatic genus) well into the late seventeenth century. (See W. C. Printz, *Satyrischer Componist* [Dresden and Leipzig, 1696] Pt. I, 31.) By the late sixteenth century, cadences on *c* or *a* (*peregrina* cadences) were used in untransposed Mixolydian and Phrygian where regular cadences would fall on *b*. In this case, Zarlino's theory did not find realization in practice until the major–minor system was adopted.

8. Orazio Tigrini, *Il compendio della musica* (Venice, 1588).

9. Zarlino, *op. cit.,* Bk. III, chap. liv; Tigrini, *op. cit.,* pp. 75*ff.;* Vicentino, *op. cit.,* f. 53ᵥ*ff.*

10. Sixteenth-century punctuation points were not always used (in the text) in the same way that we use them today; most modern historical editions punctuate the texts according to today's usage.

11. Vicentino (*op. cit.,* f. 51ᵥ) gives the prototypes of these.

12. Reproduced in Gertrude P. Smith (ed.), *The Madrigals of Cipriano de Rore for 3 and 4 voices* ("Smith College Archives," Vol. VI; Northampton, Mass., 1943).

13. Vicentino, *op. cit.,* f. 78ᵥ; Tigrini, *op. cit.,* p. 95; Pontio, *Ragionamente di Musica* (Parma, 1588), pp. 100*ff.*

14. The B-flat is raised here by Franz Espagne (ed.), in Haberl, *op. cit.,* V, 151.

15. This formed the basis of all sixteenth-century singing and sight-reading manuals as well as theory texts. See the selected list in Appendix I under "Chapter III."

16. Harry Colin Slim "The Keyboard Ricercar and Fantasia in Italy *c.* 1500–1555" (unpublished Ph.D. dissertation, Dept. of Music, Harvard University), pp. 287*ff.*

17. *Ibid.,* p. 349.

18. Max Seiffert (ed.), *Werken van Jan Pieterson Sweelinck,* Vol. I: *Werken voor Orgel en Clavecimbel* (Leipzig, 1894; Amsterdam: G. Alsbach, 1943) pp. 6*ff.;* reprinted in Adam Adrio, *Die Fuge* (Cologne: Arno Volk, 1960) I, pp. 28*ff.*

19. Diruta, *op. cit.,* Bk. II, 12.

20. Sancta Maria, *op. cit.,* Pt. II, 85*ff.*

21. The use of E-flats at times might imply Aeolian on *g,* but they are not used consistently enough to change the mode from G-Dorian. Incidental accidentals are freely used in modal works; only a consistent use throughout is considered enough to change the octave species (and hence the mode) from the one indicated by the signature. From our standpoint, this would be transitional between G-Dorian and G minor.

22. Simpson, *op. cit.,* p. 46.

23. Purcell, *op. cit.,* p. 105.

24. Solomon de Caus, *Institution harmonique* (Frankfurt, 1615), p. 21.

25. Marin Mersenne, *L'harmonie universelle* (Paris, 1636–1637), p. 315.

26. Mignot de la Voye, *Traité de musique* (Paris, 1656), pp. 74*ff.*

27. Masson, *op. cit.,* pp. 9*ff.,* 21*ff.*

28. Johann Lippius, *Synopsis musicae novae* (Strassburg, 1612), ff. H₃*ff.,* I₃v*ff.;* Johann Crüger, *Synopsis musica* (Berlin, 1630), chap. xv and Pt. I, 28.

29. Lippius, *ibid.,* f. H₂; Crüger, *ibid.,* chaps. ix, xv.

30. Printz, *op. cit.,* Pt. I, 26*ff.;* J. A. Herbst (*Musica poetica* [Nuremberg, 1643], pp. 111*ff.*) first uses this classification.

31. Furthermore, cadences were also subject to ornamental variation in performance, these also differing according to time and national style. See Putnam C. Aldrich, "The Principal *Agréments* of the Seventeenth and Eighteenth Centuries" (unpublished Ph.D. dissertation, Dept. of Music, Harvard University).

32. Helen Olive Rogers, "The Development of a Concept of Modulation in Theory from the Sixteenth to the Early Eighteenth Century (unpublished Ph.D. dissertation, Dept. of Music, Indiana University). Some German theorists of the early eighteenth century gave all twelve transpositions for each mode. See Walther, *op. cit.,* pp. 163*ff.*

33. Printz, *op. cit.,* Pt. I, 31.

34. This is a canzona in style; repetition of sections is more characteristic of the canzona than of the ricercar.

35. Seiffert, *op. cit.,* p. 18; reprinted in *GMB,* No. 158 and *MSO,* I, 98*ff.*

36. Other examples listed in Adolf Sandberger (ed.), *Werke von Christian Erbach, DTB Jahrg. IV,* II, xxvii.

37. In Banchieri, *L'organo suonarino* (Venice, 1605) and *Appendice all'organo suonarino* (Venice, 1622); Johann Woltz, *Musica organica tabulatura,* trans. and ed., Katarzyna Swarczewska in "Wkladka do Kwartalnika," *Muzyka,* II (1957), supplement.

38. A fugue acting as an inner movement of a sonata or as one of several fugues interspersed with toccata sections may end on a dominant cadence.

39. Rameau, *op. cit.,* pp. 248*ff.*

40. Béthisy, *op. cit.,* pp. 26*ff.*

41. Scheibe, *op. cit.,* pp. 472*ff.*

42. J. P. Kirnberger, *Die Kunst des reinen Satzes* (Berlin, 1771–1776), I, 103*ff.*

43. *Ibid.,* p. 108.

44. Marpurg, *op. cit.,* pp. 94*ff.*

45. J. Joachim and F. Chrysander (eds.), *Les oeuvres de Archangelo Corelli* (London: Augener, n.d.), II, 160–3.

46. *Ibid.*, III, 28–9.

47. Wrongly labeled Op. 3, No. 6 in the first edition of *HAM*.

48. Ludwig Czackzkes, *Analyze des Wohltempierten Klaviers* (Vienna: Paul Kaltschmid, 1956) lists differing analyses of these fugues by prominent theorists.

49. A. F. C. Kollman, *An Essay on Practical Musical Composition* (London, 1779), chap. v.

50. Alfred Mann's translation of Marpurg's treatise in his *Study of Fugue* (*op. cit.*) uses "exposition" for *Durchfürung* on pp. 179–184 in material selected from pp. 113 and 121*ff.* of Marpurg (*op. cit.*); but Mann, on pp. 155 and 176, also uses "exposition" where Marpurg, on pp. 18 and 93, uses *Wiederschlag*. The fault lies with English terminology and not with Dr. Mann.

51. Kollman, *op. cit.*, p. 41.

52. Marpurg, *op. cit.*, p. 121; Mann, *op. cit.*, p. 179.

53. Marpurg used a Fugue in G Minor by Luigi Battiferi (Mann, *op. cit.*, pp. 181–2) as a fugue on one subject. In the section on double fugues, he included fugues by Bach (the E Minor Fugue from Book I of *Well-Tempered Clavier* and the D Minor Fugue from Book II), both of which have very short episodes.

54. Francesco Durante, *Sei Studii e sei Divertimenti per Cembalo,* ed. Bernhard Paumgartner (Kassel: Bärenreiter, 1949); see also Gabriele d'-Annunzio ed.), *I classici della musica Italiana* (Milan: Instituto Editoriale Italiano, 1919), No. 11.

55. Starting with Printz, *op. cit.*, Pt. II, 31*ff.* See Guido Kähler, "Studien zur Entstehung der Formenlehre in der Musiktheorie des 18 and 18 Jahrhunderts [von W. C. Printz bis A. B. Marx]" (unpublished dissertation, Dept. of Music, Heidelberg University).

56. Marpurg, *op. cit.,* pp. 17–8; Mann, *op. cit.,* pp. 154–5.

57. Kollman, *op. cit.,* p. 31.

58. Marpurg, *op. cit.,* pp. 113*ff.,* 121*ff.*

59. Kollman, *op. cit.,* pp. 37*ff.*

60. Mann, *op. cit.,* pp. 95–107.

61. This shows the influence of the Italian tradition as expressed in the writings of Berardi and Bononcini. (See p. 164.)

62. "Development" is used in John Bishop's English translation of Carl Czerny's *School of Practical Composition* [(London, n.d.) p. 119] for that portion of the fugue that follows the exposition. The term is used today in this sense in certain English and American works.

63. Albrechtsberger, *op. cit.,* pp. 176*ff.,* 2nd ed., 1818; French ed., 1814; English ed., 1855.

64. Joseph Preindl, *Weiner Tonschule* (Vienna, 1827, pp. 65*ff.,* 2nd ed., 1832).

65. 9 editions to 1921; English ed., 1878; French ed., 1902.

66. Ludwig Bussler, *Kontrapunkt und Fugue im freien (modernen) Tonsatz* (Berlin, 1878; 2nd ed., 1912).

67. Jadassohn, *op. cit.,* 4 editions to 1928; English ed., 1887.

68. A. B. Marx, *Die Lehre von den musikalischen Komposition,* Vol. II; Leipzig, 1842; ten editions through 1884).

69. Edward Krüger, *System der Tonkunst* (Leipzig, 1866), pp. 364*ff.*

70. Hugo Riemann, *Grosse Kompositionslehre* (Leipzig, 1902), Vol. II.

71. Ebenezer Prout, *Fugue* (London, 1891).

72. Hugo Riemann's struggles to fit all the fugues in Bach's *Well-Tempered Clavier* into this form can be seen in his *Handbuch der Fugen-Komposition* (Leipzig, 1890–1891).

73. Czackzkes, *op. cit.,* p. 62.

74. Reicha, *Traité* . . . , Bk. II, Prt. IV, p. 25.

75. Martini, *op. cit.,* II, xxxiv*ff.*

76. Galeazzi, *op. cit.,* Morigi, *op. cit.;* of later theorists, only Fétis (*op. cit.,* Pt. II, 49–50) recommended the subdominant for the first modulation and then only when the subject is major and in such a form that it is difficult to use it in the relative minor.

77. Measure numbers here follow those used in the Breitkopf & Härtel edition (No. 1626) for chorus and piano reduction, which numbers the whole Gloria continuously, the *Cum sancto spiritu* starting with measure 260.

78. Marpurg, *op. cit.,* pp. 17–8; see also Mann, *op. cit.,* pp. 154–5.

79. *Ibid.,* p. 20; see also Mann, *Ibid.,* p. 156.

80. Kollman, *op. cit.,* p. 27.

81. Bussler, *op. cit.,* p. 134. Bussler lists the Fugues in E-flat Minor and B Minor from Bach's *Well-Tempered Clavier,* Book I, as free fugues.

82. Marpurg, *op. cit.,* pp. 19–20; see also Mann, *op. cit.,* p. 156.

83. Kirkendale, *op. cit.,* pp. 14–24.

84. Czerny, *op. cit.,* p. 125.

85. Reicha, *Traité* . . . , Vol. II, Bk. IV, pp. 222*ff.*

86. Jadassohn, *op. cit.,* p. 191.

87. Marx, *op. cit.,* II, 287.

Chapter VIII

Planning and Writing

a Fugue

Once the fugue exposition has been written, one is confronted with the question of formal continuation. Even within the framework of the expanded fugue of the eighteenth and nineteenth centuries, there exists a variety of patterns that can be followed, any of which can make a logical fugue and provide instructive challenges for the student. The most practical approach is for the beginner to decide on a plan in advance and concentrate his energies on working out a satisfactory fulfillment of that plan. The main problems then become those of craftsmanship, of adapting the musical materials to the plan so as to create a satisfactory whole.

Since this is also an exercise designed to develop certain skills—and especially to produce an awareness of the skillful use of such techniques in the fugues of other composers—each study fugue should set up precise problems and impose clear limits, for it is under these circumstances that craftsmanship must come into play. The first study fugues should then be strict fugues in Marpurg's sense of the term, fugues in which all the musical material used is derived from the exposition. The polyphonic style should be strict, as in the fugues of Bach and Handel. Each part should be an independent melody without extensive doubling in thirds, sixths, or octaves, and the separate existence of each part should be made clear by the consistent use of rests when the part has dropped out temporarily. The episodes, pedal, and coda sections should likewise be polyphonic without recourse to virtuoso keyboard figuration. Strettos, if used, should be genuine strettos.

The harmonic style should normally be based on eighteenth-century practice. The type of chromaticism found in the fugues of Schubert and Brahms discussed in Chapter VII creates special problems in writing any form, and to write a fugue in that style requires more experience in chromatic harmony than most musicians have today. Whatever the harmonic style chosen, it must be consistent throughout the fugue. A sudden irruption of chromaticism in a predominantly diatonic work is disturbing. Also, the keys should be established clearly and in the conventional way until the basic procedures of the given fugue form and its key scheme have been mastered.

As mentioned earlier, the fugues in this text have been planned for a three-voice texture because it seems more practical for the student to use his time writing as many complete fugues as possible, and the time spent in writing even one more voice in a long fugue could be used to make at least half of another three-voice fugue. The same formal procedure is involved no matter how many voices are used, the main structural difference being in the extra entry required for the exposition; the last entry in a three-voice fugue exposition is the subject whereas, in a four-voice fugue, it is the answer. No matter how many voices are involved, the fugues should be written for possible performance. It is usually most practical to write for keyboard, two hands; but, whatever the medium chosen, each fugue should stay within the performance limits agreed upon.

It is usually advisable, once a plan for a study fugue has been established, to write the different sections of the fugue separately and then join them together. If the fugue is planned precisely, the joining together of these parts should not present great difficulty. The techniques and judgments involved in linking separate parts together so as to give the impression that the whole work was composed as a unit, starting from the beginning and moving directly to the end, are a major consideration in composing in all forms. Except in rare cases, these must be learned by experience, and the difficulties encountered in joining together sections already composed will help reveal details of planning ahead that must be taken into account when composing a work straight through from start to finish. There is little opportunity or necessity today for a student to write enough fugues to gain this proficiency, but a heightened awareness of the planning and control that were involved in writing the fugues that we perform or analyze should result from even a few efforts in making a formal fugue.

There are special techniques involved in writing such parts of a fugue as the episodes, pedal, and stretto. These make more sense when composed for specific situations than as abstract entities, and certain arbitrary patterns for study fugues have been set up so as to introduce them in the actual process of writing a fugue. It is taken for granted that the expositions for these fugues have already been written; the expositions written earlier (Chapter VI) can be made the basis for these study fugues.

Preliminary Planning for the Fugue

Once the exposition is completed, the first thing that must be decided on is the number of restatements of the theme that will be used and the polyphonic ordering of their entries. No fixed rule for this has ever been given, but the accepted principle applied in fugue —that the theme should not appear in the voice that last stated it and that it should be equitably shared among the voices—should be followed. The expositions written earlier all have a regular countersubject, and this will be used with each restatement of the theme. Ideally, the later entries of the countersubject should be governed by the same rule for polyphonic distribution that governs the subject, but this is less essential here. However, since the countersubject is written in invertible counterpoint with the subject, the two (subject and countersubject) should appear in contrapuntal inversion at least once in the fugue. If it has always been above the subject in the exposition, it should appear below it in at least one restatement; if it has always appeared below the subject in the exposition, it should be placed above it somewhere in the body of the fugue. Normally, the countersubject appears in a voice adjacent to the subject. This is not absolutely necessary, but it usually is easier to write the free part (or parts) if it is done this way.

The First Study Fugue

The first study fugue projected will use three single restatements of the subject form of the fugue theme separated from the exposition and from each other by episodes. There will be no stretto, pedal, or coda. Table VI shows some possible polyphonic arrangements for this fugue.

TABLE VI
Three Possible Polyphonic Plans for the First Study Fugue

	S			Cs				S
First Polyphonic Sequence	A	Cs	Ep	S	Ep	Cs	Ep	Cs
	S	Cs				S		
	A	Cs		S				
Second Polyphonic Sequence	S	Cs	Ep	Cs	Ep	Cs	Ep	S
		S				S		Cs
	S	Cs		S				
Third Polyphonic Sequence	A	Cs	Ep	Cs	Ep	S	Ep	Cs
		S				Cs		S

S = Subject
A = Answer
Cs = Countersubject
Ep = Episode

A purist might well describe this sort of plan of the entries as the true "form" of a fugue, since fugue is a polyphonic form, and this is the basic thematic skeleton of a polyphonic work. However, as we have seen, the tonal pattern superimposed on this polyphonic structure is equally essential to the form. In this first exercise in writing a fugue, the three restatements of the subject will follow this tonal plan: first restatement of the subject in the relative minor (if the fugue is in major) or the relative major (if the fugue is in minor); second restatement in the dominant key; and the final restatement in the tonic key. For C major (1) and A minor (2) this would entail the following key scheme if the subject does not modulate at the end. (The diagram begins with the key ending the exposition, which in a three-voice fugue ends with the subject; the dashes represent episodes.)

(1) C–a–G–C
(2) a–C–e–a

If the subject modulating at the end is chosen, however, the key scheme is more complicated because each statement of the subject will end in the dominant key of the key in which it began. (Two keys are now used in each section; for clarity, a semicolon is used to mark the end of each statement in the diagram below. The exposition now ends in the dominant key.)

(1) G;–a,e;–G, D;–C,G

(2) e;–C, G;–e,b;–a,e

This shows the necessity for preliminary planning that takes into account the type of subject used as well as the key scheme and ordering of restatements. It is immediately clear that this type of modulating subject is impractical for the projected plan. The final entry ends in the dominant key, and the re-establishment of the tonic key would require further extension of the fugue. This could be rectified by having the last restatement of the subject transposed down a fourth, beginning in the subdominant and ending in the tonic (F, C; or d,a), or by using the answer form of the theme in which the modulation is reversed (G, C; or e,a), but here we will stick to the projected plan. For this first study fugue, the student must then choose an exposition made on a nonmodulating subject. It does not matter whether the subject–answer pair is tonal or real, because the brief dominant beginning of a tonal subject can usually be harmonized with the dominant chord in the tonic key, thus establishing it clearly, and the subject will end in the key (if not the chord) with which it began.

Once the exposition to be used has been chosen, the polyphonic plan of the fugue using the form shown in Table VI should be worked out, according to the form of the exposition chosen. Then a key scheme of the type just illustrated should be made, based on the key of the subject which determines the key of the fugue. The two parts of each restatement (the subject and countersubject) should then be copied out, transposed to the proper keys, and placed contrapuntally as shown in the polyphonic plan. (See instructions given in the correlative section of the Workbook.) The third voice may be left out for the present as it may be the important factor in uniting the end of the episode to the restatement and should be written after the episodes are made. The essential materials of the fugue—the exposition and restatements—are now ready. The next step is the planning and writing of the episodes.

WRITING THE EPISODES

The writing of episodes involves techniques that, in earlier centuries, were included as a matter of course in the training of musicians, but today they are often taught for the first and perhaps the only time in a course on fugue. For this reason the episode types used in this first study fugue will be quite rigidly prescribed in the manner of exercises. The episodes have, of course, two main purposes: the development of material taken from the fugue exposition and the modulation from the key of one statement of the theme to the key in which the next will appear. It is this second function that determines the basic plan of an episode. Once the plan is made, the musical materials can be chosen from the exposition and adapted to the chosen pattern.

Before any musical details have been decided on, one must consider the outlined plans of the fugue and the nature of the fugue subject. The outlined key scheme will show what keys are involved in the modulations to be used in each of the three episodes—from the key in which the preceding statement of the theme ends to that in which the next statement appears. The diagram of the polyphonic structure will show which voice will state the subject after the episode. This has already been implemented in writing out the re-statements and is an important factor in planning the episode because, in accordance with fugal tradition, the voice in which the next statement of the theme is to appear should drop out near the end of the episode in preparation for its re-entry with the subject. The nature of the subject itself must also be considered—what part of the measure it starts on, what degrees of the scale it begins with, and what will be the best harmony to prepare and accompany its entrance.

A fugue exposition is given here to be used as the basis of the illustrations of the process of creating the episodes. (See Ex. 90.) Since it is in A minor, it will follow the A-minor key scheme given above, and the polyphonic pattern that will be followed is the first of those outlined. The subject begins on the third beat and on the fifth scale degree, which will be normally harmonized with the dominant harmony. The first restatement of the subject will be in C major and will enter in the middle voice.

Aside from free improvisatory sections (which will not be used in the study fugue), there are three general types of episodes used in fugues—the sequential episode, the imitative or canonic episode, and the episode using invertible counterpoint. The nature of the first modulation, up or down a third (depending on whether the fugue is in major or minor), makes it a good one in which to use the sequential episode. The examples of the process of writing this episode will be based on the given exposition, so that the first episode will be moving from A minor to C major; but the same planning and writing processes may be applied to other modulation plans as well.

EXAMPLE 90

THE FUGUE EXPOSITION USED AS BASIS FOR EXAMPLES SHOWING CONSTRUCTION OF STUDY FUGUE.

THE SEQUENTIAL EPISODE

Although many sequential episodes in fugues extend beyond three or four repetitions of the sequence unit, it is generally accepted today that three repetitions—or, indeed, two and a half (the last half of the third repetition being slightly varied)—are sufficient. Also, most episodes are extended beyond the boundaries of the strictly organized core, so that the modulation need not necessarily be contained within the rigid sequence. Nevertheless, unless the student has had considerable experience in planning sequential modulations, it is advisable to plan the modulation within the strict sequence and to limit this to three or, at the most, four repetitions of the unit.

Once the modulation is known, the next thing to do is to see how it is possible to accomplish it within a sequence involving three or four steps. It is easiest to plan this first in a diagram in which letters representing the sequence of keys through which it will pass are thought of as the basic skeleton. These keys must be equidistant by some fixed interval, and, for the first plan, it is clearest to think of the over-all sequence pattern as a real sequence moving through the keys outlined. For a fugue based on Example 90, the first episode moves from A minor to C major, and two series of equidistant keys come immediately to mind—by upward fourths, a, d, G, C, and by upward seconds, a, B, C.

The strongest harmonic progression is the movement by upward fourths (or downward fifths) because it follows the natural order of the authentic cadence. It will not work if the episode is in a major key going to the relative minor because then the movement leads in the wrong direction, toward the flat keys. To modulate from C major to A minor by this kind of progression is impossible because going from C to F to B-flat leads one away from a, not toward it. But, because of its simplicity and because it works in other progressions beside that from the minor to the relative major, it will be illustrated first.

The sequence a, d, G, C could easily be accomplished by a simple progression of dominant seventh chords using these pitches as roots, but this does not produce as interesting a pattern as one involving two or more chords, nor will it provide as much room for development of musical material as one that spreads out over a longer space. A common pattern for the unit in any sequence is the authentic cadence V–I or V^7–I, and this can easily be arranged here. Since it starts in an established key, A minor, this tonic triad can be altered to form the dominant seventh of D minor and the tonic in D minor altered in the same way to become the dominant seventh of G major, and so forth. This pattern is the one followed in the Bach episode given in Example 85a; it is shown in the key of this study fugue in the following harmonic skeleton.

$$a{:}i, d{:}V^7 \,/\, d{:}i, G{:}V^7 \,/\, G{:}I, C{:}V^7 \,/\, C$$

Since this fugue is in ¾ time each unit can be represented by a single measure, as shown in Example 91a. The unit given here in D minor might also have been in D major, but D minor being closer to both A minor and C major, it is used here. An outline of the root movement for this episode is given in Example 90a.

The next step is to choose the musical materials from the exposition that will be used in this episode and to form a polyphonic entity on the given skeleton. (See Ex. 91b.) First of all, the bass has been arranged so that the dominant-seventh chord comes in the first in-

EXAMPLE 91

THE THREE STEPS IN MAKING A SEQUENTIAL EPISODE
MOVING FROM A MINOR TO C MAJOR BY RISING FOURTHS.

version, simply in order to give a more melodic bass. If this type of
sequence moves regularly up by fourths or down by fifths it soon gets
out of range; here, the bass moves down a fifth instead of up a fourth
for the second unit to keep that part within a normal bass range. A
fragment of the subject, motive *a* is chosen from the exposition and

put into a varied form, *a'*, in the soprano where it works well starting on the second beat. For the middle voice, a second fragment, motive *b,* is selected, and this fits well with both *a'* and the bass, starting on the up-beat of the first beat.

Before these are fixed in the sequence, the end of the exposition and the beginning of the first restatement should be checked so that the sequential part of the episode will start and end with each of the three voices in approximately the same range as the voices with which they must be connected. This results in the ranges shown. The soprano starts on *a'* and moves up by fourths, and the alto starts on *a,* moves up a fourth (*d'*), then down to *g* for the last unit. By these procedures, the sequence in Example 91b is realized.

The final step is often the most difficult of all, that of connecting up the episode with the end of the exposition and the beginning of the restatement of the subject. Here, a certain amount of experimentation must be brought into play, but, because the ranges of the voices at these points has been taken into account before writing the sequence, this is not too difficult. The finished form appears in Example 91c with the added materials circled. At the end of the exposition, the bass part moves on to avoid too final an ending, and the upper parts move into the right range. It has been possible to start the *a'* motive on *c''*, the last note of the subject, and, although by starting on this pitch it does not follow the sequence pattern, it binds together the exposition and the episode thematically. The A in the bass in the first measure of the sequence has also been moved up a beat to make better harmony. Slight changes like this in the beginning or end of a sequential episode are quite common. While it must be planned exactly, it need not be rigidly kept when adapted to its musical surroundings.

More changes have had to be made to adapt the end of the sequence to the restatement of the subject that follows. Motive *b'* has been omitted to make a rest before the entry of the subject in the alto, but an extra *a'* has been inserted on the first beat of the measure because the bass and soprano are so far apart that a note in the middle voice is needed here. To make up for the lack of rhythmic motion that results from the omission of motive *b'*, the bass now moves in eighth notes, continuing this into the next measure. The bass is the free part in this restatement, so it is the part that must be counted on to make the "joint" between the episode and restatement sections smooth. The top part has also been extended in a manner that resembles motive *a'*, giving a sense of continuity before it takes up the countersubject.

A sequential episode of this type, moving by rising fourths or falling fifths, is not easy to handle because of the large skips between repetitions of the unit. Adjustments such as that made in the bass of this one cannot be made simultaneously in all parts, and the upward motion of the soprano part in the three repetitions is the most that can be allowed without moving completely out of range. Bach solved this problem by using one motive in imitation formed so that the soprano and alto units overlap; this removes the need for a new motive in the middle part. (See Ex. 85a.) This episode may also be worked out in this way. (See Ex. 94a on p. 322.) Such a pattern takes advantage of the large interval between repetitions of the melodic unit, using it to fit the motive into different ranges in the imitation.

The sequence used in this episode is a real sequence, each unit in a different key; this is the strongest way to effect a modulaton with this sequence interval. A tonal sequence, remaining within a key, could also be managed here by counting the tonic of A minor as vi in C major and then moving by rising fourths and falling fifths within C major; *a, d, g, c* act as roots of vi, ii, V, and I in C. Using a tonal sequence, the modulation from C to a by rising fourths, which was discarded earlier because a real sequence would lead into the flat keys, might also have been accomplished, although in more steps than is allowed here. To do this, the tonic in C is counted immediately as III in A minor, and the notes *c', f, b, e,* and *a* act as roots to the chords III, VI, ii⁰, V, and i in A minor. But again, this is less strong. The long tonal sequence is normally used to establish a key after one has arrived in it, and the arrival here is made so soon that the sense of modulation, of forward movement, is missing. Also, these progressions, used tonally, leave no space for interpolated chords, and it is difficult to make an interesting polyphonic unit of motives from the exposition within a single chord. Nevertheless, Bach did use this type of episode successfully, and the first sequence in Example 85b is of this type.

The second sequence suggested above, moving the unit up or down by a series of seconds, is easier to manage in the matter of range (as is also a sequence moving by thirds). The harmonic pattern making up the unit here must, however, be more complex; it must include strong root movement, preferably using a cadence, to establish the harmonic or tonal center of each unit of the sequence. The harmonic pattern for the sequence made here will be ii, V^7, I, arranged in a two-measure unit.

The steps used in developing the episode created in Example 91 can still be followed here, but the settling of the harmonic pattern for the entire episode needs more care. It could be made a real sequence, the progression ii, V⁷, I being used successively in the keys of A minor, B major, and C major, but this type of sequence is more effective if it involves a mixture of tonal and real sequence. (See Bach's use of this in a sequence moving by seconds in Ex. 85c.)

Before the exact key and chord structure is decided on, it is advisable to work out the root movement first as if for a real sequence so the whole chord root pattern can be seen. Here the progression ii,

EXAMPLE 92

THE THREE STEPS FOR MAKING A SEQUENTIAL EPISODE MOVING FROM A MINOR TO C MAJOR BY RISING SECONDS.

V^7, I in A minor, B major, and C major creates the root pattern *B, E, A**; *c*-sharp, *F*-sharp, *B**; *d, G, c**. (The asterisks indicate the points of arrival of each statement of the pattern.) Clearly, both the first and the last unit should be kept as ii, V^7, I because these project the basic keys at the beginning and end of the episode. The middle one is the one to be tonally adjusted. The safest way to calculate this is to work from the asterisked pitch, which is the point of arrival of that unit. This is *B,* and a little thought reveals that a diminished triad on this note can fit into both A minor and C major —ii^0 in A minor, and vii^0 in C major. By changing the *c*-sharp and *F*-sharp to *c*-natural and *F*-natural, a pattern can be made that will fit in A minor (and in C as well). Here, we will treat the i in A minor that ends the first unit as the pivot, making this vi in C major, and this second unit will then consist of the progression I, IV, vii^0 in C major. This completes the harmonic pattern for the sequence, which is shown in Example 92a.

The process used to make the first episode can now be continued. Example 92b shows the realized sequence. The top part again is derived from motive *a* in the exposition, varied differently to fill in the two-measure unit. The bass is then worked out melodically to give more rhythmic and polyphonic interest, and another variant of motive *b* from the exposition is inserted. The middle part is the first measure of the bass in inversion and diminution, and the triadic pattern found in both this part and the bass can be related to motive *c* from the countersubject in the exposition. The final version, Example 92c, in which the sequence is joined to the exposition and the following restatement is in C major, should by now need no detailed analysis. As before, the portions added or changed have been circled.

The student should choose the type of sequence he considers most appropriate for his fugue and should make the first episode following the procedure demonstrated, taking special care to connect it smoothly with the exposition and the first restatement section. The continuation of the free part in the restatement may be made at this time also, making use of musical material and melodic motives that make it seem like a logical continuation of what has gone before. It is a good idea not to write the last measure of this free part until the next episode is written, for it will probably have to be changed to make a good connection with this second episode.

If difficulties arise in planning and making this episode, the student should first work the exercises on sequence in the *Workbook* in the section correlated with this chapter.

EPISODES MADE WITH INVERTIBLE COUNTERPOINT

The episode using invertible counterpoint is the most prestigious of the episode types because it exhibits skill in a restricted contrapuntal technique. From the seventeenth century through the nineteenth century, counterpoint texts included a long section on invertible counterpoint, for it was a technique used not only in fugue, but also in nearly every musical form. A brief summary of the rules of the more common types is still included in most modern textbooks on modal and tonal counterpoint,[1] but it is rarely used today outside of courses in fugue; for this reason, its use often goes unnoticed in nonfugal works of the sixteenth through the nineteenth centuries.

Invertible counterpoint is possible at nearly every interval, but the most common and most practical in a fugal episode—and the easiest to work with—is that in which the contrapuntal inversion takes place at the octave. This type has already been discussed in connection with writing the countersubject (p. 149). There are also types of invertible counterpoint in which each part can be transposed by more than one interval and still follow the rules of counterpoint, but these are not necessary for the writing of an episode. The only rules given here will be those for the writing of simple invertible counterpoint at the octave.

The rules for triple invertible counterpoint at the octave are like those of double counterpoint at the octave used in writing the countersubject but with a few more restrictions.

1. The consonances are the thirds, sixths, unison, and octave plus the augmented fourth or the diminished fifth when they are part of a chord and are treated according to regular harmonic rules.

2. In addition to the perfect fifth (which was forbidden in two-part invertible counterpoint because in inversion it becomes a perfect fourth), the perfect fourth is now forbidden even in its consonant position (between the two upper parts) because in some inversions it, too, will make a perfect fourth with the bass.

3. Thus, the perfect fourth and perfect fifth, as well as seconds and sevenths count as dissonances, and must follow the rules for dissonance treatment in tonal counterpoint.

4. To insure ease in contrapuntal inversion, the range between each pair of adjacent parts (top and middle, middle and bottom) must never go beyond the octave.

In summary, triple invertible counterpoint at the octave follows the regular rules for tonal counterpoint except that the range between adjacent parts is limited to the octave, and the perfect fourth and fifth must be treated as dissonant intervals. This last limitation means that all three notes of a triad may not sound at once, so that special care must be taken to make the harmony clear. At times, the fifth of the chord can be used along with the root; it can be treated as a legitimate dissonance such as a passing tone or an appoggiatura, but it must be watched carefully. Both perfect fourths and fifths may be used in seventh chords (especially the dominant sevenths) if the seventh is present also. One must watch, however, that consecutive perfect fourths, or a perfect fourth following directly after an augmented fourth, are not used in the upper parts even when they are parts of a seventh chord. In some contrapuntal inversions they will become parallel perfect fifths or hidden fifths. It is a good idea always to write out the different contrapuntal inversions while working out the original phrase because the rules can make the inversions correct, but cannot insure that they will sound well. A certain amount of trial and error is usually necessary to create a successful pattern.

The main advantage of invertible counterpoint is that it provides for the re-use of the same section of material in a different vertical arrangement. For a phrase in triple invertible counterpoint, six contrapuntal arrangements are possible, although not all are equally successful for a particular phrase:

$$
\begin{array}{cccccc}
A & A & B & B & C & C \\
B & C & C & A & B & A \\
C & B & A & C & A & B
\end{array}
$$

When one of these units is a complete phrase of several measures, this same phrase may be re-used in several inversions in the course of a piece. Bach's Two-Part Invention in E Major and his Three-Part Invention in F Minor are both based upon a theme written in invertible counterpoint which is re-used later in contrapuntal inversions. In some fugues an entire episode may be written in invertible counterpoint and re-used later in an inversion, but in a fugue one rarely gets the same contrapuntal section re-used more than once, and the inversion chosen is that which sounds best.

This manner of re-use of an episode written in invertible counterpoint will not be used here. It is effective only in a fugue longer than this first study fugue will be, in which a re-use of material will not result in monotony. A more common use of invertible counterpoint in an episode is the building up of a single episode through the combining of several contrapuntal inversions of one short unit, producing such patterns as the following.

(1)	A	C	B	(2)	A	C	A	(3)	A	B	A
	B	A	C		B	B	B		B	A	B
	C	B	A		C	A	C		C	C	C

Each vertical line stands for a polyphonic fragment of one or two measures, and each grouping shows three contrapuntal arrangements of the same melodic fragments A, B, and C. These are but three of many possible combinations. Each of these combinations shown— 1, 2, or 3—represents a possible pattern for a fugal episode built up from a contrapuntal unit along with two contrapuntal inversions of this unit.

The form of this episode is remarkably like that of the early *rondellus* described at the beginning of Chapter I. The main difference is that the *rondellus* repeats the material untransposed with only a contrapuntal rearrangement, whereas the episode repeats the material transposed as well as in a rearranged polyphonic order. The episode is like a sequential episode in that, for each repetition, each melodic fragment (A, B, C) is transposed by the same interval to the next pitch level, but the contrapuntal inversion prevents it from being a genuine sequence.

The second episode in this study fugue will use the first plan shown above. The episode must first have a broad modulation plan, made as if by sequence, outlining the pitch sequence that the transpositions of the unit will follow in moving from the first key to the second. This can be worked out easily. If the study fugue is in major, the modulation between the first and second restatements of the subject will be from the relative minor to the dominant (if the fugue is in C, from a to G). If it is in minor, the modulation will go from the relative major to the dominant (if the fugue is in a, from C to e). Each can be accomplished in three steps. The major fugue can go up by fourths or down by fifths (in C major, *A, D,* and *G* will be the three pitch levels used). The minor fugue can move up by seconds (in A minor, *C, D,* and *E* will be the pitch levels used). The fugue being written here as an illustration will follow the latter pattern. Being in 3/4, the pattern used will again be a two-measure unit.

Once the modulation is decided on, the next thing to do is to compose the basic unit in a triple invertible counterpoint. The great problem in this type of episode is the smooth connection of the individual voices in the inversions. Here in pattern 1, for example, in the top line, fragment A must go smoothly to C; in the middle, B to A; and in the bass, C to B; and C, A and B in the second unit will be transposed to a different pitch from the first. The safest way is to start with an incomplete version of the unit, transpose and rearrange it to fit the prescribed pattern, and then enlarge the unit to full size, working it out to the completed version.

The shortened version of the unit for this episode is shown in Example 93a. It will be noted that it is incomplete and room for expansion is left at the beginning or end of A, B, and C. This frag-ment is written according to the rules of invertible counterpoint, and the materials used are again derived from the fugue exposition. Line A comes from motive *d;* B uses a free melodic inversion of motive *b;* and the upward skip from the up-beat used in C is derived from motive *x,* the skip that precedes motive *a* in the exposition. Care has been taken to create a logical harmony in the key of C, the key in which the episode begins.

This version has then been copied out (Ex. 93b) to follow the contrapuntal plan, with the transpositions indicated. Because of the nature of the unit, it has been decided to treat it as in a real sequence; the second statement of the unit will be in D major and the third in E minor. The unit is now copied out with C on top, A in the middle, and B in the bass, each melodic fragment transposed up a whole step into the key of D major. Then, for the third step, the original melodic units are arranged with B on top, C in the middle, and A in the bottom, this time with each transposed into the key of E minor. This gives the working model of the episode. (If this combination of transposition and contrapuntal inversion seems hard to visualize in one step, the student should first do each process separately, copying out the inverted forms of the unit without transposition and then transposing these into the proper keys. An exercise in this is also provided in the correlated section of the *Workbook.*)

Once this is done, the process of connection is made by extending each melodic fragment. This is done mainly by trial and error. These extensions have been made so as to follow the rules of invertible counterpoint and so that each melodic fragment keeps its new form in each statement of the unit. Example 93c shows the completed episode. Lines A, B and C are shown in their completed forms with the added notes circled.

In some fugue texts, it is recommended that every entry of each fragment be preceded by a short rest to make the entrances clear, and this has been done here to make the structure immediately apparent

EXAMPLE 93

THE PROCESS OF MAKING AN EPISODE IN INVERTIBLE COUNTERPART.

(a.)

(b.)

(c.)

to the eye as well as to the ear. It is not necessary to do this unless the rest is wanted for musical reasons.

This episode has been worked out strictly so that the finished form is in strict invertible counterpoint, giving the impression that the finished form of the unit was the original one. Since the finished form will not be inverted later in the fugue, it is not structurally necessary to work it out so strictly, but it should be done at least once in this study fugue so as to provide the experience of working out and producing an episode of this type. Analysis of sections of invertible counterpoint in the works of past composers, however, will show that often slight changes or additions will be made so that A, for example, is not always exact in each statement of the inverted forms. Also, chromatic alterations of some notes may be used. In a work of art, a technique like invertible counterpoint is a working convenience, not a rigid technique to be exhibited for its own sake.

The connection of this type of episode to the preceding and following sections of a fugue may often require the addition of one or two measures at each end. Ideally, this should be calculated in advance, but about all that can be done here is to see that the episode begins roughly in the same range in which the preceding section ends. The combination of contrapuntal inversion and transposition makes it next to impossible to know from the writing of the first unit what range the three voices will be in in the last statement of the unit. These extensions, like those used in Examples 91 and 92, should sound like a natural continuation of the material of the fugue. The free parts in the restatement sections are the most important ones, for it is in these parts that the movement can continue beyond the entries of the subject and countersubject, so that the rhythmic and melodic continuity is kept in at least one part.

THE IMITATIVE EPISODE

To categorize the imitative episode as an exclusive type is misleading since, although there are episodes whose sole organizing principle is imitation, there are a great many episodes that combine imitation with sequence or with invertible counterpoint, sometimes with both at once. The form of episode that combines sequence with imitation was very common in the late Baroque period but was used later as well, and this use is not restricted to fugue. During the early eighteenth century, it was common in the Baroque concerto and sonata, and a section combining sequence and imitation is often found in the development section of the Classical sonata form.

Working out an imitative sequential episode involves the procedure followed in the creation of sequential episodes. (See Ex. 91 and Ex. 92.) The only difference is that, instead of using three voices for the basic unit (for a three-voice episode), only two are needed. In Example 94a, an imitative episode has to be made out of the ma-

EXAMPLE 94

IMITATIVE EPISODES (a) IN SEQUENCE (b) IN INVERT-
IBLE COUNTERPOINT

terial used for the sequential episode shown in Example 91. Here, the
sequence moves by rising fourths (or falling fifths), and this makes
for good imitation since the interval makes a natural difference in
range between repetition of the unit. The top voice and the bass of
the basic unit has been kept (the middle part not being needed), and,
in writing out the sequence, the upper melody is put alternately into
the middle and top parts. To make each part into an independent
voice, this melodic phrase has been extended (circled notes in the
first unit) to make an overlap. The bass has been changed somewhat
to give more rhythmic and melodic motion.

Imitation is also associated with invertible counterpoint. In fact,
the episode developed in Example 93 can be called imitative since

the three melodic phrases move from part to part, but the imitation
is not obvious to the ear because all three melodies are involved. A
common type of imitation in invertible counterpoint is that outlined
in the second and third diagrams given in the above section on invertible counterpoint, in which one part remains the same and the
other two are interchanged. Here, the material used for the invertible-
counterpoint episode given in Example 93 will be used to work out
an imitative episode in the following pattern.

$$A \quad C \quad A$$
$$B \quad B \quad B$$
$$C \quad A \quad C$$

The imitation is made by the interchange of the top and bottom
parts. This is done by copying out the basic unit used in Example 93,
here arranged in the above contrapuntal form and then extending
the different melodic fragments in the same manner as was done in
Example 93. (See Ex. 94b. Here, too, the added material has been
circled.) This type of imitation is more complex and less obvious to
the ear because two motives, A and C, take part, but it is clearly
imitation.

There is also a type of episode in which imitation or canon is
used and in which the imitation is the only organizing principle. The
modulation is accomplished by a good harmonic movement but is
not organized in harmonic sequence. This type of episode is found
in fugues of the late eighteenth and nineteenth centuries and was
used in the Italian school that followed the teachings of Padre
Martini and in the nineteenth-century *fugue d'école*. It will be used
here for the last episode in the study fugue, a rather simple modulation from the dominant to the tonic; in the example used here, it is
from E minor to A minor.

This kind of episode is interesting to write because it is less
rigidly controlled harmonically than the others. A melodic fragment
from the exposition is chosen (here, the second and part of the third
measures from the subject), and, beginning with the end of the restatement of the subject in E minor and going up to the re-entry of
the subject in A minor, a series of imitative entries are sketched out.
(See Ex. 95a.) Here, the motive is used in its inverted form also.
Then the entries are extended and the free parts filled in to form the
episode shown in Example 95b. In this type of episode, the entries
should be preceded by a skip or a rest to make them stand out to the
ear. If the student feels more secure in doing so, a provisional har-

EXAMPLE 95

TWO STEPS IN THE PROCESS OF MAKING A SIMPLE IMITATIVE EPISODE.

mony may be sketched out and the first sketch of imitations made to fit within it, but usually the pitches at which the entries are made and the keys that are established melodically by the motive itself are enough to chart the modulations even in the first draft.

A strictly canonic episode was greatly admired, but is rare and difficult to work out if one has not had much experience with both canon and episodes. As with all canons, this must be worked out strictly, measure by measure, but here it must also fit into a good harmonic modulation, sequential or nonsequential.

The Study Fugue as a Whole

Once the last episode has been finished and connected with the final restatement of the theme, the fugue should be brought to a close by a one- or two-measure codetta. All the free parts should by now have been filled in. It should then be played through and examined as a whole. The main thing to watch for is the sense of continuity; the rhythmic motion should not stop until the end, and the sections should all flow smoothly one to another.

Nothing has been said about cadences in this study fugue because, in a short fugue like this, strong cadences are not necessary and can even be considered inappropriate. If they do come naturally at the ends of sections, they should be de-emphasized by the use of chord inversions, delayed resolutions, and rhythmic motion in at least one part. Whether or not cadences are used to end the exposition and restatements depends mainly on the way the subject and countersubject end. The subject and countersubject in the fugue used above end with a cadence that is clear but not very final sounding, so that it presents no problem.

This study fugue should then be criticized from the point of view of proportions—relative length of exposition, restatements, episodes, and so forth; harmonic variety; and contrapuntal interest. There are no fixed criteria for these; experience in writing and analysis of good fugues are needed to shape one's judgment. A first study fugue cannot be perfect, and there is no need to try to correct any weaknesses found by rewriting this one. The point of such critical analysis is to help in planning and executing other fugues.

SUGGESTIONS FOR FURTHER WORK IN FUGUE FORM

Any number of variants of the above study fugue can be made for practice in writing a simple fugue without the use of pedal or stretto. One interesting problem is to use the answer form in some of the restatements. Depending on the subject type, this will involve careful planning of the key scheme. The fugue may also be enlarged by including both the subject and answer form of the theme in each of the restatements. This means, of course, the answer as it will appear in the key of the restatement; if the restatement is in G major, the subject will be in G major and the answer form will be as if made in an exposition in G major. This plan will work very well in the key scheme given for the study fugue just written if the subject modulates at the end. The plan had to be abandoned for this fugue when only the subject was used in the restatements, but a modulating subject combined with the answer in each restatement will mean that the restatements will begin and end in the same key. Another simple change would be the insertion of a counterexposition.

A number of changes can be made in the restatements. Inversion of the theme is easy to handle. Augmentation and diminution can be used, but they involve difficulties in the maintenance of a steady rhythmic movement. Melodic variations of the theme may be used, but they should be planned for some special effect, and they are more often found in longer fugues with more restatements of the theme.

Variations may also be made in the key scheme and in the type of episodes used. The student might like to experiment with freer use of the types of episodes already used, to re-use an episode in invertible counterpoint in another form or to extend an episode further before bringing in the next entry of the theme. Study of episodes in eighteenth- and nineteenth-century fugues may provide more ideas. The episodes shown here for the study fugue are "pure" examples of their types and need not always be so rigidly used. The important thing is to break away from the rigid pattern not because one has not planned well and things have gone wrong, but for a definite purpose, an improvement in the musical structure.

The ideal situation is for the student to make his own plan, perhaps altering it in the process of writing but always having a precise goal in mind. Following the plans of other successful fugues may have more appeal for some, and for this the simpler fugues of the *Well-Tempered Clavier*—those that do not use stretto or pedal points —are good models.[2] The expositions written earlier should be used as a basis of these fugues.

Those who prefer to stress analysis rather than writing in their study of fugue will find that even the writing of one study fugue will enable them to see the fugues of master composers in a new light. Those eighteenth- and nineteenth-century fugues analyzed in Chapter VII or those suggested there for analysis will make good material for this. Stress should be placed on the technical details—the realization of the key scheme, the proportions, and minute and detailed investigation of the episodes and their connections with preceding and following sections. For a special study of episodes and the integration of all sections of a fugue, an analysis of Fugues No. 1, No. 3, and No. 4 of Bach's *Art of Fugue* are particularly recommended.

Stretto

Stretto is the overlapping of the entries of the fugue theme in the manner of a canon. Although it should come as a surprise to the listener and as a proof of the composer's skill, the stretto is usually prepared before the fugue or even the exposition ·of the fugue is written. If there is going to be a stretto, the subject must be made so that it will stretto. There is no other way to guarantee that a subject can be put into a stretto than composing it so that it will fit with itself in canon. Thus, if a stretto is to be used, while the subject is being invented, the composer must try it out to see if it will make the type of stretto desired, and, if it will not, he must change it so that it will.

There are two main types of stretto found in eighteenth- and nineteenth-century fugues—the stretto that does not involve all the voices of the fugue and thus may be accompanied by a free part and the stretto that involves all the voices. The first is easier not only because fewer voices are involved, but also because the free part can make certain forbidden intervals (such as the perfect fourth) acceptable by the addition of another tone and can make up for any rhythmic awkwardness that might turn up in the stretto. The second kind is the most difficult and imposes the greatest limitations on the shape of the subject to be created because it involves the same problems as writing unaccompanied canon. The subject must fit with itself, be a good melody, and yet make correct counterpoint and good harmony in the stretto. Another thing that must be decided while making the subject for the stretto is whether there will be just one stretto (that is, only one melodic and rhythmic interval at which the stretto need be made) or if there will be a series of strettos of increasing closeness in the course of the fugue. J. S. Bach and his contemporaries did not mind using the same stretto, usually in different keys, in the course of a fugue. But the composers influenced by Fux, from mid-eighteenth century on, did feel compelled to have a series of ever-closer strettos in their fugues. If this is desired, then the subject must be created so as to fit with itself in several strettos, and this must be done before the final shape of the subject is decided on. The strettos then must be made before the fugue can be begun.

The first type of stretto can fit very nicely into the kind of form used for the first study fugue. Only one form of stretto will be necessary, and it can be made for only two parts, so the preliminaries are relatively simple. The process will be worked out using the subject that was used for the first study fugue illustrated here, only now it will be taken as a first sketch for a proposed fugue subject. The subject must be experimented with to see what kinds of strettos are possible; to do this, the proposed subject must be copied out in the middle of a page of music paper, and the student must then attempt to fit it against itself at different melodic and rhythmic intervals both above and below.

Since the subject was not written with stretto in mind, the only stretto found by this process that works perfectly is one with the second entry starting one measure from the end of the first, and this is too close to the end to be used when there is to be only one stretto. Another, starting one measure from the beginning, looks promising (Ex. 96a), but, at three points (x, y, and z), it is not satisfactory. The trouble at x, where there is a perfect fourth, can easily be solved by the addition of an A or c in the bass, the free part. At z, however, this cannot be done. An f-sharp in the bass could make the d'' and c'' part of a V^7 on d, but this would not fit into the harmony at this point. The subject will have to be altered here if this stretto is to

EXAMPLE 96

ADAPTING A SUBJECT SO IT WILL STRETTO.

work. The difficulty at y is simply rhythmic monotony, which could be remedied by more movement in the accompanying part. However, by using the last five notes of the theme in rhythmic condensation, the problems at both y and z are solved (Ex. 96b), and, provided the altered subject is pleasing to the composer, it can now be used as the basis of the projected fugue. The stretto can be put aside until the exposition and most of the fugue is written. The insertion of such a stretto into a fugue of the type used for the first study fugue presents no difficulties. It can be used as one of the restatements and joined to the episodes on either side of it, as were the restatements in the study fugue. The only thing that must be watched for in using the stretto is that both entries of the subject must be made clear, preferably by a short rest before the first note of each.

The stretto in which all the voices of a fugue take part is harder to work out. To create a subject that will work in such a stretto, one must start with only the beginning of the subject and, deciding on the time and pitch intervals at which the stretto will take place, compose the stretto measure by measure as a canon is composed. The leading part will then be the subject of the fugue. Fortunately, there exist lists of subjects that have been successfully used in strettos,[3] and one of these may be used here. A few subjects of this kind are provided in the *Workbook*. Having chosen one of these subjects, the student must still experiment to find the kind of strettos it will make and to work them out before starting to write the fugue in which they will be used.

A Study Fugue for Stretto

A second study fugue is proposed here in which the main problems are to work out two three-voice strettos and to fit them into a continuous fugue. It is based on the early school fugue used by the followers of Fux (see p. 263) and is a short fugue, nonmodulating, and made up of three sections. The first section is a regular exposition followed by a short extension and a cadence on either the tonic or dominant of the key. The second, the entry of which is dovetailed with the ending of the first, begins with a stretto of all three voices using either the subject or a combination of subject and answer and moves on also to cadence on either the tonic or dominant. The third section is like the second except that the stretto is a closer one. This naturally ends with a strong tonic cadence.

Example 97 shows a school fugue of this kind, taken from the early nineteenth-century textbook by Joseph Preindl, a student of Albrechtsberger.[4] It is not the exact polyphonic structure but the basic principles of construction used that the student is to emulate. In the example, each section begins with the same order of entries, moving from top to bottom, but the student does not necessarily need to follow this order. Nor does he need to make the second series of entries a counterexposition as well as a stretto, as is done here. The dovetailing of the sections begins on the resolution of the cadence. This procedure must be followed in the study fugue; it is even better if the entry can come before the cadence is finished. It will be noted also that each new entry of the theme is preceded by a rest, but two voices are always present, and continuity is strong. This is helped, too, by the fact that one of the voices from the first section continues on until the second entry of the stretto is well established. Every voice also comes to a logical end before dropping out.

EXAMPLE 97

STUDY FUGUE, JOSEPH PREINDL.

Before the two cadences or the polyphonic structure of this fugue can be planned, the two strettos that will comprise the beginnings of the second and third sections must be worked out using only the untransposed subject and answer. One of the strettos should be a fairly close one, and this will be used for the third section. The other stretto, to be used for the second section, can be at a greater distance and will be easier to contrive. Ideally, all the voices in each particular stretto should enter at the same interval. That is, if the second part enters at the beginning of the third measure of the first entry, the third should enter at the beginning of the third measure of the second entry. But this is not always possible with every fugue subject. It has not been done in the Preindl example. Here, in the second section, the second entry comes in in the third measure of the theme, but the third entry does not come in until the fourth measure of the second statement of the theme. A similar pattern is found in the final stretto. Nevertheless, both the entries in the third section are closer than the corresponding entries in the second, and this relative relationship must be followed in the study fugue. An examination of all statements of the theme in the Preindl fugue shows, too, that only the first four measures are the subject proper; the fifth measure is omitted in most later entries and should therefore be accounted a codetta to the subject. The student should be as precise in the identity of his own subject. No countersubject is needed for this fugue since there is little possibility of its re-use later in the fugue.

The best way to devise the subject for this fugue is to work it out in the process of making a canonic stretto, using some order of untransposed entries of the subject and answer. The closest stretto should be made first as a stretto with a short overlap is easy to arrange. Usually a subject that has a real answer is the easiest to work with, but in some cases a tonal answer will make a good stretto. This can be worked out only by trial and error. The subjects for stretto given in the lists mentioned above will rarely make this kind of formal stretto, but if it seems hard to work out a subject in stretto from scratch it may help to take a subject from one of these lists and adapt it in the manner shown in Example 95.

Once the two strettos are made, the order of entries for the exposition can be decided on and the exposition written. Remembering that the voice that begins the second section will be the first to drop out, the composer should not bring that voice in last. The question as to whether the first section should end on the tonic or dominant should be decided according to which cadence it will be easiest to fit with the overlapping first entry of the second section. The first section must also be planned so that the cadence will be made in those two voices that will remain when the third voice drops out to prepare for its re-entry at the beginning of section two.

The first section should be written up to and including the cadence and the beginning of the first entry of the second section over that cadence. Then the stretto that begins the second section should be copied in. Only when this has been done can the two remaining parts of the first section be extended to make a smooth overlap. This same procedure should be repeated for the ending of the second section and the beginning of the third. The third section should extend on to a final tonic cadence.

OTHER TYPES OF STRETTOS

The strettos used in this fugue and the one described earlier as a possible insertion in the first study fugue are strict strettos, called canonic strettos. Other types of strict strettos occur as well that are more complex in effect but arrived at by the same methods as those above—by experiment and trial and error. These involve regular

canonic techniques such as the use of the subject against itself inverted, in augmentation, in diminution, or in combinations of these,
for example, augmentation with inversion. The strettos illustrated
above and those used in the study fugue were made at the octave,
fifth, or fourth, but strettos may be used at any interval at which they
will work.

Many strettos are less strict; slight changes are often made to
make them fit. These changes range from the use of accidentals to
improve the harmony (but which do not change the basic melodic
line, only alter some intervals by a minor second), through slight
rhythmic and melodic changes in the theme, to radical changes or a
complete dropping out of the ending of the subject. All of these are
found in fugues in which the composer wanted the effect of stretto
but the subject itself does not make a good stretto. The one rule that
holds is that no radical changes should be made in one entry until
the next part has entered with the theme; the beginning of each entry
must be clear if it is to sound like a stretto, but, once another part
takes the lead, few listeners are aware that the theme has been altered
in the less prominent parts. Although these free strettos are found in
many fugues that are part of our regular musical repertoire, there is
little point in using them in a study fugue. The whole purpose of the
study fugue is to learn by experience the techniques involved in
fugue, and the best way to accomplish this is to use these techniques
strictly.

If desired, the general plan of the second study fugue can be
changed and expanded. The addition of more sections, the expansion
of sections to include formal episodes, modulations to other keys, and
so forth may be used. This type of fugue is the basis for a fugue like
that on *Cum sancto spiritu* by Schubert described in the preceding
chapter, and, like the Schubert work, it may have a dominant pedal
and stretto added. But this second type of exercise fugue is less used
today, mainly because it involved the introduction of the formal procedures found in Classical and early nineteenth-century fugues that
are not often studied or admired as fugues today. It is important for
a musicologist or a historically oriented theorist to understand these
forms, but it does not take a long and complex exercise fugue in this
form to elucidate the problems and techniques involved. The formal
pedal and stretto section were more often added to the *fugue d'école*
and the academic fugue of the last half of the nineteenth century, a
fugue written in a form like that used in the first study fugue. A
third study fugue will be added here using the pedal and final stretto
but following the formal procedure of the first fugue.

Third Study Fugue

A final study fugue, of a longer and more complex nature, akin to the elaborate examination fugue of the late nineteenth century but of smaller proportions, is suggested here. It is meant for those who want practice in writing a longer fugue and in the use of a pedal and formal stretto. It is also meant to act as a final fugue in which the student does the important planning as well as the execution, and, before working out such a fugue, he will need to have mastered the techniques used in the writing of the first study fugue and at least understand the process of working out a close stretto. The only technical instructions given here will be in the working out of the pedal point and its connection with the rest of the fugue.

The general plan derives from the study fugue, but it will involve not only a dominant pedal, but also a formal stretto that must be planned in advance. This stretto starts up one voice at a time after a hold on the final chord of a dominant pedal point, like that seen in the Schubert fugue on *Cum sancto spiritu.* This stretto is like a second exposition and should parallel the opening exposition, following the same order of voice entries and of statement of the subject and answer. Thus, before starting on the fugue, the student must first work out, in close stretto, an exposition of the normal order—subject–answer–subject—in the tonic key. Then, the subject fixed on, he can follow the usual order in which the parts of the fugue have been worked out, making the countersubject and the opening exposition (which will follow the order of entries used in the stretto he has just finished). Having had experience in trying to derive material for several episodes from the exposition in the first study fugue, he may want to add a codetta to the subject or a short episode in the middle of the exposition to provide more material for use later in the fugue.

The whole fugue should then be planned, the last episode arriving on the dominant chord (in the tonic key) at which point the pedal point is to begin. In comparison to the first study fugue, the proportions should be longer and restatement sections should include more than one entry of the theme. There may also be an extra entry of the subject in the exposition, a common occurrence in three-voice fugues, and a counterexposition of two or more entries may also be used. There should be, however, two restatement sections that are in related keys, and these sections should include at least two entries of the theme—either two statements of the subject, two statements of the answer form, or one statement each of the subject and the answer. If he wishes, he may use augmentation, inversion, and so forth, as well as simple two-part strettos in the restatement sections. Episodes should appear before each of these restatement sections, and another episode following the last restatement should be the one that leads to the dominant. The student should make both the key plan and the outline of the polyphonic structure of the fugue and should decide on the types of episodes to be used and the forms of the restatements. Before starting to work on the pedal, he must have sketched out the episode that precedes it, for it is in this episode that the pedal will make its entrance.

THE PEDAL POINT

The pedal point is a long, held note, usually in the bass. It does not occur only in fugue and is found in all styles and forms, but, by the nineteenth century, it had become a common practice to include a pedal point in a fugue, and it was one of the essential parts of the developed academic fugue and the *fugue d'école* of the second half of the century. The most common tones on which the pedal appears are the dominant and the tonic. The dominant pedal appears near the end, not at the very end, but as a preparation for the ending section that will center around the tonic. It builds up harmonic tension that will be resolved in this closing section. The tonic pedal, on the other hand, is normally a part of the coda. Its purpose there is to establish the tonic key and to settle down to a final ending. These harmonic functions are usually reinforced by the melodic and polyphonic movement of the upper parts. These moving parts above a dominant pedal will tend to build up tension to a harmonic climax, whereas, above a tonic pedal, they move eventually to a complete rest.

Both types of pedal are found inserted now and then in simple fugues that are constructed according to the formal principles used in the first study fugue, and they may appear under either the episode or restatement sections. In this use, they are fairly brief and can enter and leave without necessarily making a break in the rhythmic movement. They may also appear in some type of figuration centered about the note that is the basic note of the pedal, as seen in Example 86, and it is not necessary to have the pedal always in the bass. Some pedals may also involve the holding of two notes rather than just one. Here, however, the student will be working with the traditional dominant pedal point of the conventional fugue—a long note held in the bass that enters in the midst of an episode, works up to a climax, and ends on the dominant or dominant seventh, which chord is held long enough to break the rhythmic movement of the fugue.

As any harmony student knows, a pedal point must enter as a part of a chord of which it is a member and must end in a chord of which it is a member; here, in the formal pedal, it must end on the dominant or dominant seventh chord, of which it is the root. In between, however, there can and should be harmonies above the pedal that are dissonant with it. This does not mean that in a polyphonic style there is free dissonance. The dissonant treatment between the upper parts should be according to the rules for the style used, and the upper parts taken by themselves should follow these rules. But it does mean that the upper parts may outline a chord consonant in itself of which the pedal note is not a member and so make a dissonance with the pedal. The dominant of the (dominant) pedal (the V^7 formation built on D if the key is C major and the pedal is built on the dominant, G) and the diminished-seventh chord built on the leading tone of the dominant (the raised fourth degree of the scale; in C, a diminished seventh built on F-sharp) are among the "foreign" chords commonly used above a dominant pedal. One or the other of these will normally be used as the penultimate chord in a formal pedal to provide an ending cadence that will resolve to the dominant or dominant-seventh chord of which the pedal note is the root.

In addition to the tension created by dissonant harmonies above the pedal, there should be increased polyphonic and melodic-rhythmic interest. In some fugues, the pedal is the scene of strettos; of augmentation, diminution, and other scholarly variants of the theme; and of imitative sections based on fragments of the subject. This will not be the case here, as the purpose of this pedal is to produce a climax leading to and partly resolved by the stretto in the tonic key, an effect not unlike the approach to and arrival at the beginning of the recapitulation in sonata form. The pedal here will enter in the midst of an episode, and the episode will be extended on over the pedal, using fragments of the material of the episode in sequence and imitation above the pedal. The pedal will end on the dominant or dominant-seventh chord, marked by a hold, stopping all movement to prepare for the entrance of the stretto exposition in the tonic key.

As an illustration, the imitative episode made in Example 95 for the first study fugue will be used in Example 98 as the episode into which the dominant pedal, *e,* will enter. It comes in near the end of the episode where the episode has arrived at the dominant chord of A minor. Once it has entered, the episode continues, but the theme of the episode, which has been stated several times already, is shortened, the entrances coming closer together to give more rhythmic and poly-

EXAMPLE 98

PEDAL AND BEGINNING OF FORMAL STRETTO.

phonic movement. Chords dissonant with the pedal are outlined, and the pedal finally ends on a dominant chord, which is the resolution of a cadence using its dominant. This final chord is marked with a hold after which the stretto, which was prepared first of all, will enter. (As Example 98 shows, the pedal point section in a three-voice fugue is less effective than in a four-voice fugue because the active voices are limited to two. It is permitted in this case to add the pedal as a fourth voice, and the student may do so if he wishes. It should, however, drop out once the stretto has begun.)

After the stretto exposition, some composers include more strettos, perhaps a number of strettos getting gradually closer and strung together after the manner seen in the second study fugue (but without cadences separating them). Other devices such as augmentation, diminution, inversion, or strettos of the countersubject may be used in this section if the student is so inclined. But if not, the fugue may be brought to a close by a codetta-extension of the stretto that follows the pedal. This may be organized like a formal episode if desired, but the freer type of imitative episode shown in Example 95 is one of the best ways to extend and end this section, since it continues the stretto effect of close imitation and can act as a natural polyphonic extension of the stretto.

Notes

1. The one recent comprehensive study is S. I. Taniev, *Convertible Counterpoint in the Strict Style* [1909], trans. C. A. Brower (Boston: Bruce Humphries, 1962).

2. See F. C. Mayer, *Studies in Fugue Writing Based upon Models of Bach* (New York: H. W. Gray, 1931); Quincy Porter, *Study of Fugal Writing* (Boston: Loomis, 1951).

3. One that is available in most libraries is in André Gedalge, *Traité de la fugue* (Paris: Enoch, 1901). The English edition is A. Levin (Mattapan, Mass.: Gamut Music Co., 1964).

4. Preindl, *op. cit.,* pp. 79–80.

Chapter IX

Fugues with More Than One Subject

*I*n addition to simple fugues—fugues that have only one subject—there are many fugues that have two, three, four, and sometimes more subjects. Because, except for the single added countersubject, there is no important difference between the simple fugue and the fugue with one countersubject, the analytical materials used so far have been drawn from fugues using a countersubject as well as from simple fugues. Not to have done so would have meant leaving out too many interesting and important fugues. Also, in ordinary usage today, the two types of fugue are not distinguished. But, in the original and precise use of the term, the fugue with a countersubject is a type of a double fugue.

Much needless confusion has resulted from the fact that the word "countersubject" has come by usage to have a meaning that is different from the older original one. Today, one often hears or reads that a certain fugue is not a true double fugue because the second subject is "only a countersubject." But, in the eighteenth-century use of the term, *contrasubjectum* meant the second subject of a double fugue, which subject fit in double counterpoint with the first or main subject of the fugue. Marpurg, in his treatise, was very careful in his use of the word. For the free parts that accompany the theme of a simple fugue, he used the term *Gegenharmonie,* the counterparts, and the word "countersubject" was only used in relation to the double fugue.[1] Fugues using a countersubject he included as a matter of course in his section on the double fugue.

In this, Marpurg was following the usage of his time and of earlier times, and, along with Fux, he set the terminology for the early nineteenth century. In order to make sure that the terms used here are understood in this way, his definitions will be given before multiple-subject fugues of earlier periods are discussed.[2] His terms refer only to the way the second subject, or countersubject, is introduced in a double fugue, and these same ways (though with a different formal continuation) are found in earlier as well as in later fugues using more than one subject.

This countersubject may be introduced in two main ways. Either it will be introduced in a later exposition after the first subject has been given in an opening exposition, developed, and brought to a cadence that introduces the exposition of the second subject, or else the countersubject is introduced in the opening exposition of the fugue. There are three ways in which the countersubject can be introduced in the second manner—along with the first subject in the opening exposition: (1) it may enter in counterpoint with the first entry of the subject; (2) it may be stated in the entering second voice, once the first voice has finished stating the subject; or (3) it may come in as a continuation of the first voice in counterpoint with the answer that enters in the second voice. This third type of second subject is, of course, that which is today usually called the countersubject, in contrast to the new subject in the other types, which is still called a second subject.

In all of these cases, the first and second subjects are combined later on in the course of the fugue; in the first type of double fugue, in which each subject has its own exposition, this combination may appear late in the fugue as somewhat of a climax. In the others, in which the two appear in conjunction in the exposition, they will of course appear together later in the fugue. The second subject may also appear alone later in the fugue, but this does not always happen. Another way of bringing in the second subject later in the fugue, which Marpurg did not mention but which is found in actual practice, is to present the first subject alone in the first exposition and to introduce the new subject against it later on in the body of the fugue.

For Marpurg and for most German theorists of the eighteenth century, "double fugue" meant not just a fugue with two subjects in double counterpoint, but also included fugues with three, four, or more subjects. This was due to the use in their time of "double counterpoint" as synonymous with invertible counterpoint with any number of voices and not merely two, as is the usual meaning of double counterpoint today. Thus, they spoke of double fugues with three subjects, and so forth, and Marpurg's instructions really hold for all multiple-subject fugues. They refer to the entrance of the second subject in such a fugue. The actual order of bringing in third and fourth subjects was not then categorized, but in practice they are brought in either in later, separate expositions or combined with the first and second subjects in the opening exposition. At times a new subject may also be introduced in the body of the fugue against the first and second subjects. In all multiple-subject fugues, the subjects are made so that they will fit together in some type of invertible counterpoint.

Multiple-Subject Fugues in the Sixteenth and Early Seventeenth Centuries

Although this type of fugue uses more than one subject, and these subjects combine in invertible counterpoint, the origins of the fugue with two or more subjects appear to be in vocal polyphony in which more than one subject is used in a section, often without the use of invertible counterpoint. From the late fifteenth century, there are vocal works that open with a double subject, two voices entering in a duo, each with a different melody, and this pair of voices is imitated later by another pair of voices with the same two melodies. But, in most cases, these are the themes for only the first section, and, after one statement of each pair, the work moves on to a second section with new ideas. Whether or not they are written in what could be invertible counterpoint, they are not re-used in inversion.

By the late sixteenth century, there were sections in choral works that are based on two or more short themes, most commonly two, where both themes are re-used and become the basis of a more developed section. Such is the structure of the opening section of the madrigal *Scendi dal paradiso* by Luca Marenzio (1553–1599). (See Ex. 99; reprinted in *HMS,* IV, p. 12.) Here, two motives, *a* and *b,* are the basic materials of the section, and *b* enters in a way that becomes characteristic of one type of double fugue, after a rest as a continuation of *a* first in the soprano and then in the bass and alto. But the combination of the two is different from that found in the later double fugue. The two motives are not combined, as in double

EXAMPLE 99

Scendi dal paradiso (TEXT OMITTED), LUCA MARENZIO.

counterpoint, always with the same rhythmic alignment. In measure 3, motive *a* enters in the tenor against *b* in the soprano on the first beat, and, in the same measure, *a* enters in the alto against *b* in the soprano on the third beat. The motive *a* is in stretto with itself in this same measure, and, in measures 4 and 5, the stretto of *b* in these two parts takes place with *a* entering against them in the soprano on the third beat of measure 5. Similar combinations of the two motives are found in the continuation of the section, which also includes transpositions of *b*.

This is typical of the use of two subjects in choral works of this time. Whether or not the two subjects work in invertible counterpoint, they are combined in as many different ways as possible, and contrapuntal inversion is just one technique used along with stretto, transposition, melodic inversion, melodic and rhythmic variation, and rhythmic realignment to make an interesting texture, and, presumably, a polyphonic structure in which the re-use of material does not follow a predictable order and the listener can be continually surprised.

Another example of this type of double-subject construction can be seen in the opening section of the motet, *Non vos relinquam* by William Byrd (1543–1623). (Reprinted in *HAM*, I, No. 150.) Here, the second subject appears in another voice, in the bass against the first subject in the soprano. A similar use of rhythmic realignment and transposition is found, along with some melodic and rhythmic variation in later statements of the two subjects. In both of these, each motive is associated with a particular section of text so that the play on motives is also a play on two associated fragments of text.

This is the most common use for this double-theme construction, but it is also found in more "abstract" settings of the text. The first Kyrie from Palestrina's Mass for five voices on *Eripe me de inimicis meis* with only one text uses two subjects. Here, there is longer extension and more independent use of each subject, since the entire Kyrie is based on these two subjects alone.

Multiple-Subject Fugue in Instrumental Music
of the Early Baroque

Once the idea of a fugal section based on more than one theme was taken into instrumental fugue, the idea of construction based on several themes and the practical uses of invertible counterpoint were both exploited and developed to a high degree. The sixteenth-century theorist Vicentino suggested deriving a second subject from the counterpoint used against the first,[3] and this practice is found in the ricercars of Willaert and Jaques Buus (d. 1565), but this derived subject is used as the basis for a later section rather than as an entity combined with the first subject in the opening section. The clear second subject that combines with the first subject in the same section is found in the works of Andrea Gabrieli. A double theme technique that is clearly evident in the works of Giovanni de Macque (1550–1614) comes into mature use in the works of his two pupils, Ascanio Mayone (d. 1627) and Giovanni Maria Trabaci, and its use is expanded and exploited to a high degree in their works.

Example 100 shows the beginning of a ricercar from Mayone's *Secondo libro di diversi capricci* published in Naples in 1609.[4] The second subject enters as a continuation of the first, but it is clearly divided off from it by a skip in the first entry (tenor) and by a rest in the second entry (alto) where the rest is substituted for the dot used after the *a* in the first entry in measure 3. This second subject is an independent entity, contrasting melodically and rhythmically with the first subject, and it enters a little later than the first subject. The contrast in character, the entry of the second subject after the main theme has started, and the skip or rest that mark the division between the first and second subjects when they are presented consecutively in the same voice are all characteristics of this kind of double fugue exposition and become familiar regulations given for the construction of a countersubject from the seventeenth century on.

The exposition here, like many early expositions, uses the entry

EXAMPLE 100

RICERCAR FROM *Secondo libro di diversi capricci,* ASCANIO MAYONE.

order subject–answer–answer–subject. The excerpt given in Ex. 100 shows the technical problem involved in adjusting the second entry of the countersubject, which appears in the alto in measure 6, so that it works in invertible counterpoint against the answer (rather than the subject) in the bass. In measure 3, the second subject fits against the answer, with this second subject starting on c'. But in measure 6, if the second subject is to be a continuation of the answer in exactly the same way it was the continuation of the subject—and that is the way it is used here—then it must fit against the answer now starting on g', as it does in measure 6. This is accomplished by writing the countersubject in invertible counterpoint at the twelfth with the subject. The answer from measure 3 has been transposed down an octave to the bass in measure 6, and the second subject from the tenor in measure 3 has been transposed up a fifth in measure 6.

The beginning of the final entry of the subject in the soprano in measure 8 against the countersubject in the bass shows a different relationship between the two. Here, the two are in the same relation as in measure 3, both now appearing in the key of F rather than C a simple transposition. But, because of the change of key, there is a change in the melodic relationship between the first and second subjects in the bass. The second subject starts a second rather than a third up from the end of the answer form of the theme and also follows a different pattern of whole and half steps. If it were an exact transposition, the second subject would follow the *f* with an *e*-flat, but an *e*-natural is used here—a melodic change, but a very slight one compared to other melodic variations found in these seventeenth-century fugues.

Instrumental collections published in the early seventeenth century by the next generation of composers—Trabaci,[5] Banchieri,[6] and Frescobaldi[7]—not only include a good number of fugal works made on two subjects, but they also exhibit a sudden expansion of the multiple-subject fugue to include fugues with three and four subjects. Banchieri's are rather short, and both Trabaci's and Frescobaldi's pieces are long, but all of them exhibit great virtuosity in the treatment of the several subjects used. Variation, transposition, contrapuntal inversion, and rhythmic realignment are used constantly, and the more scholarly techniques such as stretto, inversion, augmentation, and *inganni* versions of the themes are also found in some of them. In studying these works, one becomes strongly aware of the great stress on artifice, ingenuity, and imagination, as well as technique, that motivated these composers of contrapuntal works.

The question of the form of the exposition becomes a complex one when there are three or four subjects. The great variety found in simple and double fugues of this time is greatly multiplied when there are more subjects to manipulate. It is impossible to outline any one pattern, and one can only generalize that all of the subjects appear somewhere near the beginning. Table VII shows the outlined entries of six expositions picked at random from Trabaci's collection published in 1603,[8] Banchieri's of 1605,[9] and Frescobaldi's *Il primo libro delle fantasie a quattro* published in 1608.[10] The manner in which they are lined up vertically in the diagram is slightly misleading because the different subjects never start together on the same beat; all that the vertical alignment means is that the subjects in one column overlap. In none of the cases here is there parallel treatment of two subjects. When two of the same subjects appear in the same column, it means a stretto pairing of two entries of the same subject.

It is hard, also, to decide when the exposition is finished ("exposition" being, after all, a term borrowed from nineteenth-century usage), so that these have been carried on to the point where all of the themes are stated and all the voices in. There is no break in the continuity at the point where the diagrams stop. All voices continue once they have entered.

To us today, a number of these beginnings do not sound at all like

TABLE VII

Subject Entries of Six Multi-Subject Expositions of the Early Seventeenth Century

TRABACI: PRIMO TONO*, CON TRE FUGHE;

```
        3
          1
    1 2     2
    1 2     3
```

QUINTO TONO**, CON QUATTRO FUGHE;

```
    1 2 3
      3
      2
        1 4
```

BANCHIERI: SONATA SESTA, FUGA TRIPLICATA;

```
    1 2 3 2
    1 2 3     2
          1 2 3 2
            1 2     3
```

SONATA SECUNDA, FUGA TRIPLICATA

```
    1 2
    2 3 1
      1
      3
```

FRESCOBALDI: FANTASIA SETTIMA, SOPRA TRE SOGGETTI;

```
    2 1
      1 1
        1 2
        2 2 3
```

FANTASIA UNDECIMA, SOPRA QUATTRO SOGGETTI

```
      2
      3 3
    1 2
        4 1
```

* Dorian
** Lydian

the beginning of a fugue, for the multiplicity of subjects disguises the imitation that is so obvious in fugue with one or two subjects. Yet, the titles show that they were considered to be fugues. The subjects, when they do enter, are treated like fugue subjects, entering on the first or fifth degree of the modal scale, and, in the body of the movement, they appear most often on these scale degrees. All of the subjects project the proper mode, after the traditions of the time, by the initial notes (1, 5, and, on rare occasions, 3), and, with Trabaci and Banchieri, tonal answers are used for the first and sometimes the second subject. As is characteristic of the time, the themes are frequently subject to melodic and rhythmic variation.

EXAMPLE 101

Fantasia sopra quattro soggetti, GIROLAMO FRESCOBALDI.

The opening of Frescobaldi's eleventh Fantasia, outlined in Table VII, is shown in Example 101. Here, the four subjects are presented in order in the opening entrances of the voices. The mode, F Ionian, is made clear by the first subject in the downward skip of the fifth from *c′* to *f,* and the other three subjects enter on *C* as well. The tendency toward variation is shown immediately in the second entry of the second theme in the tenor in measure 3, and transposition occurs in the entry of the third theme in the alto in measure 4. Most but not all of the entries are preceded by a rest or a skip in the fugal tradition. It is obvious from just this short excerpt that strict invertible counterpoint is not stressed here. It is certainly used in these works, but, most often, when there is a combination of subjects such as 3 and 1 in the alto and bass in measures 4 and 5, rhythmic realignment, variation, and transposition are involved as well. The excerpt from measures 9–11 is added at the end to show a contrapuntal exchange of subjects 1, 2, and 3 with a rhythmic realignment[11] and slight rhythmic variations. These early composers of multiple-subject fugues, like the composers of vocal fugue with more than one subject, clearly considered invertible counterpoint as only one of the techniques to be used. There is never the systematic use of rigidly worked-out contrapuntal inversions in one rhythmic relationship that characterize the double and triple fugues of later centuries.

Frescobaldi's *Fantasie* of 1608 are a musical summary of the procedures used in fugal works of his time presented in ordered form. To a degree, this collection is as important a work for understanding fugue of the early Baroque as is the *Art of Fugue* for that of Bach's time. Like Bach's work, it also shows the personal artistry and technical virtuosity of its composer and surpasses in many ways the works of his contemporaries. It includes twelve fantasias organized in groups of three. Fantasias Nos. 1–3 are made on one subject; Fantasias Nos. 4–6, on 2; Nos. 7–9, on three; and Nos. 10–12, on four. Each of the last three groups is organized so as to show different ways of combining and choosing the subjects. The opening presentation of the several subjects is different in each one. In one fantasia from each of the multiple-subject groups (Nos. 5, 8, 10), the inversion of the first subject (or subjects) is used for the additional themes. (During the seventeenth century, some considered the counterfugue in which the answer is an inversion of the subject to be a type of double fugue.)

These fantasias also use the multisection form that is typical of long fugal movements of the time. Here, the succeeding sections follow the common pattern of using a variant of the theme of the first fugue as the basis of the separate fugal expositions; in those fantasias that have more than one subject, these later sections are based on variants of the themes of the opening exposition. Example 102, from Fantasia No. 12, shows the opening section and the beginning of a later section in triple meter, where variants of the first and second themes are combined. This use of thematic transformation, in addition to the lesser variations found within each section, adds complexity to the form. It is impossible to categorize all the details of multiple-subject fugues written in the early Baroque period, but a thorough analysis of these fantasias will prepare one for a more fruitful understanding of early Baroque fugal structures.

EXAMPLE 102

Fantasia sopra quattro soggetti, GIROLAMO FRESCOBALDI.

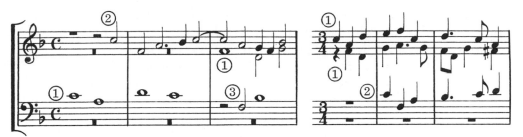

The extreme virtuosity of this early period in Italy finds an echo in Germany, but there the fugue with three or four independent subjects was less used. A fine example of such a fugue is Scheidt's *Fantasia super "Io son ferito lasso", Fuga quadruplici,*[12] which combines four themes taken from the Palestrina madrigal cited in the title. This makes a nice contrast with the *Fantasie* of Frescobaldi. The contrapuntal technique this exhibits is as formidable as that of Frescobaldi, and the themes also appear in different combinations and alignments. But the style is clearer, the variants have a more precise character, and the formal organization—a series of developments using contrapuntal manipulation and melodic figuration—is much clearer to the ear. Like Frescobaldi, however, it depends on many techniques in addition to invertible counterpoint, and there is no emphasis on simple contrapuntal inversion.

The Growth of the Multiple-Subject Fugue through Mid-Eighteenth Century

By the second half of the seventeenth century, two important trends can be seen taking place in the multiple-subject fugue. The first one is characteristic of the simple fugue as well, namely, the growing tendency to limit the subject or subjects to one distinct form in which only minor changes are made in the extension of the fugue. The other concerns only the multiple-subject fugue. This is that simple invertible counterpoint became the dominant element in the multiple-subject fugue, the contrapuntal inversion of the subjects taking place always at the same rhythmic alignment. Among seventeenth-century theorists, Reincken, (*ca.* 1670),[13] Simpson (1667),[14] Purcell (1694),[15] and Berardi (1687)[16] associated double fugue with the contrapuntal interchange of two subjects, and Reincken and Berardi definitely stated that the subjects are in invertible counterpoint.

Berardi also described the different ways in which the second subject could be brought into the fugue, and these are three of the main ways described by Marpurg—bringing in the two subjects in separate expositions and then combining them later, bringing in the second subject near the beginning in a second voice, or bringing it in as the continuation of the first voice against the answer in the second voice. Examples of all of these can be found in fugues written in the late seventeenth and early eighteenth centuries. Two movements from the *Trio Sonatas* of Corelli are double fugues in which the two subjects start together—the second movement of Op. 1, No. 3 and the third movement of Op. 3, No. 4. There are innumerable examples of double fugues in which the second subject sounds first against the answer. The *Fantasia cromatica* by Sweelinck described in Chapter VII, an earlier example, has this kind of fugue for its first section; a very clear example is the Prelude and Fugue in E Major by Vincent Lübeck (1656–1740).[17] Those in which the subjects are given in separate expositions and then combined later were less common at this time when short fugues on one or two subjects were most common. A ricercar by Pachelbel has this kind of construction.[18] The first section uses one fugue in the exposition and is extended by working with this subject. After a strong cadence, a second subject is presented in its own exposition, and only after it is over are the two subjects combined.

A similar type that is not mentioned by either Berardi or Marpurg but that was brought up at the beginning of the chapter is found in early multiple-section fugal works in the late seventeenth century and thereafter. This is where a single subject is the basis of one fugue (exposition and extension), and later this subject is combined with a second subject in the exposition and extension of both subjects in a double fugue. This can be seen in an earlier example in the *Canzona quinta* from Frescobaldi's *Canzoni alla Francese* (Venice, 1645)[19] where the opening theme returns in the final section combined with a new countertheme. The same principle is used in Buxtehude's Prelude and Fugue in E minor,[20] another work in which several fugues are strung together (separated here by toccata-like sections). Here, the subject of the second fugue section (m. 47), changed rhythmically, is combined with a new subject in the third fugue to form a double fugue (m. 66).

THE EIGHTEENTH-CENTURY DOUBLE FUGUE

By the eighteenth century it is the double fugue that is predominant among fugues with more than one subject; fugues with three or more subjects are still composed but in small numbers compared to the double fugue. The double fugue in which the second subject comes against the answer and is a continuation of the part that first stated the subject is exceedingly common and is scarcely differentiated formally from the simple fugue. Both adapt equally well to the expanded fugue form used by Bach and his contemporaries. All of the fugues from the eighteenth and nineteenth centuries analyzed in Chapter VII have countersubjects of this type, though only in the Bach F-sharp Major Fugue is it used often enough after the exposition to be included in the polyphonic diagram.

The other types of double fugue also adjust easily to the expanded-fugue form of the late Baroque period. A formal analysis of these will involve no different procedures than those used in Chapter VII except in the polyphonic outline of entries, where the placement of the two themes requires special notice. Although theorists of the time concentrated on the manner in which the second subject is made to fit with the first in invertible counterpoint and the manner in which it is introduced into the fugue, a special tradition in practice was growing up during that time concerning the polyphonic placement of the two subjects. This is very evident in the double fugues of Bach, and the polyphonic diagram of the fugue from his Passacaglia and Fugue in C Minor in Table VIII shows how these themes are parceled out among the four voices. The exposition is arranged so that each subject is stated once in each part, but, at the same time, neither one is stated twice in the same part. Yet, they also are stated together vertically each time. They are also shared out fairly equitably as they appear in polyphonic inversion in the body of the fugue. A similar balance can be seen in the polyphonic outline of Bach's F-sharp Major Fugue in Table III (p. 249).

Very fine examples in the expanded-fugue form of the kinds of double fugue in which the second subject is brought in after the exposition of the first are found in Bach's *Art of Fugue.* In *Contrapunctus IX,* a first subject is given an opening exposition. Then, after an episode, the second subject is brought in against the first subject, and the two are used together in the rest of the fugue in a balanced order similar to that shown in the C Minor Fugue in Table VIII. Bach uses here invertible counterpoint at the twelfth. This means, like the contrapuntal inversion shown in the beginning of the Mayone

TABLE VIII
Arrangement of Subjects in a Double and Triple Fugue of Bach

Fugue from Passacaglia and Fugue in C Minor

```
1  2          |  .   .   .   .   .   .   .   .   .   .   .   .
              |  .   . 2 .   .   .   .   . 1 .   .   . 1 .

1  2      Ep  | 2 .Ep . 1 .Ep . 2 .Ep .  .Ep .  .Ep . 2 .Ep . 2 . Coda

2      1      | 1 .   .   .   .   . .1 .   . 2 .   .   .   .   .

    1  2      |  .   .   . .1 . .2 .   .   . 1 .   .   .
```

Contrapunctus VIII *from* Art of Fugue

```
      1  |  .   .   .  ‖ 1  2  |  . 1 2      1.   . 2 ‖        3

  1      | Ep .1 .Ep . ‖ 2    1│Ep . 2   2 1  2.Ep .  ‖  3

  1      |  . 1 .   . 1 ‖ 1 2│  . 1   2   .   . 1 ‖    3
```
        Str   d:V–i   d:iv₆–V

```
         |  .   .   .  .   .   .   .   .   .   .
         |  . 2 .   . 2    .   . 1 3 2 .   . 3 .   . 1 ‖
         |  .   .   .   .*  .   .   .   .   .   .   .
         | Ep . 1 .Ep . 1   2 .Ep . 2 1 3 .Ep . 2 .Ep . 2
         |  .   .   .   .   .   .   .   .   .
         |  .   .   . 1   1 .   . 3 2 1 .   . 1 .   . 3 ‖
```

Ep = Episode
Str = Stretto
* = in thirds
(Very short episodes are omitted.)
Single vertical lines indicate end of Expositions
Inner double vertical lines in *Contrapunctus VIII* indicate beginning of second and third expositions

ricercare in Example 100, that in the inversion the two subjects will be at a different intervallic relation. (See Ex. 103.)

Contrapunctus X is the kind of double fugue in which the two subjects are first presented in separate expositions and then combined. The exposition of the second subject is brought in soon after the first exposition, and the exposition of the new subject is preceded by a half cadence. After this, the two subjects are stated together. As in *Contrapunctus IX,* these two subjects are not combined in double counterpoint at the octave, but at the tenth. A special characteristic of invertible counterpoint at the tenth is that one of the parts may be

EXAMPLE 103

CONTRAPUNTAL INVERSIONS (a) AT THE TWELFTH, FROM
Contrapunctus IX FROM *Art of Fugue,* J. S. BACH; AND (b)
AT THE TENTH, FROM *Contrapunctus X.*

doubled at the third or sixth and still maintain correct counterpoint
against the other subject, and Bach exploited this in this fugue.

Recognition of invertible counterpoint at intervals other than the
octave is necessary for a competent analysis of fugues using several
subjects, and this is not difficult when the pitches at which the subjects appear are noted. In invertible counterpoint at the octave or
double octave, each of the two parts will always appear on the same
letter pitch, although in different octaves. In the primary inversion of
invertible counterpoint at the twelfth, the upper part will remain on
the same pitch, but the lower one will be moved up a twelfth, so that
the lower voice of the original version will now begin on the letter
pitch a fifth above the one on which it originally started whereas the

upper voice will always be on the pitch on which it started originally. This pitch relation holds no matter in which octaves the parts may appear.

This is shown in Example 103a using the beginning of the first and second subjects of *Contrapunctus IX.* First, the combination of the two subjects where it first appears in measure 35 is given. Next, an inversion in the same key that appears at measure 89 is seen. Here, the transposition is to different octaves from what the simple transposition would be; the top voice moves down two octaves and the bottom up a twelfth, but the main effect of this transposition and the one that shows what type of invertible counterpoint is used is that now one voice, the bottom voice in the first version, starts on a different pitch than it originally did. The fact that it is a fifth higher indicates invertible counterpoint at the twelfth. Note that the part that is transposed to another pitch is adjusted tonally so as to remain in the key. This is often necessary with counterpoint invertible at intervals other than the octave.

The interval of inversion may be harder to recognize when the inversion is also transposed to another key, as in measure 45. But, if only the versions at measures 35 and 45 were available, one would still know that it was not invertible counterpoint at the octave because the first notes in measure 35 are the same, *D,* (although in different octaves), but, in measure 45, they are two different pitches (*f* and *c'*). To check, one needs only to transpose the material in the version at measure 45 back to the key in which the first version appears. This shows it to be invertible at the twelfth.

Example 103b shows the two subjects combined in invertible counterpoint at the tenth from *Contrapunctus X.* The original from measure 44 appears inverted in measure 66. Again, it is not a simple inversion, since the top voice is moved down an octave whereas the bottom part moves up the tenth, but the change in pitch location of the bottom part shows it to be invertible at the tenth. The original, in measure 44, shows the two voices a tenth apart; in the inversion, in measure 66, they are an octave apart. Measures 75 and 115 show the doubling of one of the parts at the sixth and third, which is possible in invertible counterpoint at the tenth.

THE MULTIPLE-SUBJECT FUGUE WITH THREE OR MORE SUBJECTS

Once the multiple-subject fugue became inextricably bound up with invertible counterpoint, fugues with four subjects gradually disappeared from the musical scene. Fugues with four subjects are found; both Berardi[21] and Rameau[22] included an example in their texts, but, although these are fugues in the course of which four subjects are introduced, all four subjects are not combined in invertible counterpoint. The chorus "Let old Timotheus" from *Alexander's Feast* by Handel, which the theorist Kollman cited, has four subjects, but it is not a fugue, nor are all four combined in invertible counterpoint. Evidently, the quadruple fugue that Bach projected for the finale of the *Art of Fugue* would not only have been a fitting finale, but also an outstanding show of technical virtuosity.

Although they are scarce compared to the number of simple and double fugues written during this time, numerous triple fugues were composed. They follow the same forms that were used in the double fugue, and those that introduce all three subjects in the exposition are quite common. In many cases, they enter in order in each voice as a continuation of the first subject. Once the first subject has been stated in the first voice, that voice moves on to the second subject that sounds against the answer in the second voice. The first voice then continues, now stating the third subject. This third subject sounds against the second subject in the second voice, and this combination is heard against the first subject that now enters in the third voice. This pattern is followed in the canzona movements from the first and second Sonatas in Four Parts of Purcell.[23] (See Ex. 104a.) It is also followed in the C Minor Fugue from the first book of the *Well-Tempered Clavier*. In the Bach fugue, the third subject seems rather insignificant compared to the other two but no less so than some of those cited by the theorist Mattheson in his examples of multiple-subject fugue.[24]

The triple fugue in which all three subjects are given by three voices in combination at the beginning of the fugue is more characteristic of the Italians at this time. The triple fugue for four voices on *Tu es sacerdos* from the *Dixit Dominus* in C major by Leonardo Leo (1694–1744) follows this procedure.[25] (See Ex. 104b.)

Bach seems to have preferred starting his triple fugues with the exposition of one subject, bringing in the other two later in the fugue. The Fugue in C-sharp Minor from the first book of the *Well-Tempered Clavier* follows this principle. After the first subject has had a regular exposition and is restated several times, there is a strong cadence in E major in measure 35 at which point two of the five voices drop out. Here, the subject begins in the tonic with the second subject against it, and the two voices that have dropped out re-enter, the first with the answer against the second subject and the next stating the subject again but also combined with the second subject.

EXAMPLE 104

(a) CANZONA FROM FIRST SONATA IN FOUR PARTS,
HENRY PURCELL.

(b) *Tu es sacerdos* (TEXT OMITTED), LEONARDO LEO.

This is a nicely calculated effect. It is like an exposition but not a complete one; it is just enough to exhibit the two subjects in combination. Immediately after this, the third subject enters in combination with the other two. Thereafter, all three are combined in different contrapuntal inversions and parceled out equitably among the voices. A special touch near the end is a double stretto made on the first and third subjects.

A similar but more extended triple fugue is the *Contrapunctus VIII* from the *Art of Fugue,* the polyphonic structure of which is outlined in Table VIII. Each subject is introduced in a complete exposition, the second in combination with the first, and the third alone.

[356]

The second exposition is like the regular exposition of a double fugue in which the two subjects are presented simultaneously. The exposition of the third subject sounds less like an exposition, since the other two parts do not drop out when the new subject enters. It is, nevertheless, a complete exposition, with the new subject stated in each voice. Each of these expositions is also pointed up musically by an emphasized cadence which directly precedes it. The final combinations of all three subjects in contrapuntal inversions is a logical climax to the fugue. The unfinished final fugue in the *Art of Fugue* is, up to the point at which it stops, a triple fugue made up of three separate fugues, each with a separate exposition starting with one voice only and a considerable extension before the next subject enters in its exposition. At the point where the fugue breaks off, all three are combined contrapuntally.

Nowhere is Bach's exceptional sense of structure more obvious than in these double and triple fugues. To the feeling for form that makes each fugue an individual work, there is added a sense of polyphonic structure, of arranging in a logical and effective order the subjects and their combinations among the different voices of the fugue.

The Multiple-Subject Fugue in the Classical and Romantic Eras

By the late Baroque period, the multiple-subject fugue had become definitely associated with the practice of invertible counterpoint, and it remained so as long as fugues were written in major–minor tonalities. During the late eighteenth and early nineteenth centuries, two main tendencies in the treatment of this fugue type can be observed. The first was a change in terminology and evaluation; the second, a formalizing of composition procedures.

The first change can only be observed in theory or in writings about music, since it did not affect the fugues written, but only the terms applied to them. During this time, fugues in which the second subject is presented as a continuation of the subject sounding first against the answer were no longer considered to be double fugues, and the same criterion was applied to triple fugues. Instead, these were simply called fugues with one or more countersubjects.

Fux's *Gradus ad Parnassum* was the first text to include a number of short examples of double and triple fugue, and these presented the themes in the order just described. But, in 1790, Albrechtsberger included in his section on invertible counterpoint and double fugue only those fugues in which the subjects began together at the beginning of the exposition.[26] This same treatment of the multiple-subject fugue is given in all major nineteenth-century texts and works written about music. Albrechtsberger also described in his text a fugue by Mattheson in which the subjects are first presented in separate expositions and combined later in the fugue. But this fugue type disappeared from theoretical writings about fugue until after the Bach revival; since that time, the multiple-subject fugue with separate expositions has also been listed under double and triple fugues. Pedagogically, the emphasis remained on those fugues in which the subjects sound together from the beginning.

A correlated trend was the growing assumption that the simple fugue of itself included a countersubject appearing first against the answer, in the continuation of the subject, and written in double counterpoint with it. A countersubject of this type was taken for granted by Padre Martini and his followers in Italy, and the *fugue d'école* from the time of Fétis and Cherubini likewise included a countersubject. There came about a sort of revulsion against free accompaniments to the subject, and some examples of the *fugue d'école* included a second and third countersubject as well. The German academic fugue of the second half of the nineteenth century also included a countersubject, although there was less insistence on its continued use after the end of the exposition.

A confusing terminology has resulted. In the nineteenth century and today, a double fugue is one that either starts with the two subjects at the beginning or presents them in separate expositions and combines them later, and in these cases the themes are called "subjects." When the other theme is a continuation of the subject and sounds first against the answer, it is called a "countersubject," in a fugue on one subject.

The term "countersubject" has come to mean a subject of secondary or subordinate character that fits in invertible counterpoint with the main subject. One often hears it said that a certain second theme is not significant enough either in character or in use to be "a real second subject" and that it is "only a countersubject." In some cases, this kind of evaluation is applied in a reverse way to what we now call a countersubject when it is a theme of strong character and of formal importance; here it is not "just a countersubject, but a real second subject." All of these evaluations may be illuminating and correct in present usage, but they lead to nothing but misunderstanding when applied to the works of Bach and Handel, their contemporaries, and their predecessors.

THE FORMALIZING OF THE EXPOSITION

The second important tendency of this period, the move toward fixing the formal pattern, took place in the fugue in which all the subjects appear together at the beginning of the fugue. The exposition became formalized after the principle shown in the exposition of the double fugue by Bach outlined in Table VIII. Each theme has to appear once in each voice. This is not too difficult in a double fugue, but, in a triple fugue, the problem is complex. A rule first articulated by Albrechtsberger, that a fugue should have one or two more voices than subjects, became standard. This helps in the statements of the several themes because it was also traditional that each entry of each theme should be preceded by a rest and, as the themes start one after the other, there is the same difficulty in connecting inverted statements of the theme package as is experienced in connecting the units of inverted counterpoint in making an episode of inverted counterpoint. The extra voice is imperative in a triple fugue.

This kind of exposition made for an extended exposition. Mozart's fugue on *Cum sancto spiritu* from the Mass in C Major, K. 262 repeats the contrapuntal combination of three subjects five times before ending the exposition by moving out of the tonic key, although four repetitions would have been enough for the distribution of the three subjects through the four voices. This kind of exposition, which requires much contrapuntal calculation, became standard for the nineteenth century, which may explain why so few fugues of this type were written during that time.

The rest of the multiple-subject fugue is formed after the pattern of the simple fugue except that, in restatements, some contrapuntal inversions of the combination of the subjects are expected. Usually, devices such as stretto are applied to the first subject, but in some fugues the other subjects do attain independent importance as well.

The texts on school fugues insisted that, if all of the subjects required tonal answers, these should be made; but, in most fugues of this time, the subjects were so constructed that only the first subject or the first and second subjects would require this adjustment. Calculating the exposition of such a fugue was made more complex in this tradition, but, in many cases, if the first subject requires a tonal adjustment, the second will not enter until after the point at which it must be made, so that the contrapuntal combination and inversion is not affected. It is worth mentioning, however, that, in both Bach's fugue from the Passacaglia and Fugue in C Minor and the Mozart fugue on *Cum sancto spiritu* from the Mass, K. 262, a real answer is used where the first subject would normally require a tonal answer.

(A list of multiple-subject fugues for analysis will be found in Appendix I, under "Chapter IX.")

Notes

1. Marpurg, *op. cit.*, pp. 18, 21; see also Mann, *op. cit.*, pp. 155, 157.

2. Marpurg, *ibid.*, p. 132; see also Mann, *ibid.*, p. 192.

3. Vicentino, *op. cit.*, f. 135.

4. Reproduced in Luigi Torchi (ed.), *L'arte musicale in Italia* (Milan: G. Ricordi, 1902, 1959), III, 145–8.

5. Trabaci, *op. cit.*

6. Banchieri, *L'organo suonarino* op. 13 (Naples, 1605). Excerpts reproduced in Torchi, *op. cit.*, lack full titles; Sonata No. 1 is subtitled *Fuga plagale* in the original print, and Sonata No. 6 is subtitled *Fuga treplicata.*

7. A series of publications, most of which are available in Pidoux, *op. cit.*, 5 vols. (1943–1953).

8. Trabaci, *Ricercate, canzone* . . . , pp. 1–3, 11–4.

9. Banchieri, *op. cit.*, pp. 24–5, 32–3.

10. Pidoux, *op. cit.*, V, 24–7, 40–3.

11. Taniev calls this kind of inversion with rhythmic realignment "counterpoint with horizontal and vertical shifts" (*op. cit.*, Chap. XXIII). Here, Frescobaldi also makes slight rhythmic changes in the themes.

12. Scheidt, *op. cit.*, pp. 11–5.

13. See Gehrmann, ed., *Sweelinck Werken XII,* pp. 54*ff.*

14. Simpson, *op. cit.*, p. 133.

15. Purcell, *op. cit.*, p. 118.

16. Berardi, *Documenti armoniche,* pp. 41*ff.*

17. Hermann Keller (ed.), *Vincent Lübeck, Orgelwerke* (Frankfurt and New York: C. F. Peters, 1940), pp. 9–14.

18. Max Seiffert (ed.), *Orgelkompositionen von Johannes Pachelbel,* in *DTB,* IV, i, pp. 51–2.

19. Pidoux, *op. cit.*, V, 60–2.

20. P. Spitta (ed.), *Dietrich Buxtehude, Orgelwerke,* new ed., Max Seiffert (Wiesbaden: Breitkopf & Härtel, 1952), V. I, 28–34.

21. Berardi, *Miscellanea, op. cit.*, pp. 199*ff.*

22. Rameau, *op. cit.*, pp. 340*ff.*

23. Reproduced in C. V. Stanford (ed.), *The Works of Henry Purcell* (London, 1896), VII, 2–4, 13–16.

24. Mattheson, *op. cit.*, chap. xxiii.

25. Reproduced in Ebenezer Prout, *Fugal Analysis* (London, 1892), pp. 158–162.

26. Albrechtsberger, *op. cit.*, chap. xxviii–xxxi.

Chapter X

Fugue in the Development

of Western Music

*A*s the historical investigation of the differ-
ent elements of fugue has shown, fugue as a composition procedure
based on tonality had an unbroken continuity for about four centuries, from the second quarter of the sixteenth century to the early
twentieth century. Before this time, during the late fifteenth and early
sixteenth centuries, fugue, as *fuga sciolta,* was distinguished from
canon only in the fact that a short fragment rather than a complete
melodic part was imitated exactly in the different parts of a polyphonic texture. In his use of this technique, the composer was limited
only by the melodic modal system and contrapuntal rules of his time,
and by the fact that, in the modal diatonic scales, exact imitation or
fugue could take place only at the fourth, fifth, unison, or octave.
After this time, in the twentieth century, when music was no longer
organized within a fixed tonal system, the only necessary limitation
on the composer was the technique itself, the use of a short melodic
theme, exact imitation, and whatever aesthetic limitations the composer himself might impose. From the mid-sixteenth through the
nineteenth centuries, however, fugue was shaped by the forces of
tonality and its essential characteristics remained inextricably bound
up with conventions of tonal structure.

What was the essential kernel of fugue—the exposition—was

carved out by the restrictions that tonality placed on the form of the theme and on the pitches on which the first entries of the theme were made. The basic structure of the exposition—that the theme may be stated only on two pitch levels, centered on the first and fifth degree of the mode or key in which it is written—was the direct outcome of the growing conviction, in the sixteenth century, that the opening of a piece should clearly establish the mode in which it was written by having the initial notes of the entering voices start on 1, 3, or 5 of that modal scale. This, in combination with the earlier tradition that fugue should imitate only at the perfect intervals, meant that the first entries of the theme in a fugue could take place only on two levels, the tonic and the dominant.

This tonal restriction removed fugue one step further away from canon, and the acceptance of the tonal answer—the adjustment made in the theme for the purpose of maintaining tonal unity at the beginning of the fugue by the form of the subject and answer themselves —made the final separation. Fugue, although based on the principle of exact imitation at the tonic and dominant levels could and, in some cases, should have two different forms of the theme—the subject and answer forms—these forms being governed by the conventions of tonality prevailing at the time the fugue was written. The force of tonality could overrule the principle of exact imitation.

The conventions governing the exposition were continually changing, moving from a relative freedom that was only beginning to feel the limiting rules of tonality in the sixteenth century to the almost rigid controls exercised by the complex tonal organizations of the nineteenth century. But, despite disagreements among theorists or rebellion on the part of certain composers, fugue continued to be associated with the conventions that governed its exposition. This concept of fugue encouraged dependence on tradition, a tradition rooted in the idea of tonality, and, as long as the principles of tonality were felt to be the true and only valid methods of musical construction, this tradition survived. Fugal types like the *fuga d'imitatione* and irregular fugue, which departed from the strict conventions of the exposition, still depended on these conventions. The deviations were consciously made for expressive or structural reasons; always in the background remained the abstract and ideal exposition.

The strongly fixed tradition of the fugue exposition was one of the reasons why fugue survived where other forms dropped out during the changes in musical styles and tastes that occurred during these four centuries. It adapted easily to the tonal conventions of these different times. It also was based on a short theme, and, during these four centuries, thematic organization of a piece was the dominant way of composing. Whenever polyphony based on a short theme was used, the fugal exposition was the logical way to organize its beginning. Moreover, since the continuation beyond the exposition was never rigidly fixed, fugue was adaptable to many situations.

Fugue and Texture

Fugue is a polyphonic form and its importance in the musical scene as well as its success as a composition type has always been dependent upon the type of polyphony allowed in the prevailing style. The music of the sixteenth century was highly polyphonic and by the last half of the century fugue dominated in polyphonic works. At this same time there was a strong reaction against polyphony on the part of certain theorists and composers who wished to abandon counterpoint for a new style, monody, that used only a single melody with minimal accompaniment. However, even the most ardent advocates of the monodic style were concerned only with vocal music, with a clear and expressive setting of text. Although they deplored the use of contrapuntal style for the projection of a text, especially the use of abstract and nonexpressive devices such as augmentation, inversion, stretto, and the like, it was because they were not expressive of the text. Vincenzo Galilei, one of the most impassioned advocates of monody, had no objection to contrapuntal forms and devices if they were used in instrumental music.[1] For him, these especially belonged to the impersonal and abstract instrumental style of his time. The early seventeenth century was the time of the first great culmination of instrumental works based on fugue, a time when artifice, invention, and contrapuntal skill were stressed. The instrumental works of Andrea and Giovanni Gabrieli, Mayone, Trabaci, Frescobaldi, Sweelinck, Scheidt, and many of their contemporaries abound in inventiveness and virtuosity in fugue and in intricate contrapuntal play with fugal themes. Nor did fugue long remain in the background in vocal music. During the middle and late Baroque periods, fugue was again dominant in all polyphonic media.

A significant change in musical texture that came about in the seventeenth century was the final domination of polyphonic texture by harmonic tonality. This gave to polyphonic music a stronger sense of direction and forward movement and an ever-present feeling of tonality and tonal direction. The change actually strengthened fugue because of its alliance with tonality and contributed much to the second great peak in the development of fugue, a culmination in the first half of the eighteenth century that, for most listeners today, is still expressed in the fugal works of Bach and Handel.

THE DECLINE OF POLYPHONY

The next onslaught on polyphony, which started during the lifetime of Bach and Handel, came from the advocates of the *style galant,* a style that stressed a single predominant melody with an accompaniment that provided harmonic background in as unobtrusive a manner as possible with a minimum of that contrapuntal movement that might detract from the melody. This revolution was much more far reaching. It was concerned with instrumental as well as vocal music and sought a complete change of style. Yet, even though at first the production of fugues dropped back sharply and never again did fugue regain more than a minor place in the forms of the time, still it survived, underwent further development, and retained its essential characteristics until the early twentieth century.

But the changes in texture that took place within fugue were much greater this time. Polyphony did not remain outside of the *style galant* for long, but when it re-entered it was a new kind of polyphony. It was a predominantly homophonic texture with a main melody to which the subordinate melodies gave support but which they did not supersede. Fugue was then considered a traditional style and form, a self-conscious display of contrapuntal technique of a type no longer thought natural. This had the effect, in the long run, of eroding the polyphonic texture of fugue itself. In the fugues of this period, homophonic and chordal sections abound, and there is a great deal of merely rhythmically activated harmony. This texture is found not only in the episodes of the fugue (as in Ex. 87), but also in the exposition and restatement sections, the sections that are by tradition the most polyphonic. As can be seen in Example 89, the doubling of the theme in sixths and thirds, which still retains the appearance of two parts, and the cutting-down of the accompanying parts, tend to make the aural effect one of homophony, even though all of the voices are accounted for in the written score.

Some of this change in texture is due to the development of new media and new instrumental styles that have their own traditions and that must be adapted to fugue. Even in the seventeenth century, there was a lessening at times of the consistent number of voices used in a fugue. Once instrumental fugues were written in reduced keyboard score (the two clefs, as used today for piano music) rather than in open score, it was easy to lose track of the parts, and, in some keyboard fugues, the voice leading is confusing or obscure.[2] Considerable freedom is found where the number of parts is not fixed by the number of voices or instruments used. The fugues in the Corelli sonatas for solo violin and continuo, for example, do not maintain throughout the three-voice texture that the exposition implies.

Clavier fugues by some early eighteenth-century Italian composers, such as those attributed to Alessandro Scarlatti (1659–1725), often dissolve into free two-part texture after a four-voice exposition.[3] The piano fugue likewise developed a style of its own beginning in the second half of the eighteenth century. Fugues written by the sons of J. S. Bach and by Clementi, Albrechtsberger, Czerny, Beethoven, Schumann, and Mendelssohn all include sections that use parallel thirds or sixths, piano figuration that is merely activated harmony, and the fugue from Brahms's *Variations and Fugue on a Theme by Handel* discussed in Chapter VII is in the direct tradition of this piano fugue. The net effect is not that of polyphony, yet it follows all the traditions of fugue; the several parts, although often subordinate and lacking independence, are maintained, and it is for its time a truly characteristic fugue for piano.

THE ACCOMPANIED CHORAL FUGUE

Other media, by virtue of the inclusion of more instruments or voices than the number of parts used in the fugue, made equivalent changes in fugue texture. The concertato style of the Baroque period, combining instruments and voices, ensembles and soloists, did not make too great a change at first. The basic structure of the fugue remained unchanged, the fugue appearing mainly in the chorus, often with the different voices reinforced by instruments. But in some cases the orchestra added other, independent parts or even took part in the fugue itself.

Various types of ways of using orchestra with a choral fugue can be seen in the several fugues in Bach's Mass in B Minor. In the second *Kyrie eleison,* the bass line has an independent melody line, but the other parts double the voices. In the fugue that opens the Credo, there is again a free bass part—here, one that stands out more—and the first and second violins take part in the fugue, not doubling voices, but stating the theme independently and taking part in the exposition and the strettos. The first *Kyrie eleison* does not follow the conventional fugue patterns of the time, but it nevertheless contains the basic elements of fugue and shows another common orchestral usage, that of the orchestra taking over from the chorus but still continuing the fugue with episodic material and statements of the theme. It furthermore uses both orchestral doubling of the choral voices and the addition of free accompanying parts.

The tradition of accompanied choral fugue continued in the Classical and Romantic eras. Here, the orchestral accompanying parts were often more complex, but, when they were, the composer also doubled the vocal parts to avoid confusing the singers. Often, the orchestra adds to the texture and musical excitement of the regular imitation of the fugue by imitating fragments of the themes but not adding a consistently used part, so that there is the effect of added parts without the genuine addition of another voice to the fugue. This adds to the dramatic and musical effect but also deceives the listener and, in effect, confuses the contrapuntal structure of the fugue. Temporary orchestral doubling of short motives in an individual choral part, rather than a consistent doubling of one part throughout, is also found. Beethoven uses most of these techniques in the fugue *In gloria Dei patris* from the *Missa solemnis.*

Another use of independent orchestral parts to add to the texture is seen in the fugue on *Der gerechten Seelen,* which closes the third movement of Brahms's *Requiem.* Here the fugue is made over a long pedal point that gives emphasis to the fugue's function of closing the movement. The pedal point is activated in the low strings and brass and by the kettle drums. The voices that make the fugue do not take part in the pedal point but are consistent in projecting the fugue. The other orchestral parts either double the voices or state a free accompanying figure that moves faster than the voices, completely independent of the fugue but adding to the musical effect and to the over-all texture of the work.

THE ORCHESTRAL FUGUE

The orchestral fugue, which also appeared first in the Baroque period—in the French overture and the concerto grosso—involves another problem, that of continuity of voice leading. If the exposition, for example, is stated in the strings and then the episode that follows is shifted to the woodwind section, even though the top wind instrument continues the part formerly played by the first violins, there is a change of tone color, and the continuity of that part is less obvious. This change does not always occur; in many works, the strings keep the main parts going throughout with changes in doubling but no sudden changes of range or timbre. But, in a concerto grosso that employs a concertino, perhaps of instruments of different types, the change from ensemble to soloists and the change in tone color does give the effect of interruption rather than continuation.

This happens in the fugal finale of Bach's fourth *Brandenburg Concerto,* where the ripieno is made up of a four-part string orchestra (plus continuo), and the concertino is made up of two flutes and a solo violin. It is a five-voice fugue, and, in the exposition, the violin from the concertino doubles the first violins of the ripieno, and the two flutes from the concertino make the fifth entry in unison, as one voice. In all the tutti sections that are strictly polyphonic, this combination is maintained. In those concertino sections that are fugal, restating the theme or making a stretto, the two flutes are used separately, each as a different voice in the fugue, making a change in tone color. In these sections, the violin does not state the theme, so that, in effect, one of the flutes takes over the voice originally played by the first violins. There are freer sections, episodic in character, where the ripieno and concertino combine and the virtuosity of the soloist is exhibited, as is characteristic of a concerto, but, in the fugal sections, the identity of the parts is kept clear, in spite of a change in tone color.

This type of orchestral treatment—polyphonic texture in which the identity of each contrapuntal part is maintained throughout despite changes in instrumentation—is characteristic of the Baroque but becomes less and less characteristic of the Classical and Romantic orchestral treatment of fugue. It is, of course, not at all characteristic of their treatment of homophonic or nonfugal textures.

Except for very early fugal finales in the symphonies of Mathias Georg Monn (1717–1750) and Michael Haydn (1737–1806), the orchestral fugue as a complete movement is not found in the works of the composers of the Classical and early Romantic periods. Fugatos, however, are often found within movements, and these give a good idea of the effect of the new way of orchestrating on the treatment of fugue. The identity of each voice is usually maintained by having the same instrument carry it throughout the fugato, but orchestral doublings and free parts may be added once the opening of the exposition is heard. The fugal opening of the second movement of Beethoven's First Symphony is typical. The exposition is carried by the strings, but the third entry (m. 10) is doubled by the bassoon and the horns obscure the polyphony by a long, held note. When the full orchestra comes in with the last entry (m. 12) the polyphonic texture begins to dissolve and the section ends homo-phonically.

The fugue exposition in the overture to the oratorio *St. Paul* by Mendelssohn shows an interesting use of free parts added to form a harmonic cadence at the right spot in the theme. This is a purely nonpolyphonic effect, adding neither rhythmic motion nor more contrapuntal movement, but merely giving a simple harmonic re-inforcement.

Composers in the second half of the nineteenth century and well into the twentieth century, continued to insert short fugatos into their symphonic works, but these ordinarily do not extend beyond the fugue exposition. During this same period, a number of German composers of conservative bent wrote extensive fugues for orchestra. Their musical style and approach resembles that of Brahms, and his influence is also manifest in that many of these fugues are finales to a set of variations. Some are also single, long fugues for orchestra. These composers are, for the most part, forgotten today, along with their works. Among the best known are J. G. Rheinberger, who wrote, among other fugues, an *Academic Overture,* Op. 195 in the form of a fugue on six themes, and Max Reger, whose sets of *Variations on a Theme by Hiller,* Op. 108 and *Variations on a Theme by Mozart,* Op. 132 end with big orchestral fugues.

The techniques found in the orchestral fugato were used in more imaginative and sophisticated ways in the orchestral fugue of the second half of the nineteenth and the early twentieth centuries. In these fugues, the addition of orchestral doubling and other additional techniques come only after the exposition, which is expressed clearly and often in monochrome timbre. Episodes and restatements are set off by timbre as well as texture and musical material, and orchestral means are used to build up climaxes by extensive doubling, harmonic filler, and increased rhythmic activity in the percussion section and in the repetition of rhythmic motives on one pitch in the brasses. An apparent increase in the number of voices taking part in the fugue is sometimes made by intermittent and fragmentary interjections of motives in the different instrument groups.

The fugue finale from the *Variations on a Theme by Mozart* by Max Reger uses these techniques with restraint. The strings present the exposition, the bassoon entering to double the last entry of the theme in the cellos and basses. Only in the first episode do the wood-winds enter as a group to play an independent role. The real changes in texture come in the climactic sections, when extensive doublings make the lines harder to pick out, or in those sections where short motives tossed from one instrument to another give the effect of more parts than there really are. The ending, which combines the fugue theme with the original Mozart melody on which the variations are based, uses full orchestra and is made thicker in texture by harmonic filler and a kettledrum roll. In the tradition of the orchestral fugue, it is loud (*fff*), and a broad *allargando* emphasizes the fact that the fugue has reached its close.

These fugues must today be studied from scores; they have disappeared from the orchestral repertoire since they do not appeal to modern tastes.[4] But they make a fascinating study for the student of musical style and form. Only one such fugue—written in 1927 but in a style very close to that of the nineteenth century—is still played and recorded. This is the fugue from the opera *Schwanda der Dudelsachpfeiffer* by Jaromir Weinberger (1896–), a pupil of Reger. Played as a separate piece in conjunction with the dance to which it is attached, as the Polka and Fugue from *Schwanda,* it gives a glimpse of what these orchestral fugues are like.

HARMONY VERSUS POLYPHONY

Along with these changes in the linear aspect of fugue texture went changes in the vertical relations of the parts, the details in dissonance treatment in the joining together of the parts. These can be grouped around three main poles between which stretch periods of gradual transition.

Both the sixteenth-century and the late nineteenth-century styles are predominantly consonant, dissonances for the most part unobtrusively placed on the weak part of the beat. In theory, many more types of dissonance were allowed in the nineteenth century, but the interest in harmonic color led to a tendency to treat even divisions of a beat as chord tones; this tendency was noted in the fugue from Brahms's *Handel Variations.* This late-nineteenth century stress on sensuously pleasing harmonies was partly due, as well, to the fact that the contrapuntal rules that were the basis of elementary training were those derived from Fux; even in the late eighteenth century, when the harmonic vocabulary was not greatly changed from that of the Baroque, counterpoint used much less dissonance than is found in the works of the first half of the century.

In the late Baroque, a strong harmonic structure underlaid the contrapuntal lines, but much more dissonance was used, especially on the strong beats. The style differs from that of the late eighteenth and nineteenth centuries in that the individual lines were still of primary importance, although made to fit into the harmonic skeleton. In the periods following 1750, harmony was generally more important than the individual melodic lines making up the fugal texture.

In the sixteenth century, then, the sense of forward movement was gained from the individual lines; only at the cadences was harmonic impulsion felt. In the late nineteenth century, when contrapuntal independence was not great, the main sense of movement was in the harmony. When this harmonic movement was not strong but stressed sensuous chord color and chromatic changes, the sense of movement was weak unless the polyphonic texture was made up of several active and independent melodies.

In the late Baroque fugue, all the musical elements combined to give a sense of movement—harmonic movement, melodic and rhythmic movement in each independent polyphonic line—and the melodic-rhythmic style of the themes likewise expressed melodic energy. This is the style we expect in fugue, perhaps because it is the style of most of the fugues we hear and play. It is difficult to say whether or not it is the style most appropriate for fugue, because the essence of fugue throughout its history has been imitation of a short theme in an ordered polyphonic structure. Ideally, it should be effective in any strongly polyphonic style.

The Place of Fugue in the Mainstream of Musical Activity

In its place in relation to other musical forms, fugue has followed a pattern very like that seen in the history of the canon. In the early sixteenth century, fugue took over from canon as the most popular way of organizing a polyphonic work by strict imitation. It used the same technique as canon but in a freer, more flexible way. It remained one of the leading ways of composing until mid-eighteenth century when an entirely new way of composing came into prominence—homophonic style and homophonic forms. It gave way before this new music and became a form of secondary importance; like the canon in the Baroque, it was still important but was cherished more as a tradition than a form with future possibilities for growth. Also, like the canon in the Baroque, it was accorded prestige as a proof of learning and skill, but the forms that superseded it were considered to be much more expressive and more flexible than the fugue had been.

This pattern of development was then altered by the intrusion of

a new element—historical perspective, which sought out and roman-
ticized the music of the past. In fugue, this produced a twofold effect.
The rediscovery of Bach brought about a reawakening of interest in
fugue in Germany. Not only known composers like Schumann,
Mendelssohn, Brahms, and Bruckner felt the necessity to write fugues,
but also countless composers whose works have long since been forgotten. And it brought a new influence to bear on these composers;
Bach, whose music had been forgotten by the majority of musicians
not long after his death, was used as a model for fugue writing. What
progressive changes had been made in fugue by composers like
Beethoven had less chance of development. The second result of this
searching the past for music literature was on the music heard by
composers and the audiences they wrote for. Instead of working in a
milieu of developing forms and styles, they more and more heard and
studied works of the past; and in fugue the influence of many different styles and forms was felt.

In the sixteenth century, when the *fuga sciolta* first came into
prominence, it was the new, modern, exciting way of composing. As
Zarlino put it, "this manner of singing is not only delightful, but
contains within itself elegance and artifice."[5] The structure of fugue
was fixed only insofar as the initial notes of the entries were regulated by modal tonality. The order of entries, their contrapuntal
alignment, even the forms of the answer that might be used—
whether or not the intervals agreed to the exactness of major and
minor seconds, whether or not the rhythm was exact, whether or not
the tonal answer was preferred—were left to the composer. These
were, in the eyes of Pietro Pontio, the earmarks of a composer's style,
the things a student should look at in studying the works of other
composers and watch in his own.[6] What the seventeenth century was
to name the *fuga d'imitazione*—the answer that uses only certain
elements of the subject rather than exact imitation but that has a
series of entries like the regular beginning of a fugue—was also used
when it could be more expressive than exact imitation. There were
a multitude of possibilities with which the composer could experiment.

Fugue was the first way of composing in which a polyphonic
section or even a whole movement could be made out of a short
theme, and, if many of these themes were paraphrases of pre-existent
melodies or made abstractly by what seem to us to be mechanical
calculations, still there was much thought put into the invention of
fugal themes.[7] According to Thomas Morley, the more such themes
or "points" a madrigal contained, the more it was admired.[8]

Fugue was also, as was pointed out in Chapter VII, a flexible form-building device. With it, the composer could create a form that followed a text precisely, each section being based on a short subject to which was set a meaningful fragment of text. Along with the cadences, fugue also helped to create a form based on tonality, starting in the mode, leaving it, and re-establishing it at the end.

It was associated with almost every polyphonic form, and, in the early seventeenth century, this was taken for granted, certain types of work being identified by the type of fugal subject used or the way the fugue was made. Motet, madrigal, chanson, ricercar, fantasia, and canzona all used fugue and were differentiated musically by how fugue was used. The instrumental canzona, as well as having a lively theme in the rhythmic pattern of a long note followed by two short notes, normally brought the voices of the opening fugue in in a stretto exposition.[9] The madrigal, chanson, and motet were especially associated with the *fuga d'imitazione*.[10] The seventeenth-century definitions of ricercar and fantasia expressed the excitement and interest allowed in free instrumental composition, where the composer was not bound by words, but could freely invent fugues and their themes, using his imagination and ingenuity.[11] This type of abstract thematic construction allowed by fugue in instrumental music resulted in the first long, thematically organized instrumental forms, and the pleasure certain composers took in creating these works is evident in the ricercars, canzonas, and fantasias of composers like Frescobaldi, Trabaci, Sweelinck, and Scheidt.

Throughout the Baroque period, fugue remained dominant. Other instrumental forms such as the suite, overture, sonata, concerto, variation, and chorale prelude came into prominence also, but fugue, being inherently flexible and not of necessity tied to any form, was used in all of them. During the seventeenth and early eighteenth centuries, fugue was developing rapidly. As the historical discussion of the various aspects of fugue has shown, this was the time when the structure of the exposition was becoming fixed. The form of the subject and the answer and the structure of the exposition became stylized according to the increasing strength of the major–minor system.

Also during this time, a new formal procedure became associated with the separate piece based on fugue. The simple *fuga,* an exposition with an extension based on its theme, became expanded by the insertion of developmental episodes between restatements of the theme so that, by the eighteenth century, "a fugue" was a fairly long piece that was based on relatively fixed principles, a formal procedure that may well have originated in the Baroque sonata and concerto, although later periods associated it directly with fugue. A whole literature of independent fugues based on one or two themes appeared. It became a form in its own right.

Galilei's association of instrumental music with abstraction rather than emotional expressiveness was no longer applied to instrumental music at this time. The themes for vocal fugues had long been chosen to express the words to which they were set, and, during the seventeenth century, this expressiveness became expected of the theme of the instrumental fugue. The eighteenth-century fugue, instrumental or vocal, was meant to have an appealing theme, one that set forth a certain emotion as well as establishing the key.[12] The fugues of J. S. Bach found in a collection such as the *Well-Tempered Clavier* show the contrasts of mood possible in this form when different types of subject are used.

The proponents of the *galant* style attacked fugue as not being fully expressive because of the polyphonic texture, using the same argument that the monodists had put forth against polyphonic vocal music more than a century earlier—that polyphony detracted from the full effect of the melody. But the rejection of fugue, which to the eighteenth century stood for polyphony at its worst, went even further. The new periodic instrumental melody, which, made up of short motives combined into phrases, phrases joined to make periods, and so on, followed musically the effects and structure of speech, was a more complete expression of mood. The ideal of the *empfindsamer* style, the sudden and unexpected changes of mood that were meant to lead the listener from one mood to another, emphasized also discontinuity—the opposite effect from fugue—and implied a different way of composing. Inspiration and imagination were prized. The calculation and labor that went into the writing of fugue were thought, *per se,* to prevent inspiration and expression. As Anton Bemetzrieder expressed it, "The children of the Greeks, consecrated to Apollo, were initiated into the mysteries of Orpheus. . . . There, were never heard the paltry little words *canon, fugue, filling up, interrupted cadence, subject* . . . but it was the province of music to give expression to the painting of moral sentiment, and to paint the beauties of nature."[13]

Even though fugue remained an accepted, though minor, form and technique throughout the Classical and Romantic periods, this attitude was never quite abandoned. Fugue remained the proof of learning, of musical knowledge and skill. Liszt, in his *Faust Symphony* and Richard Strauss (1864–1949) in *Also sprach Zarathustra* introduced fugatos as symbols of intellectual knowledge. Training in strict fugue was a part of the composer's training, a proof of knowledge and skill. Even Chopin wrote fugue, although not as a serious work of art. Fugue was associated with intellectual and musical engineering and with tradition. Even Beethoven, who strove to break away from its conventional and mechanical aspects,[14] looked to theory texts like Albrechtsberger's for the different techniques that he applied to the themes in his *Grosse Fuge.* Such devices as augmentation, inversion, retrograde, interrupted imitation had about them an aura of complexity and erudition although, being mechanically applied, they required less skill and imagination than the development or variation of a theme in the prevailing style.

Fugue had certain characteristics for which it was prized for itself as well. Its supposed objectivity made it appropriate for church music. Its perpetual motion and the possibilities for building up a big climax in stretto could not be matched by the melody–accompaniment texture of the pure *galant* style. For this reason it became a much-used device in the climactic closing sections of big choral works. In the Mass, the fugue provided brilliant endings for the Gloria on the text *cum sancto spiritu* and on the text *et vitam venturi* for the Credo. C. P. E. Bach used a massive double fugue for the closing of his predominantly homophonic Magnificat in D. It acted as a final movement for Haydn quartets Op. 20, Nos. 2, 5, and 6 and for Beethoven's *Hammerklavier Sonata.* Beethoven's use of it for the finales of his *Eroica Variations,* Op. 35 and the *Diabelli Variations,* Op. 120, set up a tradition that was followed not only in Brahms's *Handel Variations,* but also in numerous variation sets by minor composers including those written for orchestra.

THE ENTRANCE OF FUGUE INTO HOMOPHONIC FORM

Probably the most important accomplishment of Haydn and Mozart in regard to fugue was the amalgamation of the *galant* style and the old learned, contrapuntal style. For composers of the generation of J. J. Quantz (1697–1773) and J. S. Bach's sons, the two styles were to be kept apart, not combined in the same piece. Marpurg, however, dedicated his fugue treatise to G. P. Telemann, Bach's famous contemporary, who he felt had proved in his works that the two styles were compatible. In their early works, both Haydn and Mozart use the two, usually juxtaposed but separate, contrasting with each other. In their mature works, however, they are combined smoothly, the transition from one to the other so logical that the combination seems perfectly natural.

This amalgamation at its most complex is seen in the combination of fugue, canon, or invertible counterpoint with the simple *galant* style and especially in the combination of fugue with sonata form or scherzo, which is worked out so effectively in the works of Mozart and Beethoven. The naturalness with which this is accomplished is something that is so familiar to us that we fail to perceive the difficulties that must have attended the first attempts to combine the two, and it is hard for us to conceive of them as being incompatible. But it was a new and exciting development when it was first accomplished. J. C. Kittel, once a pupil of J. S. Bach, praised in 1808 the emergence of this new, third style, which combined the solemnity of the learned, contrapuntal style with the grace of the *galant*. He felt especially that this provided some of the rhythmic drive that was found in the fugues of Bach but was missing from the pure *galant* style.[15]

To many theorists thinking from the point of view of the new style, this combination of fugal techniques with the *galant* style was the real function of fugue. Many of them interpreted fugue more freely, separating it from the fixed forms that writers on fugues associated with it. The eighteenth-century theorist J. F. Daube asked, "What are symphonies, opera arias, concertos . . . but free or irregular fugues?"[16]

In 1827, J. A. André, author of a textbook that included traditional fugue, felt called upon to repudiate a critic who, in a review published in the *Musikalische Zeitung* of Leipzig in 1799, had called the finale of Haydn's Symphony No. 95 a fugue. In this rondo finale, Haydn first stated the theme homophonically in the *galant* tradition and then used the beginning of it imitatively in a section that does not follow the form of a regular fugal exposition since the entries come on c', e'', g'' and g, even though he did bring them in one voice at a time like an exposition—an irregular fugue, in other words. Fugal and imitative sections are used often thereafter. André insisted that it is not a fugue, showing the conventional form of the fugue and showing how Haydn's use differs.

These two opposing ideas of the fugue—as a free technique and as a conventionalized form—are found in writings about music throughout the period. For Reicha[17] and Colet,[18] as for most professional theorists and composers, there existed "the fugue," which was a strict form following fixed conventions, and the free fugue, or *genre fugué,* which they felt was truly illustrated in the quartets of Haydn, Mozart, and Beethoven. Those who followed the German meaning of free fugue used the term "fugued style." But many critics were less precise, and some theorists remained uncertain. Simon Sechter, the Viennese theorist and composer who put out a revised edition of Marpurg's work in fugue in mid-century[19] added to this edition an analysis of the finale of Mozart's *Jupiter Symphony* as an example of fugue. But his analysis is mostly in terms of sonata form, pointing out fugal devices as they appear. In searching for the beginning of the "actual fugue," he showed the confusion that was so often felt about fugue when divorced from its academic form; he finally concluded that the fugue itself starts in the midst of the coda!

LATE GROWTH OF THE FUGUE

The regular fugue as a self-contained form also developed during this period, mainly in the matter of form, a process already described in Chapter VII. Lesser composers and theorists, like Reicha, who sought to mold fugue to the ideals of the new age eventually settled for the use of fugal matter—exposition, imitation, stretto, imitative developments of theme fragments like the episodes in a fugue—in the homophonic, periodic forms. Beethoven, who excelled at combining the two, also tried to transform the self-contained fugue, convinced that "a real poetic element must be introduced into the old traditional form."[20] Regardless of how his fugues are judged as works of art, the new expressive, subjective approach of Beethoven is clearly evident, as well as his feeling for form. The sense of movement in a new direction is felt even though some may feel that he has not realized his aims successfully.

Kurt Frederick's study of the fugue after Bach through the time of Beethoven shows how Beethoven transformed the traditional, academic Viennese fugue used by his predecessors and contemporaries.[21] His innovations include much more than an enlarged form and a freer key scheme. There is experiment in form, seen in the introduction of a second theme in a new key in his fugue from the *Hammerklavier Sonata* and in the multimovement form of the *Grosse Fuge.* This new concept of form is found also in his freer use of the fugue themes, in transforming them and in treating them as he does his themes in his homophonic forms, as material for development and transformation. His many other innovations add up to an intelligent and perceptive use of the form, modelled to fit his own aesthetic and his own sense of musical construction.

Whatever might have come from this new approach was negated by the reawakened interest in the past and in the rediscovery of Bach. Bach now became the model to which the German composers and

theorists (and, later, those of other nations) looked. The Bach influence was unsettling on theory, which now tried to readjust the
nineteenth-century tradition to the fugues of Bach and to rationalize
the usages of Bach according to the rules of the Fux-Martini tradition.
Composers tried to imitate Bach while following the nineteenth-
century form, which avoided the tonic key between the exposition
and the final section of the fugue and which ended with a climactic
pedal and stretto and a brilliant coda. They also tried vainly to adjust their style to Bach's.

The main effect of the Bach restoration was in the increased
number of fugues written, particularly in Germany. Otherwise totally
Romantic composers looked to Bach for inspiration. Mendelssohn
and Schumann wrote fugues, but they did not resemble Bach's so
much as fugues in the nineteenth-century tradition, freer than the
academic fugue but not so free as the fugues of Beethoven nor, to be
honest, of Bach. Many minor composers who today have been forgotten wrote fugues, especially for organ and in liturgical music and
oratorios. The collection of forty-eight fugues by the older composer
A. A. Klengel (1783–1852) in imitation of the *Well-tempered
Clavier* followed directly in the tradition of the post-Bach piano
fugues.[22]

Only Schumann managed to turn the fugue to his own purposes.
For him, the fugue was a "character piece" in which the character of
the theme defined the mood of the work just as it did in the freer
forms of his day. His Op. 60, *Fugues on the name BACH* for organ
or pedal-piano shows a clear attempt to work out interesting forms
within the fugue tradition. Perhaps the fugue from Liszt's *Prelude
and Fugue on the Name BACH* for organ is the freest of all. Once
the exposition is over, it is scarcely polyphonic, almost a nineteenth-
century fantasia rather than a fugue; the freedom is a lack of control
rather than the controlled effort at new order seen in Beethoven's
fugues. Except for the theme, the resemblance to Bach or to any other
fugue composer is faint.

Minor German composers of the late nineteenth and twentieth
centuries who made no break with the traditional styles of composing
continued to write fugues following the nineteenth-century tradition.
New elements in their works show the nineteenth-century concern
with form. Alongside the experiments in combining fugue with
homophonic forms, composers of fugues sometimes tried to bring
certain aspects of homophonic forms into their fugues. In the fugue
in his eighth Sonata for Organ, Op. 132, Rheinberger combined the
rondo-principle with the elements of strict fugue and in his seven-

teenth, Op. 181, he brought elements of sonata form into his otherwise conventional fugue. Formal techniques were also exaggerated in those fugues, which followed conventional fugue form. Composers like Max Reger used the elements of dynamics, tone-color, and variations in tempo to emphasize the formal divisions of his fugues.

THE END OF TRADITIONAL FUGUE

Like canon, fugue remained an important structural element in the new music of the twentieth century. But, unlike canon, once the all-pervading organization of music according to major–minor tonality was abandoned the traditions associated with fugue lost their meaning. Its structure, much more than canon, had been based on tonal principles; now these very principles had been abandoned.

Fugue then seems to have moved in two different directions. One, the "neo" approach, stressed techniques used in the tonally oriented fugue of the seventeenth, eighteenth, and nineteenth centuries. It used sometimes the old exposition form, or followed the episode-entry alternation of the eighteenth- and nineteenth-century fugue, or picked up certain developmental techniques associated with the form. The *Twenty-four Preludes and Fugues, Op. 87* of Dmitri Shostakovitch (1906—) follow this approach. There are even some fugues that use the tonal answer. Paul Hindemith (1895–1963) applied structural elements taken from fugues of the sixteenth through the nineteenth centuries in the fugues of his *Ludus Tonalis.* These techniques—such as retrograde, inversion, stretto, sequence— are not in themselves based on modal or major–minor tonality and they are used in fugues that do not depend tonally on the conventions of the modes or the key system. Here the approach is nearer to the early *fuga sciolta* where the tonal restrictions governing it were not yet rigidly limited, and the entries of the opening exposition may come at various different pitches. The main thing missing in this new use of old techniques is the tension between restrictive vertical controls and the use of horizontal elements of structure that existed in fugues of earlier periods. Fugue here is no longer a show of skill because there is no longer the problem of fitting a horizontally conceived technique into strict vertical controls. There is, for example, no problem in making a stretto when the overlapping statements no longer have to be so arranged as to be in accord with contrapuntal or harmonic rules. It needs only to fit with the aesthetic ideals of the composer.

For this reason it is the second, more experimental approach that seems more logical in twentieth-century fugue. Fugue in the general sense, as the use of a short theme in exact imitation to organize a polyphonic piece, provides great scope in the working-out of new structures that do not ape structures based on tonal principles. An interesting movement of this type is the first movement from the *Music for Strings, Percussion and Celesta* of Bela Bartok (1881–1945). Here is a musical structure that is unique. From the fugue of the past he takes the ideal of a short theme used in imitation at the interval of a fifth, but extends it to include entries on every pitch of the chromatic scale. The order and arrangement of these entries in the movement give a logical "tonal" form, but this is a form characteristic of this movement alone; it bears no resemblance to earlier fugue forms. Other techniques from the past, such as stretto, mirror, and inversion are used also, but with a formal logic that grows out of the unique structure of this fugue, and they gain most of their effectiveness from the intervallic structure of the particular theme of this fugue.

In both approaches to the use of fugue in twentieth-century styles, however, the traditions and conventions that attended fugue in its growth from the sixteenth through the nineteenth centuries are no longer essential to fugue nor do they have the same significance they had in the past. What new usages have been developed have not yet achieved the status of accepted convention, and the future of fugue cannot be predicted. In any case, the long tradition of fugue that survived during four centuries of our development has been broken.

FUGUE AS MUSIC LITERATURE

In a form like fugue, where the techniques of contrapuntal manipulation and the existence of a certain number of fixed devices—such as stretto, the combination of subjects, and the like—make it necessary for the composer to master precise techniques, the exhibition of contrapuntal skill, the kind of skill that can be learned and can also be easily recognized, is an outstanding element. In studying the vast numbers of fugues that have been written during four centuries, one is made aware of the great ingenuity of composers, both major and minor. One sees also that the fugues most often performed are not necessarily those that are the most ingeniously contrived.

Another aspect of fugue that has always been associated with it is the problem of formal extension, to which a number of different solutions have been found. Here is the aspect that most interests the composer and the analyst, and, in every period, there are fugal works that delight because of the skill and logic of the form. Usually, it is the peculiar individuality of a particular form that pleases, the solution that grows in part from the conventions of the time but also from the character of the subject itself. This is true of the works of many sixteenth-century composers, such as Gombert, Willaert, de Rore, Marenzio, and Palestrina. The flexibility and variety of their forms and uses of fugue, their smooth transitions from fugue to fugue, the subtle ingenuity of the tonal progressions are all seen in the minute details of their works. But they must be discovered by attention to minute detail; in performance, they pass swiftly by, and it is other elements—the themes, the interweaving of parts, and the special flavor of the different modes—that provide the main pleasure to today's listeners.

In all periods, there are fugal forms that please because of their logic. The long fantasias of Sweelinck and Scheidt, extended by augmentation and double augmentation and diminution and double diminution of the theme, provide satisfying forms. These forms are perhaps the most logical fugue forms and the ones that are the most consistently "fugal" because there are so few measures in which the theme is not present. They provide a continuously growing intensity toward the end, the result of techniques always associated with fugue —diminution and double diminution of the theme and stretto—that bring the rhythmic and polyphonic motion to a climax. Yet, the theme itself is rarely appealing; rather, it is abstract, and the effects that are most often enjoyed are the figurations surrounding it in the different statements.

Today, we are so used to reacting to a work first according to the character of its theme (and also to the harmonic and polyphonic style) that the works that we choose to perform and to listen to are almost unconsciously chosen according to the nature of the theme and the emotive associations that it has for us. This way of judging a fugue came in only in the late Baroque period, but it has had a major influence on composers and listeners for over two centuries. The new athematic manner of composing that has come into prominence and that substitutes other elements just as pleasing to many musicians may change the attitude of succeeding generations, but few listeners today, even among professional musicians, derive great pleasure from listening to fugues in which the significant elements are those of ingenuity of construction and form. Fugue is, after all, a thematic form. One must concentrate on the theme either to follow abstractly its technical adventures or simply to enjoy its musical nature.

The fugues from the last quarter of the seventeenth century on—beginning with those of the instrumental school of Bologna typified by the fugues in Corelli's sonatas—do not follow a form so inherently *fugal* as those of earlier periods. The episode, not new, but stressed more as a pleasing developmental play with motives from the theme, is not a basically fugal technique and is used to give relief from the continuous use of the theme. The expanded fugue of the late Baroque—although it uses fugal devices, is consistently polyphonic, and opens with a strict exposition—lacks the intensive fugal logic of earlier forms and has a lower concentration of such technical devices as stretto. Yet, it is this fugue that, since the Bach revival of the nineteenth century, has remained the one most enjoyed by the majority of listeners, musicians and nonmusicians.

And it is still the fugues of Bach that lead the list of fugues performed. The reason for this must lie inherently in the musical content as a whole, for analysis has yet to decide the question by mechanical investigation of his works. One can find many tangibles to praise, however. The thematic content, the themes themselves and the episodic elucidation of their constituents, are important, because each fugue is thus given a particular unity of mood based on the theme that dominates. There is always contrapuntal ingenuity, but often in a single fugue there will be no stretto, no inversion or augmentation of the theme, only statements of that theme separated by episodic developments. Bach's forms lack the inexorable logic of the academic fugue form of the Classical and Romantic eras with their final climactic stretto, and they lack the strictly fugal logic of the formal prototype used by Sweelinck and Scheidt. Yet, one finds among his fugues an amazing variety of form within the tonal and polyphonic principles that governed the fugues of his time. Each has a slightly different pattern from the next, and the pattern used seems to grow directly from the form and character of the theme itself and of the materials and shape of the exposition. It may be that his fugues please because there is a balanced use of theme, form, and technique —no intensive concentration on ingenuity or fugal form, but a comfortable ease in their use and a sense of what is appropriate for each individual fugue.

If there is any one monument that stands out in the literature of fugue, it is Bach's *Art of Fugue.* He combines in this series of fugues and canons a summary of all the techniques of the past as well as new and more logical uses of them. There is variety of form and a tremendous concentration of fugal devices—stretto, augmentation, inversion, diminution, variation, mirror—not displayed at once in a single fugue, but introduced fugue by fugue, each of which has its own balance and logic. The theme on which the work is based may seem rather abstract and introspective at first, but, even in the most complex of the fugues, there is a sense of subjective communication. In addition to the unity provided by basing the work on one main theme, there is a tremendous variety in the countersubjects used against the theme, in the free parts, and in the variations of the main theme as it is used in the different fugues. Although the work is unfinished, the ordered presentation of the fugues and canons it contains gives it a broad sense of total form that is felt when the work is heard as a unit. It remains the only unfinished work that is played clear through, to the last remaining note of the final unfinished fugue.

The *Art of Fugue* is a work that reveals new aspects each time it is studied, and any detailed analysis of it seems in time to be incomplete. It is a work that each musician must study for himself and evaluate according to his own insight and interests. A familiarity with it in detail and as a whole is not gained quickly, but a study of it is the fitting and natural conclusion to a study of fugue.

Notes

1. Vincenzo Galilei, *Dialogo . . . della musica antica et della moderna* (Florence, 1581), p. 87.

2. William Presser, *The Fugue before Bach* (Ph.D. dissertation, University of Rochester, Eastman School of Music, 1947; Rochester, N.Y.: University of Rochester Press, Microcard Publications, 1957), p. 446.

3. *Ibid.,* pp. 69–73; see also Alessandro Scarlatti, *Toccate per Cembalo* ed. John S. Shedlock (London: Bach & Co., 1908).

4. A small collection of out-of-print scores can be found in the Music Collection of the Boston Public Library. See also Norbert Linke, "Die Orchesterfuge in Spätromantik und Moderne" (unpublished Ph.D. dissertation, Hamburg University, 1959).

5. Zarlino, *op. cit.,* Bk. III, chap. li.

6. Pietro Pontio, *Dialogo della Theorica, e della prattica de musica* (Parma, 1595), pp. 54*ff.*

7. *Ibid.,* pp. 43*ff.*

8. Morley, *op. cit.,* p. 172; Harman ed., *op. cit.,* p. 282.

9. Michael Praetorius, *Syntagma musicum* (Wolfenbüttel, 1619), III, 17.

10. Cerreto, *op. cit.,* p. 212.

11. Praetorius, *op. cit.,* III, 21, 22; Morley, *op. cit.,* p. 181; Harman ed., *op. cit.,* p. 296.

12. Walther, *op. cit.,* p. 185; Mattheson, *op. cit.,* pp. 206, 207; see also Samber, *op. cit.,* p. 235.

13. Anton Bemetzrieder, *Account of a New Way of considering Musick* (London, 1783), p. 39.

14. See Ignaz X. Ritter von Seyfried, *Beethovens Studien* (Vienna, 1832), p. 172.

15. J. C. Kittel, *Der Angehende praktische Organist* (Erfurt, 1808), p. 14.

16. Johann Friedrich Daube, *Der musikalische Dilettant* (Vienna, 1773), p. 216.

17. Reicha, *Traité,* Vol. II, Bk. IV, p. 233.

18. Colet, *op. cit.,* p. 251.

19. Simon Sechter (ed.), W. F. Marpurg, *Traité de la fugue* (Vienna, c. 1850).

20. From one of Beethoven's conversations quoted in Paul Bekker, *Beethoven,* M. M. Bozman, trans. (London: J. M. Dent, 1925), p. 332.

21. Kurt Frederick, *Fugal Writing from 1750 to 1827* (Ph.D. dissertation, University of Rochester, Eastman School of Music, 1957; Rochester, N.Y.: University Press, Microcard Publications, 1957).

22. A. A. Klengel, *Canons et Fugues* . . . (Leipzig: Breitkopf & Härtel, 1854). Published posthumously.

Appendix I

Below are listed additional works for analysis and suggested reading arranged according to chapter.

Chapter II

Canons amalgamated into larger forms

 Haydn, String Quartet, Op. 76, No. 2: minuet

 Mozart, String Quartet, K. 172: minuet

 Schubert, Trio, Op. 100: scherzo and trio

Canons with free added parts

 Most collections of sixteenth-century Masses include canonic movements. The following are Masses using canon with free parts in all or nearly all movements.

 Des Près, *Missa sine nomine; Missa ad fugam*

 Palestrina, *Missa ad fugam; Missa Repleatur os meum; Missa sine nomine à 5*

 Bach, *Canonic Variations on Vom Himmel Hoch:* Nos. III and IV

(Both the Mozart and Schubert works above also have free added parts.)

 Schumann, *Jugend-Sonata,* Op. 118, No. 2: second movement; *Album Blätter,* Op. 124, No. 20

Forms built up of several different canons strung together, with or without free interpolated sections

 Des Près, *Missa Hercules Dux Ferrariae; Christe eleison*

 Michael Praetorius, duets on *In dulci jubilo* and *Wer in dem Schutz* in Friedrich Blume, ed., *Gesamtausgabe der musikalischen werke von Michael Praetorius* IX, (Wolfenbüttel-Berlin: George Kallmeyer Verlag, 1929), pp. 13 and 161

 Heinrich Schütz, *Historia der Auferstehung Jesu Christi* (most of the duets have this kind of structure)

 Bach, *Canonic Variations on Vom Himmel Hoch:* No. V

Chapter III

The following is a list of late fifteenth- and sixteenth-century theory books and music textbooks teaching the modes, arranged in chronological order.

Theory

Tinctoris, Johann. *Liber de natura et proprietate tonorum* [1476]. In *Oeuvres théoriques de Jean Tinctoris*. Edited by E. de Coussemaker. Lille, 1875.

Gaffurio, Franchino. *Pratica musica,* Bk. I. Milan, 1496; Venice, 1512.

Aaron, Pietro. *Compendiolo di molti dubbi, segreti et sentenze,* chaps. i–l. Milan, *ca.* 1550.

Vanneo, Stephano. *Recanetum de musica aurea,* Bk. I. Rome, 1533.

Glarean, Heinrich. *Dodekachordon.* Basel, 1547. See also Clement A. Miller (trans.). "The *Dodecachordon* of Heinrich Glarean." Unpublished Ph.D. dissertation, University of Michigan, 1951.

da Picitono, Angelo. *Fior Angelico di musica,* Bk. I, chaps. xxx–lix. Venice, 1547.

Finck, Hermann. *Pratica musica,* Bk. IV. Wittenberg, 1556.

Zarlino, Gioseffo. *Istitutione armoniche,* Bk. IV. Venice, 1558.

Aijguino, Illuminato. *Il tesoro illuminato.* Venice, 1581.

Pontio, Pietro. *Ragionamente di musica.* Parma, 1588. Pp. 99–121.

Tigrini, Orazio. *Il compendio della musica,* Bk. III. Venice, 1588.

Elementary Textbooks

Cochlaeus, Johann. *Tetrachordum musices.* Nuremberg, 1511.

Rhaw, George. *Enchiridion utriusque musicae practicae.* Wittenberg, 1520.

Spangenberg, Johann. *Quaestiones musicae.* Nuremberg, 1536.

Listenius, Micolaus. *Musica.* Nuremberg, 1537.

Agricola, Martin. *Rudimenta musice.* Wittenberg, 1539.

Heyden, Sebald. *De arte canendi.* Nuremberg, 1540.

Vogelsang, Johann. *Musica rudimenta.* (N. p.), 1542.

Faber, Gregorius. *Musicae practicae.* Magdeburg, 1553.

Lossio, Luca. *Erotemata musicae practicae.* Nuremberg, 1563.

Dressler, Gallus. *Musicae practicae.* Magdeburg, 1571.

Chapter V

Studies discussing the answer forms in Bach's works

Czackzkes, Ludwig. *Analyze des Wohltempierten Klaviers.* Vienna: Paul Kaltschmid, 1956.

Dickinson, A. E. F. *Bach's Fugal Works.* London: Putnam, n.d.

Oldroyd, George. *The Technique and Spirit of Fugue.* London: Oxford University Press, 1948.

Reutter, Fritz. *Die Beantwortung des Fugenthemas dargestellt an dem Themen von Bachs Wohltemperierten Klavier.* Leipzig: C. F. Kahnt, 1929.

Riemann, Hugo. *Katechismus der Fuge.* Leipzig, 1890–1891.

Chapter VII

The following are collections of fugues for analysis. Short references only are given; if only the publisher is given, this means that the collection is available through the publisher.

Sixteenth and early seventeenth century

The following are mixed collections.

Adrio, Adam (ed.). *The Fugue.* Vol. I: *From the Beginnings to J. S. Bach.* Cologne: A. Volk.

Fitzwilliam Virginia Book. 2 vols. Broude.

Slim, Harry Colin (ed.). *Musica nova.* Chicago: University of Chicago Press.

Torchi, Luigi (ed.). *L'arte musicale in Italia.* Vol. III. Milan: G. Ricordi, 1902, 1959.

The following are collections by one composer.

Bull, J. *Keyboard Music.* Vol. I. Stainer and Bell.

Frescobaldi, G. *Orgel- und Klavierwerke.* Vols. I, III, IV, V. Bärenreiter.

Gabrieli, A. *Ricercari für Orgel.* Vol. I. Bärenreiter.

———, and Gabrieli, G. *Musiche Strumentale.* In *Istituzione e monumenti dell' arte musicale.* Vol. I. Milan: Ricordi, 1931.

Gabrieli, G. *Werke für Tasteninstrumente.* Bärenreiter.

Hassler, H. L. *DTB,* IV, 2.

Scheidt, S. *Tabulatura nova. DDT,* I.

Sweelinck, J. P. *Selected Works.* Vol. I. Peters.

Late seventeenth and early eighteenth century

The works of Bach and Handel have been omitted.

Böhm, G. *Werke für Klavier und Orgel.* Vol. I. Breitkopf & Härtel.

Buxtehude, D. *Orgelwerke.* Vol. I. Peters.

Dandrieu, J. F. *Premier livre de pièces d'orgue.* Schott. (In addition to pieces called fugue, the duos and trios are fugues.)

Erbach, C. *DTB,* IV, 2.

Eberlin, J. E. *Neun Tokkaten und Fugen.* Altötting: A. Coppenrath.

Fischer, W. C. F. *Ariadne musica.* Schott.

Froberger, J. J. *DTÖ,* IV, i; X, ii.

———. *Selected Works for Cembalo.* Kalmus.

de Grigny, N. *Livre d'orgue.* Schott.

Kreiger, J. *DTB,* XVIII.

Kerll, J. R. *DDT,* II, 2.

Lübeck, V. *Orgelwerke.* Peters.

Mattheson, J. *Die wohlklingende Fingersprache.* Breitkopf & Härtel.

Pachelbel, J. *DTB,* IV, 1.

Telemann, G. P. *Easy Fugues.* Kalmus.

Walther, J. G. *DDT,* XXVI.

Late eighteenth and nineteenth centuries

So few collections of fugues from this time are now in print that a few collections available in American libraries (but now out of print) are given here. These may be available also at other libraries than those listed, nor is this meant to include a complete list of their holdings. Arranged in chronological order.

Albrechtsberger, J. G. *DTÖ*, XVI, 2.

——. *Six fugues en forme de quatuors.* Vienna, n.d.

——. *Douze fugues pour le clavecin ou l'orgue,* Op. 1. Berlin, 1778?. (Both in the Library of Congress, Washington, D.C.)

Bach, C. P. E. (Six fugues originally published in different collections and listed in A. Wotquenne, *Thematisches Verzeichnis,* are to be found in a clear manuscript copy at the Library of Congress.)

Martini, G. B. *Venti composizioni originali per cembalo.* Padua: G. Zanibon. (Movements in sonatas, as well as the separate *fuga,* are fugues.)

Czerny, C. *School of Fugue Playing,* Op. 400. 2 vols. (In the Boston Public Library.)

Mendelssohn, F. *Organ Fugues,* Op. 37. Peters.

——. *Six Preludes and Fugues,* Op. 35 (At the Library of Congress.)

Schumann, R. *Fugen,* Op. 60. Peters.

Klengel, A. A. *Canons et fugues.* 2 vols. Leipzig, 1854. (In the Newberry Library, Chicago, Ill., and the Music Library, Harvard University.)

Reger, M. (Fugues for organ, published separately, by Universal and Peters.)

Rheinberger, J. G. Finales of his organ sonatas, Nos. 1–24, are fugues. Novello.

Chapter IX

The following is a list of additional fugues with more than one subject, arranged in chronological order.

Ferrabosco, A. *Fantasia.* In *Jacobean Consort Music.* Edited by T. Dart and W. Coates. ("Musica Brittanica Series," Vol. X.) London: Stainer & Bell, 1955, pp. 30–2.

Lupo, T. *Fantasia.* In *ibid.,* pp. 35–6.

Froberger, J.J. Canzona I and Ricercar III. In *DTÖ,* IV, 1.

Bach, J. S. Organ Fugues in C Minor B.W.V.546 and E-flat Major B.W.V.552; Cantata No. 31, *Aus der Tiefe;* chorus, *Und er wird Israel;* Cantata No. 25, *Es ist nichts Gesundes:* first chorus.

Handel, G. F. *Israel in Egypt:* choruses, "And I will exalt them" and "Egypt was glad"; *Judas Maccabaeus:* chorus, "We worship God."

Bach, C. P. E. Magnificat in D Major: chorus, *Sicut erat.*

Haydn, J. String Quartets, Op. 20, Nos. 2, 5, and 6: fourth movements.

Mozart, W. A. *Requiem, K. 626: Kyrie eleison, Christe eleison.*

Beethoven, L. *Diabelli Variations,* Op. 120: finale; *Grosse Fuge,* Op. 133: first fugue.

Bruckner, A., Fourth movement of *Symphony No. 5.*

Reger, M., *Fugue on BACH for Organ, Op. 46.*

Appendix II

The following is a selected list of sources for the history of fugue theory, arranged in chronological order from first printing.

Aron, Pietro. *Libri tres de institutione harmonica.* Bonn, 1516.

————. *Il toscanello in musica.* Venice, 1523.

Buchner, Johannes. *Fundamentbuch* [ms. *ca.* 1525]. Ed. K. Paesler in *Vierteljahrschaft für Musikwissenschaft* V (1889), pp. 1–192.

Vicentino, Nicola. *L'antica musica ridotta alla moderna prattica.* Rome, 1555.

Finck, Hermann. *Practica musica.* Wittenberg, 1556.

Zarlino, Gioseffo. *Institutioni harmoniche.* Venice, 1558, 1562, 1573, 1589.

Lusitano, Vincentio. *Introduttione facillissima.* Venice (1561).

de Sancta Maria, Tomás. *Arte de tañer fantasia.* Valladolid, 1565.

Artusi, Giovanni Maria. *L'arte del contrappunto.* Venice, 1586–1589.

Pontio, Pietro. *Ragionamento di musica.* Parma, 1588.

Tigrini, Orazio. *Il compendio della musica.* Venice, 1588.

Calvisius, Seth. *Melopoeia.* Leipzig, 1592.

Pontio, Pietro. *Dialogo della theorica, e della prattica de musica.* Parma, 1595.

Morley, Thomas. *A Plaine and Easie Introduction to Practicall Musicke.* London, 1597. (New ed.: Edited by R. Alec Harman. New York: Norton, 1952. Harman uses "imitation" where Morley uses "fugue.")

Cerreto, Scipione. *Della pratica musica.* Naples, 1601.

Diruta, Girolamo. *Seconda parte del transilvano.* Venice, 1609.

Coperario, Giovanni. *Rules How to Compose* [ms. *ca.* 1610]. Facs. ed. Edited by M. F. Bukofzer. Los Angeles, E. E. Gottlieb, 1952.

Lippius, Johann. *Synopsis musicae novae.* Strassburg, 1612.

Cerone, Pietro. *El melopeo y maestro.* Naples, 1613.

Banchieri, Adriano. *Cartella musicale.* 3rd ed. enlarged. Venice, 1614.

de Caus, Salomon. *Institution harmonique.* Frankfurt, 1615.

Trabaci, Giovanni Maria. *Il secondo libro de ricercate.* Naples, 1615.
(Not a text, but has comments written into the score.)

Praetorius, Michael. *Syntagma musicum.* Vol. III. Wolfenbüttel, 1619.
(Facs. ed.: Kassel: Bärenreiter, 1958.)

Angleria, Camillo. *La regola de contraponto e della musical compo-sitione.* Milan, 1622.

Zacconi, Lodovico. *Prattica di musica.* Pt. II. Venice, 1622.

Crüger, Johann. *Synopsis musica.* Berlin, 1630.

Picerli, Silverio. *Specchio secondo di musica.* Naples, 1631.

Butler, Charles. *The Principles of Musick.* London, 1636.

Mersenne, Marin. *L'harmonie universelle.* Paris, 1636–1637.

[Schonsleder, Wolf.] *Architectonice musices.* Ingolstadt, 1641.

Herbst, Johann Andreas. *Musica poetica.* Nuremberg, 1643.

Denis, Jean. *Traité de l'accord de l'espinette.* Paris, 1650.

Nivers, Guillaume Gabriel. *Traité de la composition de musique.* Paris, 1667.

Simpson, Christopher. *A Compendium of Practical Musick.* London, 1667.

Bernhard, Christoff. *Tractatus compositionis augmentatus* [ms. *ca.* 1670]. In *Die Kompositionslehre Heinrich Schützens in der Fas-sung seines Schülers Christoph Bernhard.* Edited by J. M. Müller-Blattau. Leipzig: Breitkopf & Härtel, 1926.

Reincken, Jan Adams. *Kompositionslehre*[ms. *ca.* 1670]. Vol. X of *Jan Pieterson Sweelinck Werken.* Edited by H. Gehrmann. Leip-zig: Breitkopf & Härtel, 1901.

Penna, Lorenzo. *Li primi albori musicali.* Bologna, 1672.

Bononcini, Giovanni Maria. *Il musico prattico.* Bologna, 1673.

Berardi, Angelo. *Documenti armonici.* Bologna, 1687.

———. *Miscellanea musicale.* Bologna, 1689.

Purcell, Henry. "Of Fuge or Pointing," in John Playford, *An Intro-duction to the Skill of Musick.* 12th ed. London, 1694.

Masson, Charles. *Nouveau traité des règles pour la composition de la musique.* Paris, 1694.

Speer, Daniel. *Musicalischen Kleeblat.* Erbe, 1697.

Scorpione, Domenico, *Riflessioni armoniche.* Naples, 1701.

Werckmeister, Andreas. *Harmonologia musica.* Frankfort and Leipzig, 1702.

Tevo, Zaccaria. *Musico testore.* Venice, 1706.

Samber, Johann Baptist. *Continuatio ad manuductionem organicum.* Salzburg, 1707.

Walther, Johann George. *Praecepta der musicalischen composition* [ms. *ca.* 1708]. Vol. II of *Jenaer Beiträge zur Musikforschung.*

Edited by Peter Benary. Leipzig: Breitkopf & Härtel, 1955.

Rameau, Jean Philippe. *Traité de l'harmonie.* Paris, 1722.

Fux, Johann Joseph. *Gradus ad Parnassum.* Vienna, 1725. (Section on fugue translated by Alfred Mann in *The Study of Fugue.* New Brunswick, N.J.: Rutgers University Press, 1958.)

Mattheson, Johann. *Der vollkommene Kapellmeister.* Hamburg, 1739.

Scheibe, Johann Adolph. *Der Critischer Musicus.* Nos. 49–50 (1739). (See pp. 447–92.)

Spiess, Meinrad. *Tractatus musicus.* Augsburg, 1746.

Marpurg, Friedrich Wilhelm. *Abhandlund von der Fuge.* Berlin, 1753–1754. (Selections translated by Mann, *op. cit.*)

de Béthisy, Jean Laurent. *Exposition de la théorie et de la pratique.* Paris, 1754.

Paolucci, Giuseppe. *Arte prattica di contrappunto.* Venice, 1765–1772.

Daube, Johann Friedrich. *Der musikalische Dilettant.* Vienna, 1773.

Eximeno, Antonio. *Dell'origine e delle regole della musica.* Rome, 1774.

Martini, Giambattista. *Exemplare o sia saggio fondamentale prattico di contrappunto.* Bologna, 1774–1775.

Azopardi, Francesco. *Le musicien pratique.* Paris, 1786.

Albrechtsberger, Johann George. *Gründliche Anweisung zur Composition.* Leipzig, 1790. (Eng. ed., 1855.)

Galeazzi, Francesco. *Elementi teorico-pratici de musica.* Vol. II. Rome, 1796.

Kollman, Augustus F. C. *An Essay on Practical Musical Composition.* London, 1799.

Sabbatini, Luigi Antonio. *Trattado sopra le fughe musicali.* Venice, 1802.

Morigi, Angelo. *Trattado di contrappunto fugato.* Milan, [1802].

Reicha, Anton. *Über das neue Fugen-system.* Vienna, 1804–1805.

Momigny, Jerome-Joseph. *Cours complet d'harmonie.* Paris, 1806.

Choron, Alexander. *Principes de composition des écoles d'Italie.* Paris, [1808].

Langlé, H. F. *Traité de la fugue.* Paris, [1808].

Fétis, Joseph Francois. *Traité de la fugue.* Paris, 1824.

Reicha, Anton. *Traité de haute composition musicale.* Paris, 1824–1826.

André, Johann Anton. *Lehrbuch der Tonsetzkunst.* Offenbach, 1832–1842, II, iii.

Preindl, Joseph. *Wiener-Tonschule.* Vienna, 1827.

Cherubini, Luigi. *Traité de la fugue.* Paris, 1837. (Eng. trans., 1854. Actually, this is notes on Cherubini's course by his pupil J. F. Halevy.)

Colet, Hippolyte Raymond. *La panharmonie musicale.* Paris, 1837.

Marx, Adolf Bernhard. *Die Lehre von den musikalischen Komposition.* Leipzig, 1837–1847.

Czerny, Carl. *School of Practical Composition.* Op. 600. London, n.d.

Elwart, Antoine A. E. *Le contrepoint et la fugue appliqués a la composition.* Paris, 1840.

Weinlig, Christian Theodore. *Theoretisch-Praktische Anleitung zur Fuge.* Dresden, 1845.

Birnbach, W. *Der volkommene Componist.* Vols. III–IV. Berlin, 1846.

Dehn, S. W. *Lehre vom Contrapunkt, dem Canon und der Fugue.* Berlin, 1859.

Richter, Ernst Friedrich. *Lehrbuch der Fuge.* Leipzig, 1859. (Eng. ed., 1878.)

Lobe, Johann Christian. *Lehrbuch der musikalischen Komposition.* Leipzig, 1860.

Krüger, Edward. *System der Tonkunst.* Leipzig, 1866.

Gore Ouseley, Rev. Sir F. A. *A Treatise on Counterpoint, Canon and Fugue.* Oxford, 1869.

Hauff, J. C. *Die Theorie der Tonsetzkunst.* Frankfurt a. M., 1874.

Bussler, Ludwig, *Kontrapunct und Fuge im freien (modernen) Tonsatz.* Berlin, 1878.

Higgs, James. *Fugue.* London, 1878.

Jadassohn, Salomon. *Lehre vom Canon und von der Fuge.* Leipzig, 1884. (Eng. ed., 1887.)

Prout, Ebenezer. *Fugue.* London, 1891.

———— *Fugal Analysis.* London, 1892.

Dubois, Théodore. *Traité de contrepoint et de fugue.* Paris: Heugel, 1901.

Gedalge, André. *Traité de la fugue.* Paris: Enoch, 1901. (Eng. translation by A. Levin. Mattapan, Mass.: Gamut Music Company, 1964.)

Riemann, Hugo. *Grosse Kompositionslehre.* Leipzig: Breitkopf & Härtel, 1902.

Appendix III

The following is a list of modern books on the history of fugue, arranged in alphabetical order.

Adrio, Adam. *The Fugue. Vol. I: From the Beginnings to Johann Sebastian Bach.* Cologne: Arno Volk, 1961.

Burns, Joseph Albert. "Neapolitan Keyboard Music from Valenti to Frescobaldi." Unpublished Ph.D. dissertation, Harvard University, 1953.

Busse, Renate. *Das Problem der Fuge in der musikalischen Frühromantik.* Unpublished Ph.D. dissertation, Munich University, 1941.

Crocker, Eunice C. "An Introductory Study of the Italian Canzona for Instrumental Ensembles." Unpublished Ph.D. dissertation, Radcliffe College, 1943.

Dickinson, A. E. F. *Bach's Fugal Works.* London: Putnam, n.d.

Frederick, Kurt. *Fugal Writing from 1750 to 1827.* Ph.D. dissertation, Eastman School of Music, 1957. Rochester, N.Y.: University of Rochester Press, Microcard Publications, 1957.

Ghislanzoni, Alberto. *Storia della fuga.* Milan, 1952.

Kirkendale, Warren. *Fuge und Fugato in der Kammermusik des Rokoko und der Klassik.* Tutzing: Hans Schneider, 1966.

Linke, Norbert. "Die Orchesterfuge in Spätromantik und Moderne." Unpublished Ph.D. dissertation, Hamburg University, 1960.

Mann, Alfred. *The Study of Fugue.* New Brunswick, N.J.: Rutgers University Press, 1958.

Müller-Blattau, Josef Maria. *Geschichte der Fuge.* 3rd ed. Kassel: Bärenreiter, 1963.

Oldroyd, George. *The Technique and Spirit of Fugue.* London: Oxford University Press, 1948.

Presser, William. *The Fugue before Bach.* Ph.D. dissertation, Eastman School of Music, 1947; Rochester, N.Y.: University of Rochester Press, Microcard Publications, c1962.

Slim, Harry Colin. "The Keyboard Ricercar and Fantasia in Italy *c.* 1500–1555." Unpublished Ph.D. dissertation, Harvard University, 1960.

Sutherland, Gordon. "Studies in the Development of the Keyboard and Ensemble from Willaert to Frescobaldi." Unpublished Ph.D. dissertation, Harvard University, 1942.

Trapp, Klaus. *Die Fuge in der deutschen Romantik von Schubert bis Reger.* Fraskfurt: Hessen, 1958.

Index